The Collected Writings of
JESSIE FORSYTH
1847-1937

The Good Templars
and Temperance Reform
on Three Continents

Edited by
David M. Fahey

The Collected Writings of
JESSIE FORSYTH
1847-1937

The Good Templars
and Temperance Reform
on Three Continents

Edited by
David M. Fahey

Interdisciplinary Studies in
Alcohol Use and Abuse
Volume 1

The Edwin Mellen Press
Lewiston/Queenston
Lampeter

Library of Congress Cataloging-in-Publication Data

Forsyth, Jessie, 1847-1937.
    [Selections. 1988]
    The collected writings of Jessie Forsyth, 1847-1937 : the Good Templars
and temperance reform on three continents/edited by David M. Fahey.
      p. cm.--(Interdisciplinary studies in alcohol use and abuse : v. 1)
    Includes bibliographical references and index.
    ISBN 0-88946-296-8
    1. Forsyth, Jessie, 1847-1937. 2. Temperance--Biography.
3. International Order of Good Templars--History. I. Fahey, David
M. II. Title III. Series
HV5218.F67A3 1988
363.4'1'0924--dc19
[B]   87-35002
                                                   CIP

> This is volume 1 in Interdisciplinary
> Studies in Alcohol Use and Abuse
> Volume 1 ISBN 0-88946-296-8
> ISAUA Series ISBN 0-88946-295-X

For information contact:

The Edwin Mellen Press

Box 450   Box 67
Lewiston, New York   Queenston, Ontario
USA 14092   CANADA L0S 1L0

Mellen House
Lampeter, Dyfed, Wales
UNITED KINGDOM SA48 7DY

Printed in the United States of America

To my Mother and Father,
and my two Sisters,
with love

TABLE OF CONTENTS

Preface

This book is not the one I had planned. I began with a book on Joseph Malins and the English Good Templars and then became interested in the international conflict within Good Templary over black membership in the American South. In the course of my research, I met the name of Jessie Forsyth, a British-born resident of Boston, who edited Temperance Brotherhood in the mid-1880s. One summer while I was in London working at the library of the United Kingdom Alliance, I happened upon her memoir, "Thirty Years of Good Templary," published in the International Good Templar, 1903-04. A few weeks later I returned to the United States and travelled by car from New York State to my home in southwestern Ohio. I decided to stop in Columbus for a couple of hours to browse in the library of the Ohio Historical Society. It has much temperance material which formerly belonged to the Anti-Saloon League of America, including overseas publications. There I found the Australian Temperance World which had published additional Jessie Forsyth memoirs. At that point I decided I had a new book to do.

The book has two overlapping subjects, the Good Templar Order--one of the great unknowns in temperance history--and Jessie Forsyth, a fascinating, yet forgotten reformer. Begun as an edition of her memoirs, the book has grown to encompass some of her letters and a great deal else, what I have called representative writings, including official reports, a variety of didactic essays, even fiction and verse. I have kept my focus on her, on one particular Good Templar, and have postponed writing a history of the Good Templar Order which might claim comprehensiveness. This book attempts to evoke one woman's world.

I regret that I have been unable to locate Forsyth's heirs and hope that through this book I shall find them.

I have many debts. I owe the beginnings of the book to the United Kingdom Alliance, its general secretary, the Rev. Bernard Kinsman, and its librarian, Mrs. Lois Brown. In Britain I also did research at the Good Templar headquarters in Birmingham before its historical records had been removed to the Alliance; at the British Library, particularly the newspaper library in Colindale; at the Mitchell Library in Glasgow; and at St. Catherine's House, London, for records of birth and death.

Most of my research took place in America. In the course of my investigation of Good Templar history I have benefited from many libraries and archives, but here will specify only those which directly helped in the preparation of the present book. For unpublished letters I thank the manuscripts section of the University of Washington Libraries for its George F. Cotterill papers; the archives/manuscripts division of the Minnesota Historical Society for its George Henry Hazzard papers; and the State Historical Society of

Wisconsin archives for its Grand Lodge of Wisconsin papers. For print material I am grateful to the Cornell University, Department of Manuscripts and University Archives, where I consulted the Edward C. Sturges temperance collection; the Michigan Historical Collections, Bentley Historical Library, University of Michigan, for its Good Templar collection; the State Historical Society of Wisconsin; the Ohio Historical Society; the Earl W. Hayter Regional Historical Center, Northern Illinois University, for its Good Templar collection; the Library of Congress; the New York Public Library, for its James Black temperance collection; the University of Wisconsin, particularly for its Guy Hayler temperance collection; and the Minnesota Historical Society, library division.

For Australian sources I began with the serials conveniently located at the Ohio Historical Society and then sought help from Australia. This assistance came from another Mitchell Library, that in Sydney; the State Library Service of Western Australia, Perth; the Registrar General, Western Australia; and the Public Trustee, Western Australia; and also from Vivienne Parsons, who acted as my agent in Sydney; Nola A. Adams, State President, Woman's Christian Temperance Union of Western Australia; Doreen Blum, formerly secretary, WCTU of Western Australia; and Margaret Medcalf, Principal Librarian, Battye Library, Perth.

I could not have written this book without the cooperation of the library staff at the King Library, Miami University, who patiently and skillfully coped with my unending requests for loans and purchases. I particularly want to acknowledge the help of social science librarians Karin Ford (now at the Idaho State Library) and Chris Africa (now at the University of Iowa) and interlibrary loan librarians Sarah Barr and Karen Clift.

I also am grateful to Susan and David Mann for their generosity in allowing me to write this book on their computer and printer while they taught in Luxembourg. This kindness converted a stubborn CP/M user to MS-DOS and the convenience of WordPerfect.

I wish to acknowledge material assistance: the National Endowment for the Humanities for a travel to collections grant to do work at Cornell; the Faculty Research Committee, Miami University, for a summer research appointment, as well as several travel grants, to do research in Britain; and Miami University for a research leave.

A number of scholars read versions of my introduction or gave advice. I should mention by name Jack S. Blocker, Ruth Bordin, Jack T. Kirby, Ronald E. Shaw, Lilian Lewis Shiman, and Beverly A. Smith. I appreciate their counsel. On several pages my wife Mary Fuller, who teaches writing, saved readers from my native obscurity. Most of all, I owe a very heavy debt to Frank J. Merli, a candid friend, for repeated and effective criticism. Finally I want to thank my friends and colleagues at Miami University and elsewhere for putting up with my relentless talk about the Good Templars and my favorite Good Templar--Jessie Forsyth of London, Boston, and Fremantle.

One Woman's World

Who remembers Jessie Forsyth? A half-century after her death this remarkable woman is virtually unknown, largely because the organization which she served suffers so badly from neglect. History has failed to notice a life which touched on many of our contemporary concerns: opportunities for women, dignity for blacks, the need for community, the threat of substance abuse--especially among the young--and the necessity for international cooperation on behalf of reform. During her long life (1847-1937), she demonstrated a rare capacity for growth, a talent for seeing and seizing opportunities for service and self-fulfillment. Although she, no doubt, would have modestly declined the accolade, she became very much a citizen of the world.[1]

---

1   The most useful biographical writings are James Yeames, "Miss Jessie Forsyth, R.W.G.V.T.," <u>International Good Templar</u>, Jan. 1889, pp. 11-12; <u>Boston Traveller</u>, reprinted in <u>International Good Templar</u>, Nov. 1889, p. 683; Ernest Hurst Cherrington, ed., <u>Standard Encyclopedia of the Alcohol Problem</u>, 6 vols. (Westerville, OH: American Issue, 1925-30), art. Jessie Forsyth (which misreports her birth date); and the obituaries in (Melbourne) <u>White Ribbon Signal</u>, Dec. 1937, p. 224; <u>International Good Templar</u>, Jan. 1938, p. 6.

The memoirs which she wrote, together with her reports, essays, letters, stories, and poetry--previously
inaccessible and unknown--enable readers to glimpse one
woman´s world of temperance reform. They also open up
the history of a forgotten organization, once the largest temperance society in America and Britain, and a
pioneer in affirming equal rights for all members of
the human family.[2]

---

2   Early documents and eye-witness reports are
preserved in I. Newton Peirce, The History of the Independent Order of Good Templars (Philadelphia: Daugha-
day and Becker, 1869), whose name is often misspelled
as Pierce. The most accessible histories are anniversary works by William W. Turnbull, The Good Templars: A
History of the Rise and Progress of the Independent
Order of Good Templars: 1851-1901, Jubilee Volume, ed.
James Yeames (n.p.: IOGT, 1901); and Lars Larsen-Ledet,
Good Templary Through [a] Hundred Years (Aarhus, Denmark: International Supreme Lodge, 1951). The only
detailed study by an outsider is Joanne Judd Brown-
sword, "Good Templars in Wisconsin, 1854-1880," unpub-
lished M.A. thesis, University of Wisconsin, 1960.
Turnbull and Larsen-Ledet regarded the beginning of
their fraternal society as 1851, when the Order of Good
Templars was organized. The Independent Order of Good
Templars, a secessionist group, was founded in 1852.
In 1902 the IOGT was renamed the International Order of
Good Templars and in 1966 the International Organization of Good Templars. The recent history of the Good
Templars can be followed in the pages of the Interna-
tional Good Templar, succeeded in 1975 by the Globe.

For the rise of fraternal ritualism in mid-nine-
teenth-century America and its decline in the early
twentieth century, see Mark Christopher Carnes, "A Pil-
grimage for Light: Fraternal Ritualism in America,"
Ph.D. dissertation, Columbia University, 1982, which
includes the Good Templars; and the comparative study
by Mary Ann Clawson, "Brotherhood, Class and Patri-
archy: Fraternalism in Europe and America," Ph.D.
dissertation, State University of New York at Stony
Brook, 1980.

Forsyth served the Good Templars and the temperance movement for almost fifty years before age and
ill health left her a semi-invalid. These years—from
the early 1870s through the early 1920s—comprise a
period notable for socio-economic, cultural, and
political change. Forsyth's life and work must be seen
within this context. During these years the agitation
against alcohol won its greatest triumphs, including
National Prohibition in America. On the other hand, in
its other English-speaking and Scandinavian strongholds
the temperance tide had begun to ebb prior to the First
World War.

Since the 1960s historians have taken drink and
the temperance movement seriously.[3] Research has

---

3   For America, see Frank L. Byrne, Prophet of Prohibition: Neal Dow and His Crusade (Madison: State
Historical Society of Wisconsin, 1961); Joseph R. Gus-
field, Symbolic Crusade: Status Politics and the American Temperance Movement (Urbana: University of Illinois Press, 1963; 2nd ed., 1986);   James H. Timber-
lake, Prohibition and the Progressive Movement, 1900-
1920 (Cambridge: Harvard University Press, 1963); Norman H. Clark, The Dry Years: Prohibition and Social
Change in Washington (Seattle: University of Washington
Press, 1965; 2nd ed., 1988); John C. Burnham, "New Perspectives on the Prohibition `Experiment´ of the
1920´s," Journal of Social History 2 (Fall 1968); Norman H. Clark, Deliver Us from Evil: An Interpretation of
American Prohibition (New York: W. W. Norton, 1976);
Jack S. Blocker, Jr., Retreat from Reform: The Prohibition Movement in the United States, 1890-1913 (Westport: Greenwood Press, 1976); Ian R. Tyrrell, Sobering
Up: From Temperance to Prohibition in Antebellum America, 1800-1860 (Westport, CT: Greenwood Press, 1979);
William J. Rorabaugh, The Alcoholic Republic: An American Tradition (New York: Oxford University Press,
1979); Robert L. Hampel, Temperance and Prohibition in
Massachusetts, 1813-1852 (Ann Arbor: UMI Research

focused on the English-speaking world, Scandinavia, and
other parts of Europe.[4]

Press, 1982); Mark Edward Lender and James Kirby
Martin, Drinking in America: A History (New York: Free
Press, 1982; 2nd ed., 1987); Perry R. Duis, The Saloon:
Public Drinking in Chicago and Boston, 1880-1920
(Urbana: University of Illinois Press, 1983); Jed
Dannenbaum, Drink and Disorder: Temperance Reform in
Cincinnati from the Washingtonian Revival to the WCTU
(Urbana: University of Illinois Press, 1984); Harry
Gene Levine, "The Alcohol Problem in America: From
Temperance to Alcoholism," British Journal of Addiction
79 (March 1984); Mark Edward Lender, Dictionary of
American Temperance Biography: From Temperance Reform
to Alcohol Research, the 1600s to the 1980s (Westport,
CT: Greenwood Press, 1984); David E. Kyvig, ed., Law,
Alcohol, and Order: Perspectives on National Prohibi-
tion (Westport, CT: Greenwood Press, 1985); K. Austin
Kerr, Organized for Prohibition: A New History of the
Anti-Saloon League (New Haven: Yale University Press,
1985); Robert Smith Bader, Prohibition in Kansas: A
History (Lawrence: University Press of Kansas, 1986);
Jack S. Blocker, Jr., American Temperance Movements:
Cycles of Reform (Boston: Twayne, forthcoming 1988). A
later footnote identifies important works on women.

    For further bibliography, see Jacquie Jessup, "The
Liquor Issue in American History: A Bibliography," in
Jack S. Blocker, Jr., ed., Alcohol, Reform, and Soci-
ety: the Liquor Issue in Social Context (Westport:
Greenwood Press, 1979), supplemented since 1980 by the
publications of the Alcohol and Temperance History
Group, currently the Social History of Alcohol Review.

4   For England, see Brian Harrison, Drink and the
Victorians: The Temperance Movement in England, 1815-
1872 (London: Faber, 1971); Lilian Lewis Shiman, Crusade against Drink in Victorian England (London: Macmillan, 1988); John R. Greenaway, "Bishops, Brewers and
the Liquor Question in England, 1890-1914," Historical
Magazine of the Protestant Episcopal Church 53 (March
1984); and Stephen G. Jones, "Labour, Society and the
Drink Question in Britain, 1918-1939," Historical
Journal 30 (March 1987). For other parts of the British Isles and the British Empire, see W. R. Lambert,
Drink and Sobriety in Victorian Wales (Cardiff:
University of Wales Press, 1983); Elizabeth Malcolm,
`Ireland Sober, Ireland Free´: Drink and Temperance in

5

The Good Templars deserve a prominent place in
this revisionist scholarship, but rarely get more than

Nineteenth-Century Ireland (Syracuse: Syracuse Univer-
sity Press, 1986); T. C. Smout, _A Century of the
Scottish People, 1830-1950_ (London: Collins, 1986), ch.
6, "Drink, Temperance, and Recreation;" Lucy Carroll,
"The Temperance Movement in India: Politics and Social
Reform," _Modern Asian Studies_ 10 (July 1976); and
Wallace Mills, "Cape Smoke: Alcohol Issues in the Cape
Colony in the Nineteenth Century," _Contemporary Drug
Problems_ 12 (Summer 1985). For a transatlantic per-
spective, see Bernard Aspinwall, _Portable Utopia:
Glasgow and the United States, 1820-1920_ (Aberdeen:
Aberdeen University Press, 1984), ch. 4, "The Demon
Drink: The Drift to Prohibition."

Outside the English-speaking world scholarship is
either scanty or, for Scandinavia, available only to
those who read the national languages. (I am not one of
these fortunate readers.) Recent books include Kettil
Bruun and Per Frånberg, eds., _Den svenska supen: En
historia om brannvin, Bratt och byråkrati_ (Stockholm:
Prisma, 1985), on the Swedish restrictive system; and
Irma Sulkunen, _Raittius kasalaisukontona: Raiittius ja
järjestäytyminen 1870-luvulta suurlakon jälkeisiin
vuosiin_ (Helsinki: Jyväskylä, 1986), on "temperance as
a people's religion" in Finland. The most important
Norwegian book is Per Fuglam, _Kampen om alkoholen i
Norge, 1816-1904_ (Oslo: Universitetsforlaget, 1972).
Ole-Jorgen Skøg, "The Long Waves of Alcohol Consumption: A Social Network Perspective on Cultural Change,"
Social Networks 8 (1986), based in part on statistics
of alcohol consumption in Norway, 1851-1982, illustrates Scandinavian innovation in methodology.

English-language books for the Continent include
James S. Roberts, _Drink, Temperance, and the Working
Class in Nineteenth-Century Germany_ (Boston: Allen &
Unwin, 1984); Boris M. Segal, _Russian Drinking: Use
and Abuse of Alcohol in Pre-Revolutionary Russia_ (New
Brunswick: Rutgers Center of Alcohol Studies, 1987);
and Thomas Brennan, _Public Drinking and Popular Culture
in Eighteenth-Century Paris_ (Princeton: Princeton University Press, 1988). Patricia E. Prestwich, author of
"French Workers and the Temperance Movement," _Interna-
tional Review of Social History_ 25, pt. 1 (1980), has
completed a book on the French anti-alcohol movement.

a brief reference.[5] Even specialists in temperance history risk a stumble when they venture to discuss Good Templary. Although this is not the occasion for a full portrait of the Order, a sketch is indispensable. Who were the Good Templars? What did they want? What did they do?

ALL KINDS OF PEOPLE

The Independent Order of Good Templars evolved into a worldwide organization within two or three decades. The first lodges had been organized in central New York State in 1851-52, a district known as a nursery of reform movements and a time known for its moral causes. After the first dozen years in which growth and decline alternated, the Order grew impressively. At the end of 1868, it claimed more than 500,000 members in the United States and Canada.[6] Although the North American membership subsequently declined, the Order spread overseas and attracted large memberships in Britain and Scandinavia.

The Good Templars welcomed everyone: the life-long abstainer and the reformed drunkard, male and female, black and white, young and old, prosperous and

---

5   In explaining what he excluded from his monograph, one temperance historian mentions, among other topics, "the curious but neglected Independent Order of Good Templars." A. E. Dingle, The Campaign for Prohibition in Victorian England: United Kingdom Alliance, 1872-1895 (New Brunswick: Rutgers University Press, 1980), p. 9.

6   Peirce, The History of the Independent Order of Good Templars, p. 503.

poor.[7] Unlike other fraternal societies it avoided
mutual insurance which might exclude those whose health
or age made them poor risks or who could not afford the
high dues needed to fund a beneficiary scheme.

At a time when virtually all movements for moral
reform denied women equal rights, the Good Templary
offered comparative equality.[8] Within a few months of

---

7   Occasionally Good Templars called themselves by
the shorter form, Templars, and this shorter form ordinarily will be used here.

8   Most of the scholarship devoted to women in the
temperance movement deals with America. The Woman's
Christian Temperance Union, organized in 1874, has
dominated the field. Some of the more important recent
works include: Harry Gene Levine, "Women and Temperance in 19th-Century United States," in Oriana Josseau
Kalant, ed., Alcohol and Drug Problems in Women [Re-
search Advances in Alcohol and Drug Problems, vol. 5]
(New York: Plenum Press, 1980); Ruth Bordin, Woman and
Temperance: The Quest for Power and Liberty, 1873-
1900 (Philadelphia: Temple University Press, 1981);
Barbara Leslie Epstein, The Politics of Domesticity:
Women, Evangelism, and Temperance in Nineteenth-Century
America (Middletown, CT: Wesleyan University Press,
1981); Ian R. Tyrrell, "Women and Temperance in Ante-
bellum America, 1830-1860," Civil War History 28 (June
1982); Jack S. Blocker, Jr., "Give to the Winds Thy
Fears": The Women's Temperance Crusade, 1873-1874
(Westport, CT: Greenwood Press, 1985); Ruth Bordin,
Frances Willard: A Biography (Chapel Hill: University
of North Carolina Press, 1986).

One can also benefit from looking more generally
at feminist theory and women's history, such as Estelle
Freedman, "Separatism as Strategy: Female Institution
Building and American Feminism, 1870-1930," Feminist
Studies 5 (Fall 1979); Mary P. Ryan, Cradle of the Mid-
dle Class: The Family in Oneida County, New York, 1790-
1865 (Cambridge: Cambridge University Press, 1981),
which examines the district where the original Good
Templar lodges were organized in 1851; and Mary Ann
Clawson, "Nineteenth-Century Women's Auxiliaries and
Fraternal Orders," Signs 12 (Autumn 1986).

its birth the IOGT had declared that women should exercise rights to vote and hold office which society at large restricted to men. Recognizing that few women controlled much ready cash, the Order charged them lower dues. Typically women made up at least a third of the membership. In local lodges and Grand Lodges women almost always held the office of Vice Templar, frequently headed the juvenile auxiliary, occasionally served in the important office of Secretary, but very rarely became Counsellor or Chief Templar, the two highest offices. In the international organization a woman was briefly Secretary in the 1850s. Otherwise women held only the titles of International Superintendent of Juvenile Temples and International Vice Templar (and lost those offices to men in 1908 and 1911). Despite the theory of equality, "brothers" dominated the higher offices. On the other hand, a great many "sisters" took active roles as speakers and organizers.

To appeal to all kinds of people the Order had to provide a variety of opportunities for enjoyment and service, for personal growth and moral witness. It

---

For women and temperance in other parts of the English-speaking world, see the historical pamphlet written and published by the National British Women's Total Abstinence Union, A Century of Service, 1876-1976 (London, n.d.); David Wright and Cathy Chorniawry, "Women and Drink in Edwardian England," Historical Papers/Communications Historiques (1985); Lilian Lewis Shiman, "'Changes are Dangerous': Women and Temperance in Victorian England," in Gail Malmgreen, ed., Religion in the Lives of English Women, 1760-1930 (Bloomington: Indiana University Press, 1986); and A. R. Grigg, "Prohibition and Women: The Preservation of an Ideal and a Myth," New Zealand Journal of History 17 (Oct. 1983).

offered a non-sectarian religiosity, as well as colorful regalia and secret handshakes, passwords, and rituals. It developed an elaborate organization, with an abundance of offices bearing ostentatious titles. Not content with personal abstinence, Templars worked as a "Temperance Missionary Society," dedicated to saving the fallen and to protecting abstainers, particularly young ones, from temptation.[9]

The Templars attracted more than one kind of teetotaler. Ex-drinkers regarded the lodge as a means of stabilizing the teetotal pledge. A reclaimed drunkard declared, "Thank God! the Good Templar Order saved me from lapsing again through the sheer want of proper associates."[10] The lodge also could be a sanctuary for those who had never been drinkers, particularly the young. The leader of a Band of Hope--the great

---

9   John B. Collings, The I.O.G.T.: What It Is and What It Does; Who Are the Good Templars? (Birmingham: Grand Lodge of England, n.d.), p. 9. A recent history of alcohol treatment states that the Good Templars (and the Sons of Temperance) "increasingly devoted their attention to alcohol control [legislative] measures and by the 1880s had lost interest in the individual inebriate." Jim Baumohl and Robin Room, "Inebriety, Doctors, and the State: Alcoholism Treatment Institutions before 1940," in Marc Galanter, ed., Recent Developments in Alcoholism, vol. 5 (New York and London: Plenum Press, 1987), p. 141. It would be more accurate to say that by the late nineteenth century the Good Templars everywhere showed a diminished interest in the individual inebriate and in some countries developed a great interest in children.

10   Good Templars´ Watchword, June 16, 1906, p. 217. The Good Templars incorporated some of the mutual-help functions later seen in Alcoholics Anonymous. Harry Gene Levine, "Demon of the Middle Class: Self-Control, Liquor, and the Ideology of Temperance in 19th-Century America," Ph.D. dissertation, University of California at Berkeley, 1978, p. 53 n. 66.

teetotal organization for children--overcame his
distaste for secret societies such as the Templars,
out of a desire to bring his teenaged members into "an
ark of safety during their youthful years."[11] As an
instrument for temperance work beyond the membership,
the Order attracted temperance activists. "The Good
Templar life is one of warfare."[12] The Order worked to
reclaim drinkers through evangelism and to strengthen
the resolve of nondrinkers by pledging them to abstinence. In the early 1890s a Temperance Van Mission
wandered England as "Good Templar Gipsies."[13] Drink
inflicted a cruel disease which no one had a right to
choose; wanting to drink was itself an illness. As the
militant "Spartans" of the temperance movement, the
members of the Order refused to serve guests or cus-
tomers alcohol and did whatever they could to make the
State stop the sale of drink.[14] The Order worked for
enforcement of the existing law and for new legislation. In the late 1850s the Templars endorsed prohibition, paradoxically at a time when many other temperance reformers had lost confidence in the so-called
Maine Law for state prohibition. The Order supplied
workers for virtually every prohibition campaign,
local, state, and national. In the late 1860s Templars
took the lead in the formation of the Prohibition Party

---

11 (London) Temperance Star, Nov. 19, 1868, p. 5.

12 Grand Lodge of Illinois, Proceedings (1898), p. 13.

13 Jessie Forsyth, "Good Templar Mission Van," International Good Templar, Nov. 1891, pp. 340-44.

14 (London) Temperance Journal and Treasury, Jan. 9,
1879, p. 17.

in the United States. They stood among the most
resolute advocates of Direct Local Veto in Britain.[15]

Few remained in the Order long. Many had joined
in their teens or early twenties, attracted by the
prospect of good times and fellowship as much as by the
temperance cause. The enthusiasm of these youthful
recruits in most cases cooled.[16] Former members, most
of whom continued to be abstainers, greatly outnumbered
active Templars. Ex-members comprised a reserve army
of sympathizers, or so the leaders of the Order hoped.
At the Jubilee meeting in 1901, for example, the Grand
Lodge of Georgia reported that since 1867 the Order in
that state had initiated 225,636 members and had
pledged 66,270 Juvenile Templars.[17] These impressive
figures must be set against the modest number of dues-
paying members for any particular year. Making the
best of the situation, the Templars depicted their
Order as a kind of training school for the temperance
movement and for social reform in general.

Although all kinds of people joined the Templars,
most members lacked the property and the education
which might have assured them a comfortable

15   On the militancy of the Good Templars in England
and Scotland, see David M. Fahey, "Temperance and the
Liberal Party--Lord Peel's Report, 1899," Journal of
British Studies 10 (May 1971): 151-57.

16   The clearest evidence for the youthfulness of the
membership can be found in the Grand Lodge of Minnesota
obituary lists for 1890-1901 which record the age at
death for 130 members, with the mean a little over age
22. Grand Lodge of Minnesota, Proceedings (1890-1901).
Few remained long enough to die as members in middle
age or old age.

17   International Good Templar, June 1902, pp. 208-9.

independence.   A detailed Swedish study of an agricul-
tural parish near an industrializing city concluded
that in the 1890s "lodge members came for the most part
from the categories that had been pushed aside from all
communal influence or from groups that never possessed
any political position."   About the time of the First
World War, "the children of the farmers (whose parents
seldom joined), smiths, carpenters, an occasional
soldier, the railway guards, the station hands, and a
few workers" provided active members, while "the mid-
wife and the elementary school teachers" became
leaders.[18]

The record book of Triumph Lodge, Altamont, New
York, near the cities of Schenectady and Albany, hints
at the occupations of the rank and file in North
America.   This book identified new members in 1899-1902
and 1906-12.   In the latter years many students were
admitted, inflating their number to 77.   In the second
largest category, 28 women identified themselves as
housekeepers or housewives.   There were 17 clerks, 11
teachers (including two music teachers), and 10
farmers.   The remainder of the members was scattered
among many livelihoods.   There were five stenographers;
three ministers, drivers (or chauffeurs or coachmen),
seamstresses, and painters; and two lumbermen, com-
positors, and embroidery workers.   There was an
attorney (elected Chief Templar when the lodge was
organized and the record book began), a bookkeeper, a
tinsmith, a mechanic, a dressmaker, a "counter jumper,"

---

18   Torkel Jansson, Samhällsforändring och sammans-
lutningsformer: Det frivilliga föreningsväsendets upp-
komst och spridning i Husby-Rekarne från omkring 1850
till 1930 [Uppsala University] (Stockholm: Almqvist &
Wiksell, 1982), pp. 294, 297 (English summary).

a laborer, a hostler, an "operator," a pantsmaker, a
barber, a telegrapher, a blacksmith, a laundryman, a
butcher, a plumber, a milliner, a letter carrier, a cat
and dog catcher, a "sheetwalker," a "sandbanker," and a
baggageman.[19]

In 1889 the international organization reported
that 215 men and 91 women had registered for a three-
year reading program created two years earlier. These
people ranked among the most committed members of the
Order. The registrants included 33 housekeepers
(presumably women who lived with their own families);
28 teachers; 21 students; 18 clerks; 15 farmers,
soldiers, and lecturers (probably temperance ones); 12
merchants; 11 lawyers; eight bookkeepers; seven
carpenters; six printers; five manufacturers; four
machinists, railway agents, engineers, postmasters,
Grand Superintendents of Juvenile Work (a Templar
office), dressmakers, and secretaries; three (otherwise
unspecified) agents, as well as three insurance agents,
carriage-smiths, laborers, telegraph-operators, and
photographers; two drapers, travelling salesmen,
stewards, pattern-makers, auditors, mechanics, black-
smiths, editors, and draftsmen; and one each of the
following: book-agent, molder, jeweler, minister,
Grand Secretary (a Templar office), surveyor, watchman,
secretary of an insurance company, miller, glovemaker,
paving-cutter, orange grower, liveryman, barber,

---

19   Four had no occupation listed. Box 17, Edward C.
Sturges temperance collection, Cornell University
Library, Department of Manuscripts and University
Archives. Sturges became Chief Templar when the lodge
was organized in December 1899, a few weeks before his
twenty-second birthday. A graduate of Albany Law
School in 1900, he spent most of his life as a State of
New York civil servant.

founder, genealogist, pastor, canvasser, spinner,
cashier, cabinet-maker, railway postal clerk, retired
spinster, correspondent, miner, plumber, traveller (or
sales agent), potter, hospital superintendent, nursery-
man, real estate agent, publisher, bookmaker, paper-
hanger, salesman, factory superintendent, mason, and
coal operator.[20] One might have expected more divines
to have registered for the reading program and also
farmers as the latter constituted a very large part of
the general population.

Such members peopled Jessie Forsyth's Templar
world. In the nineteenth and the early twentieth
centuries, Good Templary attracted skilled workers and
the lower middle class more than persons from any other
social stratum, but its membership also included many
common laborers and a sprinkling of solidly middle
class professionals and entrepreneurs.

By the end of the nineteenth century Good Templary
emphasized the worldwide scope of its brotherhood and
sisterhood. More than anyone else, Joseph Malins made
the IOGT an international organization. He joined the
Order in Philadelphia where he had worked as a decora-
tive painter of railway coaches. In 1868 he returned
to his native England with a commission to organize
Templar lodges. In addition to building a strong Grand
Lodge, Malins assisted sailors, soldiers, and emigrants
in planting the Order throughout the British Empire and
on the European Continent. By the end of the

---

20   Right Worthy Grand Lodge, <u>Proceedings</u> (1889), p.
304.   Only 42 came from outside North America, with
none from Scotland or Sweden and fewer from England
than New Jersey. Nearly half of those registered lived
in Wisconsin. Apparently not all listed livelihoods.

nineteenth century Sweden had the Order's largest Grand
Lodge. With the help of lodges in English-speaking
communities on every continent, the IOGT circled the
globe. The slogan "the world our field" became popular, and a few idealists tried to promote the use of
Esperanto as the official language. Early in the
twentieth century, the Order replaced its old name--the
Independent Order of Good Templars--with one which
stressed its new sense of universalism--the International Order of Good Templars. Eventually international fellowship and world peace became as much a
part of the Templar program as the elimination of
alcoholic drink.

Nowhere did the Order grow more dramatically than
in England in the early 1870s. Three years before
Jessie Forsyth joined the Order, England counted fewer
than a hundred Templars, but when she was initiated in
October 1872 the Grand Lodge claimed more than a
100,000 members. Forsyth joined an exuberantly self-
confident Order which took this extraordinary growth
for granted. By the end of the next year--when membership exceeded 200,000--leaders dreamed of a million
English Templars.

Although this kind of optimism helped shape the
first years of Forsyth's Templar world, that world was
more a home than an empire. Good Templary provided an
extended family of friends and acquaintances in the
lodge-room, and functioned as a fraternal society as
well as a temperance organization. The Order offered
fellowship, recreation, and an opportunity to be important, all in a morally uplifting atmosphere. It was
described as "a mild form of freemasonry tempered by

Methodism."[21]   Good Templary enhanced Forsyth´s life
and the lives of countless others by creating a world
of commitment and fellowship, of work and good times,
in which members became part of a community, enlivened
by personal relationships, ennobled by a sense of purpose.[22]

FROM LONDON TO BOSTON

On April 29, 1847, Jessie Forsyth was born to a
family of London Scots.[23]   Although she loved London,
and once in her memoirs called herself a cockney, she
clearly saw herself as a daughter of Scotland, whose
people, she said, had a national character sharing
"much of the strength and stability of their native
hills."   As a child she listened to the tales of Sir
Walter Scott and the verse of Robert Burns, and learned
the "old Jacobite melodies" at her aunt´s knee.[24]

---

21   Joseph Malins, "Good Templary in England," United
Temperance Gazette, March 1898, p. 29.   Probably the
ritual was borrowed from the Odd Fellows rather than
from the Freemasons.

22   Lodges varied enormously, but many of them provided members with opportunities otherwise closed to
them.   For instance, some lodges produced "manuscript
magazines," such as Carter Lodge, No. 535, Thorn Grove,
Tennessee, which in 1879 issued a magazine edited by a
millwright.   Grace Leab and Charles Z. Roettger, "A
Good Templar `Journal,´" East Tennessee History
Society´s Publications 31 (1959): 83-94.

23   General Register Office, London, Certified Copy of
an Entry of Birth, for Jessie Forsyth.   She was born in
Kentish Town.

24   For "cockney" reference, see Forsyth, "Thirty
Years of Good Templary," International Good Templar,
June 1903, chapter 6.   {TEXT} (This symbol will mark
writings reproduced in this volume.)   For the "hills"

Years later she recalled that when a "wee bairnie" a remnant of grandfather Forsyth's kilt had become her frock.[25] She visited Scotland four times and on one occasion was able to spend a day at Elgin, the kilted grandfather's birthplace.[26] Her love of history began, it seems, with "Bonnie Scotland."

Illness was another formative influence in her early life. Until the age of twelve she could not attend school. She spent long hours alone, frequently on nearby Hampstead Heath, where, as a semi-invalid, she "could only play very quietly, or sit still and read." When her health improved she joined a children's temperance society, a Band of Hope, in whose choir she sang. Her love of nature and its beauties provided one consolation during her years of illness and solitude.[27] Religion provided another. Decades later she remembered how as a little girl she enjoyed attending church services and how she loved the kindly

quotation, see Forsyth, "Some Notes of Travel," _International Good Templar_, Dec. 1905, chapter 2. {TEXT} For the references to the Scottish writers and songs, see Forsyth, "Incidents in a Good Templar Life," subtitled "Some Little Visits to Scotland," _Australian Temperance World_, June 1929, p. 6. Forsyth visited Scotland in 1885, 1891, 1897, and 1905.

25 Forsyth, "Thirty Years of Good Templary," _International Good Templar_, March 1904, chapter 15. {TEXT}

26 Forsyth, "Some Notes of Travel," _International Good Templar_, Dec. 1905, chapter 2. {TEXT}

27 Forsyth ("Auntie Jet"), "Our Young People," _West Australian White Ribbon_, May 1927. {TEXT} She did not specify the nature of her illness.

rector.[28] Her family worshipped in the Church of England. She said that the only moment more solemn in her life than initiation as a Templar was her confirmation in the Church.[29] As a devout Anglican she was something of an anomaly: a Templar activist more typically was a Methodist or a Congregationalist or a Presbyterian.

Although Forsyth wrote abundant memoirs, this sketch of her early life, pieced together from miscellaneous sources, is frustratingly blurry. Any psychological portrait must be tentative, no more than informed hypothesis. As Templar memoirs, her reminiscences, unfortunately, have a narrow focus and rarely allude to her personal or business life.

Forsyth said little about her parents. When she was born her mother was nearly 50. Eliza Maria (Kitteridge) Forsyth died in 1862, from cirrhosis of the liver and jaundice, which suggest a drinking problem.[30] At 15 Jessie had to "leave school and earn her own living."[31] Three years later her father, a baker, died in a workhouse, which might indicate destitution or simply that, in need of a hospital, a

---

28 Forsyth, "Our Monthly Letter," International Good Templar, Sept. 1894, p. 281.

29 Forsyth, "Thirty Years of Good Templary," International Good Templar, Jan. 1903, chapter 1. {TEXT}

30 General Register Office, London, Certified Copy of an Entry of Death, for Eliza Maria (Kitteridge) Forsyth. She was 63 when she died on June 11, 1862.

31 Yeames, "Miss Jessie Forsyth, R.W.G.V.T.," International Good Templar, Jan. 1889, p. 11.

person of humble circumstances, such as Andrew Forsyth, had no alternative to a workhouse infirmary.[32]

Her real sense of family seems to have been with her sister Maria and the two aunts with whom Jessie made her home from the death of her parents until her departure for the New World.[33] The sisters remained close emotionally even when thousands of miles apart, as Jessie's decision in old age to emigrate to live near Maria indicates. Their only brother George had moved to Western Australia the year that their father died and became harbor captain at Fremantle. Maria and her husband later followed George to Western Australia. Eventually, many years after George had died, Jessie joined them. She mentions only one other relative, her great-uncle, the caricaturist George Cruikshank, who visited her home and once spoke to her Band of Hope.[34]

---

32   General Register Office, London, Certified Copy of an Entry of Death, for Andrew Forsyth. He was 60 when he died on August 23, 1865, as a result of a stomach ulcer.

33   Forsyth never mentions the names of her aunts or any details of their lives, other than a reference to a tea party in their home. Considering the age of Eliza Maria Forsyth when Jessie was born, it is likely that Maria was older than her sister Jessie.

34   Forsyth ("Auntie Jet"), "Our Young People," West Australian White Ribbon, May 1927. {TEXT} See also Thomas F. Parker, History of the Independent Order of Good Templars from the Origin of the Order to the Session of the Right Worthy Grand Lodge of 1887 (revised ed., New York: Phillips and Hunt, 1887), pp. 292-93. Cruikshank, who suffered from a serious drinking problem much of his life, drew a number of anti-drink pictures, such as "The Drunkard's Children," "The Bottle," and "The Gin Trap." He died in 1878.

In 1872, when she was 25, Jessie Forsyth made a decision that changed her life and enlarged her world. That decision was made casually, as such decisions often are. In search of companionship and good times, she joined a Templar lodge in the district of north London known as Islington. At that time, a respectable young woman enjoyed few opportunities for recreation, so Forsyth longed to enter a safe and convivial circle of like-minded men and women. According to her memoirs, she, like other members of her household, had been an occasional drinker of ale and wine, and, despite her childhood membership in a Band of Hope, she had not been attracted to teetotalism. Hatred of drink apparently played little part, if any, in her decision to join the Templar Order. "I knew nothing about the temperance question beyond the fact that I had seen the evil effects of drink on one near and dear to me.[35] She did not name that person, but very likely it was her mother. Toward the end of her life Forsyth suggested that the temperance work of her great-uncle George Cruikshank inspired her to become a temperance activist, but the weight of evidence in her memoirs is that she became committed to temperance reform and prohibition only after joining the Templars. Although at first "the idea that total abstinence should be demanded of everyone seemed a very extreme measure," she learned to see teetotalism and prohibition as the only practical response to an appalling social scandal and as something more, a moral crusade.[36]

---

35   Forsyth, "The Worth of Good Templary," New York Templar, July 1925. {TEXT} Reprinted in Australian Temperance World, April 1927.

36   Ibid.

Like youth in other times and other places, she
soon was disappointed that middle-aged members dominated the life of her lodge "and that there seemed
little for new members to do."[37] Forsyth joined other
young people who "swarmed" to create a more congenial
new lodge. She took an active role in its affairs and
soon received appointment to minor office and later was
elected Vice Templar. There her sister Maria met her
husband, and from there Jessie embarked on her journey
to the New World. When she applied for her clearance
card--a sort of license to transfer from one lodge to
another--her lodge asked the popular young officer to
say a few words of farewell. This, her first public
speech, ended with her in tears. No one could have
imagined that in a few years she would grow into a
self-confident speaker.

Believing that her health would benefit from a new
environment, her aunts had persuaded her to take a job
in America. Originally Forsyth intended to stay in the
United States for only two years, but she remained
until 1911. When she next saw England her aunts had
died, her sister had emigrated, and Jessie Forsyth knew
she was only a visitor. Massachusetts had become home.
She spent all her American years at the Boston Printing
and Numbering Company. Her progress can be traced
through the Boston directory. First called a
bookkeeper, she was listed as manager beginning in 1886
and then as proprietor, with the firm operating under
her name, beginning in 1903. As the business was
classified under numbering, paging, perforating, and

37   Forsyth, "Thirty Years of Good Templary," _Interna-
tional Good Templar_, Jan. 1903, chapter 1. {TEXT}

eyeletting, it presumably specialized in printing tickets.[38]

Until she found new friends in a Templar lodge, Forsyth was desperately unhappy in her new home. When cautioning prospective emigrants in 1884, she asserted that winters in the northern States were too severe for people with poor health.[39] But more important than frigid temperatures and icy streets, a sense of loneliness amounting almost to despair colored her comments on her early life in Massachusetts. She, who had always lived amid relatives and longtime friends, felt very alone, even though she originally roomed with other British immigrants whom she had known in the old country. Despite her love of children she never alluded to the possibility of having a family of her own or to marriage.

As a single woman Forsyth boarded in a succession of homes. Once while she lived with an American couple, Yankees from Maine, she became very friendly with their young son, a baby when she first entered their home, four when she left, and eleven when he died. At age 79 she told the readers of her column for children that she "gratefully remember[ed] how his love comforted me in some days of sorrow and homesickness,"

---

38   Boston City Directory (1877), p. 344; (1885), p. 416; (1886), p. 441; (1902), p. 628; (1903), pp. 676, 2114.

39   Forsyth to editor, <u>Good Templars´ Watchword</u>, Jan. 28, 1884. {TEXT}

and adopted the pen name, Auntie Jet, in memory of his childish pronunciation of Jessie.[40]

Forsyth escaped from her isolation through the Templars. She located a lodge two or three months after she arrived in Boston. Warmly received by the Americans when she arrived to deposit her clearance card, she entered fully into the life of local Good Templary and soon was elected lodge secretary. In later years the Order developed many national differences, but in the mid-1870s a member who had learned to love the rituals, odes, and regalia of Templar life in London would find most things in a Boston lodge familiar. "For the first time since my arrival in America, I felt at home."[41]

THE "NEGRO QUESTION"

Soon, to her distress, she had to break with her new friends. In 1876, two years after her arrival in Boston, the Grand Lodges of England and Scotland led a secessionist movement which broke away from the old international organization, the Right Worthy Grand Lodge, and organized a rival Right Worthy Grand Lodge of the World. Frequently the supporters of the old organization were known as the Hickmanites, after John J. Hickman of Kentucky, who headed the Order in 1876. The seceders were known as the Malinites, after Joseph Malins, the chief of the Grand Lodge of England. In a

---

40 Forsyth ("Auntie Jet"), "Our Young People," West Australian White Ribbon, July 1926. {TEXT}

41 Forsyth, "Thirty Years of Good Templary," International Good Templar, Feb. 1903, chapter 2. {TEXT}

few years Hickman faded into obscurity, but Malins remained the dominant personality in his Order.

Among the causes of this complex quarrel, racial prejudice stands out as the most obvious and the most fundamental. In the nineteenth century blacks often regarded drink as a form of slavery and temperance as liberation.[42] Many blacks wanted to join the Good Templar Order, but whites members in the South rejected racially mixed lodges and Grand Lodges. Most Templars in the northern and western States and in Canada acquiesced to the formation of racially segregated organizations in the South, so that white Templars there would not quit. Was this racism, or simply a practical compromise to make the IOGT available for both races? Most of the Templars in Britain answered racism and seceded from the American-dominated organization in 1876 to form an Order which claimed to be the true IOGT.

The Americans blamed the schism on the personal ambition of the British leaders. The large Grand Lodges in Britain had grown restive over American and Canadian dominance in the Order, a dominance which continued despite the decline in membership in North

---

42 Almost nothing has been published on the temperance movement in black organizational life. For an introduction, see Denise Herd, "`We Cannot Stagger to Freedom´: A History of Blacks and Alcohol in American Politics," in Leon Brill and Charles Winick, eds., The Yearbook of Substance Use and Abuse, vol. 3 (New York: Human Sciences Press, 1985). See also Herd´s contributions in Susanna Barrows, Robin Room, and Jeffrey Verhey, eds., The Social History of Alcohol: Drinking and Culture in Modern Society (Berkeley: Alcohol Research Group, Medical Research Institute of San Francisco, 1987).

America. The North Americans wanted to break up the Grand Lodges of England and Scotland--to form smaller, provincial Grand Lodges--which would have reduced the power of Malins.

Despite her social and psychological dependence on her lodge, Forsyth took an outspoken position on the unpopular side of the debate. As a recent immigrant she knew more about the British point of view than most American Templars. She was one of the few people in Boston to read the weekly organ of the Grand Lodge of England, the Good Templars´ Watchword. She also received frequent letters from her sister and brother-in-law arguing the secessionist case--that under its existing leadership the Order had failed to protect the rights of blacks. She had already encountered racial prejudice and had begun to form her lifelong dislike for it. In her first speech outside her own lodge, at a meeting to form a county organization, she defended the British position on equal rights for blacks and the English leader Joseph Malins. She had heard Malins speak in England, admired his "wonderful power, and zeal, and earnestness," and regarded him as the greatest man in the Order.[43] Although she was elected County Vice Templar, she rejected the office and withdrew to join a newly formed American affiliate of the Right Worthy Grand Lodge of the World.

Because this breakaway group had few adherents in North America, it offered abundant opportunities to its members. A talented, hardworking woman, with some experience as an office-holder, could rise quickly.

43 Forsyth, "Thirty Years of Good Templary," International Good Templar, Jan. 1903, chapter 1. {TEXT}

Although she did not see herself as ambitious, Forsyth
in practice soon became a leader in the new organization.   When a secessionist Grand Lodge was organized
in Massachusetts on the last day of 1877, she became
its Grand Vice Templar and three years later achieved
the much more important office of Grand Secretary.
Until his death she worked closely with Dr. William
Wells Brown, the Order's most prominent black member,
"one of the most distinguished members of the African
race which this country has ever produced."[44]   By hard
work and dedication, by endless devotion to the affairs
of the Grand Lodge, she prepared herself to enter onto
a still wider stage.

The crucial moment for her Templar career came
when the British-dominated Right Worthy Grand Lodge of
the World met in Halifax, Nova Scotia, in 1883.   If the
meeting had been held in Europe she could not have
attended, but she travelled the short distance between
Boston and Halifax as a delegate of the Grand Lodge of
Massachusetts.   At Halifax British members won nearly
all the elections for the offices which made up the
Executive Council.   The delegates wanted to provide the
Americans with a seat and elected Forsyth to the
office of Right Worthy Grand Vice Templar.   The
Englishwoman who presented her name knew so little
about her that she failed to make the customary
nominating speech.   Until they met her some delegates
had assumed that she was black.

The other members of the Executive Council
promptly turned to Forsyth to implement their

44   Forsyth, "Thirty Years of Good Templary," _Interna-
tional Good Templar_, March 1903, chapter 3.   {TEXT}

missionary work in the United States. The Negro
Mission Committee, largely funded by English Quakers,
appointed her its American agent. She also took on the
editorship of a monthly newspaper, Temperance Brotherhood. At 36 Forsyth began what amounted to a four-year
apprenticeship as writer and editor.[45] Optimistic
about the future, practical about the present, increasingly comfortable about her place in the Order's
leadership, she earned the respect of her colleagues in
the Templar hierarchy and also won their friendship.
Although she lacked time for "social pleasures" or even
adequate sleep, she enjoyed her work. She said that as
a result of her correspondence with Templars outside
Massachusetts, "my outlook became broader day by day,
and, in a word, I learned unconsciously that `mankind
is one, in its rights and wrongs,´ and that the field
of Good Templary was indeed the world."[46]

Her first surviving photograph dates from her
years as Right Worthy Grand Vice Templar. She appears
to have been a plain, rather serious-looking woman,
dark-haired, and perhaps below average in height. In

---

45   From October 1885 through May 1887 Forsyth's
monthly incorporated the International Good Templar
which previously had been published in Britain. For
this period Forsyth's own copy of Temperance Brotherhood survives at the State Library Service of Western
Australia, Perth, as part of a run of the International
Good Templar. No other newsprint copy seems to exist.
A microfilm is available at the King Library, Miami
University.

46   Forsyth, "Thirty Years of Good Templary," International Good Templar, June 1903, chapter 6. {TEXT}

later pictures she had become somewhat stocky.[47]
Apparently she fitted the model of the Victorian woman,
soft-spoken, gentle, and "womanly." In her account of
the Halifax meeting of 1883 she reported that "some of
the British representatives who had met me in Boston
had amused themselves by describing me to those who did
not know me as a tall, angular woman, with a loud
voice, a nasal twang, and a very aggressive manner."
Consequently Forsyth attracted many stares when people
first saw her. "I suppose that when I appeared the
contrast between the real and the imaginary individual
must have seemed funny."[48]

As an international officer she became a traveller, much to her delight. Her memoirs report her
enthusiasm at seeing new places--an enthusiasm
strengthened by her love of history, nature and the
arts--and her knack for making new friends. One advantage of travelling as a Templar, she said, was that she
often stayed in the homes of ordinary people rather
than in hotels. By the end of her service as an
international officer she had picked up a smattering of

---

47   See, for instance, Parker, History of the Independent Order of Good Templars, p. 245; International Good
Templar, Jan. 1889, p. 11; April 1902, p. 111; Sept.
1908, p. 303; (Glasgow) Good Templar, March 1894, p.
41; Cherrington, Standard Encyclopedia, p. 1019. In
the 1890s she was characterized as "worth her weight in
gold, and she isn´t very light either," and further
described as "business looking." Iowa Temperance Magazine, June 1896, p. 8; Oct. 1896, p. 11.

48   Forsyth, "Thirty Years of Good Templary," International Good Templar, chapter 5, May 1903. {TEXT}

languages, understood "some French and a very little German," and spoke a bit of Swedish.[49]

It was a Templar meeting in Europe which enabled her to return to England and for the first time see something of her native country outside London. In 1885 she attended the Right Worthy Grand Lodge session in Stockholm, travelling there by way of England, Germany, and Denmark, and returning by way of Norway, Scotland, and Ireland. She published reports of these travels in <u>Temperance Brotherhood</u> which show a keen eye for local color.

In addition to describing churches and fiords, railway journeys and peasant costumes she reported her encounters with foreign Templars, which in the case of Sweden meant she chronicled both their politeness and their prejudice. The Swedes, unaccustomed to women office-holders, relegated Forsyth and other women leaders to the back of the speakers' platform. Unhappy with these arrangements, the Englishman who presided, Joseph Malins, asked all the officers to give a brief speech, followed by a Swedish translation. Forsyth had little experience in speechmaking and none at all before an audience of 2000 people. But her anger over this blatant rejection of the equality of the sexes made her ready and eager to stand up and speak out. She regarded sexual equality as one of most important of the causes which the Order championed.

---

49   For her French and German, see "Some Notes of Travel," <u>International Good Templar</u>, Jan. 1906, chapter 3. {TEXT}   For a sample of her limited Swedish, see "Incidents in a Good Templar Life," <u>Australian Temperance World</u>, July 1929. {TEXT}

We were quite out of sight of the
audience and when my name was called and I
had to push my way through a crowd of brethren, I was conscious of a distinct feeling of
surprise on the part of the audience when
instead of a big man responding to the rather
imposing title of Right Worthy Grand Vice
Templar they saw only a little woman. But,
for once, I was equal to the occasion and I
began my speech with an apology for the embarrassment which I must necessarily feel at
standing before such an audience, because I
represented "a country in which it was not
the custom to put the women in the back
seats."[50]

REUNION

Upon her return to America she soon became active
in the movement to end the schism which divided Good
Templary. As editor of Temperance Brotherhood she made
it a point to send copies of the newspaper to her
fellow Templars, the leaders of the rival Hickmanite
branch of the Order. Moreover, as this organization
began to encourage the formation of black lodges in the
South, conflict developed among black reformers, some
belonging to lodges affiliated with Forsyth's Order
and others with the Hickmanites. She worried that

---

50   Forsyth, "Thirty Years of Good Templary," International Good Templar, July 1903, chapter 7. {TEXT}
See also Forsyth, "Good Templar Memories: Some Outstanding Templars," Australian Temperance World, May
1928, p. 12. She said nothing of this incident in a
contemporary account. "Some Notes of Travel," Temperance Brotherhood, Oct. 1885-April 1886. {TEXT}

this destructive rivalry obstructed the advance of
Good Templary and temperance reform among the black
people of the southern States. Forsyth served as a
delegate at the Boston union conference in 1886 and
helped draft the terms of reconciliation. In addition,
she participated in the meetings of the two Right
Worthy Grand Lodges at Saratoga Springs the following
year, which ratified the Boston treaty. Her memoirs
preserve many anecdotes from these two important years,
but as a loyal and discreet Templar she revealed little
about the politics of the negotiations.

After more than a decade of bitter conflict, the
rival organizations reunited, with the terms of the
settlement not much different from what had been un-
acceptably racist to the secessionists eleven years
earlier. The compromise created Junior Grand Lodges
for blacks not welcome in the original or Senior Grand
Lodges.

Forsyth took a practical view of the schism and
the reunion. She justified the original secession, but
recognized that the quarrel had become scandalous and
unproductive. Although she strongly supported and
sincerely rejoiced in the reunion, one suspects that
she was troubled that Catherine Impey of England, previously a close friend, condemned the Boston treaty.
Forsyth was personally committed to racial equality,
but unlike some of her closest associates on the
Mission Committee, insisted that the terms of reunion
did not betray that principle. She believed that the
schism had slowed temperance reform for both whites
and blacks. She herself belonged to a racially mixed
or integrated lodge in Boston, whose Chief Templar was

black.[51] It was sad for Forsyth to quarrel with some
of her old friends, black and white. But for her
temperance always came first among social and moral
reforms. She also loved the Order and wanted its
success.

In later reflections on the 1876-87 split, she
emphasized that, through a wise Providence, the conflict had brought about a number of positive achievements: it enabled the Order to attain "a higher conception of its principle of universal brotherhood"
than it might otherwise have done; it aroused Malins
and his allies to plant the Order in new lands; and
this in turn gave Templar leaders a wider perspective,
allowing them to cast their eyes "over all the
world."[52]

For Templar unity to become more than nominal, the
leaders from both factions had to learn how to cooper-
ate. At Saratoga, in a conciliatory gesture toward the
American ex-secessionists, the delegates elected Forsyth to the third highest office in the united Order.
A few months later she made a sacrifice which contributed toward strengthening the union which she had
helped forge.

The leader of the reunited Order, John B. Finch of
Illinois, died on October 3, 1887. As the constitution
provided, the Right Worthy Grand Counsellor, William W.

---

51   "Debate on Reunion in R.W.G. Lodge of the World,
Saratoga, New York, May 25, 1887," Good Templars'
Watchword, June 27, 1887. {TEXT}

52   Forsyth, "Thirty Years of Good Templary," International Good Templar, Oct. 1903, chapter 10. {TEXT}

Turnbull of Scotland, succeeded him. "Thus by a
strange providence, one who had been for years a leading member of the [secessionist] Right Worthy Grand
Lodge of the World, became head of the [re]united
body."[53] The unexpected death of the charismatic
Finch, a victim of a heart attack at age 35, had the
potential for reigniting the flames of factional
strife.

Although empowered by the constitution to take
over the vacant post of Counsellor, Forsyth decided
that the times required "a strong and influential man"
in that office, a leader of what until recently had
been the Hickmanite Order.[54] Perhaps she believed that
gender made her an impolitic choice for the senior
office. Certainly she knew that history disqualified
her: people from her old dissident organization could
not monopolize the highest offices in the reunited
Order. Some Templars might regard a woman as inadequate, but what made Forsyth's succession intolerable
was her Malinite past. To strengthen the bonds of
union, she put aside her own ambitions and nominated in
her stead the Mohawk Indian physician from Canada, Dr.
Oronhyatekha. The doctor had been outspoken in the
fight with Malins in 1876 and had been conciliatory as
a delegate at the Boston conference in 1886. Oronhyatekha was fully committed to the terms of the Boston
treaty and, as one of Finch's closest allies, was well-
informed on the deceased leader's plans for the reunited Order. Although Forsyth made the decision on

---

53   Forsyth, "Thirty Years of Good Templary," *International Good Templary*, Nov. 1903, chapter 11. {TEXT}

54   Ibid.

her own, she was pleased to learn that it coincided
with the wishes of her colleagues on the Executive
Council and that it had the blessings of Malins. Years
later she said that she had "never regretted" her re-
fusal to be tempted by "a foolish ambition."[55] Not
for the last time, she put the interests of the Order
above any personal aspirations.

She did not stand for re-election as Right Worthy
Grand Vice Templar in 1889. For the first time in a
dozen years she held neither Grand Lodge nor international office. This respite gave her time for other
interests, including a flirtation with the kind of
utopian socialism which Edward Bellamy promoted in his
book Looking Backward (1888). When the Second Boston
Nationalist Club was organized in 1889, she became a
charter member and its first secretary.[56]

Although Bellamy had little stomach for prohibition, Forsyth felt an affinity between his aims and
those of her Order. She knew that the principle of
human equality had been recognized in lodge-rooms

---

55   Forsyth, "A Memorable Executive Meeting," New York
Templar, May 1925, p. 13.   {TEXT}

56   Boston Traveller, reprinted in International Good
Templar, Nov. 1889, p. 683; Nationalist, Nov. 1889, p.
226.   She resigned as secretary to attend a Good
Templar meeting in Europe. New Nation, May 31, 1891,
p. 259.   The First Boston Nationalist Club, exclusive
in membership, abstract in argument, and under the
influence of theosophy, had attracted such temperance
reformers as Frances Willard, the WCTU leader. The
more democratic Second Boston Nationalist Club advocated immediate reforms such as municipal ownership of
gas and electric utilities. Its first president was a
woman lawyer. For an account of the appeal of Bellamy's ideas to women, see Bordin, Frances Willard, pp.
145-48.

around the world. She knew that the Order recognized no rank except that which it bestowed through election. She knew that the fundamental principle of Good Templary proclaimed that "there are no classes or races, but one human brotherhood." She regarded the teachings of the Order as "distinctly socialistic."[57] The essence of her socialism appears to have been a rejection of rule by the rich and the well-born, together with a belief that love and enlightened self-interest should unite humanity, one great family under God. Despite her sympathy for the ideas of Bellamy and socialism as she understood it, she refused to subordinate her temperance work to it or to believe that ending poverty would solve the drink problem.

Like many reformers who discovered how resistant to change the present generation was, Forsyth turned to education to shape a new generation. As Good Templary aged, its confidence in revivalistic conversion faded. Repentant drinkers appeared to be poor material for an effective reform movement. Forsyth indicted drink as guilty of many crimes. Most important, she argued, or more precisely assumed, that drinking alcohol signified a weakness in character and caused a weakness in character. She did not say that a repentant drunkard never could reclaim his character, but did say that he had to pay a bitter price.

We may if we believe him to be truly penitent, venture to assure him of God´s

---

57   Forsyth, "Some Side Issues of Good Templary," International Good Templar, April 1895. {TEXT} Reprinted from (Massachusetts) Templar. Also appeared in (Glasgow) Good Templar, Jan. 1895.

forgiveness, but we cannot prevent him from suffering the penalty of his misspent life, and realizing the truth of the inevitable law that "what a man sows, he reaps."

In her essay, "Begin at the Beginning," Forsyth urged "that the rising generation shall be spared these `wounds of the soul.´" Better a child preserved from the taint of drink than a reclaimed drunkard, "haunted by the remorseful memories of his wasted years and opportunities."[58] Elsewhere she hinted at another motive for pledging the young: forestalling "the hereditary appetite."[59]

Forsyth devoted her middle years to the children gathered in the Order´s Juvenile Temples. In 1890 she was elected Grand Superintendent of Juvenile Work for Massachusetts. In 1893 when the Right Worthy Grand Superintendent of Juvenile Work died, Forsyth succeeded her.[60] Her new responsibilities introduced her to an even wider world. Until 1908 she supervised children´s organizations and their adult advisors on six continents.[61] She devoted her salary to Templar purposes,

---

58   For the three preceding quotations, see Forsyth, "Begin at the Beginning," (Glasgow) Good Templar, March 1896. {TEXT} Also printed as a pamphlet.

59   Forsyth, "Urge the Pledge," (Boston) Temperance Cause, Sept. 1901. {TEXT}

60   Later the office was renamed the International Superintendent of Juvenile Work, and the Right Worthy Grand Lodge was renamed the International Supreme Lodge.

61   For a representative letter to Grand Superintendent of Juvenile Work, see Forsyth to H. A. Lawson, Oct. 19, 1899. General Correspondence, Grand Lodge of Wisconsin, I.O.G.T., Wis/Mss/JT, State Historical

particularly in travel to places where otherwise she
could not have gone.[62]   Although she did most of her
work through correspondence, she travelled widely, and
in her memoirs she can be found in Budapest and Winnipeg, Zurich and Des Moines, as well as in her Boston
home.

During her years of leadership, Juvenile Templary
faced two major problems. First, the controversy over
tobacco made it difficult to enforce a universal
system.   In 1899 the International Supreme Lodge
reluctantly authorized Grand Lodges to set up Junior
Lodges (which only required a pledge against drink),
and to allow Juvenile Temples to admit associate
members who only pledged themselves not to drink.
Details were left to the particular Grand Lodges, and
the old fourfold pledge, which included a promise not
to use tobacco, was encouraged.[63]   Unlike Juvenile
Temples, the Junior Lodges had the ability to enroll
youthful smokers.   The concession that associate
members of Juvenile Temples could smoke, addressed the
needs of jurisdictions, such as those in India, where
soldier Templars comprised most of the prospective
adult advisors for the children, and, like the non-
abstainers in the army, enjoyed their pipes.

Society of Wisconsin, Madison. {TEXT}

62   "Report of the International Superintendent of
Juvenile Work," International Good Templar, July 1908.
{TEXT}

63   Joseph Malins, "The Changes in the Juvenile
Templar Work," International Good Templar, Oct. 1899,
pp. 346-47.

For the other problem, the weakness of Juvenile
Templary in North America, no solution could be found.
Despite evidence that adult lodges needed Juvenile
Temples to recruit new members, only a few jurisdic-
tions made organizations for children a priority.[64]
The Grand Superintendent for Juvenile Work in Prince
Edward Island lamented, "I don´t know what to do; no
one seems to care anything about our Juvenile work."[65]
In addition to this lack of enthusiasm, Templar efforts
often had to compete with those of the various churches
and the Woman´s Christian Temperance Union in organizing children and young people.

Under Forsyth´s leadership Juvenile Templary
prospered statistically. When she was appointed, there
were almost 170,000 members in nearly 2900 juvenile
branches. Fifteen years later the juvenile membership
approached 240,000 in nearly 3500 branches. But this
represented the growth of the Juvenile Temples in
Europe. The weakness of the Order in North America
undermined the position of all American officers in the
international organization during the twentieth
century. People who in earlier times might have
belonged to the Templars preferred the Prohibition
Party or the Woman´s Christian Temperance Union or the
Anti-Saloon League or a denominational society. As a
result of the decline of the Order in America, Forsyth

---

64   Right Worthy Grand Lodge, Proceedings (1902), p.
243. California took the lead in such efforts.

65   Adelia E. Horton to Forsyth, n.d., in International Good Templar, July 1902, pp. 224-26.

had difficulty in winning re-election over the leader of the English Juvenile Temples in 1905.[66]

In 1908 Forsyth, then over 60, intended to retire from her post as International Superintendent of Juvenile Work. Perhaps that explains why she chose to be a candidate for Grand Secretary of Massachusetts. In the election, held in April 1908, she led on the first ballot with 143 of the 151 votes needed for victory. On the second ballot, a 28-year-old minister defeated her.[67] When the International Supreme Lodge convened in Washington in June 1908, Scandinavian representatives--among them her old friend Oskar Eklund, Grand Chief Templar of Sweden--persuaded her to change her mind and be a candidate for another three-year term.[68] On the first ballot she received 62 votes: J. W. Hopkins of England got 58, and a third candidate four votes. Election had required 63 votes. On the second ballot Hopkins was elected.[69] Forsyth

66 International Supreme Lodge, Proceedings (1905), p. 209.

67 Grand Lodge of Massachusetts, Proceedings (1908), pp. 10-11, 13.

68 Bessie Santesson to editor, Sept. 16, 1908, in International Good Templar, Oct. 1908, p. 365. The other Scandinavian leaders who urged Forsyth to be a candidate for re-election were Hugo Thorne, Grand Secretary of the Scandinavian Grand Lodge of New York, and Peder Swenson, of Norway, Past International Marshal.

69 International Supreme Lodge, Proceedings (1908), pp. 330-31. This was not a generational change, as the two candidates both had been born in 1847 (and both died in 1937).

often mentioned the presents which she received, but
not her retirement gifts, a gold chain and locket.[70]

The elections in 1908 also ended Forsyth´s work at
the International Good Templar which she had edited
since January 1901.[71] The American who had been
International Secretary was defeated for re-election.
For $500 he transferred to the International Supreme
Lodge the monthly newspaper which he had owned.[72] The
new International Secretary took it home with him to
Glasgow. Forsyth said her farewells as editor in
December 1908. Since 1901 her unpaid editorial work
had supported the Order´s sense of itself as an
international society with a proud history. As editor
she had commissioned herself to write her memoirs in
twenty-four parts, "Thirty Years of Good Templary,"
published in 1903-04.

Her work for the International Good Templar, as
editor and as writer, constituted her most important

---

70   International Good Templar, Aug. 1908, p. 288.
Martha B. O´Donnell, a veteran children´s advocate,
wryly noted that women had headed international
juvenile templary from 1874 until 1908, "when a Brother
from England superseded our highly esteemed, universally beloved and honored Sister Jessie Forsyth."
O´Donnell, "Reminiscences," New York Templar, Dec.
1909, p. [3].

71   Many Templar editors were women. For instance,
Mary Magdalene Forrester became the fifth editor of the
Good Templars´ Watchword in 1903 and served until 1932.
Joseph Malins, A Brief History of Good Templary in
England (3rd ed., Birmingham: Grand Lodge Offices;
London: R. J. James, [1922]), p. 9 note; Good Templars´
Watchword, Oct. 1932, p. 244. She also edited the
Juvenile Templar.

72   For the price, see Larsen-Ledet, Good Templary
Through Hundred Years, p. 26.

contribution to Templar journalism, but since the reunion of the Order she had written for several other
papers and in the 1890s had helped edit the (Massachusetts) _Templar_. She also wrote fiction and a little
poetry. Some of her short stories about children,
particularly the Elsie Foster series, seem to have
autobiographical moments, glimmers of Jessie Forsyth's
own childhood.

Seemingly the first decade of the twentieth
century marked the end of her career as a temperance
activist. After her defeat for re-election in 1908,
Forsyth held a few appointed offices. Immediately
after the loss of her International Grand Lodge office,
she had described herself as "ready in the future, as
in the past, to perform any task assigned to her."[73]
She took charge of the Course of Study--the Templar
home study program--late in 1908 and early in 1909 when
its director was dying, and she served on a couple of
committees in the new National Grand Lodge of the
United States, which had been organized in 1905.
(Forsyth had been a member of the "committee of seven"
which had drafted its plan of organization in 1904.)[74]
In 1910 she assumed responsibility for the international section, "Our Field--The World," in the National

73   _International Good Templar_, July 1908, p. 262.

74   "Brief History Leading to the Organization of the
National Grand Lodge, I.O.G.T., of the United States of
America," in National Grand Lodge, _Proceedings_ (1905),
pp. 6-9. Forsyth represented the Grand Lodge of
Massachusetts, "the prime mover" in the creation of the
National Grand Lodge. Willard O. Wylie to Lars O.
Jensen, Oct. 10, 1924. Box 8, Folder 48, George F.
Cotterill papers, University of Washington Libraries.

Grand Lodge´s new paper, the <u>National Good Templar</u>.[75]
But she had no expectation of ever again winning a
major elective office. Moreover, she suffered from
ill-health and longed to see her Australian relatives.

She decided to close her printing business and
leave Boston, her home since 1874. Unfortunately, only
scraps of information survive about her Massachusetts
days. Predictably she belonged to other temperance organizations, such as the Sons of Temperance, which had
a mutual insurance scheme, the Citizens´ Law and Order
League, the Woman´s Christian Temperance Union, and the
Massachusetts Total Abstinence Society (on whose board
of directors she served). She also joined the Woman´s
Suffrage Association.[76] At the turn of the century she
served on a committee, consisting of representatives of
the WCTU and Massachusetts officials, which drafted a
temperance syllabus for the public schools.[77] As a
devout Anglican she headed the Women´s Guild at the
Church of the Ascension for a time and taught in its
Sunday School.[78]

Forsyth had many women friends, particularly among
the leaders of the Juvenile Temples, but her closest

---

75   Willard O. Wylie to George F. Cotterill, Feb. 1,
1910. Box 24, Folder 16, George F. Cotterill papers,
University of Washington Libraries.

76   Yeames, "Miss Jessie Forsyth, R.W.V.T.," <u>Interna-
tional Good Templar</u>, Jan. 1889, p. 12; <u>Boston Travel-
ler</u>, reprinted in <u>International Good Templar</u>, Nov.
1889, p. 683.

77   <u>International Good Templar</u>, June 1900, p. 209;
Nov. 1903, p. 385.

78   <u>International Good Templar</u>, Jan. 1912, p. 12.

friend in Boston was a man, James Yeames. Like her he
had dedicated his life to children: he directed the
Juvenile Temples in England for several years, edited
the Juvenile Temple Review in that country, and wrote
many hymns and songs for young reformers. In the 1870s
he helped establish an illustrated temperance weekly,
the Templar, which reached a circulation of 30,000
under his editorship. Yeames, the first Right Worthy
Grand Templar in the secessionist Order, emigrated to
Boston late in 1883. He was a minister in the Methodist Episcopal Church. When Forsyth travelled overseas
in 1885, he substituted for her at the editorial desk
of Temperance Brotherhood. According to the Boston
city directory, Yeames and his family lived at the same
Boston boarding house as Forsyth during the years 1886-
91. When he removed to one of Boston's suburbs, one of
his sons, a printer, stayed on in that boarding house
home. On a couple of occasions James Yeames addressed
the Second Boston Nationalist Club when Forsyth was its
secretary. After Forsyth emigrated to Australia, she
corresponded with him every month until his death in
1931 and then with his widow and daughter.[79]

Forsyth had another close friend in Boston, Miguel
Sereque, by trade a printer. A native of the Azores,
he published a Portuguese-language newspaper widely
circulated in New England. He succeeded Forsyth in her
old Massachusetts office, Grand Superintendent of
Juvenile Temples, and later was elected Grand Chief

---

79 Forsyth to George F. and Cora R. Cotterill, Jan.
18, 1932. Box 23, Folder 27, George F. Cotterill
papers, University of Washington Libraries. {TEXT}

Templar. He named his daughter Jessie and his son
Forsyth.[80]

In the autumn of 1911 the Templars of Massachusetts held a farewell reception for Forsyth. She
thanked the Order for giving her "opportunities for a
nobler, more useful, and, therefore, a happier life"
than that which she might have experienced had she not
been invited to join the Templars.[81] In addition to
opportunities for service the Order had provided her
with dear friends. Forsyth often pointed out that
isolation from her only relatives made her value
friendship more than other people did.[82] The Yeames
and the Sereque families provided a large part of the
small group which said goodbye to her at the Boston
railroad station. When her friends could no longer see
her, she allowed herself some tears. She knew that she
would never again look upon those faces which had been
a familiar, comforting part of her existence. She had
begun the first stage of a journey to the other side of
the world. In her mid-60s Forsyth bravely looked
forward to life in Australia and joining her family,
most of whom she had never met.

AUSTRALIA

The Smiths made up this Australian family. In
1876 Jessie's sister Maria had married Thomas Smith, a

---

80   *International Good Templar*, April 1906, pp. 125-
26, May 1908, p. 175.

81   *International Good Templar*, Jan. 1912, p. 12. The
quoted words were reported as a paraphrase.

82   Forsyth, "Thirty Years of Good Templary," *International Good Templar*, Dec. 1903, ch. 12. {TEXT}

few years after they had met in an Islington lodge. In
1881 they had emigrated to Western Australia where the
only Forsyth brother, George, had settled. Thomas
prospered as a tailor and outfitter. He became mayor
of Fremantle, the port city for Perth, and Grand Chief
Templar of Western Australia. Maria also held office
in the Grand Lodge, as did the eldest of their four
daughters. Jessie Forsyth-Smith, named after her aunt,
became Grand Superintendent of Juvenile Work at age
21. Her parents had taken Jessie to her first lodge
meeting when she was two months old.[83] Thomas Smith
died shortly after his sister-in-law reached Western
Australia. Her brother George had died many years
earlier. Thus, in the last years of her life Forsyth
entered a family of women: her widowed sister, her
widowed sister-in-law, and her four nieces. Apparently
only one of the nieces married, Jessie's namesake and
favorite: Jessie Forsyth-Waugh had her daughter
christened Jessie Forsyth.

The oldest of the three Jessies sailed from Vancouver to Sydney late in 1911 and arrived in Fremantle
in January 1912, with her health much improved by the
restful sea voyage.[84] Instead of a life of retirement
she began a new chapter of temperance activism in this

---

83   "A West Australian Good Templar Family," _Interna-
tional Good Templar_, Feb. 1896, p. 40; "Jessie Forsyth-Smith, G.S.J.T., Western Australia," _International
Good Templar_, Nov. 1898, pp. 363-64; "Two West Australian Workers," _International Good Templar_, June 1903,
pp. 208-9.

84   Forsyth to Cora R. Cotterill, July 13, 1929. Box
4, Folder 5, George F. Cotterill papers, University of
Washington Libraries. {TEXT}

new world.[85] In 1912 she was elected Grand Superintendent of Juvenile Work, serving a single term, and could have been elected Grand Chief Templar in 1914.[86] Although she insisted that Good Templary remained her greatest love, Forsyth did most of her temperance work in Western Australia through the Woman's Christian Temperance Union.[87] In 1912 she was elected president

---

85 For some details of Forsyth's work in Australia, see an obituary sketch written by the WCTU of Western Australia, "Veteran Pioneer Woman Social Welfare Worker Passes: A Tribute to the Memory of the Late Miss Jessie Forsyth," (Melbourne) White Ribbon Signal, Dec. 1, 1937, p. 224.

86 Forsyth to George H. Hazzard, Feb. 25, 1915. A.H431, Hazzard (George Henry) papers, Archives/Manuscripts Division, Minnesota Historical Society. {TEXT} The Grand Lodge which Forsyth could have headed was very small, only 273 members in nine lodges, with 419 children in seven Juvenile Temples.

87 The most accessible introductions to the WCTU in Australia are Anthea Hyslop, "Temperance, Christianity, and Feminism: The Woman's Christian Temperance Union of Victoria, 1887-97," Historical Studies 17 (April 1976); and three comparative studies: Ross Evans Paulson, Women's Suffrage and Prohibition: A Comparative Study of Equality and Social Control (Glenview, IL: Scott, Foresman, 1973); Richard K. Evans, The Feminists: Women's Emancipation Movements in Europe, America and Australasia, 1840-1920 (New York: Barnes & Noble, 1977); and Ian R. Tyrrell, "International Aspects of the Woman's Temperance Movement in Australia: The Influence of the American WCTU, 1882-1914," Journal of Religious History 12 (June 1983). For an analysis of what Australians drank, see A. E. Dingle, "'The Truly Magnificent Thirst': An Historical Survey of Australian Drinking Habits," Historical Studies 19 (Oct. 1980). For bibliographies on women and on drink, see Phyl Garrick, "'People of Glass': Women Becoming Visible in the History of Western Australia," Studies in Western Australian History 7 (Dec. 1983); and David M. Fahey, "Australia and New Zealand: A Bibliography of Drink and Temperance," Alcohol in History: A Multidisciplinary Newsletter (since renamed Social History of Alcohol Review), no. 11 (Spring 1983).

of the Fremantle WCTU and became the salaried superintendent of a WCTU mission for seamen in Fremantle, the
Sailors' Rest, where she resided.[88] During 1913-16 she
served as State President of the WCTU.[89] In 1915 the
WCTU of Western Australia reported a membership of 312
women organized in 10 unions.[90] In 1916 Forsyth left
the Sailor's Rest and, at age 69, opened a drygoods
shop.[91]

In 1917 she moved to Melbourne to become organizing secretary of the newly founded Australian National
Prohibition League.[92] To her disappointment the League

---

88   International Good Templar, May 1912, p. 90. When
a Good Templar lodge was organized at the Sailors' Rest
in 1914, Forsyth became its treasurer. An English-born
friend from Massachusetts, Mrs. Bessie H. (Mountford)
Santesson, served as Chief Templar, and her Swedish-
born husband also held office in the lodge. International Good Templar, May 1908, pp. 161-62; New York
Templar, Feb. 1915, p. 9. Bessie Santesson replaced
Forsyth as corresponding secretary of the State WCTU in
1922, a year before the former returned to America.
Report of the 31st Annual Convention of the WCTU of
Western Australia (1923), p. 13. She provides another
illustration of the internationalism of the temperance
movement.

89   The Minute books show that Forsyth first chaired
an Executive Committee meeting as State President on
Sept. 9, 1913, and signed the minutes as State President for the last time on March 14, 1916. Nola A.
Adams (State President, WCTU of Western Australia) to
the author, April 10, 1986.

90   Minutes of the Ninth Triennial Australasian WCTU
(1915), p. 51.

91   Forsyth to Laura D. Rudy, New York Templar, June
1916. {TEXT}

92   Forsyth to Cora R. Cotterill, March 17, 1917. Box
26, Folder 9, George F. Cotterill papers, University of
Washington Libraries. {TEXT}

merged in the following year with another, less militant organization behind the program of the "Strength
of the Empire" movement for wartime prohibition. Although she considered an offer to join the staff of
the merged organization, she returned to Western Australia where she remained for the rest of her life.
Her family wanted her back, and she had suffered a bad
bout of grippe.[93]

She set about making herself useful in Western
Australia. In 1919 she served as the founding editor
of The Dawn, then the organ of the Fremantle Women's
Service Guild.[94] In the same year she resumed work for
the WCTU of Western Australia. She became press superintendent and, in December, corresponding secretary.[95] Her WCTU friends described her as "a great
lover of children and of books and mankind in general."[96]

---

93 The "Strength of the Empire" movement was Australia's version of the "Strength of Britain" movement,
which beginning in 1916 had argued for wartime prohibition in the United Kingdom. In Australia the movement
also emphasized social (or sexual) purity.

94 International Good Templar, Jan. 1920, p. 247;
Country Women's Association of Western Australia,
Pioneer Women's Memorial Fund (1976), PRS 8894/3,
Battye Library, Perth (a reference I owe to Margaret
Medcalf, principal librarian).

95 The Minute books identify her as press superin-
tendent on June 10, 1919 and report her appointment as
State corresponding secretary on December 16, 1919.
She also was secretary of the Fremantle WCTU in 1919.
Nola A. Adams to the author, April 10, 1986.

96 Obituary by WCTU of Western Australia, in (Melbourne) White Ribbon Signal, Dec. 1937, p. 224.

In 1921 she fell desperately ill and expected to die. Before she made a partial recovery she had shrunk to less than a hundred pounds. For the rest of her life she needed a stick to walk.[97] At the beginning of 1922 she resigned.[98] "This is rather a trial to me, as my brain is as active as ever and my memory as good, but having rounded out my fifty years of active service I must not complain at being compelled to be still."[99]

Thereafter, she had to be content to serve the cause with her typewriter and seldom attended temperance meetings.[100] She accepted a vice-presidency of the West Australian Alliance in 1925, a militant new organization which adopted an old name, after a split in the ranks of local temperance reformers. On the first day of May 1926, she made a rare public appearance to deliver the opening address at a banquet commemorating the fiftieth anniversary of the Grand Lodge of Western Australia. Later that year she took over a children's column in the West Australian White

---

97   Forsyth to Willard O. Wylie, New York Templar, Sept. 1921. {TEXT}

98   Forsyth to WCTU, n.d., in West Australian White Ribbon, Feb. 1922. {TEXT} The WCTU Executive accepted the resignation on Jan. 10. A farewell meeting honored Forsyth on Feb. 23. New York Templar, April 1922, p. 5.

99   Forsyth to Willard O. Wylie, New York Templar, June 1923. {TEXT}

100   In declining an invitation from the North Leederville League of Hope, she said that "I cannot be out at night alone, and so have to lose a great many pleasant times." "Auntie Jet" (pen name), "Our Young People," West Australian White Ribbon, Nov. 1929, p. 4. I owe this reference to Margaret Medcalf, principal librarian, Battyle Library, Perth, Western Australia.

Ribbon under a pen name, Auntie Jet.[101] It was in this
semi-anonymous format that Forsyth offered glimpses of
her early life which her formal memoirs had ignored.
In the late 1920s she published a number of articles of
Templar reminiscence in the Australian Temperance
World, the organ of the Grand Lodge of New South Wales,
some of which also appeared in the New York Templar.
For the most part these memoirs duplicate her earlier
ones in the International Good Templar, but sometime
add details and seem more candid about her own feelings.

In her active years she had been a tireless
letter-writer, and in the final fifteen years of her
life, as a semi-invalid, she continued to correspond
with old friends throughout her Templar world and
enjoyed their letters and the papers which they often
enclosed.[102] "In fact, the receiving and replying to
letters is now my chief occupation, for I cannot do

---

101   For the column, "Our Young People," Forsyth used
the pen name Auntie Jet. She explained that it was a
name "which a dear little boy who loved me very much,
but who long ago went to the `Better Land´ used to call
me." West Australian White Ribbon, June 1926, p. 4.
The column consisted of letters and other contributions
from children. When the children failed to write,
Auntie Jet filled the column with her opinions and
memories.

102   For instance, she received the (Capetown) Tribune
from its editor, F. E. Dexter, who had been Grand
Superintendent of Juvenile Work for the Grand Lodge of
Western South Africa, and the WCTU organ, Our Message,
from Massachusetts friends. West Australian White
Ribbon, Oct. 1927, p. 4; June 1928, p. 4.

much active work."[103] Gradually, as her old friends
died, however, her world of temperance reform and Good
Templary began to shrink. So did her family. Her
favorite niece and namesake died in 1931, and her
sister in 1932.[104]

Jessie Forsyth died on September 18, 1937, in
Leederville, a suburb of Perth. At the time of her
death she was a member of Unity Lodge, No. 12, Grand
Lodge of Western Australia.[105] Her death certificate
ascribed her death, at age 90, to cardiac failure and
bronchopneumonia. She was buried in the Methodist
cemetery, Fremantle, with an Anglican clergyman
officiating.[106] No one applied for a Grant of Administration for her estate "which would seem to indicate
that she left no assets requiring administration."[107]

Forsyth had remained loyal to Good Templary for 65
years. With the exception of a Swedish colleague, and

---

103   Forsyth to George F. and Cora R. Cotterill, Jan.
18, 1932, cited earlier. {TEXT} During the 1926
Christmas season she received a "shower" of letters and
cards from Sweden, with a dozen arriving in a single
postal delivery. Forsyth ("Auntie Jet"), "Our Young
People," West Australian White Ribbon, March 1927, p. 4.

104   International Good Templar, April 1931, p. 125;
July 1932, p. 226.

105   (Perth) West Australian, Sept. 21, 1937, p. 1.
There were only 130 members in the Grand Lodge of
Western Australia in 1937. International Good Templar,
July 1946, p. 63.

106   Western Australia, Certified Copy of an Entry in
the Register of Death, column no. 1667/37, for Jessie
Forsyth.

107   Public Trustee, Public Trust Office, Western
Australia, to the author, Jan. 24, 1985.

perhaps one or two others, she was the last survivor of the bitter schism of 1876-1887 and the healing of the Order at Boston and Saratoga.[108]

Although Forsyth told much about herself, her silences were vast. Her energy and her humanity stand out clearly, but it is impossible to be certain about her motives, why Forsyth lived the life that she did, or her attitude toward drunkards and moderate drinkers and those teetotalers who did not share her program. Some things are certain. She lived during the heyday of the WCTU and served as one of its officers in Western Australia, but preferred the IOGT which joined men and women in a common organization. Although she had no children of her own, there were thousands of boys and girls in the Juvenile Temples whom she called "my big family."[109] In Good Templary and the temperance movement she found more than a moral cause. She discovered her home, her family.

CONCLUSION

Jessie Forsyth´s world of Good Templary still lives in her memoirs, correspondence, and other writings. She is both a historian of the Order and a source for later historians. Since she wrote to strengthen the commitment of fellow members, she did not dwell upon the struggles within the Order or make her memoirs a weapon in such conflicts. It was not that Forsyth had a bland personality. "Strong in her

---

108 Oskar Eklund, who had taken part in the meeting at Halifax in 1883, died in 1940.

109 Forsyth ("Auntie Jet"), "Our Young People," West Australian White Ribbon, March 1927, p. 4.

likes and dislikes," she had a temper and could be sarcastic.[110]   She replied vigorously when Catherine Impey criticized her for helping to organize a segregated Junior Grand Lodge in Virginia.   Forsyth carefully marshalled her evidence to suggest that the Quaker champion of racial equality had insulted "the intelligence of the colored Virginians" by insinuating that they had been manipulated.[111]   In a very few instances Forsyth judged someone harshly in private correspondence, notably her condemnation of Albert Sutcliffe, sometime Grand Chief Templar of Massachusetts, as a none too scrupulous troublemaker.[112]   In public she ordinarily was a gentle critic--when she criticized at all.

Her strength as a historian lies elsewhere.   She evokes a sense of the fabric of Good Templary: what it was like to be a member and an officer in the late nineteenth and the early twentieth centuries.   Although her memoirs are her most important writings, they must be supplemented by her other work.   Her biographies of Oronhyatekha, the Mohawk physician, and Charlotte Gray, the Templar missionary on the European Continent, illustrate the diversity within the Order's leadership.

---

110 For the quoted words, see the obituary by the WCTU of Western Australia, in (Melbourne) White Ribbon Signal (Dec. 1937), p. 224.

111 Forsyth to editor, Good Templars' Watchword, May 1, 1888, as printed in International Good Templar, May 1888. {TEXT} The letter appeared under the title "Dual Grand Lodge."

112 Forsyth to George F. Cotterill, Nov. 11, 1905, Nov. 24, 1925. Box 23, Folders 4, 27, George F. Cotterill papers, University of Washington Libraries. {TEXT}

Forsyth's short stories, some set in Templar lodges and others in the lives of small children, open another, charming vista on the world of Good Templary, one peopled with humble folk. Her official reports, and a variety of essays on the Order and the temperance movement, show the practical temperament of a woman of business, while her correspondence--which confirms that portrait--reveals a lively and vigorous personality.

Her witness is invaluable on three topics with which her life had been intertwined: the Juvenile Temples, Templar internationalism, and the "Negro Question" of 1876-87. Templar writers always recognized the importance of the work among the children, but, unlike Forsyth, they did little more than report statistics and legislation. Although internationalism became a major theme in the Order, few members embodied the worldwide life of the Order as impressively as she did. After the reunion, official histories avoided detail on the bitter schism, and no other account provides the perspective of the American supporters of the British-dominated Right Worthy Grand Lodge of the World.

As a writer Forsyth ranks among the better journalists who, without pay, filled the pages of the many hundreds of publications sponsored by voluntary organizations in the late nineteenth and the early twentieth century. She made no stylistic contribution to literature. Her memoirs often stagger under the weight of her co-workers' names and the lengthy initials of their official titles. Sentimentality overwhelms any literary art in her fiction. But Forsyth knew her audience and her purpose. She wanted to be an effective teacher--lively, intelligible, reasonable--and she succeeded.

Through her writings she also helps us understand how the Templars differed from the more conventional branches of the temperance movement. The Order attracted radicals of all sorts. Forsyth, without being an ideologue, deserves to be counted as a determined critic of the kind of respectability which preferred appearance to work and love.

She strongly advocated equal rights for women. From age 15 she earned her own living and took "a pardonable pride in being able to say that she has always maintained her independence and taken care of herself."[113] As already noted, she fought back in 1885 when she saw herself and her sisters relegated to the back of the speakers´ platform. In an article published in that year, she described Swedish peasant women "doing men´s work and--what is better--receiving men´s wages."[114] The accomplishments of women in Good Templary had shown that women possessed equal ability. In the mid-1890s she proudly declared "that it is hardly possible to find an intelligent male Good Templar who is not a woman suffragist."[115] Probably a few unintelligent male Templars existed. She had to chide a Right Worthy Grand Templar in 1893 because of

---

113 Yeames, "Miss Jessie Forsyth, R.W.G.V.T.," _International Good Templar_, Jan. 1889, p. 11.

114 "Some Notes of Travel," _Temperance Brotherhood_, Jan. 1886, p. 5. {TEXT} Reprinted with minor changes in _International Good Templar_, March 1902.

115 Forsyth, "Side Issues of Good Templary," _International Good Templar_, Jan. 1895. {TEXT}

the "very few sisters" he had appointed to committees. Angrily dismissing speculation about his gallantry, she described the question as "simply one of justice."[116] In discussing "Some Reasons for the Decline of Good Templary in the United States," she pointed out that many of the women prominent in the WCTU had started their temperance work as Templars. "And let it be whispered in passing that a little less greed for office on the part of the brothers and little more readiness to give the sisters the equal rights promised by the Order might have prevented the defection of some of these good women."[117] She later criticized the International Supreme Lodge for not electing any women officers between 1911 and 1930.

> I do not like my sex to be slighted, and I am sure that there are many women members now who are equally deserving of international honors, [sic] and equally capable of fulfilling the duties which go with them, as are the brothers who monopolise the offices.[118]

116 Forsyth, "Des Moines Driftwood," International Good Templar, Aug. 1893. {TEXT} It first appeared in (Massachusetts) Templar.

117 Forsyth, "Some Reasons for the Decline of Good Templary in the United States," International Good Templar, May 1911. {TEXT}

118 Forsyth, "Incidents in a Good Templar Life," Australian Temperance World, Aug. 1929. {TEXT} Joseph Malins denounced the absence of women among the elected international officers as "a barbarism." Joseph Malins to Edvard Wavrinsky, July 7, 1916. Box 23, Folder 6, George F. Cotterill papers, University of Washington Libraries.

In filling international offices the Order had posted a better record in the nineteenth century.

Despite these reluctant complaints, she remained convinced that Good Templary and the temperance movement in general advanced the cause of women. She rejoiced when she could report a meeting in Dresden where all the speakers were women: contrary to the image of the passive German hausfrau, German women had joined "the fight against the great foe of the family and the home."[119] Forsyth did not argue for a feminist analysis of the family or the economy or political power, but she instinctively took a stand for the equal rights and the equal abilities of women.

She almost certainly accepted the nineteenth-century concept of "separate spheres," which assigned women functions related to the home, but she chose to work through a temperance organization not segregated by gender.[120] It would have been easy for Forsyth to have turned to the WCTU in the late 1870s and have made it her principal temperance organization, after she had left the branch of the Templars which was dominant in America, but she did not. Although women played a disproportionate role in the management of the Juvenile Temples, this was not considered women's work in Good Templary. It was a man who defeated Forsyth for re-election as International Superintendent of Juvenile Templars in 1908, and men led many of the local

119 "Some Notes of Travel," International Good Templar, Jan. 1906, chapter 3. {TEXT}

120 In her preference for an organization which combined men and women, Forsyth makes a striking contrast with Frances Willard.

Juvenile Temples, particularly in Europe. On the other
hand, although she claimed that her heart still lay
with the IOGT, Forsyth spent most of her time in Western Australia working for the WCTU.

Forsyth was a deeply committed Christian. She
declared in a private letter that "I never can imagine
how people who do not believe in God can endure life."
She added that "I regard it as something to be devoutly
thankful for that I can look, with the faith of [a]
child, up to the Father of all and trust my hopes and
plans, and wishes in His hand." Yet Forsyth despised
"the frothy and wordy religion professed by some people
. . . which has so little influence upon their
lives."[121] She had no use for the respectable religious folk who kept aloof from the IOGT because of its
egalitarianism and its embarrassing admission of
reformed drunkards. In one of her serialized short
stories, a factory foreman rejected the rector´s invitation to come to church with a sharp reproof: "I
will come to church, sir, when some of those stuck-up
Christians come and join our Good Templar lodge."[122]
In her fiction she often represented initiation in the
Order as a preparation for church membership, but in
these stories the favored churches enjoyed the leadership of Templar ministers.

She confidently saw the hand of God in this world.
Without "the influence of the Holy Spirit" the Templar

121 Forsyth to George F. Cotterill, Sept. 2, 1903. Box
23, Folder 4, George F. Cotterill papers, University of
Washington Libraries. {TEXT}

122 Forsyth, "A Little Leaven," International Good
Templar, April 1899, p. 123.

reunion deliberations in 1886 would have failed.[123] Not even the horrors of the First World War could shatter her serene confidence in Divine Providence. "It is all very sad and it is difficult to believe that some good purpose is behind it all, but we must believe that. If we refuse to believe that we must doubt the wisdom and goodness of God."[124]

Her socialism of brotherhood and sisterhood sprang from a sense of what was morally right, not from economic analysis. She never mentioned a socialist writer other than Edward Bellamy, and she quickly abandoned her enthusiasm for his "New Nation." Although there is little evidence that she remained a socialist after the 1890s, she made no contrary commitment to <u>laissez-faire</u>, or to a society which supported inequality of status or power. Her opposition to the drink-sodden <u>status quo</u> helped make her a radical for life. Socialists were well-represented in Good Templary in Britain and Sweden, and a Labour ministry took power in Western Australia before the First World War, so, even after her Second Boston Nationalist Club days, Forsyth knew something about alternatives to the capitalist state. Although she firmly rejected the contention that socialism could solve the problem of poverty without help from the temperance movement, she

---

123 Forsyth, "The Historic Union Conference," <u>New York Templar</u>, Nov. 1923, p. 6.

124 Forsyth to Laura D. Rudy, in <u>New York Templar</u>, June 1916. {TEXT}

also dismissed as naive the claim that teetotalism by itself could end poverty.[125]

Although not the only needed reform, temperance raised a banner behind which other reforms could rally in the knowledge that they joined an ally. Somewhat like the environmentalist movement in the late twentieth century, the temperance movement in the late nineteenth century managed to combine traditionalism and radicalism, individualism and collectivism, piecemeal change and utopian vision, and--although seeing its agitation as paramount in importance--recognized that men and women of goodwill must join the battle against a host of evils. These tensions and this openness toward all kinds of reform--from vegetarianism to pacifism--characterized the more radical sections of the temperance movement such as the Good Templars.

Good Templary educated its members. Forsyth hoped that in fighting "that mighty foe drink," Templars learned "to overcome all distinctions of race or nationality, sex or creed." She believed that the Templar brotherhood rejected the class system, and saw similarity between the aims of the Order and the spirit of socialism. In the 1890s she asserted that the internationalism of Good Templary aided "the work of the Peace Societies" in making war obsolete.[126]

---

125 Forsyth, "Drink versus Poverty," _International Good Templar_, July 1912. {TEXT} Reprinted in _New York Templar_, Aug. 1912; and (Perth, Western Australia) _Reformer_.

126 Forsyth, "Some Side Issues of Good Templary," _International Good Templar_, April 1895. {TEXT}

(Despite this hope she reported at the end of the First
World War that a third of the members of the Grand
Lodges of Western Australia and Victoria had served
with the Australian expeditionary forces.)[127]

Her feminism, reform-minded Christianity, and
radical instincts enhanced her portrait of Good Templary, and so did another more personal characteristic.
She had a need and a gift for friendship. She never
forgot that the Templars were a fraternal order as well
as a temperance society. Her memoirs and other writings make fellowship a theme as important as reform.
She often reminded her readers that Templars liked to
laugh, to tell stories, to sing, and to enjoy a good
time. She also recognized in the Order "its power to
awaken ambition and to inspire many of its members to
cultivate their natural gifts."[128] Good Templary
demanded self-sacrifice, but it rewarded its members
generously. Her friends honored her as the "Little
Duchess."[129]

Forsyth knew that the Templars had opened up a new
life for her, had given her access to a much wider
world, and had saved her from "what might otherwise
have been a dull and colorless" existence and

---

127 Forsyth to Laura D. Rudy, in New York Templar,
March 1919. {TEXT}

128 Forsyth, "The Worth of Good Templary," New York
Templar, July 1925. {TEXT} Reprinted in Australian
Temperance World, April 1927.

129 George W. E. Hill, Some Good Templars I Have
Known: Brief Biographies of Our Most Eminent Workers
(Grand Valley, MI: Valley City, 1893), p. 34.

unspeakable loneliness.[130] She repaid the Order by preserving for history the world of the Good Templars, her world.

---

130 "Thirty Years of Good Templary," International Good Templar, Dec. 1904, chapter 24. {TEXT}

Abbreviations

The lengthy Templar titles were often abbreviated. The head of a Grand Lodge would be:

G.W.C.T.   Grand Worthy Chief Templar
G.C.T.   Grand Chief Templar

These titles refer to the same office; in 1886 "Worthy" was dropped.

A person formerly holding this office would be:

P.G.W.C.T.   Past Worthy Grand Chief Templar
P.G.C.T.   Past Grand Chief Templar

The head of a District Lodge would be District Chief Templar, or D.C.T., the former head of a District Lodge would be a Past District Chief Templar, or P.D.C.T., and so forth.

The head of the Right Worthy Grand Lodge would be:

R.W.G.T.   Right Worthy Grand Templar

When the Right Worthy Grand Lodge was renamed the International Supreme Lodge, its head would be:

I.C.T.   International Chief Templar

Most other titles can be understood by analogy. A Grand Chief Templar appointed liaison officers who would be:

```
L.D.                    Lodge Deputy
D.D.                    District Deputy
```

Similarly a liaison officer for the International Chief Templar would be:

```
D.I.C.T.               Deputy International Chief Templar
```

In order to avoid confusion with another office, words in some titles were not contracted to a single letter. Treasurer was ordinarily abbreviated "Treas.," or "Tr."

The names for the supreme bodies were often abbreviated:

```
R.W.G.L.               Right Worthy Grand Lodge
I.S.L.                 International Supreme Lodge
```

The local lodge was called a Subordinate Lodge, or Sub-Lodge, or most commonly and most simply, a Lodge.

Brother was commonly abbreviated as "Bro." or "Br.," while Sister became "Sis."

Editorial Note

I have organized Jessie Forsyth´s writings into three sections: memoirs, 1872-1912, from her decision to join the Order until her arrival in Western Australia; letters from Australia, 1913-1934, which continue her autobiography; and a grand miscellany which I have called representative writings, 1882-1932. They include official reports, short stories, letters (written before she emigrated to Australia), and a great many didactic essays urging Templars to pursue some particular policy or encouraging them to remain confident of the worth of the Order. The divisions separating these three categories are not rigid. Forsyth wrote no account of the important year 1908, so her final report as International Superintendent of the Juvenile Work is reprinted as part of the memoirs. A few memoirs, particularly from 1885-86, poorly fit the structure of the memoir section and consequently appear under representative writings. Other memoirs, which she wrote in old age, have been excerpted in extended footnotes in the first section.

When citing monthly publications I omit the day of the month. When Forsyth or her printer misspelled a word I silently correct the error. In nearly all instances I have left her punctuation alone.

I have located a couple dozen unpublished letters. The most important are part of the George F. Cotterill papers, University of Washington Libraries, Seattle. Two letters, one of them important, are preserved in the George Henry Hazzard papers, Minnesota Historical Society, manuscripts/archives division, St. Paul. Many routine letters appear in the Grand Lodge of Wisconsin papers, State Historical Society of Wisconsin, Madison.

Jessie Forsyth published extensively. Unfortunately for the historian her work appeared in serials which survive in few copies. A good deal of detective work has been necessary to gather together her published writings.

I first stumbled upon her "Thirty Years of Good Templary" while reading the International Good Templar at the United Kingdom Alliance, which maintains an excellent temperance library at its London headquarters. The Grand Lodge of England recently had turned over to the Alliance a substantial collection of Templar publications. Britain too is the place to read the Good Templars' Watchword, at the British Library newspaper library in Colindale, and the (Glasgow) Good Templar, at the Mitchell Library, Glasgow. (Colindale lacks the years when Forsyth published in the Good Templar.)

The United States has many excellent, if rarely used, collections of Templar publications. For this book the most important has been the Edward C. Sturges temperance collection, Cornell University, Department of Manuscripts and University Archives, which includes most of the International Good Templar and a nearly

complete New York Templar. I filled the gaps in what
Cornell had of the International Good Templar with the
holdings of the State Historical Society of Wisconsin,
Madison, and the Library of Congress, and missing
numbers in Cornell's New York Templar with those at the
Michigan Historical Collections, Bentley Historical
Library, University of Michigan. I copied the speech
published in the Temperance Cause at the State Historical Society of Wisconsin. The Ohio Historical Society,
Columbus, provided parts of two Australian temperance
papers in which Forsyth published, the Western Australian White Ribbon and the Australian Temperance World.

I obtained copies of memoirs which Forsyth had
published in other volumes of the Australian Temperance
World from the Mitchell Library, Sydney. The State
Library Service of Western Australia, Perth, has Jessie
Forsyth's own copy of Temperance Brotherhood, for
October 1885 through May 1887, when it incorporated the
Right Worthy Grand Lodge of the World's International
Good Templar. The King Library, Miami University, has
a microfilm.

Part One:
Memoirs, 1872-1912

This section combines "Thirty Years of Good Templary," published in 1903-04, with subsequent memoirs and an abridged version of Forsyth´s final report as International Superintendent of the Juvenile Work in 1908. When the memoirs which Forsyth published in the late 1920s do not duplicate what she had written earlier, the new material has been placed in footnotes in this section or assigned to the section, "Representative Writings." Her first extended piece of writing, "Some Notes of Travel," originally published in 1885-86, has been placed in "Representative Writings" in order to reproduce it in full.

THIRTY YEARS OF GOOD TEMPLARY

[<u>International Good Templar</u>, Jan. 1903-Dec. 1904]

Chapter I

I JOIN THE ORDER AND MEET ONE OF ITS GREATEST MEN

"I tell you what it is, girls, you will have to join the Good Templars."

The speaker was a young man friend of the family,
who was remarkable for the enthusiasm with which he
entered upon any new enterprise. We, my sister [Maria]
and myself, and the two elderly aunts who had shared
their comfortable and pretty London home with us, since
the death of our parents, were, with our guest, seated
around the tea-table and the sudden announcement quoted
above almost made me drop one of my aunt's delicate and
precious china teacups.[1] My sister, who was an

---

1   Forsyth ignores her childhood in "Thirty Years of
Good Templary," but gives a brief account of it in a
column for children which she wrote as an old woman
under the pen name Auntie Jet.

"I think children always like to hear anything
about the childhood days of older people, so perhaps,
Sylvia [a 12-year-old correspondent] will be interested
in hearing that Auntie Jet was not able to go to school
until she was twelve years old, because of ill health.
She lived in a suburban part of the great city of
London, near the famous Hampstead Heath. That part is
now built upon, but in those days it was almost like
country, and one had only to go across the road to be
in beautiful green fields, which were often covered
with buttercups and daisies and clovers, and through
which there ran a lovely clear brook with the banks
covered with quantities of watercresses, which used to
be gathered and sent to market. In these fields, when
she was well enough Auntie Jet used to play, but she
could only play very quietly, or sit still and read.
When she began to be a little better, she joined a Band
of Hope which was started near her home, and she used
to sing in a little choir composed of the members. She
had a great uncle [George Cruikshank] who was a very
famous artist, and who, when he died, was buried in St.
Paul's Cathedral, where his tomb may be seen in one of
the crypts. In the latter days of his life this
gentleman became a very ardent Temperance worker, and
used often to make public addresses. One evening he
was engaged to talk to the children of this Band of
Hope, and he came to tea in Auntie Jet's home. The
little girl felt very proud as she walked up to the
platform, holding his hand. Some of the other children
whispered, `do you know him?´ And Auntie Jet said,
with much dignity, `He is my Uncle.´ This great uncle

exception to her sex in the fact that she was not given
to many words, tossed her head disdainfully and said,
"The idea!" I said, "Why, it is only the other day
that you were making fun of the Good Templars." "I
know," replied Mr. Brooks, as I shall call our friend,
for as he is not a member of the Order at present, his
true name does not belong to my readers.[2] "I know, but
I have changed my mind about them. I have been a Good
Templar a whole week, and I am getting all my friends
to join."

This statement was a signal for much merriment on
the part of Mr. Brooks´ audience. Remember, that
thirty years ago the Order was a comparatively new
thing in Great Britain and our actual knowledge of it
was limited to the facts that its members wore something they called a regalia and pledged themselves not
to drink intoxicating liquors.[3] At that time, we knew

(great in more senses than one) lived to be eighty-six
years of age, and not long prior to his death, Auntie
Jet heard him deliver a lecture on temperance before a
large audience. Very likely his influence had a great
deal to do with Auntie Jet becoming a temperance
worker." West Australian White Ribbon, May 1927, p. 4.
Probably Forsyth exaggerates the influence of Cruikshank on her temperance work. Certainly she did not
mention it in the memoirs which she published in 1903.

That Forsyth and Cruikshank were related is mentioned in Thomas F. Parker, History of the Independent
Order of Good Templars (revised ed.), pp. 292-93.

2   He was W. Wells, later Worthy Chief Templar of
Favourite Lodge. Templar, July 31, 1873, p. 101.

3   The first Good Templar lodge in England was
established in 1868. The Grand Lodge of England was
organized in 1870 and reached its largest membership,
more than 210,000 adults, in 1874. See Malins, A
Brief History of Good Templary in England; E. H.

nothing about the dangers of the moderate use of alcohol; we supposed that the Order was intended only for the reclamation of drunkards, and it seemed a huge joke that a sober young man like Mr. Brooks should identify himself with it. The fact that our guest had, only a few weeks before, kept us amused for a long time with a description of a Good Templar initiation, which, as I afterwards learned, was not based upon fact, made the joke seem all the funnier, and many were the shafts of ridicule aimed at the devoted head of the proselyte. He, however, managed to parry them with equal wit and with unfailing good humor, and when our mirth had subsided, he gave us a calm and lucid explanation of the purposes and methods of the Order, such as could not fail to make an impression upon a fair-minded person.

Our household was not composed of total abstainers; we belonged to the class of very, very moderate drinkers. A glass of ale, once in a while at home; a still rarer glass of wine when in company, these were the limits of our potations and it seemed absurd to think of giving up such trifling indulgences. But the social features of the Order, as set forth by our visitor, attracted me. There were pleasant times to be enjoyed in the Lodge and, in order that I might share them, I decided, unwillingly, it is true, to give up my occasional glass and run the risk of being laughed at for joining "a peculiar people."[4] So when Mr. Brooks

---

Welfare, _The World Our Field: A History of the Good Templar Order_ (Birmingham: Templar Press, [1954]).

4   "Like many other Good Templars I was attracted to the Order by its social features. At the time I joined I was living in London, and in those days there were

left our home that evening he carried with him my name
for proposition in his Lodge.

A week or so later, on the 14th of October, 1872,
I made one of nine persons who were initiated into the
"Henry Ansell" Lodge of North London. This Lodge is
still strong and active and the veteran Henry Ansell
for whom it was named, and who was presiding officer on
the night of my initiation, is still one of its most
faithful members. I remember that I felt a little shy
and nervous as I entered the Lodge-room. When the door
was thrown open I had a confused impression of the
presence of many people and of a glow of warmth and
light and color, while in the burst of song which
greeted us I could detect the words, "Welcome, welcome." Even then I was conscious of the fact that I
was entering a fraternal circle whose bond could never
be broken. But, as I listened to the charges, I
realized that I was doing something much more serious
than I had contemplated. As I stood before each
officer in turn, all my frivolous anticipations of
amusement faded from my mind and I felt that I was
indeed undertaking "a life-long work." And, although,
as I listened, I felt that I was not "sufficient for
these things," I am glad that I was able then, as I
have been ever since, to look to the true source of

---

not the opportunities for enjoyment for respectable
young people that are to be found now. An occasional
tea meeting at one´s church; a visit to the theatre occasionally in the winter, and a picnic or two in the
summer contributed the total of one´s diversions, aside
from such as we found in our own homes or in the
immediate circle of our friends." Forsyth, "Good
Templar Memories: Some Outstanding Templars," Australian Temperance World, Jan. 1928. p. 7. Also printed as
Forsyth, "Some Good Templar Memories of a Long Life,"
New York Templar, Jan. 1928, p. 11.

enabling strength "for His blessing." There are those
who have failed to receive such a serious impression
from our initiation ceremony, but I can say that no
event of my life, except my confirmation in the Church
of England, has ever seemed so solemn as the taking of
the Good Templar obligation. Thus it has happened
that, amid all the varied experiences of this thirty
years of my life and with all the demands for service
which come to me, from other quarters, I have always
felt that my best work belonged to the Order.

Notwithstanding the impression I received during
my initiation it was several months before I became an
actual working member of the Order. This was, no
doubt, due to the fact that the Henry Ansell Lodge was
a very large and strong one and that there seemed
little for new members to do. It was not very interesting or inspiring to young people to sit in the back
row of seats at session after session with nothing to
do but watch the older folks transacting the business.[5] I do not remember finding fault with this
condition of things, but I am frank to say that I found
it somewhat dull. That I was not the only one who
found it so was evidenced by the fact that an application for a new charter was soon in circulation among
some of the young members and to it my name was
affixed. This resulted in the institution of Favorite
Lodge, No. 3155, [in July 1873] which became in a short
time one of the most flourishing and lively Lodges in

---

5   The Good Templars tended to be youthful, and the
older members probably were not very old. Henry
Ansell was born around 1830, and so was only in early
middle age when Forsyth joined the Lodge which bore his
name. International Good Templar, Nov. 1907, pp. 386,
389.

London.[6] My friend Mr. Brooks was the first Chief Templar of this Lodge; a Brother Bannister, who is still, I believe, in active connection with the Order, was its Deputy Grand [sic] Chief Templar, and Mrs. Bannister was the Vice Templar for several terms. Into this Lodge, soon after its institution, my sister was initiated, and it was here that she formed the acquaintance of Brother Thomas Smith, to whom she was happily married a couple of years later.

Very soon after the starting of Favorite Lodge it was decided to hold a public meeting and the Grand Chief Templar, Joseph Malins, was invited to attend it.[7] By that time I had become familiar with the appearance of some of the District Lodge officers and other prominent members. I do not remember the names of many of them, but I recollect that some of them were men of large and imposing presence and that they wore resplendent scarlet regalia. They appeared to my youthful mind to be very great personages indeed and, in my innocence, I expected that the one who had arrived at the position of the head of the Order, [sic] would naturally be bigger and more important in appearance than any of them. It is not surprising, therefore, that when I saw the much-heralded officer my first sensation was one of extreme disappointment. Instead of the magnificent being my fancy had painted, I found him to be a small, smooth-faced, unassuming

6   In its second month of existence, Favourite Lodge had nearly 50 members, while at the same time Henry Ansell Lodge had 183 members. *Templar*, Aug. 31, 1873, p. 167.

7   See the biography by his second son, Joseph Malins, *The Life of Joseph Malins* (Birmingham: Templar Press, 1932).

young man, certainly not "looking the part" as I had
pictured it.[8]   But my disappointment vanished when I
listened to the Grand Chief Templar´s address. He was
not an orator, but every word he spoke expressed the
wonderful power, and zeal, and earnestness which have
done so much to make the Order what it has been and is
in England, and to inspire the work in other lands.   I
have heard many great orators in my time and I have
forgotten what some of them said, but to this day I can
remember many of the words spoken by Joseph Malins that
evening in the Britannia Row Chapel, and can recall
that they led me to consecrate myself anew to the work
of Good Templary.

Chapter II

I GO TO AMERICA.   THE DISRUPTION IN THE ORDER

Although I have intimated that I soon learned the
Order existed for something more than the providing
amusement for its members, it must not be supposed that
pleasant times were overlooked.   On the contrary, I
have recollections of many most enjoyable social
occasions in connection with Favorite Lodge, such as a
Christmas Tree and some very largely-attended tea

---

8   "Some delay occurred in the train which was
bringing the G.C.T. from Birmingham and the meeting
opened before he arrived.   While it was proceeding, I
was told that the G.C.T. had entered and looking
towards one of the side aisles I saw, instead of the
splendid figure my imagination had pictured, a short,
slight young man with a smooth face.   He looked so
boyish that I could scarcely believe he was indeed the
veritable Joseph Malins."   Forsyth, "A Tribute to
Joseph Malins," New York Templar, June 1918, p. 9.   See
also Forsyth, "Joseph Malins: A Few Words of Appreciation," Australian Temperance World, April 1926, p. 6.

parties, at which I sometimes had the pleasure of waiting on table. Then our regular meetings were, as a rule, most pleasant and profitable affairs. Our Lodge soon became very popular and visitors came to us from all parts of London. It was during my connection with Favorite Lodge that I became acquainted with some of the incidents which have furnished the material for two or three of my short stories. I learned to do my part as a worker on committees and I also contributed something towards swelling the membership of the Order, as will be seen when I mention that on one evening I proposed the names of eight of the young people from my place of business.

After filling a term as Right Hand Supporter [an appointive office], I was elected Vice Templar, and no office I have ever held has come to me as a greater honor than did this one, whose duties I undertook with much inward fear and trembling.[9] Altogether, my two years spent in a London Good Templar Lodge were very happy ones and my interest in the Order increased from day to day, as did my knowledge of the philosophy of the temperance movement. And let me say here that through hearing those speak who were better informed than myself, and by reading the Good Templar and other temperance papers, I almost insensibly acquired a temperance education which brought about, in the course of time, an entire change in my views regarding moderate drinking and other phases of the question.[10]

9   She was elected Vice Templar on July 25, 1874. Templar, Aug. 6, 1874, p. 529.

10   The paper was not the Good Templar, a monthly which was published in Scotland, but instead the Templar, the first Good Templar weekly in England,

In fact it was not long before I was sufficiently
advanced to be classed among the temperance fanatics.
I mention this as an example of what the Order has been
doing in the way of educating temperance workers during
the many years of its existence.

In 1873 the Right Worthy Grand Lodge met in
London. I was not able to attend any of the meetings,
but I caught the echoes from them as they were talked
of in the Lodge, and I was full of interested curiosity
regarding the great men and women who had come from
America to attend this wonderful gathering. Among those
whose names became most familiar to me were
Hon. S. D. Hastings and Hon. S. B. Chase. They were
honored names then; they are no less honored now, and
our Order has been greatly blessed in retaining the
valued services of such men. An amusing incident
happened at this time when a young brother belonging to
my Lodge was displaying with much pride some of the
autographs of prominent members which he had secured.
Among them was that of Brother Chase, and I remember
listening almost with envy to the brother´s account of
a few words he had exchanged with that eminent man.
After displaying his autographs somewhat boastfully,
the young man remarked, "I shall keep this book for the
names of distinguished persons." Then, I suppose,
fearing that my feelings might be hurt, he added in a
rather patronizing tone, "Well, as you are V.T. in our
Lodge, I don´t mind you writing your name on the last
page." This I refused to do, telling him rather pertly
that I should be sorry to spoil his collection of
distinguished names by adding my own insignificant one.

published from 1871.

Towards the close of 1874 I received the offer, most unexpectedly, of a business position in Boston, Massachusetts [as a bookkeeper in a printing house]. Although, like many other young people, I often wished for a chance to travel, I do not remember that I felt at all drawn towards the United States, and if it had rested with myself, I think that I should have refused the opportunity. But my health had not been of the best for some little time and my good aunts decided in their wisdom that such a change would be most desirable for me. As the way seemed to be open without any effort on my own part, I concluded that it must be for the best and I wrote accepting the engagement for two years. I had scarcely two weeks in which to prepare for my voyage, but I found time to go to my Lodge and apply for my clearance card. I shall never forget that evening. It had been my intention to get my card and steal quietly away with only a word of good-bye to my most intimate friends. But when the application for the card was read, members rose from all parts of the room and said all manner of kind things. It was voted that in addition to the card, a letter should be written to the members of the Order in America, recommending me to their fraternal regards. Overcome with the kindness shown by my fellow members, I tried to escape, but was told that I must say a few words. I endeavored to express my gratitude for all the kinds words and wishes, but this, my first attempt at a speech in a Lodge room, ended in my bursting into tears. The letter ordered by the Lodge reached me a few days after my arrival in Boston and I have it now among some other treasured souvenirs of my Good Templar career.

I pass over my other farewells and my voyage to
Boston, which was a very stormy one, by the way,
occupying fourteen days. I landed in Boston on
December 22d, 1874, when the thermometer stood at eight
degrees below zero and the ground was covered with
frozen snow. I pass over, also, the weeks of homesickness which followed, for I do not like, even now, to
recall them. I was boarding with friends who had
settled in America a few years before, so perhaps my
situation was not as bad as it might have been, but I
was very unhappy. And not the least of my troubles
was that I never met a Good Templar and that I could
not hear of a Good Templar Lodge. My place of abode
was a few miles out of town and the strange locality,
the icy streets, and the intense cold combined to keep
me a prisoner of an evening. As the end of the quarter
[when Good Templar dues should be paid] approached,
however, I felt that I must find a Lodge in which to
deposit my card so as to maintain my standing in the
Order. A few more inquiries resulted in my being
directed to "Undine" [named after the water-sprite in
folklore] Lodge of Boston, and I summoned all my
courage and wended my way to the hall in which it met.
I was warmly welcomed, and what a delight it was to be
once more in a Lodge room, listening to the familiar
words of the ritual and the odes and wearing a familiar
regalia. This was before the days of badges, and our
Lodge rooms presented a much more uniform appearance
than they do now. For the first time since my arrival
in America, I felt at home and I have always cherished
with pleasure the memory of the kind greetings that I
received. "Undine" was a good Lodge, with an active,
earnest membership, which included a number of young

people, among whom I soon became popular. I filled the
office of Secretary for several quarters in this Lodge
and gained much valuable experience. On one never-to-
be-forgotten evening, General George P. Hawkes, at that
time Grand Chief Templar of Massachusetts, came to
install the officers. In the intermission he busied
himself in looking over the books, a thing I have never
seen any other G.C.T. do, I think, and I felt exceedingly pleased and proud when he told me that he was
glad the Lodge had re-elected a good Secretary. About
this time I met another Grand Lodge officer in the
person of Miss Amanda Lane, Grand Secretary, who had
reached distinction in the Right Worthy Grand Lodge and
had filled the office of R.W.G.V.T. I remember being
much impressed with her appearance and address. This
lady, now Mrs. Root, is still living, and holds her
membership in the Order.

Looking back to those days of loneliness and
homesickness, when my surroundings were utterly uncon-
genial and when the two years I had agreed to spend in
Boston stretched before me like a lifetime, I realize
how much I owe to Good Templary, for in the Lodge room
I found pleasure and friendship free from the
temptations which so often assail the young stranger in
a strange city. I found too a continual incentive to
make the best of myself and to cultivate such gifts as
I possessed. And mine was not an isolated case, for
the Order has been a haven of refuge to many such
lonely ones in every part of the world.

Time passed on and I was daily becoming more accustomed to my new conditions.[11] My interest in the

---

[11] In old age Forsyth wrote about a special friend in Massachusetts. "He was an American child; his parents belonged to the State of Maine, the first place in the world to adopt a law prohibiting the manufacture and sale of intoxicating drink. But when I knew them many years ago, they were living in Boston, and for a few years I made my home with them. They were very good, kind people, and although they would sometimes make a little fun of my English ways, for I had only lately come from London, and I used to retort by ridiculing some of their Yankee expressions; it was all good natured, and I was very happy with them."

"Their little boy, whose name was Ray, was a dear loving little fellow, only a baby when I first knew him, and it was when he first began to talk that he called me `Jet.´  By and bye he quite took possession of me, and then he used to say `My Jet.´ I played with him a great deal, and we used to have great fun together."

"When Ray was about four years old circumstances made it necessary for me to leave his home, and [as] I was a very busy person, I could not see him very often. But one night, just as I was about to prepare for bed, I was told that a gentleman wished to see me. I went into the sitting room and found Ray´s father, who burst into tears when he saw me, and sobbed out, `Our little Ray is very ill; we think he is dying, and he keeps calling for his Jet.´"

"I hurried to Ray´s home and found him lying very still and pale in bed, but when he saw me his dear little face was transfigured by a most beautiful smile and he said in a very faint voice, `My Jet,´ and tried to reach out his arms to me. I stayed with him that night and gave him as much of my time as I possibly could afterwards, until we had the happiness of seeing him grow better. But he never became very robust, and he died when he was about eleven years old. I spent some time with him before he left us and one day I said `Oh, Ray, how you used to love me when you were little.´  He put his arms around me and said, `I love you just the same now, My Jet.´"

"It was a great grief to me to part with my dear

Order remained unabated, the more so, perhaps, because
I received the Good Templars' Watchword from London
every week and kept myself informed regarding the work
in England and other places.[12] In 1876 came the
disruption in the Order, of which I was probably one of
the first of the subordinate members to learn, thanks
to the English Good Templar papers. From the first my
sympathies were with those who were called "seceders."
This was partly due to the influence of my sister and
her husband, who wrote constantly regarding the
conflict, but more, I think, to the fact that there
were hardly any colored people in the Order in Boston
and that the members to whom I spoke regarding the
matter, showed a distinct aversion to that race and
openly expressed objection to having them in the
Order. By degrees the question came up for discussion

---

little friend, but I always think of him now as loving
his `Jet´ just the same as ever. And I think of the
words of the poet Longfellow:--"

> "he is not dead, that child of our affection,
>   But gone into that school,
>   Where he no longer needs our poor protection,
>   And Christ himself doth rule."

"And I gratefully remember how his love comforted
me in some days of sorrow and homesickness, and I like
to think that--"

> "My remembrance, though unspoken,
>   May reach him where he lives."

Forsyth ("Auntie Jet"), West Australian White Ribbon,
July 1926, p. 4.

12 The Good Templars' Watchword, published from 1874,
replaced the Templar as the official organ of the Grand
Lodge of England. The Templar continued for several
years and often was at odds with the Good Templars'
Watchword.

in Lodge meetings, although an effort was made on the part of the then G.C.T. to prevent such discussion. In the heat of the debates, many things were said by partisan speakers which were not true. The leaders of the "secession" were assailed most bitterly, Joseph Malins, Grand Chief Templar of England, being especially an object for vituperation. My first speech ever made outside of a subordinate Lodge was at a largely-attended County Lodge session, when a prominent member, now deceased, made a savage onslaught on the individual to whom he facetiously referred as "Joe Malins." It is probable that the speaker believed he was telling the truth, but I was better informed regarding the matter and my indignation was great. I sprang to my feet and forgetting where I was and who I was, I made what must have been a fairly eloquent speech in defense of the "seceders." I do not remember what I said except that before I sat down I sarcastically advised the preceding speaker to make himself acquainted with the facts before he ventured to talk on the question again. My remarks were greeted with hearty applause and my opponent did not attempt any reply. At this session I was elected County Vice Templar, but by the next session the Order had divided in Massachusetts, and I never filled the office. I may say here, that with regard to the unkind things which were said in the heat of the controversy, I am now aware that neither section of the Order was free from blame in that respect. We were all human and we sometimes forgot that we were Good Templars. On the evening to which I have referred, a fine-looking and dignified lady was acting as County Secretary. That lady was Mrs. Lizzie M. Robinson, now the G.S.J.T. of Massachusetts.

Chapter III

DR. WM. WELLS BROWN--THE REORGANIZED GRAND LODGE

It was during the agitation of what was known as the "Color Question" in Massachusetts that I became acquainted with the late Dr. William Wells Brown, who was one of the most distinguished members of the African race which this country has ever produced.[13] An ex-slave, who had as a boy run away from his Southern master and whose freedom had later been purchased by some English philanthropists, he had acquired a fine education, had graduated as a physician and was practicing in Boston at the time when I first met him. Dr. Brown was a fine-looking mulatto, with a keen intellect, a genial manner, and a kind heart. He was a gifted writer and a most eloquent speaker. With all these traits, which made his white associates ready to condone the fact of his negro blood and to admit him to equality with themselves, he was intensely proud of and loyal to his race. This determination to stand by his own people often stood in the way of his personal interest, and it is to the credit of this noble and large-hearted man that, after having devoted his life to the cause of humanity he died poor. In the anti-slavery agitation Wm. Wells Brown had labored side

---

13 Brown explained the relationship between temperance reform and his concern for his race in "The Elevation of the Coloured Race," Temperance Brotherhood, reprinted in Good Templars´ Brotherhood, Nov. 5, 1883, pp. 705-6. He concluded his article by saying that "a large portion of the coloured men and women in the Northern States are recently from the South, and need the Temperance pledge and the spelling book more than they do advice on politics."

by side with [William Lloyd] Garrison and [Wendell]
Phillips and he retained the friendship of these men as
long as they lived.

Dr. Brown was one of the few individuals of his
race who was identified with the Order in Massachusetts prior to the disruption, and he never had reason
personally to complain of the treatment he received
from his white brethren. He had held several positions
of honor and was a cause of offence to the Southern
representatives at the session of the Right Worthy
Grand Lodge held in Boston in 1874, when he represented
Massachusetts. His wife, who died very recently, and
who was a handsome, light-complexioned woman, well
educated and cultured, had served as G.V.T. of Massachusetts.[14]

It was, of course, perfectly natural that a man
who possessed such an intense love for his own race
should be greatly interested in the "Color Question"
when it was being agitated in the R.W.G. Lodge, and it
is not surprising that, when the disruption finally
occurred, he cast his lot with the men and women who
had withdrawn from the original body and had reorganized under the title of the Right Worthy Grand
Lodge of the World. At the time when I made his
acquaintance, Dr. Brown had already left the Grand
Lodge of Massachusetts and was holding a commission as
Special Deputy, under the Right Worthy Grand Lodge of
the World. I remember that it was often charged by

---

14   Annie G. Brown, Brown's second wife, died in
1902.   Until her sight and health deteriorated during
the last years of her life she remained an active Good
Templar. International Good Templar, Oct. 1902, p. 318.

those who resented this action that financial induce-
ments had been offered to the Doctor to cause him to
transfer his affiliation. It was a common thing to
hear some one express the opinion that he had been
"well paid" and the price was more than once stated to
be as high as $20,000. It is hardly necessary now to
say that there was no truth in these assertions. The
Right Worthy Grand Lodge of the World, while it claimed
to be the supreme head of the Order, had not been able
to secure the Order's funds, and it had no money with
which to purchase his allegiance. Consequently
Dr. Brown found in this agitation another opportunity
for the sacrifice of himself to his people.[15]

There were others beside Dr. Brown, however, whose
sympathies were with the Right Worthy Grand Lodge of
the World. Several of the leading members of the Order
in Massachusetts, not colored men, nor Englishmen, but
good, true Americans, championed the cause of the
so-called "Seceders." At the session of the Grand
Lodge, held in 1877, the matter was very keenly debated. The report of a majority of a committee appointed to consider the question expressed the opinion
that "the action of the Right Worthy Grand Lodge at the
Louisville session was contrary to the principles of
our Order, and of human liberty," and stated that the
continued loyalty of the Grand Lodge to the supreme
body would depend upon its adherence to the cause of
universal humanity. A minority report demanding "a

---

15   Brown died in 1884 at age 68. There is an
obituary in R.W.G.L. of the World, Proceedings (1885),
pp. 1355-56. The standard biography is that by William
Edward Farrison, William Wells Brown, Author and
Reformer (Chicago: University of Chicago Press, 1969).
Brown's temperance work remains unstudied.

repeal of all class legislation in the Right Worthy
Grand Lodge and the enactment and enforcement of such
laws as shall secure to every person throughout our
land the benefits of our Order," was submitted by James
H. Roberts and received large support. But Brother
S. E. Vinal went a long step beyond this by offering a
substitute for both reports, which included the
following resolution, "That the Grand Lodge of Massachusetts feels that it is in duty bound to stand by the
principles which a majority of the delegates comprising
the twenty-second annual session of the Right Worthy
Grand Lodge have forsaken, and in consequence must
recognize the Right Worthy Grand Lodge of the World
(Brother James Yeames, R.W.G.T) as the true and loyal
body, and supreme head of the I.O.G.T." This substitute was favored by the late Rev. George F. Clark,
P.G.C.T., among others, but the majority report was
finally adopted.

The action of the Grand Lodge decided some of us
who believed in the R.W.G.L. of the World to begin
organizing under its jurisdiction. The first Lodge was
formed in Allston, and it included Brother S. E. Vinal
mentioned above in membership. The second one was
named "Favorite," in memory of my old London Lodge, and
I became a charter member of the organization. Prior
to its institution it was of course, necessary that I
should leave Undine Lodge, and the doing so was a very
severe test of my principles. I had been well treated
in Undine Lodge and had many friends among its members. It was difficult to make some of them understand
why I need leave them, and I was accused of fickleness
and ingratitude by those whose good opinion I valued.
However, I felt that I could not do otherwise than

throw in my lot with the "seceders," and my doing so
was the first step toward the entire devotion which the
Order has demanded of me ever since. Other Lodges
followed Favorite, until we had the necessary ten for a
Grand Lodge charter, and the Grand Lodge was instituted
by Dr. Wm. Wells Brown on December 31, 1877. Although
I had been a member of the Order for between five and
six years, and had been entitled to the Grand Lodge
degree for the greater part of that time, I had never
attended a Grand Lodge session, and was much interested
in the proceedings. I had not given a thought to the
officers, and it was a matter of great surprise to me
when I was elected Grand Vice Templar. Our first Grand
Chief Templar was Rev. George W. Mansfield, a Methodist
minister of high standing, and our Grand Secretary was
Mrs. Wm. Wells Brown.

The organization of our Grand Lodge was the
beginning of a long struggle to uphold what we believed
to be the right in the face of adverse conditions. The
large Grand Lodges in the British countries, which
constituted the bulk of the membership of the Right
Worthy Grand Lodge of the World, could have no conception of the effort it required to maintain our slender
hold in a jurisdiction in which a strong Grand Lodge
already existed. Then we were living up to the principles which we had proclaimed and were giving absolute
equal rights to our colored members, and this, while it
won for us the respect and admiration of many
right-thinking people, was somewhat of a hindrance to
our speedy growth. However, with all the hard work and
discouragements which filled the next ten years, they
were very happy ones. On account of our Grand Lodge
being so small, its members were able to become

acquainted with one another, and we were a very
harmonious and united little band. Our sessions were
like family reunions and we looked forward to them
during the year with pleasurable anticipation. Many
friendships were formed among the members, some of them
enduring until the present time. We held a high ideal
of the Order in other matters besides the question of
human brotherhood, and our little Grand Lodge was never
disgraced by political trickery or selfish office
seeking. Our Subordinate Lodges, also, with rare
exceptions, maintained a high standard and were
remarkable for their activity, harmony and
sociability. This was peculiarly true of "Joseph
Malins" Lodge, which for several years had a membership
of over one hundred, about equally divided between
white and colored. It seemed as if the representatives
of the one race were stimulated by fellowship with the
other to make the very best of themselves, and vice
versa. In this Lodge [which Jessie Forsyth joined
after leaving Favorite Lodge] we had at one time
members representing ten different nationalities--Amer-
ican, Canadian, English, Scotch, Irish, South African
(a white man), French, German, Norwegian, and West
Indian. A visitor once remarked that he never saw a
Lodge of which it might more truly be said, "Behold how
good and pleasant it is for brethren to dwell together
in unity."

Chapter IV

BRIEF MENTION OF SOME OLD CO-WORKERS

The story of the "Joseph Malins" Lodge would be
incomplete if I were to neglect to mention one who was

identified with it from its institution until his death
occurred a few years ago. This was Brother Wm. H.
Clark, a colored man of high character. Brother Clark
was a generous giver and an active worker, and was one
of the most valuable members of the Order. Like some
others of his race, he had a remarkable history. He
lived in slavery until set free by the emancipation
proclamation, and was owned by the family in Richmond,
Va., who gave up their house to be a headquarters for
Jefferson Davis. Brother Clark, who was at that time a
mere youth, was given to Mr. Davis to act as his body
servant, and he was able to relate some amusing incidents which occurred at the time. He was a man of keen
intellect, and although handicapped by the lack of
education, he was able to make a most interesting
address, while his personal integrity was so generally
acknowledged that he was invariably chosen as treasurer
of any organization with which he was connected. He
served as Treasurer of the Grand Lodge for several
years. There are many old workers, who, like myself,
can look back with pleasure to association with this
brother, and remember his unfailing neatness, his
courteous manner and pleasant temper.

Another remarkable Lodge which worked from the
first under our little Grand Lodge was composed
entirely of women and was called "Edward M. Thomas"
Lodge. It was formerly an organization of the Order of
Good Samaritans and its members were attracted to us by
our attitude on the "Color Question." They voted to
come over to us in a body, and I was present on the
evening when the whole membership, consisting of more
than seventy women, nearly all of the African race,
became Good Templars. It was, of course, understood

that the Lodge could not constitutionally limit its
membership to one sex, but the question never arose,
for no man was ever found brave enough to apply for
admission, except occasionally as a visitor. For a
number of years "Edward M. Thomas" Lodge flourished,
but as its original members grew old and passed away,
it was not able to recruit its ranks from among the
younger women, who preferred to join a mixed organization. So the Lodge died "from natural causes" a few
years ago, leaving behind it a long record of useful
work for humanity.

Many bright and clever women were members of this
Lodge, one of the most remarkable being the late
Mrs. Harriet Hayden, who, with her husband, Lewis
Hayden, was well known in connection with the anti-slavery movement. The Hayden home on Phillips
street, Boston, was renowned as one of the stations of
the famous "Underground Railway," and it was mobbed on
at least one occasion when Wendell Phillips was within
it, at the time of the great agitation. The Haydens,
who had themselves escaped from slavery in their
youthful days and who had encountered numerous strange
and dangerous adventures in their effort to obtain
their freedom, were exceedingly interesting people. It
is a matter for regret that the story of their lives
and work should only live in the memories of those who
were privileged to hear them tell it. I can recall the
vivid interest with which I listened to Sister Hayden's
graphic recital of her flight from bondage. How at
times she and her husband were obliged to be separated
as they were helped from point to point by friends,
some of whom suffered punishment for assisting them to
escape, and how they rejoiced when they reached Canada

and set foot for the first time upon free ground. Although Sister Hayden lacked the advantages of an early education, she was a woman of great mental power and possessed the ability to tell a story with almost dramatic intensity. She survived her husband for a short time and at her death [in 1894] her property went by her wish to found a scholarship for colored youths at Harvard University.

Another remarkable member who still lives and who still holds the position of a leader among her people is Sister Miss Eliza A. Gardner, a highly educated and cultured woman, who is a gifted speaker and whose graces of character are equal to her intellectual endowments. Sister Gardner is an active worker in connection with the Zion A.M.E. Church, especially its mission work, and her fame extends far beyond her native State of Massachusetts.[16]

---

16   "There is nothing, I think, in the story of the peoples of the world finer than that of the American colored people. When released from slavery they were destitute and, for the most part, unlearned, owning nothing and dependent very largely upon the charity of their former owners, themselves impoverished by the loss of their `property´ in human flesh and blood. Now they have their colleges, their churches, men and women who, from being the `hewers of wood and drawers of water,´ have distinguished themselves in some of the professions, and others who have been successful in business and have made money. Looking back over the past I can recall many earnest and faithful workers, among them Sis. Eliza Gardner, who died recently at over ninety years of age. She was devoted to her race, and did her utmost for its moral uplift. She was possessed of great gifts, was a splendid speaker and reasoner, and, but for the handicap of her color, might have held first rank among the noted women of the world." Forsyth, "Some Outstanding Templars," Australian Temperance World, Nov. 1928, p. 5.

I mention these persons as examples of the race with many of whom I labored happily in past years and whom I learned to love and honor. Among all the members surrounding my past work in the Order there are none more valued than those which cling around my labors with and for the colored people. I have never known truer or more loyal friendships than theirs have been and I prize the regard of those of the co-workers who still survive.

But all our members did not belong to the African race. There was our Brother C. A. Stevens, who was for about seven years our Grand Chief Templar, and whose death occurred less than three years ago.[17] Brother Stevens was a Yankee of the most pronounced type who had served his country in the Civil War. He and his good wife were among the first members to come over to us after the disruption. It was a matter of principle with them and they, and other Americans who stood with us, are deserving of more honor for their attitude than were members who were of British birth or family, because it might be said of the latter that they were somewhat influenced by their National prejudices. Brother Stevens was a most honorable, upright and unselfish man and his wife was a fitting mate for him. Bro. Reuben Forknall, P.G.C., is still living and can look back with satisfaction upon many years of useful work in connection with "Charity" Lodge of Newton.[18] Then there is the Mountford family of Lowell, whose Lodge, "Mount Zion," celebrated its twenty-second anniversary recently. The elder members of this

17 _International Good Templar_, April 1901, p. 1222.

18 He died at age 71 in 1928.

family were active workers in our little Grand Lodge,
and they have continued their labors since the union,
while the younger members have grown up to be no less
earnest in the cause. "Mount Zion" Lodge is one of the
very few Lodges in Massachusetts which owns its own
hall and the fact that it does so is due to the
Mountford family.

In the latter part of 1883 Rev. James Yeames,
P.R.W.G.T., came from England and settled in our
state.[19] His name had been almost a household word

19   "Bro. Yeames joined the Order soon after its
introduction into England and became deeply interested
in it, particularly in its juvenile branch, and the
rituals of that branch are very largely his work.   He
acted as honorary editor of the first organ published
by the English Good Templars [the Templar], and wrote
and set to music several odes.   While faithfully
fulfilling the onerous duties of a [Methodist] pastor
he was ready to help in the public work of the Order
and became a very able and attractive platform speaker.   He was one of the representatives from the Grand
Lodge of England to the famous Louisville session of
the R.W.G. Lodge, and was elected the first R.W.G.T. of
the reorganised body [the Right Worthy Grand Lodge of
the World in 1876].   Bro. Yeames removed to Boston in
1884 [actually late 1883] and immediately transferred
his membership to the little struggling Grand Lodge
where his presence was a great help and inspiration.
In his ministerial work he has always given special
attention to the young, and is rewarded in his old age
by constantly receiving testimonies to his good work in
the past from those whom he helped to train in habits
of temperance and right living.   Mr. Yeames is now 85
years of age, and he and his good wife [Amy L. Cam-
burn], who has always shared and sympathised with his
labors, have lived together for nearly sixty years.
Their family of six surviving sons and daughters [out
of eight born to them] are all good and clever, and are
filling worthily various responsible positions.   I may
add that Bro. Yeames has been the host, both in England
and America, of many eminent members of the Order.   He
was a close friend of Joseph Malins and that distinguished brother always found time when he visited the

among the members of our Grand Lodge and his coming was
hailed with rejoicing. His services were of great
value to us, as they are still to the Order at large.
Brother Yeames is too well known to render any introduction necessary, and I will only say that those of us
who had believed in him as an earnest and zealous Good
Templar when we only knew him by reputation were not
disappointed when we met him face to face.

In 1878 the Right Worthy Grand Lodge of the World
held its session in Boston and the effort to entertain
the Supreme body called forth all the energies of our
little organization. I think that, considering our
resources, we acquitted ourselves fairly well. I was
not qualified to attend the sessions, but greatly
enjoyed the public occasions and the opportunities for
meeting some of the representatives from other countries, about whom I had heard and read. Chief among
the visitors was, of course, Joseph Malins, who in the
interval which had occurred between the time when I
heard him speak in London and the occasion of meeting
him in Boston had become one of the most abused men in
this country. Although not more responsible than his
colleagues for the action taken at Louisville in 1876,
the great force of character possessed by Brother
Malins caused him to be regarded as the leader in the
"split," and we of the Right Worthy Grand Lodge of the

United States to spend a few days with his old col-
league." Jessie Forsyth, "Good Templar Memories: Some
Outstanding Templars," Australian Temperance World,
Feb. 1928, p. 7. Yeames died in 1931. International
Good Templar, Oct. 1931, p. 165. See also "Rev. James
Yeames, P.R.W.G.T.: Editor of `Our Children's Corner',"
International Good Templar, Dec. 1888, pp. 742-43,
which is strong on Yeames in England; and Lender, Dic-
tionary of American Temperance Biography, pp. 533-34.

World soon came to be known as "Malinites." Except for the fact that some of us were opposed on principle to being labelled with the name of any individual, I am sure that no one felt anything but pride in the sobriquet which linked us with our honored leader.

At this time I first met Rev. Wm. Ross, of Scotland, one of the noblest men in the Order; Brother Wm. W. Turnbull, of Scotland, who for several years prior to the reunion of the Order was our most efficient Right Worthy Grand Secretary; Sister Catherine Impey, of England, for several years the leader in our mission work and the collector of its funds, and Mrs. Elizabeth Browne, of London, who has rendered valiant service to the Order in England in the past and is still active. There were many others present deserving of especial mention, but I recall these because I have met them many times since and have long counted them among my personal friends. At the Boston session of 1878 Rev. Wm. Ross was elected Right Worthy Grand Templar; Mrs. H. N. K. Goff (recently deceased) [1901], of New York, Right Worthy Grand Vice Templar; Mrs. Elizabeth Brown of London, Right Worthy Grand Supt. Juvenile Temples; Rev. S. C. Goosely of South Carolina, a distinguished colored man, was elected Right Worthy Grand Counsellor and Joseph Malins was re-elected Right Worthy Grand Secretary.

Among the public occasions which I remember were an elaborate banquet tended to the representatives by Joseph Malins Lodge, and a mass meeting in Tremont Temple, at which Wendell Phillips was one of the speakers, and a message was read from Wm. Lloyd Garrison.

Chapter V

I BECOME AN OFFICER OF THE RIGHT WORTHY GRAND LODGE
OF THE WORLD

In 1879 I was elected Grand Secretary upon the retirement of Mrs. Wm. Wells Brown and I was continued in the office, by unanimous vote, until the reunion of the Order in Massachusetts in 1888.[20] The position was an honorary one, as we never reached the point of being able to pay salaries to any of the officers. As I have said before, it was sometimes difficult for us to maintain our organization in a jurisdiction where a strong Grand Lodge existed. Of course there were times of discouragement and generally the Grand Secretary was the one who would be most affected by such seasons of depression. Many a time have I lain awake at night worrying over the condition of some weak Lodge, or planning some method of reviving interest in places where it was waning. The loss of a Lodge meant so much when we had so few and it required constant, patient and faithful effort to hold our "slender handful" together. It was fortunate for me and for the cause, that I always possessed plenty of hope and courage and cheerfulness. It was fortunate also that the hands of the officers of our little organization were always upheld by the loyalty, earnestness and good-feeling which existed among our members.

---

20   It was actually 1880 when she first was elected Grand Secretary. Forsyth to editor, September 30, 1880, in Good Templars´ Watchword, October 25, 1880, p. 679.

As time went by and we lost some of our earlier
workers, more and more of the burdens fell upon my
shoulders. Brother Stevens was not a strong man and it
was often my lot to represent the Grand Chief Templar
or perform some duty which properly belonged to him. I
used to get around the fact that I had no authority to
render a decision, by telling the members that I was
only able to give them fraternal advice. As a rule,
the "fraternal advice" was taken and some trouble
averted. This was especially true in the case of one
Lodge to which I was sent by the G.C.T. to straighten
out a terrible tangle. It was quite impossible to find
any constitutional provision that would fit the case.
The proceedings had been so irregular in the matter of
the trial of a member that the Lodge could have been
disciplined. But I knew that the errors were uninten-
tional and the Lodge was too good a one to lose. My
fraternal advice in this instance was certainly not
constitutional, but it was acted upon and the Lodge was
saved. When I reported my action to the G.C.T. he
laughed and said that my methods would do very well if
no appeals reached him. Notice had been given of an
appeal, but, to my joy, it never materialized, and the
Lodge went on with its work in as satisfactory a manner
as if it had been extricated from its dilemma by the
most approved methods. I am not recommending such
easy-going practices, however, but simply showing that
there are cases sometimes where a little common sense
may smooth over a matter when more constitutional
methods fail. The Lodge I have referred to is alive
to-day and doing good work.

In performing the duties of my office it was
necessary sometimes to correspond with some of the

officers of the Right Worthy Grand Lodge of the World
and I still cherish lively feelings of gratitude
towards Brothers Joseph Malins and Wm. W. Turnbull for
the encouraging and appreciative words they often wrote
to me. It was very helpful to know that such men
could spare a thought from their own large organizations for our little Grand Lodge and it made us
realize that we were indeed, as I expressed it in one
of my earlier reports, "a link, though a small one, in
the chain of brotherhood which encircles the globe."

In 1883 the Right Worthy Grand Lodge of the World
held its session in the Parliament House of Halifax,
Nova Scotia, and it was my good fortune to be able to
attend the session. There were four of us who went
from Massachusetts, Brother Stevens, Brother Reuben
Forknall, another Brother and myself. We reached
Halifax quite early in the morning and were taken care
of by Brother Rev. Wm. G. Lane, whom I met then for the
first time. After breakfasting and making some changes
in our dress, we were escorted to the Grand Lodge of
Nova Scotia which was in session. The delegation from
Massachusetts was announced and received in proper
form. As we stood in front of the G.C.T. during the
reception ceremony, I noticed some of the visitors on
the platform gazing in my direction and exchanging
smiles and significant glances with one another. I
felt very uncomfortable at being the object of such
scrutiny, but learned afterwards that some of the
British representatives who had met me in Boston had
amused themselves by describing me to those who did not
know me as a tall, angular woman, with a loud voice, a
nasal twang, and a very aggressive manner. I suppose
that when I appeared the contrast between the real and

the imaginary individual must have seemed funny. A different idea concerning me had been conceived by Rev. George Gladstone who, when he was introduced, regarded me attentively for a few moments and then said: "Why, Miss Forsyth, I thought you were a colored woman and I have been referring to you as one of the remarkable specimens of the race." I told the Brother that if he would come to Boston I would show him some real colored women who were as much credit to their race, or to the human race as a whole, as any women could be. I may not have occasion to mention Brother Gladstone again, as I have not met him many times, so I will say here that he was one of the principal speakers in the Louisville debate which resulted in the disruption of the Order; [and I should add] that I had become familiar with his name for this reason and had read his speeches upon the question with much enjoyment. Consequently, it was a great pleasure to meet him. Brother Gladstone is a very eloquent speaker and his touch of Scottish accent is just sufficient to give an additional charm to his voice.

At this time Brother Malins, who was R.W.G. Templar, was recovering from a long and severe illness and was still very lame and weak. Everyone rejoiced over the prospect of his recovery and during the session resolutions expressing our gratitude to Almighty God were adopted. At this session I became acquainted with a Brother who, until his death, a few years ago [in 1892], was numbered among my closest friends in the Order. This was Gilbert Archer, for several years Grand Chief Templar of Scotland, one of the best and kindest and most true-hearted of men. Here also I became acquainted with Brother Oskar Eklund of Sweden,

at that time a very young man, but who had even then
become a power in the Grand Lodge of Sweden.[21] I need
hardly refer to the well-known fact that Brother Eklund
has never swerved from his fidelity to the Order, but
that he is still one of the foremost workers in his
jurisdiction. Here also I renewed my acquaintance with
Sister Catherine Impey and laid the foundation for
several other long-standing friendships.

Under the rule which existed then, but which has
since been abolished, I had been appointed proxy
representative for South Australia and my instructions
from that far-away Grand Lodge was that I was to "vote
with Scotland." I may mention here that an occasion
arose during the session when I could not conscien-
tiously act upon these "general orders" and I took the
liberty of voting according to my own convictions. I
was called to account afterwards by one prominent
Scottish member, but I think that even he, as well as
others in the body, thought none the less of me for
having a mind of my own. When I made my report to the
Grand Lodge which I represented, I mentioned my action
in this matter, but received no reprimand for it.

The election of officers is always an interesting
feature of any assembly and was especially so on this
occasion to the members from Massachusetts, as we had
gone to the session intending to make it understood
that our jurisdiction deserved some recognition. On
the way to Halifax, Brother Forknall and I had decided,
without consulting the individual in question, that

21   Eklund was one of the few of Forsyth´s contem-
poraries to outlive her. He died in 1940. _Interna-
tional Good Templar_, Jan. 1941, p. 3.

Brother Stevens ought to be elected Grand Marshal,
which was an executive office in the R.W.G. Lodge of
the World. We had determined to do all we could in the
direction of securing his election, but we were not
very good wire-pullers and, even if we had been, we
were in a gathering where anything in the nature of
canvassing for office for ourselves or our friends was
frowned upon.[22] So the only way to do [sic] was to
wait until the nominations were open and then present
the name of our candidate in the best manner possible.
The rule was for only one nominating speech and that
was made, after the candidate had been asked to retire,
by the member who had made the nomination. I have
always thought that method an improvement on the one of
allowing a number of speeches to be made on behalf of a
candidate. I nominated Brother Stevens for Counsellor,
not expecting that he would be elected, but hoping that
it would pave the way for his election as Marshal, when
we should reach that office. For the same reason, I
accepted a nomination for R.W.G.S.J.T., but was greatly
relieved at my defeat, as at that time I should hardly
have known what to do with the office if it had come to
me.[23] That office held the third place on the

---

22   "I ventured, when an opportunity occurred for a
quiet word with Bro. Malins, to hint at our wishes [for
international office for Bro. Stevens] and received in
return a reprimand for my temerity in canvassing for
anyone. I retired rather crestfallen, but this did not
hinder me from proposing Bro. Stevens for Counsellor,
although I felt dreadfully alarmed at hearing my own
voice in such a dignified assembly." Forsyth, "Good
Templar Memories: Some Outstanding Templars," Australian Temperance World, March 1928, p. 7; also New York
Templar, May 1928, p. 8.

23   Forsyth was defeated by the narrow margin of 20
votes to 17. R. W.G.L. of the World, Proceedings
(1883), p. 1304.

R.W.G.L. of the World Executive Committee and next in order came R.W.G.V.T., for which also I received a nomination. There were other candidates, among them a very popular English lady.[24] I had no expectation of being elected, but thought that another defeat for Massachusetts only made our prospects the better when we came to the election of Marshal.

I was told afterwards that when I had retired with the other candidates to the ante-room, Sister Mrs. [A. M.] Green of England, who had nominated me, was asked to speak regarding my qualifications, and she said that she was unable to do so as she had no acquaintance with me, but she thought Massachusetts deserved recognition. Brother Stevens, with his usual unselfishness, felt sorry that my nomination could not be backed up as the others had been by a eulogistic speech and he asked for the privilege of speaking in my behalf. But he was informed that the rule of the body could not be departed from. When I re-entered the Lodge-room, I went and sat with some English acquaintances in the rear of the hall. I was so sure of being defeated that I did not feel much interest in the result of the ballot, and while talking to my new friends I did not hear the report of the tellers. I noticed a burst of applause, however, and was startled when a Brother sitting in front of me turned and, holding out his hand, said: "Sister Forsyth, I congratulate you," and in this way I learned that I had

Lizzie Osborn, Henry Osborn's first wife.

been elected Right Worthy Grand Vice Templar.[25] I was
the subject of a good deal of fun among my Massachusetts friends when I returned bringing the honors
which I had promised to secure for Brother Stevens. It
was characteristic of that good man that he showed not
a particle of envy or disappointment, but honestly
rejoiced in the office which had come to me and which
he said had been worthily bestowed. I have sometimes
wondered whether the honor would have been so easily
won if I had been anxious to obtain it for myself as I
was for another, but it is certain that, having come by
it honestly, I could afford to enjoy the distinction
with a clear conscience.

Chapter VI

I BECOME EDITOR OF "THE TEMPERANCE BROTHERHOOD"

The officers elected at the Halifax session of the
Right Worthy Grand Lodge of the World in addition to
myself were:-

R.W.G.T., Joseph Malins, England.

R.W.G.C., Rev. W. G. Lane, Nova Scotia.

R.W.G.S.J.T., Rev. Enoch Franks, England.

R.W.G. Secretary, Wm. W. Turnbull, Scotland.

R.W.G.Tr., Gilbert Archer, Scotland.

R.W.G.Ch., Rev. Hugh J. Boyd, England.

R.W.G.M., Oskar Eklund, Sweden.

---

25   Forsyth was elected by a vote of 24 votes to
Lizzie Osborn´s 13 votes. R.W.G.L. of the World,
Proceedings (1883), p. 1304.

These officers were installed by Rev. George Gladstone, P.R.W.G.T.

My first public address outside of my own juris- diction was delivered in connection with the Halifax session at a meeting in a little church at Dartmouth, where Brother Gilbert Archer and I were the speakers. I remember that I was requested to speak regarding the Juvenile work, and did so to the best of my ability, little dreaming that I should ever be so intimately connected with that branch of the Order as I have been since then.

At the meeting of the new Executive Committee, which was held before we left Halifax, it was voted that I should have charge of the mission work in North America and that the funds should be disbursed by me subject to the instructions of the Mission Committee. This seemed rather a heavy responsibility, but it was not the only one which my office brought to me.

For some time prior to the R.W.G.L. session, Rev. Charles P. Wellman, a young Methodist minister, had been doing mission work for us among the colored people in the Southern States. In connection with his work he had published a little paper called The Temperance Brotherhood. Mr. Wellman had died just before the Halifax session, and it had become a question whether the little paper should be continued or not. It was finally [two years later, in 1885] decided to combine it and the little International Good Templar, which had been published from the office of the R.W.G. Secretary, and make The Temperance Brother- hood and International Good Templar the organ of the

R.W.G. Lodge. At this, to me, memorable Executive
meeting it was voted to place this also in my charge
and in spite of my protests I was appointed editor.
The appointment struck me as being almost an absurdity
as, at that time, I knew nothing about such work. But
my objections were overruled and I could only submit
to the inevitable and resolve that, in this case as in
other matters, I would do the best I could.[26] I
remember that, filled as I was with misgivings, it was
a tremendous help and inspiration to me when Brother
Malins said at the close of the meeting: "My little
sister, we are placing heavy burdens upon your shoulders, but I think you can carry them." Like many
others, I have been helped all along the way by just
such words of kindly encouragement from those whom I

---

26   "It took me some little time to realise that I,
the secretary of a very little organisation, was raised
to the dignity of an office on the Executive of the
International body, but I soon found that my position
was not be a sinecure, and I think it is seldom that a
Vice-Templar has so many duties placed upon her. At
the Executive meeting following the session I was give
the task of editing a little paper called "The Temperance Brotherhood," which had been published in the
interests of our scattered membership in America, and
whose founder and editor, a young Wesleyan minister,
had recently died. In addition I was given charge of
the mission work among the colored people. This
included the disbursing of the money collected by the
Mission Committee in Great Britain, subject, of course,
to the Committee's instructions. It also included
sending out the password when received from the
R.W.G.S., collecting the tax, sending out supplies and
collecting payment for same. I felt a little overwhelmed. . . ." Forsyth, "Good Templar Memories: Some
Outstanding Templars," Australian Temperance World,
March 1928, p. 7.

have looked up to as leaders.[27] Their confidence in me
has helped to develop my best gifts and I can only hope
that, in my turn, I may have sometimes said some words
to cheer others onward.

Before they returned to Europe, Brothers Malins
and Eklund, accompanied by Brother and Sister Henry
Osborn of England, visited some parts of this country
and we had the pleasure of having them with us for a
few days in Massachusetts. We held some successful
meetings at which, next to the R.W.G. Templar, Brother
Eklund was always the drawing card. His youth, his
fine appearance, and his quaintly-worded English made
him a great attraction.

The two years which intervened between the Halifax
session and the Stockholm session of 1885 were filled
with hard work and many cares. The editing of The
Temperance Brotherhood was not an easy task for one so
inexperienced as myself, but with the help and advice,
first of Brother Stevens and later of Brother Yeames,
who settled in Boston in the autumn following the
Halifax session, I succeeded in making it a fairly

---

27 "One characteristic of Joseph Malins was the
readiness he always showed to help less experienced
members by a word of information or advice. This
appeared in many ways which some persons would never
have thought of. On one occasion I happened to be
present when he was giving some counsel to a young
brother who was about to take up organising work. The
young man was clever and earnest, but he was rather
slovenly in his appearance. I remember that in a most
kindly and delicate manner Joseph Malins called his
attention to this, as a father might to a son, and
suggested that a neat appearance would be a great help
to him in his public work." Forsyth, "Good Templar
Memories: Some Outstanding Templars," Australian
Temperance World, Jan. 1928, p. 7.

readable paper and now, after the lapse of years, I can
look over my two little bound volumes without having
any reason to blush for my first attempts at journalism. The mission work gave me an ever-increasing
correspondence and with my duties as Grand Secretary
and the work of my own Lodge, I had little idle time.
It must be remembered that my work was all voluntary
and that in addition to the work for the Order, I
earned my own living in a business position which was
by no means a light one.

I had little time for social pleasures, and the
"burning of the midnight oil" was a common occurrence
with me. But the work, like all work I have undertaken
for the Order, was a great source of enjoyment. The
correspondence awakened my interest in other jurisdictions and my sympathies with the workers and their
difficulties. My outlook became broader day by day,
and, in a word, I learned unconsciously that "mankind
is one, in its rights and wrongs," and that the field
of Good Templary was indeed the world.

But notwithstanding the ever-growing interest
attaching to the work, I became very tired and looked
forward with keen anticipation to the session of 1885.
It was a very weary little woman who set sail on the
Cunarder "Scythia" for Liverpool, England, in the May
of that year, and I always look back gratefully to that
trip, which gave to me renewed health and strength,
coming as it did just when it was most needed. Added
to the delightful rest and change was the joy of
visiting my own country again after nearly eleven
years' absence. This joy was tempered with sorrow,
however, for the old home I had left existed no

longer. The dear aunts who had sheltered their orphan nieces had passed on to their reward, and my sister, with her husband and two little daughters, had gone to Western Australia, about four years prior to my visit to England, to join my brother [George], who was at that time Harbor Master of Fremantle.

But whatever of loneliness I felt was softened by the kindness of Good Templar friends. As soon as the steamer reached port, I found letters awaiting me from members of the Order, bidding me welcome to England and offering hospitality. My first day in Liverpool was spent in the home of Sister Mrs. Green, the lady who had nominated me at Halifax and who now gave me the kindest of welcomes. Later I was the guest of the late Brother John B. Collings and his wife [Caroline], who were always very kind and dear friends.

A visit of several days was given to the lovely home of Sister Catherine Impey at Street, Somerset-shire. This place was almost ideal, situated in a most beautiful part of England and surrounded with every-thing needed to make life happy and wholesome. The Impey family were very earnest Good Templars and their efforts for the Order extended for miles around their home. A garden party held in their grounds during my visit brought together representatives of the various Lodges of the district and was a most enjoyable affair. Although English-born, my life before leaving the old land had been entirely spent in London and vicinity, and this charming English country home, built of grey stone, situated in an old-fashioned garden filled with a wealth of blossoms of all kinds, and surrounded by places of historic interest, was almost as much of a novelty to me as if I had been really an American. In fact, during this visit, I became acquainted with my own country and learned that London did not comprise all that was admirable in England. Nevertheless, I may say in passing, I felt a keen enjoyment in the few days which I spent later with an old friend in London. Like all true Cocknies, I have never lost my love for the old city.

While I was staying at Street, I went for a day to Bristol to visit the Henry Osborns and to address a public meeting called in the interests of the Mission Fund of the Order. I have pleasant recollections of this visit on account of the fact that I was very cordially welcomed and kindly treated by everyone, and also because I scored a success in the talk which I gave. At that time I was so little used to speaking except in my own Lodge and Grand Lodge that it was a delightful sensation to find that I could interest an audience of strangers.

Chapter VII

THE STOCKHOLM SESSION OF 1885

The journey to Stockholm was taken in company with Sister Impey. We made part of a detachment of representatives headed by our R.W.G. Secretary, Brother Wm. W. Turnbull, who showed himself to be as capable in the capacity of guide to a party of untravelled people as he was in so many other directions. The party included several prominent English and Scottish members, who were hospitably entertained in the home of the late Brother Wm. Woodall at Hull. We were given a

"send off" by one of the Hull Lodges in the shape of a
fine meeting, and were afterwards escorted to the
steamer which sailed for Hamburg that night.

At Hamburg we were met by a few members of our one
little Lodge in that city, which to-day numbers its
members by the thousands.[28] The next day at Copenhagen, other members met us and escorted us about
during the few hours we were able to spend in that
beautiful and interesting city.[29] Here we found Sister
Charlotte A. Gray awaiting us to continue her journey
in our company.[30] Sister Gray was at that time
employed by the W.C.T.U, and it was not until somewhat
later [in 1891] that she became our missionary and
entered upon the remarkable work which has done so
much for the spread of our Order upon the European
continent. Sister Gray was then, as now, a very
earnest and devoted Good Templar. The first Lodge
which ever existed on the continent of Europe outside
of Scandinavia was organized under her auspices in

---

28 "Hamburg, which is now, and has been for many
years, a great centre of Good Templar activities, at
the time of my first visit possessed only one small
Lodge, carried on by the English Mission at the
Seamen´s Bethel, and chiefly composed of British
sailors." Forsyth, "Good Templar Memories: Some
Outstanding Templars," Australian Temperance World,
April 1928, p. 4. See Der Guttempler-Order in Deutsch-
land (Hamburg: Neiland-Verlagsgellschaft, 1979-81), the
first volume on 1889-1945 by Theo Gläss and Wilhelm
Biel, and the second on 1945-80 by Theo Gläss and
Martin Klewitz.

29 See also Forsyth, "Good Templar Memories: Some
Outstanding Templars," Australian Temperance World, May
1928, p. 12.

30 Gray wrote a short memoir published in International Good Templar, Oct. 1903, pp. 353-55.

Antwerp, where she and her sister were residing. I believe the Lodge was chiefly composed of English-speaking seamen and it did a good work. I had heard about this Lodge and was glad to meet Sister Gray in the flesh and make a beginning of the friendship which has endured to the present time.

At Malmo we were greeted by more Good Templars and during our very brief sojourn in the town we visited the fine Good Templar hall. When we arrived in Stockholm we were greeted, as we were last summer [in 1902] (on what was the second visit for a few of us) by a large concourse of members, carrying banners and singing odes of welcome. Such a reception was enough to inspire anyone and I have never forgotten the effect it produced upon me. At that time Sweden had somewhere in the neighborhood of thirty-five thousand members, I think, but even the number, small as it appears beside the one hundred and twenty thousand of to-day, was a wonderful record for the time the Order had existed in the country. Indeed so rapid had been the progress that some of the more conservative members of the Right Worthy Grand Lodge of the World shook their heads over it and feared for the permanence of the Order in a land where its growth had been so phenomenal. But these pessimistic ones did not know our Scandinavian brethren; events have proved that they had not only been able to keep what they had won, but also to go on winning fresh victories.[31]

---

31   The standard monograph is Hilding Johansson, <u>Den svenska godtemplarrörelsen och samhället</u> (Stockholm: Oscar Eklunds Bokforlag, 1947).

At this session I renewed my acquaintance with Brother Oskar Eklund, and became acquainted with that good, faithful member, Brother Edward [Edvard] Wavrinsky. I also met and learned to esteem many other prominent members, some of whom have since passed away. There were present among the representatives from Norway, Brother Lars O. Jensen, then a student, now a distinguished professor, and the late Brother M. Laumann, who was a most faithful worker for the cause up to the time of his death a few years ago. From Denmark came the late Dr. Selmer and his beautiful wife, who, since her husband´s death, has become well-known in connection with the W.C.T.U.

In addition to Brother Malins, R.W.G. Templar, England sent several well-known members, including Brother and Sister John B. Collings, Mrs. Elizabeth Browne, the late Brothers Winton and Woodall, and others. From Scotland there were Brothers Rev. Wm. Ross, Archer, Hamilton, Craig and others. From Wales the now venerable Brother Cooke, Grand Secretary, and the late Brother [W. T.] Raper. From Ireland Brother Charles F. Allen, a cousin of Sister Impey, and, like her, a member of the Society of Friends. New Zealand was represented in the person of the late Sir William Fox, a fine old gentleman, ex-Premier of the colony and a P.G.C.T. Then there were Brother Rev. W. G. Lane and Brother R. R. Duncan from Nova Scotia and many others whose names I cannot now recall.

Our session was held in the Rigsdaghuset (Parliament House), where we again met last summer. There were many interesting events during the meetings, but I remember one in particular. That was a debate upon the

Scandinavian beer question [as to whether drinking beer with a low alcohol content would violate the Good Templar obligation]. There was much conflict of opinion and at one point the feeling was most intense. Just when it seemed to be impossible that we could ever come to an amicable settlement of the question, Rev. Wm. Ross rose and moved that a few moments should be given to silent prayer. It was so ordered and for a brief space all heads were bowed and silence prevailed. When the discussion was resumed the air seemed clearer, and a moderation, which had been lacking before, seemed to govern the speeches of even the most fiery debaters. This was my first experience of the effect of prayer in "stilling the troubled waters" of a heated argument. I had taken no part in the debate myself, but had become somewhat "nerved up" in sympathy with others, and I shall never forget the peaceful influence which seemed to surround me during those moments of silence. Truly "more things are wrought by prayer than this world wots of."

It was during this session that the now world-famous gavel was presented to Brother Malins. As presiding officer Brother Malins had used the gavel belonging to the Swedish parliament. It was a very large and handsome one, inlaid with mother of pearl, and Brother Malins had expressed his admiration for it. The generous Swedish brethren, who were ready to bestow anything they possessed upon our R.W.G. Templar, had an exact duplicate of the gavel made and gave it to the honored chief. Brother Malins carried this gavel around the world with him on his recent tour.

I had not thought of being a candidate for re-election as R.W.G.V.T., but Sister Impey believed that my continuance in office was necessary to the welfare of the mission work in America and she exacted from me the promise that I would stand again. I am frank to confess that I fully expected to be defeated, however, for I knew that the Scottish brethren, albeit they were all my very good friends, had conceived the idea that the R.W.G.L. Executive should be composed entirely of men. So when Brother A. H. Berg, G.C.T. of Sweden, a very fine man, who by reason of his power as an orator was known as "the Spurgeon of Sweden," [after the Nonconformist preacher in London] was nominated by Rev. William Ross, I would very gladly have retired from the field but for the pledge that I had given to Sister Impey. When it was found that, notwithstanding the strength of my opponent, I had received about two-thirds of the whole vote cast, I felt that a majority of the body must have agreed with Sister Impey and I accepted the compliment gladly.

It was a great shock to the R.W.G.L. to have Brother Malins decline positively to be re-elected to the office of R.W.G.T., for we had become so accustomed to looking upon him as our leader that the thought of his relinquishing the position caused a feeling of almost consternation. But we had to bow to the inevitable and for the first time in the history of the R.W.G.L. of the World the office was bestowed on a member from North America, Rev. W. G. Lane of Nova Scotia. Brother Lane is a Methodist minister, able and eloquent. He recently served with distinction in the South African war as Chaplain to one of the Nova Scotia regiments. Although forced to give up Bro. Malins as

R.W.G. Templar, we insisted upon retaining him upon the
Executive by electing him as R.W.G. Counsellor. The
other officers elected at the session were
R.W.G.S.J.T., Gilbert Archer, Scotland; R.W.G. Sec-
retary, Wm W. Turnbull, Scotland, who was, of course,
re-elected unanimously; R.W.G. Treasurer, Charles
F. Allen, Ireland; R.W.G. Chaplain, A. H. Berg,
Sweden; R.W.G. Marshal, Dr. H. Selmer, Denmark. The
appointed officers included Sister Charlotte A. Gray as
R.W.G.D.M., and represented New Zealand, Channel
Islands, Norway and Wales. The officers were installed
by Rev. Wm. Ross of Scotland, P.R.W.G.T.

Among the many pleasant occasions which had been
arranged in connection with this session was a great
public welcome meeting in one of the largest churches
of Stockholm which was attended by about 2,000 people.
At that time it was not a very common thing for ladies
to appear upon the public platform in Sweden. There
were not very many women connected with the Order even,
and the few who were privileged to belong had not taken
a prominent position. It was therefore somewhat of a
shock to some of the Swedish brethren to find that some
of the representatives from abroad were women and that
one of the Executive officers belonged to the gentler
sex. Perhaps, if Brother Malins and some other of our
leaders had held the same ideas as prevailed at that
time in Sweden, the women of the Order might have been
overlooked on the public occasions, but as it was, I
shared with Sister Mrs. E. Browne of London,
P.R.W.G.S.J.T., the honor of representing the sex. I
remember that when I stepped upon the platform on the
evening of the meeting, I was politely ushered to a
seat with the ladies in the rear, instead of being

placed with the other R.W.G.L. officers in front of the
platform. We were quite out of sight of the audience
and when my name was called and I had to push my way
through a crowd of brethren, I was conscious of a
distinct feeling of surprise on the part of the
audience when instead of a big man responding to the
rather imposing title of R.W.G.V.T. they saw only a
little woman. But, for once, I was equal to the
occasion and I began my speech with an apology for the
embarrassment which I must necessarily feel at standing
before such an audience, because I represented "a
country in which it was not the custom to put the
women in the back seats." I then in the few moments
allotted to me told what I could of the work woman was
doing for the temperance cause and urged the Swedish
members to enlist her efforts if they desired to make
the Order a permanent success. The audience showed
their approval of my remarks in an unmistakable manner
and many individual Swedish brethren expressed their
approbation later. The English-speaking members, some
of whom were indignant at what they considered a slight
to the office when I had not been given a seat with the
others, congratulated me warmly and altogether my
little speech "made a hit."[32]

---

32   "When it was learned that the representatives from
abroad included several sisters, a prominent gentleman
on the reception committee expressed his fear that the
fact might cause a prejudice against the Order in
Sweden. So when he escorted the R.W.G.L. officers to
seats on the front of the platform, he left out the one
woman on the Executive, and with great politeness
seated her at the back, `with the other ladies.´ But
Bro. Malins was not one to allow the sisters to be
ignored. As soon as the preliminary exercises, the
addresses of welcome and responses, etc., were ended,
the meeting was put into the hands of our R.W.G.T. He
began by saying that in a great assembly of people, few

I may say here that, although some of the Swedish
members were willing to ignore a woman in an official
position, there was no lack of courtesy shown to us
otherwise. Everything that kindness and politeness
could suggest was done to make our visit to Sweden
comfortable and pleasant. It may be well also to
mention here that at least one-third of the present
membership in Sweden are women and that a lady speaker
at a public meeting is no longer a novelty. I believe
that our Order has been a great factor in bringing this
change about, as it has been in other lands.

There were two other amusing incidents at this
meeting. One was when Brother Turnbull tried to bother
Professor Thorelli, who was acting as interpreter, by
reciting some poetry in very broad Scotch and Brother
Thorelli extricated himself from the difficulty by
announcing that it was a Scotch song and that Brother
Turnbull would sing it. Another was the receipt of a
cable despatch from Florida which read: "We in our warm
South land, greet you in your Northern iceland." This

---

of whom would ever meet again, it would be more satisfactory if they heard brief remarks from a great many
of those who had come from other countries, instead of
lengthy addresses from two or three. His suggestion
was applauded, and after a few introductory words from
himself, he announced that the speakers would be
limited to five minutes for themselves and five for the
interpreter. He then introduced the members of the
Executive, and when my name was called, I was conscious
of a distinct sensation in the audience, when instead
of another man, a little woman appeared."

"I was not then very much accustomed to public
speaking, and had never addressed such a large audience
before, but I determined to vindicate the right which
the Order had always given to my sex." Forsyth, "Good
Templar Memories: Some Outstanding Templars," Australian Temperance World, May 1928, p. 12.

message, when translated, raised a very hearty laugh,
for at that time it was exceedingly hot in Sweden and
the reception we had that evening was warm in every
sense of the word.

I must not linger over the many other pleasant
things connected with this session. They included a
great parade, a banquet in the Pavilion of the Queen's
Summer Palace at Ulrichsdahl, a visit to the Grand
Lodge of Sweden, and other never-to-be-forgotten
events. And in addition there were the beauty and the
historic associations of the buildings in Stockholm, at
Upsala, and in other places. The events were dupli-
cated and improved upon last summer; the city, beautiful as it was in 1885, has been improved, and the
hearts of the Swedish people I found to be as warm as
at my previous visit. But this does not prevent me
from recalling with pleasure the events of 1885, events
which have left in my memory a never-fading series of
delightful pictures, and in my heart a strong regard
for Sweden and her people.

Chapter VIII

A GLIMPSE OF NORWAY--THE GRAND LODGE OF IRELAND

It had been arranged that special sessions of the
R.W.G. Lodge of the World should be held in Copenhagen,
Denmark, and in Christiania [later renamed Oslo],
Norway, and to meet these plans it became necessary to
divide up the members of the Executive into two
parties. It fell to my lot to be one of the number who
went to Norway and to that fact I am indebted for a
delightful addition to my experiences. Among the

members of my deputation were Rev. Wm. Ross, P.R.W.G.T.; Wm. W. Turnbull, R.W.G. Secretary; Miss Catherine Impey; Sir Wm. Fox of New Zealand, and his niece; Bros. Osborn, Woodhall, Hamilton, and some others. We also had with us Brothers Laumann and Jensen of Norway, who were able to point out the interesting objects along the route.

The journey to Norway was made by night. It was slow and fatiguing, but the scenery was charming. It was impossible to sleep when there was so much that was beautiful to be seen and we were a weary little party when the train arrived at Christiania on the following afternoon. I remember that I not only felt tired, but dreadfully untidy and travel-worn when I alighted from the train, and it was therefore distinctly embarrassing to be met by a number of gentlemen in spotless evening attire, who had come to welcome us and escort us to the hotel. When I was shown to my room, it was a great relief to find that I did not look quite so dishevelled as I felt. A bath and a change of dress made the ladies feel like themselves again, and we were soon ready to be escorted to the grand banquet which awaited us. At this banquet our sex was in the minority and we English-speaking women received all the attention that one could desire. Many of the brethren spoke English well and their kindness and courtesy were unbounded. The usual exercises followed the dinner, and the whole affair gave us a good impression of Norwegian hospitality.

The special session of the R.W.G.L., which follow-ed, was a very impressive affair. It was held in the Good Templars' own hall and was presided over by

Rev. Wm. Ross, P.R.W.G.T. The fatigue of the journey
had, however, been too much for me and I was obliged to
go away before the session closed, leaving Sister
Impey to fill the R.W.G.V.T.'s chair. On the evening
of this same day a tremendous meeting was held in the
Drill Hall, which was capable, we were told, of seating
4,000 people, and which was filled. The audience
included all the notabilities of the city and it
exhibited wonderful patience throughout the long
exercises which followed. Brother Torjus Hanssen (the
brother who has recently retired from the office of
G.C.T. which he had filled for many years) presided.
His address of welcome was of the most cordial character, delivered first in his own language and afterwards
translated by himself into English. Some fine vocal
music enlivened the meeting, which was a magnificent
one in every respect. But it had been a long day for
us and I imagine that I was not the only one of our
party who was glad to get to bed that night.

The next day brought us a delightful change in the
shape of a long and beautiful drive up a mountain, from
the summit of which we could get a magnificent view of
Christiania and its surroundings. Sister Impey and I
were in a comfortable open carriage with Brothers
Laumann and Jensen. Sister Impey did some botanizing
and some digging up of rare plants, but as I had no
garden at home to think of, I was glad to remain in the
carriage and drink in the invigorating mountain air and
the scent of the pine trees.

Our stay in Norway was all too brief, but it was
long enough to impress me with a sense of the kindness
and hospitality of its people and with the many noble

characteristics which have enabled them to make a wonderful success of our Order in their wild and beautiful land. The kindness of the Norwegian brethren accompanied me for quite a way along my homeward trip, for it took a final expression in the shape of a basket of magnificent roses which was presented to me at the wharf where we took [a] steamer for Scotland.

In these reminiscences I do not intend to describe the scenery of the countries I have visited. If I were to attempt to do so I should give many paragraphs to the beauties of the voyage down the Christiania Fjord to Christianland, the harbor which delighted our representatives so greatly last year [in 1902], when we lay for a few hours outside of it. I spent a day or two in this charming little place awaiting the steamer for Scotland, but, with the exception of a little public meeting arranged by the local Lodge, the days were uneventful. The same may be said of the brief time spent in Scotland, the land of my ancestors, as far as Good Templary was concerned, for the short time I had in the bonnie country was given to seeing a little of Glasgow and Edinburgh. I was the guest of Brother [James] Hamilton and his family and have grateful recollection of the kindness I received from his wife and daughter. But I was obliged to hurry away to attend the Grand Lodge of Ireland and a further acquaintance with Scotland and with Scottish Good Templary had to be postponed to a later date.

I had been instructed to attend the session of the Grand Lodge of Ireland at an Executive meeting of the R.W.G.L., which was held before we left Stockholm. A request had come for the attendance of a R.W.G.L.

officer and the privilege was very kindly given to me
by my colleagues. I was very glad to have this addition to my experiences before returning to America.
The session was held in Londonderry, the famous walled
city around which so many historic associations
cling. The meetings were in progress when I arrived
and I received a most cordial welcome. Here I met the
late Brother [James] Caithness, G.C.T., a most noble
man; Rev. John Pyper, the present D.R.W.G.T., who is a
distinguished author; Brother Shippobotham, the present
G.S.J.T.; Brother [Robert] Semple, who had since served
many years as Grand Secretary and who is a lecturer and
author of no mean repute, and many others. I also met
Brother John Sutherland, P.G.C.T., who has always
ranked as one of the foremost workers of Scotland. In
connection with this session I had my first experience
in conferring the Grand Lodge degree, and it also fell
to my lot to install the officers, the first time I had
ever performed this duty outside of my own Grand
Lodge. A particularly pleasant recollection in
connection with this latter service was that I had the
privilege of installing a woman, Sister McKensie, as
Grand Chief Templar.[33]

153   Elsewhere Forsyth names the wife of the secretary
of the Irish Temperance League as the woman Grand Chief
Templar of Ireland. ". . . the G.C.T. I had the honor
of installing was a woman, Mrs. [William] Wilkinson, a
most faithful and zealous member. I have installed
many Grand Lodge officers, but this, I think, was the
only experience I have had of putting the G.C.T. collar
on one of my own sex." Forsyth, "Some Good Templar
Memories: Some Outstanding Good Templars," Australian
Temperance World, July 1928. (On the photostat copy
which I received from Australia, the page number is
indecipherable.)   These statements are puzzling, as in
her report at the time she said that James Caithness
had been reelected unanimously to head the Grand Lodge
of Ireland for another term. Forsyth, "Some Notes of

A fine public meeting gave me an opportunity to discover that an Irish audience is a good one to talk to, as the people are extremely responsive and sympathetic. Making one of a party to visit the wonderful natural formation, the "Giant's Causeway," I was enabled to become better acquainted with our Irish brethren (who, by the way, proved in many cases to be Scottish) and in particular established a lasting friendship with Brother Robert Semple and his late beautiful wife. They had with them their little daughter, Mary Gladstone Semple, now a grown young lady who is achieving distinction as a musician.

The time had now come to turn my face homewards, and a pleasant voyage brought me back to Boston, with renewed health and vigor, after an absence of three months, able and willing to take up again the everyday routine.[34] I had many things to tell my friends, and the faithful little band of workers, who constituted what we now refer to as the Junior Grand Lodge of Massachusetts, were never tired of hearing about the work which our great Order was accomplishing in Europe. They realized, as all our members should realize, that it is a great thing to belong to such a world-wide brotherhood, and each rejoiced to be known as a Good Templar.

Travel," Temperance Brotherhood, April 1886, p. 5.

34   During Forsyth's absence, James Yeames had edited Temperance Brotherhood and had served as mission agent. Forsyth, "Some Outstanding Good Templars," Australian Temperance World, Aug. 1928, p. 12.

For myself, I knew that I should continue my work in Subordinate and Grand Lodge, and that I would work harder than ever for the success of the mission work of the Order, but I hardly expected any further experiences in connection with the R.W.G. Lodge. The next session was appointed to be held in Cardiff, Wales, and it did not seem possible that I should be able to cross the Atlantic again in the short space of two years. But those two years were destined to be crowded with events, the telling of which must be left for another chapter.

Chapter IX

INDICATIONS OF UNION---THE UNION CONFERENCE

Some little time before the Stockholm session of the Right Worthy Grand Lodge of the World, indications pointing to the direction of a reunion of the divided forces of Good Templary began to appear. The late beloved and honored John B. Finch had been elected R.W.G. Templar of the American section and under his sagacious leadership, some resolutions had been adopted which practically removed the reasons for a longer separation.[35] In pursuance of this new policy, mission work was undertaken among the colored people of the South by the Right Worthy Grand Lodge of North America. This brought about a curious complication and for a time, added considerably to our difficulties. I remember the perplexity which it caused me when I found that our work in the South was being hindered and our

---

35   See Frances E. Finch and Frank J. Sibley, John Finch: His Life and Work (New York and London: Funk and Wagnalls, 1888).

members harassed, not by white Good Templars, but by colored people enrolled in the opposition camp. It was not long before I was convinced that it was a foolish expenditure of money and effort for two organizations, bearing the same name, to be doing mission work in the same place. Instead of promoting our principle of universal brotherhood, we were helping to divide those who would otherwise be content to work together. When it came to the point (as was the case in one jurisdiction) of a Lodge more than once changing its allegiance from one Grand Lodge to the other, with the consequent bitterness of feeling engendered by the transfer, I felt sure that something would have to be done to prevent such a condition of affairs from continuing.[36]

---

36   "During the previous year [1884] our American friends, acting on a ruling by John B. Finch, their R.W.G.T., had secured the institution of some [black] Lodges in the Southern States. A Grand Lodge had been formed of colored people in Virginia, where we had for some time had one at work, and one of the results of this was that the members of the two bodies came into conflict. Members drifted from one organisation to the other, and letters kept coming complaining of grievances which, of course, I had no power to deal with. The best I could do in the circumstances was to advise patience and forbearance, and remind my correspondents that, although they were working under different charters, they were bound by the same pledge and must remember that they were brethren and not opponents. But I became convinced that the only way to settle the various problems was for a reunion to take place. It soon appeared that the same idea was arising in the minds of members in many places. It is probable that the growth of our Order [the Right Worthy Grand Lodge of the World] in the Scandinavian countries and the great success of our meeting in Stockholm may have had something to do with this impression among R.W.G.L. members. . . ." Forsyth, "Some Outstanding Good Templars," Australian Temperance World, Aug. 1928, p. 12. (As in this case the series sometimes had slight variations in title from month to month.)

In the meantime, John B. Finch had been delivering
some addresses in the Eastern States and on one Sunday
afternoon he and Brother Rev. James Yeames, P.R.W.G.T.,
were the speakers at a temperance meeting in Tremont
Temple, Boston. After the meeting closed, these two
men became acquainted with each other, with the result
that Brother Yeames accepted an invitation to meet
Brother Finch the next day and talk over the affairs of
the Order. I have no doubt that this interview was one
of the first (if not the very first) steps in the
direction of reunion.

Another factor was the <u>Temperance Brotherhood</u>. I
had adopted the custom of sending this little organ to
every G.C.T. and G. Secretary under the Right Worthy
Grand Lodge. I think it had the effect of showing some
of the members from whom we were separated, that the
Right Worthy Grand Lodge of the World was not, as some
of them had supposed, simply a small faction, but a
large, prosperous and <u>growing</u> body. I had several kind
little notes from leading members of the American
section and it is a cause for satisfaction to me now
that more than one of them referred to the spirit which
was revealed in the page of the paper. Among those who
thus wrote was the late Captain [John F.] Cleghorn of
Wisconsin, a most noble man, who hoped he might see the
day when the Order should again be one. The late
Hon. S. D. Hastings, P.R.W.G.T., wrote enclosing a
dollar towards the expense of publishing "such a useful
little sheet," and saying: "Although, as we have been
looking at some things from different standpoints,
there have been many things in your paper with which I
could not entirely agree, the most of your editorial
articles have met with my cordial approval." To have

129

won such approval from Brother Hastings was worth all
the labor bestowed upon the paper. Our Brother Colonel
B. F. Parker, who was then as now, the honored and
efficient R.W.G. Secretary, wrote that he was glad to
get the Temperance Brotherhood and considered it ably
edited. This was the first compliment--indeed the
first word--ever received from Brother Parker, who has
said other nice things about me since, as some of our
readers know.[37] Well, these little amenities, trifling
as they may seem, had their part in helping to bring
about a better understanding between our long-divided
brotherhood.

The next move in the direction of union came in
the shape of a letter from Brother Rev. W. G. Lane, the
R.W.G.T. of the Right Worthy Grand Lodge of the World,
enclosing a communication from the late Colonel J.[ohn]
J. Hickman, P.R.W.G.T. Colonel Hickman had been lecturing in Nova Scotia and had met and had some conversation with Brother Lane. As a result he made what
we all thought a rather extraordinary proposition, to
the effect that the two bodies should continue to
exist, but should agree to work amicably together, the
one to have jurisdiction in the Western and the other
over the Eastern hemisphere. When I met Colonel
Hickman, after the union, he mentioned some slightly
sarcastic references which I made to this proposition
in the Temperance Brotherhood and said, "Well, anyhow,
Sister Jessie, my letter helped to bring about the
union." And this was true, although it hardly seemed
likely at the time to produce the result.

---

37   Parker appointed Forsyth editor of the International Good Templar, effective January 1901.

Colonel Hickman's letter went the round of the
Executive Committee of the R.W.G.L. of the World, and
we unanimously agreed to instruct Brother Joseph Malins
to communicate with Brother John B. Finch and ask him
whether Colonel Hickman was authorized to make such
propositions. Brother Finch in reply repudiated the
Colonel's overtures in language that was rather more
curt and less courteous than might have been desired.
The next incident was the visit of F. G. Keens,
P.R.W.G. Secretary to England, and during a call which
he made upon Brother Malins he referred to the question
of reunion. As the interview was a very brief one,
Brother Malins wrote fully in reply to Brother Keens
who, upon his arrival in the United States, laid the
letter before Brother Finch.

In the interval between the Hickman incident and
the letter to Brother Keens, it is probable that
Brother Finch had been studying up the question, or
that he had taken counsel with other leaders, for his
reply to this communication showed a very different
spirit from his previous letters. The result of the
correspondence was that it was decided that a conference to consider first "whether union is desirable,"
and second "whether union is possible," should be held
during September, 1886, in Boston. The commissioners
appointed by the Executive of the Right Worthy Grand
Lodge of the World were: Rev. W. G. Lane, Nova Scotia,
R.W.G.T.; Joseph Malins, England, P.R.W.G.T.; Rev.
Wm. Ross, Scotland, P.R.W.G.T.; Jessie Forsyth, Massachusetts, R.W.G.V.T.; Wm. W. Turnbull, Scotland,
R.W.G.S.; Wm. Artrell, G.C.T., Florida, and Wm. P.
Hastings, D.R.W.G.T., Tennessee. Those representing
the Right Worthy Grand Lodge were: Hon John B. Finch,

Illinois, R.W.G.T.; Dr. Oronhyatekha, Canada, P.R.W.G.C.; W. H. Lambly, G.C.T., Quebec; N. B. Broughton, G.C.T., North Carolina; Charles L. Abbott, G.C.T. of Massachusetts; W. Martin Jones, P.G.C.T. of New York, and Mrs. Francena C. Bailey of New Hampshire. When the conference assembled it was found that Brother N. T. Collins of our Grand Lodge in New South Wales was in Boston and it was thought advisable to add an Australian member to the commission.[38] Consent to this was granted by the representatives of the American section and to make matters even, Brother George A. Bailey, G.C.T. of New Hampshire, was added to their number.

The representatives of the Right Worthy Grand Lodge of the World arrived in Boston a day or so before the date of the conference, which was fixed for the 27th of September, 1886, and the intervening time was largely spent in conferring with trusted leaders of the Order, such as Brother Rev. James Yeames, P.R.W.G.T.; Brother C. A. Stevens, G.C.T.; Sister Eliza A. Gardner, G.V.T., and others. On the morning of the 27th, our representatives all assembled at the Adams House a little before the hour named for the conference to begin, which I think was 9:30. The time arrived and passed and no one from the American section appeared. An hour passed and still no one came. We began to grow impatient and, as noon approached without any word or sign from the American commissioners, some us were

---

38 See Collins' reminiscences of the Union Conference, "Good Templar History," Australian Temperance World, Dec. 1926, p. 4. Collins, born in Massachusetts in 1853, had emigrated to New South Wales in 1877. "A Notable Good Templar: Bro. N. T. Collins, P.G.C.T.," Australian Temperance World, Jan. 1927, pp. 5-6.

outspoken in our indignation. Just as we were at fever
heat, a rap at the door announced the arrival of John
B. Finch. I am afraid that we did not regard him with
very friendly eyes, for we were angry over the lost
time and I, for one, was prejudiced against him on
account of the letters I have referred to above. But I
shall never forget how quickly my feelings changed when
I came into close touch with that wonderful man, and I
imagine that my experience was similar to that of all
the other members. Brother Finch first apologized,
with that peculiarly winning ease and grace which
distinguished him, for his own tardiness and that of
his colleagues.[39] Then he clasped the hand of us each
one of us, saying some pleasant words to each in his
delightfully frank and genial manner. In a few moments
he had won us all to a love and allegiance which was
never to falter during the few brief months we were
privileged to claim him as a friend. I can recall him
now, as he sat with his chair slightly tilted back,
gazing from one to another with that keen yet kindly
glance, his face lighted up with his almost boyish
smile, talking as easily and unconcernedly to us as if
there had never been a difference between us and as if
he knew that we were all henceforth to be his true
friends. He did believe this, I think, and he found it
to be so. The last time that I saw him before he died
he told me that he had never had more sincere and loyal
friends and supporters than those who had been members
of the Right Worthy Grand Lodge of the World.

---

39   Finch "had met Rev. William Ross of Scotland in
another part of the building and had learned of the
contretemps, so was not surprised to find our party
looking a little annoyed and unsociable." Forsyth,
"The Historic Union Conference," New York Templar, Nov.
1923, p. 6.

The conference was called to order when all had
assembled except Dr. Oronhyatekha. The good feeling
which Brother Finch had awakened had been extended to
his colleagues and when the famous Indian arrived we
were sitting together discussing matters quite amicably. I had been extremely anxious to see Dr. Oronhyatekha and at the same time just a little afraid of
him. I scarcely know what I expected to see, certainly
not exactly a "big chief" in feathers and war paint,
but at the same time I was hardly prepared to meet a
handsome, kindly, genial gentleman who, as events
proved, was just as anxious to "bury the hatchet" as
anyone could be.

With the Doctor's arrival, our numbers were
complete and we settled down to business in earnest. I
am not going to write of the transactions of the conference, because they are all a matter of printed
record. But I just wish to repeat what I have often
said that if I had gone into that series of meetings an
atheist, I should have been converted to a belief in
the Divine power which had brought us together and
whose guidance was so evident in all our deliberations. During the years of separation, many changes
had been made in both sections of the Order and the
harmonizing of all differences, without yielding any
principle, often presented a difficult problem for our
consideration. Sometimes an apparently insurmountable
obstacle loomed up, but as we approached it, it faded
away and at the close of our sittings which lasted
nearly a week, we were all able to affix our names,
with clear consciences, to a basis of union which

secured to both sides the opportunity for "peace with honor."

On that memorable afternoon, Brother Finch, who was jubilant over the happy results of our meeting, insisted upon our accompanying him to photographer and sitting together for a picture which has become known in history as the Union Conference Group. With characteristic generosity, Brother Finch presented a copy of this picture to each one of us and mine is one of my most cherished possessions. It hangs on the wall of the room in which I am writing, a constant reminder of the conference and of the beloved donor. If my readers will turn to our frontispiece, they will find a miniature reproduction of this historic picture.[40]

Chapter X

THE UNION SESSION

It is unnecessary to mention that although the members of the Conference on Union had come to such an amicable agreement, there was still much to be done before the union could be an accomplished fact throughout the worldwide Order. There was considerable conflict of opinion and some of those who were members of the Conference had difficulty in bringing the Grand Lodges they represented to consent to the terms. One action agreed to by the Conference, however, was a great help in smoothing the way. This was the decision

---

40   Forsyth gave this picture to the West Australian Alliance which had it hung in the Temperance Hall, Perth. Forsyth, "A Glimpse of Past History," New York Templar, April 1922, p. 5; reprinted in International Good Templar, July 1922, p. 122.

that both R.W.G. Templars should issue the same passwords during the interval between the Conference and
the session of the two Supreme Lodges, and that visita-
tion should be allowed between the Lodges of both sections. The result of this was that in jurisdictions
where the two branches existed, the union had, to all
intents and purposes, taken place among the subordinate
members, before the question could be considered in
either Grand Lodges, or R.W.G. Lodge.

I remember that, after being shut out of fellowship with Lodges of the original body in Massachusetts
for so long, it was a delightful experience to be able
to exchange visits with them and some very pleasant
times were enjoyed. Among the first members from the
American section to visit us were Frank I. Jefferson
and J. Sydney Hitchens, both of whom have since filled
the chair of G.C.T. Just prior to the Conference
meeting I had become acquainted with Mrs. Sarah A.
Leonard, the lady who was then as now the Grand Secretary of Massachusetts. A rather singular coincidence
was the fact that Sister Leonard and myself were holding the office of R.W.G.V.T. in our respective Supreme
Lodges at the same time. Someone jestingly referred to
us as the "rival queens," but the rivalry was not a
very keen one.

In accordance with a tacit agreement, those who
had signed the basis of union kept each other informed
of the progress that was being made. Thus I sometimes
heard from John B. Finch and occasionally he did me the
honor to ask my opinion on some matters relating to the
work in the South. On one or two occasions when
Brother Finch was in Boston, he sent for me to talk

matters over with him and at one of these interviews I
was able to give some information which enabled him to
overcome the scruples of one prominent member.

Having agreed to the terms of union, Brother Finch
threw himself with characteristic zeal into the effort
to bring his constituents around to his views. This
necessitated a tremendous amount of travel and personal
effort and I have little doubt that these labors, in
addition to his numerous other duties and cares, acting
upon an already debilitated constitution, helped to
bring about his lamented death a few months later. It
has been said that the union of the Order caused the
death of John B. Finch, but, if that were so, I am sure
that he himself would never have grudged the sacrifice. The great work of uniting the two branches of
the Order was a fitting crown to his noble life.

Among the pleasant occasions to which I have
referred was a reception tended by Tremont Lodge of
Boston to John B. Finch, Rev. James Yeames, and myself. The officers of both Grand Lodges were among
the guests and were all, of course, invited to the
platform. Our G.V.T. of the Junior Grand Lodge was
Sister Eliza A. Gardner, an educated and cultured
colored woman. Just before the meeting opened I
noticed Miss Gardner enter and take a seat in the rear
of the hall and I said to Brother Finch: "There is our
Grand Vice Templar." He replied: "She ought to be here
with the rest of us," and leaving his seat, he went to
our Sister and escorted her to the platform. Sister
Gardner has never forgotten this kindly and courteous
act. She was used to such treatment from the members
of the R.W.G.L. of the World, and when she met with it

from the representative man of the American section, it
went far to banish any misgivings she might have had
regarding the union.

Thus filled with more than ordinary interests and
duties the months speedily passed until it was time for
the sessions of the two Supreme bodies to be held at
Saratoga, New York. The R.W.G.L. of the World was to
have met in Great Britain, but the prospect of union
had made it necessary to have the two bodies near
together, so our session was called for the same place
(Saratoga Springs, N.Y.) and time (May 24th, 1887) as
that of the Right Worthy Grand Lodge. Those who went
from our little Grand Lodge, Brother James Yeames,
Reuben Forknall, and myself, arranged to travel with
the representatives of the New England Grand Lodges and
we were a large party, filling a special car. I
remember that I had with me a roll of the little ribbon
badges, with the globe woven into them, worn instead of
a button by the members of the R.W.G.L. of the World,
and it was not long before our fellow travellers
noticed them and begged them from me. Before we
reached our destination everyone of the party was
wearing the insignia of the R.W.G.L. of the World, but
as it was the legitimate emblem of the Order, the
wearing of it involved no sacrifice of principle upon
their part. We became pretty well acquainted with one
another upon the journey and in particular I gained one
friend in the person of Mrs. Martha M. Ruslow of New
Hampshire, who has always been a very kind and loyal
one and in whose pleasant home at Manchester I have
since spent many happy and restful days.

I had secured accommodation at the headquarters of
the American section as I had not been informed where
the members of my own Executive would stay. But when I
reached Saratoga, I learned that all of my colleagues
were quartered at another house and I stopped at the
Worden House to see whether I could relinquish the room
I had engaged. While I was waiting for an opportunity
to speak to the clerk, Brother John B. Finch entered
the parlor and after we had exchanged greetings he took
up my handbag and cloak and "personally conducted" me
to the other hotel, telling me that he would make it
all right at the Worden House. I mention this as
another example of the kindness and courtesy of Brother
Finch. Although R.W.G. Templar and head of the
National Prohibition Party, and by reason of these
offices, the foremost man among the temperance people
of America, he was never too busy or too much uplifted
to perform the "little kindnesses, which most leave
undone or despise," and it was this trait in his character, perhaps, even more than his greater gifts (if
any gifts can be greater than the unselfish thought
for others) which won for him the love and admiration
of all.

I was so much later than the other members of our
executive in arriving at Saratoga that I had missed the
opportunity which their earlier arrival had given them
of becoming acquainted with some of the leading representatives of the American section. Brother Finch
realized this and after supper on the day of my
arrival, he called for me and Brother Yeames and took
us over to the Worden House, where he introduced us to
those who, prior to that time, had only been known to
me by name. It was a delightful experience to meet

such men as Brother Hastings and Brother Chase in the
flesh and to listen to their cordial words of greeting,
to receive the warmest of sisterly welcomes from those
grand women, Mrs. M.[artha] B.[arnum] [Dickinson]
O´Donnell, Mrs. Mattie McClellan Brown, Amanda Way,
Mrs. A. A. Brookbank, and others. Then there were
Doctor Oronhyatekha (who greeted me like an old
friend), Brother Parker, R.W.G. Secretary, Dr. [D. H.]
Mann, Brother [Eugene] Chafin of Wisconsin, Brother
and Sister Chisholm of Nova Scotia, with whom I have
since labored side by side in Massachusetts, Brother
Thomas R. Thompson of Connecticut, John N. Stearns of
New York and others too numerous to mention. I heard
enough kind and complimentary speeches that evening to
have turned my head if it had not fortunately been a
tolerably level one.

The sessions of the two Right Worthy Grand Lodges
were opened the next day.[41] Their proceedings are a
matter of published record, so I shall briefly state

41   The Right Worthy Grand Lodge united with the
R.W.G.L. of the World only after some angry debate.
One of the members of the former described the scene
when the Boston Basis of Union was presented. "There
was some sharp debate and some amendments were insisted
on. The discussion was warm, and after a strong speech
assailing the proposed Basis, before anyone had time to
`get the floor´ for a reply, Bro. Finch, announced in a
perfectly calm voice, `I declare the effort to reunite
the Good Templar Order a failure, and we will take up
the next order of business.´ It was as good as a
circus to see those objectors run to cover. It was not
more than ten minutes afterwards, as I remember, until
the Basis of Union was declared adopted." R. J. Hazlett to Jessie Forsyth, n.d., quoted in Forsyth,
"Incidents in a Good Templar Life," Australian Temperance World, April 1929, p. 11. Hazlett´s wife Genie
F. Hazlett, who died in 1921, had been Forsyth´s
predecessor as literary editor of the International
Good Templar.

that in the R.W.G. Lodge of the World we adopted the basis of union with only one dissenting vote and that we then finished up all our business.[42] Although we rejoiced at the union, the last moments of our existence as a separate body were naturally somewhat sad. Many kind words were said of our leaders and testimonials were voted to Brothers Malins, Turnbull and Lane, and to myself. Mine took the form of a writing desk and bookcase combined and has always been a most valued and useful gift. When it was done, we were escorted by the Committee on Reunion, which consisted of Brothers S. B. Chase, P.R.W.G.T.; S. D. Hastings, P.R.W.G.T.; J. J. Hickman, P.R.W.G.T.; Geo. B. Katzenstein, P.R.W.G.T.; W. Martin Jones, Nelson Dingley, Jr., and Dr. Oronhyatekha, to the hall in which the R.W.G.L. was holding its session.

It is impossible to describe the scene which ensued; it was one of the most intense excitement. I have a confused remembrance of a crowded room and a sound of cheering. I quote from the printed minutes of this session which record that "A recess was taken for congratulations and hand-shaking. For a time, the members of various lands shook hands, their hearts beating in unison in the bonds of a common purpose, and happiness reigned supreme."

---

42   Catherine Impey cast the sole negative vote and later withdrew from the Order. She regarded the terms of union, which allowed separate Grand Lodges on the basis of race or language, as a violation of the principle of equal rights. Impey subsequently published a small magazine called Anti-Caste to continue her fight against racism.

"Being called to order, the officers of both
branches occupied the various official positions. The
hymn entitled "Blest be the tie that binds" was sung
and all present seemed to feel the premonition of the
grand results which would follow the union thus happily
consummated."[43]

I came to myself as from a dream, when order was
restored, and found myself sitting beside Sister
Mrs. Francena C. Bailey of New Hampshire, R.W.G.V.T.
My face was wet with tears and as I glanced at those
around me I saw that mine was not the only countenance
which bore traces of the supreme emotion through which
we had all passed. The first order of business was the
election of officers and John B. Finch was put in
nomination by Joseph Malins for re-election as
R.W.G.T. His election was by unanimous vote, amid
tremendous enthusiasm. I had naturally expected to be
retired from the office of R.W.G.V.T. at this session,
but after several other nominations had been made, my
name was submitted by Thomas R. Thompson of Connecticut. Very much to my surprise, with three other
candidates in the field, I was elected on the first
ballot, having received one more than half of the whole
vote cast. This election gave me the record of six
years as R.W.G.V.T., a longer term than has ever been
served by anyone else in that office. I am glad to say
that the defeated candidates have never borne me any
malice, but have always been counted among my best
friends. The whole board of officers chosen at this
session was as follows: R.W.G.T., John B. Finch, Illinois; R.W.G.C., Wm. W. Turnbull, Scotland; R.W.G.V.T.,

43 See also Forsyth, "The Union Session," New York
Templar, March 1924, p. 12.

Jessie Forsyth, Massachusetts; R.W.G.S.J.T., Mrs. America A. Brookbank, Indiana; R.W.G.S., B. F. Parker, Wisconsin; R.W.G. Treas., Uriah Copp, Illinois; R.W.G. Chaplain, Dr. D. W. Thomas, India; R.W.G.M., O. G. Tolnaes, Norway; R.W.G.L.M., Mrs. S. E. Bailey, Virginia; R.W.G.C., Esther J. Blakey, England; R.W.G. Sent., J. A. Kelly, Bahamas; R.W.G. Messenger, Mrs. Denholme, Cape Colony; P.R.W.G.T., Rev. W. G. Lane, Nova Scotia.

These officers were then installed by Hon. S. B. Chase, P.R.W.G.T., and the R.W.G.L. entered upon its work as a united body representing the Good Templars of the whole world.

As was to be expected, however, although the essential conditions of union had been adopted, some difference of opinion occurred over the adoption of some of the minor conditions. On some occasions the conflict waxed strong, notwithstanding the fact that everyone was in a generous and conciliatory mood. But here, as at the Boston Conference, the difficulties were providentially removed. Some of the leaders strove hard to maintain the good feeling with which the sitting had opened. In particular I want to bear testimony to the work done by Dr. Oronhyatekha in this direction. I feel that we can never sufficiently admire and appreciate his attitude in the circumstances, because he had been the worst-abused of all the R.W.G.L. leaders during the years of disruption, as Brother Malins was the mark for the attacks of the American section. The magnanimous spirit shown by members of both sides of the Order in general, was intensified in the case of these two great men who had

been for so many years antagonistic to each other.
When they clasped hands it was indeed in token that all
past differences were forever buried and so at Saratoga
we found them standing side by side, fighting for the
adoption of the resolutions agreed upon at the Boston
Conference. Dr. Oronhyatekha had been a formidable foe
and at Saratoga he proved himself a noble friend.

I am not one of those who regret that the disruption in the Order ever occurred. I believe that it was
just as much a Providential leading as any other event
in the history of our great movement. Mistakes were
made, of course, and much bitterness of feeling was
engendered. But the stand taken by the so-called
"seceders" at Louisville, [sic] led the Order to attain
to a higher conception of its principle of universal
brotherhood, [sic] than it might have done under other
circumstances. Then, too, it gave Brother Malins, as
the leader of the R.W.G.L. of the World, a better
chance to seize every opportunity of planting the Order
in other lands and we see the results of this to-day in
the most cosmopolitan membership ever gathered in one
organization. At an executive meeting held before we
left Saratoga, one of those who had been a member of
the R.W.G.L. of the World remarked that Brother Malins'
eyes were "over all the world," and our R.W.G. Secretary, Bro. Parker, quickly retorted that it was well
for us that it was so as it had led to our becoming a
truly International Order.

But if I never regretted the disruption, I sincerely rejoice in the reunion. I believe that the fact
that we were able to come together again after eleven
years of separation, and to agree to stand shoulder to

shoulder henceforth proves that the fraternal bond which unites us is not simply a figure of speech, and that our motto of "Faith, Hope and Charity" has a vital and enduring influence upon the lives of all true Good Templars.

Chapter XI

UNION IN MASSACHUSETTS--THE DEATH OF JOHN B. FINCH

In the month of September following the Saratoga session of the Right Worthy Grand Lodge, an attempt was made to unite the two branches of the Order in Massachusetts. The Senior Grand Lodge at that time held a semi-annual session and it occurred in 1887 in the city of Lowell. The Junior body arranged for a special session at the same time and place. Prior to this, committees appointed by the two Grand Lodges had met and agreed upon a basis of union upon lines similar to those followed in the R.W.G. Lodge. When our little Grand Lodge convened, this basis was considered and readily adopted. But it met a different fate in the Senior organization. Much to our surprise--considering the good feeling which had existed during nearly a year between the Lodges of the two sections--the Senior body rejected the Committee's proposals and the message was conveyed to us in a manner calculated to arouse the strongest feelings of indignation in our members.

When the Committee, consisting of three prominent members from the Senior Grand Lodge, was announced, the Junior body received it in proper form and with every mark of respect. We were not anticipating that any antagonism would be shown and it was a tremendous shock

to us all when the chairman of the Committee reported
the action of his Grand Lodge and followed up his
report by making, on his own account, a most unkind and
unfraternal attack upon us, telling us practically that
we were guilty of great presumption in expecting to be
allowed to make terms with his Grand Lodge, that if we
wanted to come back, we must be satisfied to accept the
terms they offered.

I may say that this Brother (who is not now a
member of the Order) was an active member of the Grand
Lodge at the time the disruption occurred. He was a
man of strong prejudices and he had not forgiven "the
seceders." He did not seem to realize that many of
those he was addressing had never been members of the
original Grand Lodge and that they had never known any
other Order of Good Templars than the one in which he
found them. So he lectured us as if we had been the
"original sinners" and great was the wrath which his
words inspired in each breast. I am quite sure that in
speaking as he did he misrepresented his Grand Lodge
and the other members of the Committee, who looked
ashamed of him while he was speaking, as well they
might.

Our Brother, C. A. Stevens, G.C.T., was a
mild-mannered man, not given to many words, but he
astonished us all on this occasion. While the rest of
sat in amazed silence after the scolding we had
received, Brother Stevens sprang to his feet and made a
reply which was most eloquent, and powerful, and con-
vincing. It silenced our antagonist and the Committee
retired. I am afraid that not many of us felt anxious
for union after this experience, but we were loyal

members and were willing to do our part to carry on the work so well begun by the union of the two Right Worthy Grand Lodges.

It is known to all that the union was amicably effected a few months later. The brother to whom I have referred must have experienced a change of heart, for he was among the first to give us a cordial welcome when the union was happily consummated. We closed up the proceedings of our little Grand Lodge with mingled feelings of joy and sadness. Joy that we were henceforth to work together in harmony with Good Templars throughout the world and grief at the severing of the bonds which had held our little company of workers together for so many years. The last paragraph in my report to this session will express something of my feelings and I venture to quote it here: "I cannot close this, my last report, after nearly eight years´ service as Grand Secretary, without a reference to the harmonious relations which have always existed between the members of the Executive, the membership generally, and myself. I take pride in believing that our members are loyal and earnest and that these qualities will go with them into the larger organization and help to make them useful and valuable. There are those in our little company who have been associated together for years and the thought of the probable change which today will make in our relations, has in it much of sadness. I thank every member for the kindness and courtesy which has always been accorded to me personally, and--whatever the future may hold for us--I shall always look back upon my connection with the Junior

Grand Lodge of Massachusetts as among the pleasantest experiences of my life."[44]

After the lapse of more than fifteen years I am glad to be able to count many of the surviving members of the little Grand Lodge among my best and truest friends and in some cases the sons and daughters of these members have inherited a love and loyalty, not only for the Order, but for the one who honestly did what she could for the cause while she filled the honorary office of Grand Secretary.

But before these events transpired, a sad and unlooked for blow had fallen upon us in the death of our beloved leader, John B. Finch [on October 3, 1887]. Shall I ever forget the morning when, thinking over some matters about which I wished to consult our Right Worthy Grand Templar at an interview which he had appointed for that forenoon, I took up the newspaper and was overwhelmed by the news of his sudden death at the railroad station in Boston on the previous night. It seemed too dreadful to be true and the consternation we felt in Massachusetts was shared by Good Templars everywhere as the tidings was [sic] spread throughout our worldwide Order.[45]

---

44   "There existed a spirit of loyal comradeship among ourselves, fostered by the frequent interchange of visits, and I remember with satisfaction that we paid a due regard to the educational features of the Order, and our programmes, as a rule, were kept free from trivialities." Forsyth, "Good Templar Memories: Some Outstanding Templars," Australian Temperance World, Feb. 1928, p. 7.

45   "It became my duty to cable to Scotland to inform Bro. Turnbull. . . ." Forsyth, "Good Templar Memories: Some Outstanding Templars," Australian Temperance

It is a testimony to the admirable construction of our organization that this event did not cause entire confusion. But our Constitution makes provision for such emergencies and our Order was safely piloted through the difficulties which confronted it by Brother Wm. W. Turnbull who, as R.W.G. Counsellor, was called upon to take the place so sadly made vacant. Thus by a strange providence, one who had been for years a leading member of the Right Worthy Grand Lodge of the World, became the head of the united body.[46]

It had never occurred to me that this sudden loss could have any effect upon the office of R.W.G. Vice Templar, but my attention was called to the fact that I was entitled by Constitutional provision to assume the office of Counsellor. I decided that we at that time needed a strong and influential man in the position with a residence in North America. In mentally looking over the field, my thoughts turned to Dr. Oronhyatekha, partly because I knew him to possess the necessary wisdom and knowledge, and partly for the reason that he was a most intimate friend and valued counsellor of the lamented Finch. But I held my peace until the R.W.G.L.

World, Oct. 1928, p. 8.

46 ". . . Bro. Turnbull did not possess the faculty of winning affection possessed by his predecessor. He was a man of strong character, and of rather stern appearance, and it was only those who knew him well who realized how much there was of gentleness, of kindness, and sympathy beneath his apparently hard exterior." Forsyth, "Good Templar Memories: Some Outstanding Good Templars," Australian Temperance World, Dec. 1928, p. 10.

officers arrived to attend the Executive Committee
which had been called.[47]

Brother Lane, P.R.W.G. Templar, came first, and he
immediately agreed to my proposition, as Brother
Yeames, P.R.W.G. Templar, had already done. When
Brother Turnbull, who had been hastily summoned from
Scotland, to assume a position he had not coveted,
reached Boston, he brought to me a message from Brother
Malins and other British leaders to the effect that
they hoped I should be unselfish enough to waive my
claim to the office of R.W.G. Counsellor. It is unnecessary to say that Brother Parker was warmly in
favor and other prominent members from different parts
of this country who came to Boston about that time
commended the idea, and it is a fact that the choice of
Dr. Oronhyatekha to fill the vacancy was not only a
very wise one but was entirely unanimous.[48]

---

47   "In the interval before that date [of the meeting
of the Executive], I was the recipient of much advice
and many suggestions regarding the office of R.W.G.
Co., which I learned I was entitled to assume. Friends
came to me suggesting that in the event of my doing so
I should nominate such or such a lady to the post I was
vacating, or if I preferred to decline the office I
should nominate such an one to it. The suggestions all
pointed to very worthy people, but it happened that no
one named the person I had in mind. I had already made
my decision, and was glad to find when other members of
the Executive arrived that it agreed with their
ideas." Forsyth, "Good Templar Memories: Some Outstanding Templars," Australian Temperance World, Oct.
1928, p. 8.

48   W. W. Turnbull published the following account of
Forsyth's nomination of Oronhyatekha. "The nomination
having been cordially seconded by R.W.G.S. Parker, I
explained that before leaving Scotland I had consulted
my colleagues and Bro. Rev. Wm. Ross, P.R.W.G.T., and
they had been unanimously of opinion that the vacancy

Chapter XII

A MOURNFUL MEETING--A VISIT TO VIRGINIA

The Executive meeting [October 20, 1887] referred
to in the previous chapter was naturally a very sad and
trying occasion. When the roll of officers was called
Bro. Parker could hardly utter the name of John B.
Finch, so great was his emotion, and the silence which
followed, to indicate respect for our dead leader, was
really needed to enable us to regain some measure of
composure. Then in a broken voice Brother Wm. W. Turnbull, of Scotland, announced his assumption of the
vacant office, according to constitutional provision.
It is certain that the honor never fell to one who
sought it less, and I am sure there was no feeling of
exultation in Brother Turnbull's heart as he stepped
into the position at the call of duty. I remember his
manly words upon this occasion and his tribute to the
lamented leader. And I remember, too, my own feeling

---

should be filled by a brother who belonged to the
former American section of the Order, who was in full
sympathy with the policy of Bro. Finch and the Boston
Treaty, under which the Order was united, and who was
believed to enjoy the confidence of the Order in
America. The only name that had occurred to us was
Bro. Oronhyatekha. Again, at Liverpool, Grand Chief
Templar Malins had kindly come to see me off, and had
charged me with a message to Sister Forsyth. It was,
`Advise her from me to decline the Counselorship, and
to nominate Dr. Oronhyatekha.´ I was afterwards told
that a meeting of American leaders, held at Bro.
Finch's funeral, the only name suggested was that of
our respected Brother." Irish Templar, Dec. 1887, p.
135; and Good Templars´ Watchword, Dec. 5, 1887,
p. 777. Reprinted from (Glasgow) Good Templar.

of thankfulness that the position was to be filled by
one so tried and true.

I was then informed that it was my privilege to
assume, if I pleased, the office of R.W.G. Counsellor.
But I waived my claim upon condition that I might make
the nomination for the office. This was agreed to and
I nominated Dr. Oronhyatekha, who was elected by a
cordial unanimous vote. Like Bro. Turnbull, I think
the Doctor cared little at that time for the new honor;
his heart was too full of grief.[49]

A little later some time was given to a sort of
memorial service, when those who could control themselves sufficiently to do so, gave voice to their
appreciation of the high character and the great work
of John B. Finch. It was an occasion never to be
forgotten. I think I was the only woman present, as
Sister Brookbank, R.W.G.S.J.T., did not arrive until
later in the day, and it was an impressive sight to see
strong men so overcome with grief. I cannot now name
all who were there, but I remember Bro. Chase's serene
presence and uplifting words; the impassioned tribute
of Bro. Colonel Chevis; the calmer, yet no less
sincere, testimony of Bro. Yeames, and the eloquence of
Bro. Lane. I remember, too, that Dr. Oronhyatekha

---

49   Forsyth said about her decision not to take the
office of Right Worthy Grand Counsellor herself, "This
is one of the acts of my Good Templar life which I have
never regretted. It has always been a satisfaction to
remember that I did not allow a foolish ambition to
tempt me to take what seemed to be an upward step,
which would have deprived our Order of the services of
one so eminently qualified as was the famous Indian."
Forsyth, "A Memorable Executive Meeting," New York
Templar, May 1925, p. 13.

frankly abandoned the traditional stoicism of his race
and wept like a woman--or like the large[-]hearted man
his friends know him to be.

I have said I was the only sister present during
the first part of the meeting, but during the day we
had many callers, among them Sister Leonard, Grand
Secretary, who had served with Bro. Finch on the
R.W.G.L. Executive and was well able to testify to his
worth. Other prominent Massachusetts members, including Charles L. Abbott, G.C.T., and William Leonard,
P.G.C.T., also came.

Among the many items of business transacted at
this meeting was one relating to the colored membership
in Virginia. At the time of the Saratoga Union
session, two Grand Lodges composed of people of the
African race existed in Virginia. One of them,
belonging to the R.W.G.L. of the World, was several
years old; the other had been recently organized by the
R.W.G. Lodge. Some time before Bro. Finch's death he
had authorized me to correspond with the officers of
the first named body and arrange for a union of the two
Lodges. Owing perhaps to the influence I had acquired
while I was in charge of the mission work for the
R.W.G. Lodge of the World, I was successful in conduct-
ing the negotiations and a joint session was arranged
for the early part of December of that year (1887), at
which Bro. Finch intended to be present and at which it
was hoped the union would be consummated. It was
necessary someone should be sent to fill the appointment, and, bearing in mind the fact of my long correspondence with some of the leaders, the Executive

decided to send me. This was another occasion when an honor came to me unsought.

Dr. Oronhyatekha was appointed Superintendent of Missions for North America and, prior to leaving for the South, I wrote to him for instructions. His reply was characteristic, "Go with my blessing and do the best you can." This left me free to use my own judgment and I am glad to say that the mission was successful.

Although my business was only with our colored brethren, I considered that courtesy required me to notify the senior (or original) Grand Lodge of my intention to visit its territory. A letter to Brother Geo. W. Hawxhurst, the efficient Grand Secretary, evoked a most kind reply in which he bade me a cordial welcome and offered any assistance in his power. He also extended an invitation to attend his Grand Lodge which was to convene a few days later in Charlottesville.

When I arrived in Richmond I found Brother Hawxhurst waiting to escort me to a hotel. Later I received calls from Bro. [J. R.] Miller, G.C.T., Bro. and Sister Julius Hobson, and other members. Everyone was most kind and thoughtful in providing for my comfort and showing me every attention. I knew that our Southern brethren did not see "eye to eye" with some of us on the race question, but I realized that as an individual and as the R.W.G.V.T., I was to receive all due honor, even if they disagreed with some of my convictions.

Perhaps, from the fact that I have been for so large a part of my life practically alone in the world (the only relatives I have being in Australia), I am more ready than some people to appreciate the kindness and sympathy of friends. However that may be, I know I was very much touched by the good feeling shown to me in Virginia; and, lest I might appear to be receiving all this kindness under false pretenses, I found it necessary to tell them that in my own Lodge in Boston there were numerous colored people. I did not succeed in shocking the Virginians, however, and from the first day to the last, my stay in the Old Dominion was made pleasant by their hospitality and fraternal courtesies.

The union of the two colored Grand Lodges [on December 5, 1887] was effected harmoniously and a good staff of officers elected to carry on the work. Although so long familiar with the race in Massachusetts, and knowing their abilities in many directions, I was hardly prepared to find them so far advanced in the South. But I have seen some Grand Lodge officers among white people who were not so well qualified to conduct the work of the Order as were those representatives of the African race whom I installed as officers of the Junior Grand Lodge of Virginia. Especially was I impressed with Bro. Rev. D. N. Vassar, G.C.T., Principal of the Richmond Theological Seminary, and with Mrs. Lucy Woodin, G.S.J.T., an old correspondent of mine, who was doing a most wonderful work among the children. These were two very noble types of the race, such as would have done honor to any people.

When the united session closed, I went to Charlottesville to the Senior Grand Lodge. The Order was

very strong in Virginia at that time and many prominent
people were in active membership. The session was a
magnificent one in every respect and I listened with
interest to the many debates. A funny incident occurred when I entered the hall. Senator [J. M.] Thorne
had been reading the report of the representatives to
the R.W.G. Lodge at Saratoga and it was laid over for a
few moments while I was introduced. As I stepped upon
the platform, Sister Mrs. S. E. Bailey, G.S.J.T., with
whom I had become well acquainted at Saratoga, greeted
me very warmly. When Senator Thorne resumed the
reading of his report, I noticed that he seemed rather
embarrassed, and I found out the reason as he proceeded
somewhat in this manner: "Our Sister Bailey, G.S.J.T.,
would undoubtedly have been elected R.W.G.V.T. but for
the fact that the circumstances attending the union of
the Order made it seem necessary to elect a member of
the R.W.G.L. of the World, and Sister Jessie Forsyth,
of Boston, was chosen." Sister Bailey and I exchanged
glances of amusement. I had not remembered that we had
been rivals at Saratoga, nor had she. Afterwards she
said, "ar´nt [sic] you glad we were able to greet each
other so cordially and show the Grand Lodge that there
was no hard feelings between us?" There has never been
anything but the best of feeling between Sister Bailey
and myself and I was sincerely glad when she was
elected R.W.G.V.T. a few years later.

From Charlottesville I travelled to Norfolk, where
a great meeting had been arranged. Here I met with a
large gathering of Good Templars in which mine was the
only white face. I had a most enthusiastic reception
and spent about three hours addressing, advising, and
instructing in the unwritten work, an intelligent,

receptive and appreciative audience. I had to shake
hands with everyone when the meeting closed and I well
remember one dear old white-haired woman, whose face,
[although] marked by great age and many sorrows, yet
wore a most serene expression. She said solemnly, as
she clasped my hand, "The Lord bless you and keep you,
child. I don´t never ´spect to see you no more on
earth, but I´ll meet you ´fore the throne." With tears
in my eyes, I reverently said "Amen to this benedic-
tion.[50]

Chapter XIII

THE CHICAGO SESSION OF 1889

In 1888, as I stated in a previous chapter, the
two Grand Lodges of Massachusetts were united. The
Grand Chief Templar elected at that session was Edgar
W. Whittemore, of whom I have very pleasant and
appreciative recollections on account of the courtesy
and kindness he showed to me and to other former
members of the Junior Grand Lodge. Brother Whittemore
has resided for several years past in Kentucky, but
still holds his membership in Massachusetts.

During Brother Whittemore´s term of office, I
received invitations to many pleasant occasions, held
under the auspices of Lodges in different parts of the
State. The members were pleased to welcome a R.W.G.L.
officer and ready to listen to news of the work in

---

50   See also Forsyth to Oronhyatekha, Dec. 13, 1887,
in International Good Templar, Jan. 1888, p 26; and
"Good Templar Memories: Some Outstanding Templars,"
Australian Temperance World, Nov. 1928, p. 8.

other jurisdictions. I was glad of the opportunity of
enlarging my circle of Good Templar acquaintances and
enjoying the privileges of visiting in a larger jurisdiction than I had been connected with. In addition to
the many enjoyable events in my own State, I paid a
visit to New York in response to a summons to meet with
the Literature Committee and assist in selecting books
for the Course of Study.

The publication of The Temperance Brotherhood
ceased at the time of the Union Conference so my labors
as editor were no longer needed. The International
Good Templar was started in January, 1888, and was
edited by Dr. Oronhyatekha. I did a little sometimes
for this publication, but it was mainly in the direction of looking up selections, and keeping the editor
supplied with little corner scraps. On one occasion I
forwarded to Dr. Oronhyatekha a number of valuable
quotations from the best authors and felt that, having
supplied all that would be needed for a time, I could
afford to take things easy. To my surprise and
vexation, however, when the next number of the magazine
came out, my carefully culled quotations appeared altogether, occupying nearly a page. I wrote the editor
that when I sent him those pearls, "I did not intend
them to be all hung on one string." His answer was,
"You can´t feel any worse about those pearls than I do;
I was away when the paper was printed and when I
returned and saw what had happened I said things. And
it was all in English, too, for you can´t swear in
Mohawk." In reply to this I thanked the Doctor for
telling me that important philological fact and added,
"Now, I understand why Mrs. Oronhyatekha insists upon
the Mohawk language being exclusively used in your

home." Dr. Oronhyatekha, like many other of our Good
Templar leaders, dearly loves a joke and it does not
hinder his enjoyment if the point happens to be turned
upon himself.

The next session of the Right Worthy Grand Lodge
was held in Chicago, May 28th to June 5th, inclusive,
1889. A party of ten of us went from Massachusetts,
including Rev. James Yeames, Edgar W. Whittemore,
F. I. Jefferson, Charles L. Abbott and Mrs. S. A.
Leonard. The attendance at this session was very large
and the debates were full of interest. It was a great
pleasure to meet many old friends again and to form new
acquaintances. Among the prominent members present
from abroad were Bro. Theo. Schreiner, Miss Harriet
R. Schreiner [later Mrs. John Stakesby-Lewis], and
their niece, Mrs. K. H. R. Stuart, all from South
Africa. These members made a great impression by their
earnestness and eloquence. There was also Bro. N. T.
Collins, P.G.C.T., of New South Wales, who had been a
member of the Union Conference three years before, and
Bro. Eklund of Sweden. I met again some of the grand
women of the Order, Mother Stewart, Mrs. Mattie McClellan Brown, Mrs. M. B. O´Donnell, Amanda Way, Mrs.
L. C. Partington, Mrs. Annie Weichmann, Mrs. Brookbank
and many others. Among the brethren were, of course,
the honored Past Right Worthy Grand Templars, Hastings
and Chase; Dr. D. H. Mann, B. F. Parker, R.W. Secretary, E. W. Chafin, etc. At this session I first made
the acquaintance of the late Sister Mrs. [Ellen] Oronhyatekha, who from that time became a valued and very
kind friend. I also met Brother George W. E. Hill of
Iowa and his wife, both of whom I have seen many times
since. I became quite intimate with Sister Mrs. Knapp

of Michigan and Mrs. Genie F. Hazlett, of Illinois, and have since been hospitably entertained in the homes of both ladies. Then there were old friends from Great Britain, including Brothers Malins, Turnbull and Archer and some who were to be numbered among my friends in the future, such as Rev. J. D. McKinnon and wife, Mrs. [B.] Shipman, and others. A great deal of the pleasure of these sessions consists in the meeting with dear friends from all parts of the world.

A memorial service was held in honor of our departed leader, John B. Finch, and like the one in Boston written of in my last chapter it was a very trying occasion. Tender and beautiful tributes were paid to the memory of this great man by those who loved him and many tears were shed. Later in the day more than 150 Good Templars traveled in a driving rain storm to Rosehill cemetery where in the little chapel a service was held, with prayer by Hon. S. B. Chase and a touching memorial address by Brother Turnbull, R.W.G.T. A procession was then formed, headed by the R.W.G.L. officers, to the grave, where numerous and exquisite floral tributes, from members in many parts of the world, were laid upon the massive granite slab which covers our leader's resting place.

There were not very many social occasions connected with this session. One largely attended and magnificent public meeting was held at which the speakers were Brother Turnbull, R.W.G.T.; Joseph Malins, for Great Britain; Oskar Eklund for Scandinavia; Dr. Oronhyatekha for Canada; George B. Katzenstein for the United States; N. T. Collins for Australasia; Walter E. Webb for India, and Theo. Schreiner for

Africa. It was a most representative gathering and the addresses enabled the audience to gather some idea of the vast extent of our work.

At this session I retired from office and Mrs. John B. Finch was elected my successor. The Committee on Procedure in their report recommending the thanks of the body to retiring officers included the following paragraph: "The R.W.G.L. places on record its grateful appreciation of the special services rendered to the Order by Sister Jessie Forsyth, P.R.W.G.V.T., during the six years she has held position as a R.W.G.L. officer." Bro. Turnbull was unanimously re-elected R.W.G.C.T., Dr. Oronhyatekha was elected R.W.G.C. on the first ballot by a large majority over several contestants for the office, Sister Brookbank was re-elected R.W.G.S.J.T., Brother Parker was unanimously re-elected R.W.G.S., and Bro. W. M. Jones was chosen for R.W.G. Treas. The officers were installed by Hon. S. D. Hastings, assisted by Rev. James Yeames and Sister Amanda Way.

There were many things discussed at this session which tended to make it a particularly important one and the last sitting was prolonged well into the small hours. During the debate over one question, I have forgotten what it was, in which Brother Malins and Oronhyatekha were both intensely interested it was discovered that the genial Doctor, who, like everyone else, was dreadfully tired, was taking a nap. Brother Yeames arousing him and reminding him of the business before the house when the Doctor asked: "Is Brother Malins awake?" "Oh, yes," replied Brother Malins, "I am awake." Then said Oronhyatekha, "It´s all right, while Malins watches, I can sleep." This raised a laugh among the members and one of them remarked, _sotto voce_, that this was quite a change from a few years ago and that the attitude of the two Brothers, formerly so antagonistic to one another, was a "veritable illustration of the lion and the lamb." "That is so," said another, "but, please, Mr. Showman, which _is_ the lion and which the lamb?"

Certainly that session proved, as other occasions have, that the lion-like qualities of the two men which had made them formidable opponents in the past, rendered them almost invincible when their united influence was given to the same side of a question.

On the way home from Chicago, several of the British representatives stopped over to attend a great banquet which had been arranged in their honor by the Canadian brethren. I was favored with a special invitation to this function and was only too happy to accept it. When we arrived in Toronto, Dr. and Mrs. Oronhyatekha very kindly took me with them to their Toronto home and I spent three or four very pleasant days with them. The famous banquet was a great occasion. Many of those who had long been leaders of the Order in Canada were present, among them Brother Daniel Rose, Brother and Sister Cumner, Brother Wilson and Brother Naismith. With the exception of Brother Malins and Brother C. Stacy-Watson, I think all the guests from Great Britain were Scotchmen and as so many of the Canadians were of Scottish descent, there were many tributes paid to the "Land o´Burns." I remember that Brother Turnbull referred to me as "the Scotch lassie who had been for six years the R.W.G.V.T.," and even

Dr. Oronhyatekha was claimed as a kinsman by some of the more enthusiastic of the canny Scots. In the course of my remarks, I raised a laugh by saying that this was not the first time I had found myself in Scotland when I supposed I was in another place. A previous occasion was when I attended the Grand Lodge of Ireland in 1885 where, at a reception meeting, every speaker representing the Grand Lodge of Ireland avowed himself a Scotchman, and the only Irishman on the program was the representative from the Grand Lodge of Scotland.

A little party of us, Brother Turnbull, [line missing, with one of two omitted names being that of Stacy-Watson] Archer, Naismith, Stansfield, and myself, paid a visit to Niagara before we left Canada and were photographed together. The pictured group has a mournful interest attaching to it now as three out of the seven comprising it, Brothers Stacy-Watson, Archer and Naismith, have passed to the land beyond.

Chapter XIV

BRIEF MENTION OF WORK AND WORKERS

In March, 1890, in response to the request of many friends, I consented to be a candidate for the office

of G.S.J.T. [for the Grand Lodge of Massachusetts].
The whole vote was 349, and of this I received 257.[51]

---

51   "While holding the office of G.S.J.T. of Massachusetts, I was sent on one occasion to a small town
about fifty miles from Boston, with instructions to
deliver an address and, if possible, to institute a
Lodge. Arriving at the place I was met by two gentlemen, who were expecting a brother instead of a sister
to perform the duty. However, they greeted me very
kindly, but expressed the fear that the institution
could not take place as their pastor was very much
opposed to it, and some of the intending members had
become discouraged in consequence. After some hesita-
tion they decided to call upon the pastor and tell him
that a lady had come and asked him to meet her. I
waited while they went on their errand, and presently
they returned accompanied by the pastor, who responded
rather stiffly when they introduced him to me. On the
way to the Church in which the meeting was to be held
the reverend gentleman favored me with his views
regarding our Order, which I need not say did not
coincide with mine. Arrived at the Church, a cosy
little building, well-warmed and lighted, he gave me a
seat in one of the side aisles, sat down himself, and
folding his arms maintained a dignified silence. It
was not quite time for the meeting, but a few people
had assembled, and seeing a little organ near the
pulpit I suggested to the pastor that he might ask
someone to play. He very unwillingly arose and
escorted a young lady to the instrument, and we soon
had some lively hymns. After that he conducted me to
the platform, and in response to my request invited the
two gentlemen who had met me to take seats on it also.
He then placed the meeting in their hands, and told me
that he was very busy and I must excuse him if he left
the Church while I was speaking. But he asked in a
very resigned tone whether there was anything else I
wished him to do. I answered that it was usual for us
to begin our meetings with a request for the Divine
blessing, and I should be glad if he would offer
prayer. He assented, not too willingly, and I could
not help feeling that he was not altogether in the
right spirit."

      "Nevertheless the meeting was a good one. I did
my best to set forth the many good features of our
Order, and a number of people handed in their names to
join the Lodge. And the pastor did not leave."

I may as well state here that I was unanimously
re-elected at the three succeeding annual sessions and
resigned the office in the fall of 1893, when I was
appointed R.W.G.S.J.T.

Our Grand Lodge session of 1890 was rather remarkable, from the fact that an entirely new executive was
elected to take charge of the affairs of the Grand
Lodge. Sister Leonard, Grand Secretary, had given
notice of her intention to withdraw from her office for
at least a year, at the previous semi-annual session,
and Brother Rev. E. P. F. Dearborn was elected as her
successor. Brother Dearborn was an old and faithful
member of the Order; he has for some time resided in
Arizona, but retains his membership in a Boston Lodge.
The G.C.T. elected at this session was James L. Bowen
of Springfield, one of the oldest members of the Grand
Lodge, who had previously held office, and who was well
known and highly respected. It was my privilege to
serve during three years upon the same executive board
as Bro. Bowen, and I have the pleasantest recollections
of his invariable kindness and courtesy to his associates;[sic] his earnestness and zeal in the work of
the Order, and his good judgement and perfect impar-
tiality in dealing with the membership.

"The next morning when I took my seat in the train
for Boston I was surprised to have the pastor as a
companion. He had thawed out since the evening before,
and was quite genial and sociable. He told me that
after hearing what had been said about Good Templary he
had changed his mind, and would do his best for the
Lodge and would himself become a member." Australian
Temperance World, Feb. 1929, p. 10.

The other elective officers were G.C. Willard O. Wylie, G.V.T. Mrs. Lizzie M. Robinson, Grand Treasurer Hon. Loyed [sic] E. Chamberlain, Grand Chaplain Francis M. Harrington, and G.M. Samuel G. Wait. Of these, Sister Robinson was another long-term member, who had always been a hard worker in the Order, and several times filled the office of G.S.J.T. Brother Chamberlain, although a young man, had been identified with the Order since boyhood. He is a distinguished lawyer, a judge and an ex-senator. He has held his membership for over thirty years in Fraternal Lodge, Brockton. Brother Francis M. Harrington, like Brother Bowen, G.C.T., is a distinguished veteran of the Civil War. Brother Wylie was a comparatively young member of the Order, although he had belonged to it for several years. Thus our executive, although a new one, was formed of good material, and was well fitted to grapple with the problems which presented themselves.

Among these problems was the adoption of the Uniform Constitution, which had been for several years a much discussed question in Massachusetts. During the three years of Brother Bowen's administration the state was mapped out into districts, and the twelve District Lodges, which are in active working order today were organized. In the prosecution of my own department I traveled over the state extensively during the nearly four years that I held the office. I have very grateful remembrances of help and sympathy shown by the larger proportion of the membership, and if I occasionally met with a little opposition, it only served to stimulate my zeal. Among the many friends whose kindness I recall was Brother Wm. Leonard of Salem, P.G.C.T., who, with his excellent wife, was always

ready to extend hospitality to Good Templars. Brother
Leonard is still living, although not able to be active
in the work at present. He is a man of high character,
and has been more than once nominated for Mayor of his
city. He was a close friend of the late Hon. Jonathan
Orne, P.R.W.G.T., whose funeral, by the way, I attended
as an executive officer in 1890.

My acquaintance with Brother Orne was but a brief
one, but was long enough for him to win my sincere
respect. He deserves to be held in remembrance, no
less for his own noble characteristics than for the
fact that he was the Right Worthy Grand Templar whose
hand signed the Commission, which empowered our present
Right Worthy Grand Templar, Joseph Malins, to plant the
Order in England. It is hardly to be supposed that
Brother Orne dreamed of the results which followed this
official act. As he said himself, when speaking of it
once to me, "he builded better than he knew," but I
think he always felt glad and grateful that he had been
given a share in making our Order world-wide. It was
one of the coincidences resulting from the union of the
Order that it fell to the lot of Brother Rev. James
Yeames, P.R.W.G.T., to be the principal Good Templar
speaker at Brother Orne's funeral.

During the year 1893 I organized the Massachusetts
Institute of Juvenile Templar Workers, which, for
several years, was an efficient adjunct to the Juvenile
work in the state. I also organized a District Institute in my own District and this helped to keep up
the interest among the local Temples. While speaking
of my local work, I may as well mention that I served
one year as District Secretary and one year as

D.S.J.T. I also served for two or three years as
President of the Massachusetts Good Templars' Mutual
Benefit Association and rendered some assistance in
the organization of the Good Templar Veteran Association of Massachusetts [for those who had been members
for at least twenty-five years], of which Brother
Herbert E. Phinney, P.G.C., was the originator. During
all these years my active work in subordinate Lodge
never ceased and for several years I was S.J.T. of an
active Temple [associated with the Church of the
Ascension, Boston].

At the session of the Grand Lodge of Massachusetts
in 1891 I was elected head of the delegation to the
R.W.G. Lodge, which was to hold its session in Edinburgh, Scotland, in June of that year. The other representatives were Hon. L. E. Chamberlain and Sister
Sarah A. Leonard. Brother George A. Leonard was the
first alternate and accompanied his wife to the
session, and Bro. Rev. E. P. F. Dearborn also went. We
joined a party of over 120 Good Templars who sailed
from New York on the Steamer "City of New York" for
Liverpool. This goodly company included prominent
members from many parts of the U.S. and Canada. Among
the sisters were Mrs. A. A. Brookbank, R.W.G.S.J.T.;
Mrs. John B. Finch, R.W.G.V.T.; Mrs. T. B. Knapp, of
Michigan; Mrs. L. C. Partington, of Maine; Miss Altie
Reed (now Mrs. Walker), of Wisconsin; etc. The list of
brothers was headed by Dr. Oronhyatekha, R.W.G.C., who
was accompanied by his wife and daughter; Hon. S. D.
Hastings, P.R.W.G.T.; Colonel B. F. Parker, our
honored R.W.G. Secretary, who also had his daughter
with him; Geo. W. E. Hill, of Iowa; the late General

Payne [died, 1901], of Ohio; [George] O. W. Blain and P. J. Connell, of Michigan, and many others.[52]

Such a large party of temperance people could not fail to attract considerable attention even on a steamer as crowded as was ours. Some of the other passengers regarded us with a great deal of curiosity and a little amusement was created in our ranks by the naive remark of a lady passenger to one of our sisters with whom she became on speaking terms during the voyage. The lady in question asked what the Good Templars represented and when she was informed regarding the objects of the organization, she raised her eyeglass, regarding some of us in a slightly supercilious manner, while she said, "Well, really, for temperance people, they seem quite intelligent." The person addressed informed her that our party included a distinguished physician, an ex-Secretary of State, an ex-consul, two or three judges, several clergymen, etc., but she could only arouse a languid surprise that such people should be willing to attach themselves to a temperance organization.

It was my good fortune on this trip to be included in Dr. Oronhyatekha´s party and the kindness which I received from the Doctor and his wife and daughter made a substantial addition to my already large debt of gratitude in that quarter. Nor was I the only one indebted to them. Our Brother Chamberlain was taken

---

52   There were two other parties of Good Templars crossing the Atlantic for the Edinburgh session. Forsyth, "Good Templar Memories: Some Outstanding Templars," Australian Temperance World, Jan. 1929, p. 10. This article was the twelfth and concluding one in its series.

seriously ill at the beginning of the voyage with a
sharp attack of pneumonia which might have ended
seriously but for the skill of Doctor Oronhyatekha and
for the assistance which Mrs. and Miss Oronhyatekha
gave in taking care of him. Such events as this illness are a test of true friendship, and I have never
forgotten the sympathy and helpfulness of these two
dear women. Their kindness was all the more valuable
by reason of the fact that so large a number of our
party who would otherwise, no doubt, have been glad to
assist in caring for the sick man, were prostrated by
sea-sickness. On this voyage and the return one also,
I shared the stateroom with Miss Oronhyatekha and we
were together also in Edinburgh, so I had ample
opportunities for becoming well[-]acquainted with and
sincerely attached to her.

Chapter XV

THE EDINBURGH SESSION

When the "City of New York" reached Queenstown a
quantity of letters awaited some of our party, as well
as papers containing information of the forthcoming
I.S.L. [International Supreme Lodge] session and
programmes of the various events. Many of these
letters were from Good Templar leaders in Great Britain
and contained words of welcome and greeting to the
American representatives. As Dr. Oronhyatekha was, of
course, by reason of his office of R.W.G. Counsellor,
regarded as the head of the party, most of the letters
were addressed to him, and after the steamer resumed
her voyage to Liverpool, the Doctor convened a meeting
of the Good Templars in the dining room and laid the

various communications before them. When the 123 Good
Templars assembled in the saloon, they made quite an
imposing gathering, and they fairly rent the air with
their cheering as the plans for their entertainment
were read.

Upon arrival at Liverpool we were met by a number
of Good Templars and I particularly remember the
cordial greetings of my friends, the late John B. Collings and his dear wife. A few minutes sufficed in
"free trade" England to get our baggage clear of the
Custom House and we were soon comfortably quartered in
the temperance hotels of Liverpool.

A public meeting and banquet had been arranged by
the district lodge for that evening and when we arrived
at the hall, we found Brother Malins, G.C.T., and other
well-known English members awaiting us. Although not
holding office at that time in the I.S.L., I was
assigned a place upon the program, which was a very
interesting one and had drawn together a large and
enthusiastic audience.

The next evening found us in Glasgow at a great
meeting in the City Hall. Here we were met by our
R.W.G. Templar Brother Turnbull, and many other leading
Scottish members. During the exercises which followed
the bountiful repast provided for us, the American
speakers delighted their Scottish brethren by claiming
kin with them. It was interesting to note how everyone
"trotted out" his Scottish ancestors, or if he could
not possibly claim that his family tree was originally
transplanted from "bonnie Scotland," he quoted "Robbie
Burns." (one brother called him "Bobbie ? Burns"), or

"Walter Scott." I was not among the speakers on that occasion, but at a meeting at Leith a few days later, presided over by the late dear Brother Archer, G.C.T., I made a little fun by telling the audience that I had a better claim than some to a Scottish ancestry (as my good old name indicates) for my grandfather was a Highlander and when I was a "wee bairnie" I wore a frock made from what was left of his kilt.

Well that great meeting in Glasgow would not soon be forgotten by the American brethren of Scottish descent or not. It was most enthusiastic and no one could doubt the warmth of the welcome extended.

The next day some of us took a delightful trip through the Trosachs and reached Edinburgh, the fair "Ladie City," at night. We were quartered at the Cockburn House, a temperance hotel, and one of the best and most comfortable houses I have ever stayed at. In this city also we were given a great welcome meeting and again were the genealogical records of some of the speakers overhauled in search of progenitors who hailed from the land of the thistle. But these claims of kinship, though ever so well founded, were not needed to win Scottish hearts. They recognize, as all true Good Templars do, the universal brotherhood of the Order, and at every possible occasion they showed by their enthusiasm how glad they were to greet their guests from afar.

Among the many pleasant social occasions, perhaps the most interesting was the reception by the Lord Provost and other city officials in the Museum of Fine Arts. The Lord Provost and the councillors were

attired in their robes of office; the names of the
guests were announced, and as we bowed to the official
receiving line, we were glad to note that at least one
of the councillors wore a Good Templar regalia over his
robe. After the reception the evening was spent in
viewing the beautiful works of art in the no less
beautiful building, in listening to the fine music
discoursed by the band of the Queen's Own Cameronian
Highlanders, or in partaking of the dainty refreshments
furnished by the city of Edinburgh. It was a delightful occasion and one never to be forgotten by those who
shared its enjoyment. I spent a large part of the
evening in company with our late dear Brother Hastings
and can recall how delighted he was with everything and
how pleased when some who had met him at the London
session of 1873 recalled themselves to his memory.

A visit to Roslyn castle and chapel was another of
the pleasant events which had been planned for us and
there were others of lesser moment, but all tending to
make the few days spent in Edinburgh very happy ones.

The session itself was largely attended and most
interesting, and among the representatives were many
prominent men and women. The English contingent
included Brother Malins, the late John B. Collings and
his wife, the late William Sutherland, the late
C. Stacy-Watson, Brothers H. J. Osborn, Guy Hayler,
Sisters Charlotte A. Gray, Elizabeth Browne, Brother
and Sister Haefner, and many others. From Ireland
Brother and Sister J. L. Yule, Bro. and Sis. George
Gray, the late J. S. Lyttle, etc. Those two faithful
workers, Brothers Wavrinsky and Eklund, and others,
represented Sweden, and another equally faithful

brother, Lars O. Jensen, came from Norway. The two
Grand Lodges of Wales [Welsh-speaking and English-
speaking], the Channel Islands, and Denmark were ably
represented. India, and Australia sent delegates, and
among the representatives from the four Grand Lodges of
South Africa, were Sister Harriet R. Schreiner, Brother
James Brunton, Mayor of Beaconsfield, and Brother
E. Pickering. Scotland naturally had many of its best
men and women out in force. They made an imposing
array and carried such weight in the session that the
places assigned to them might almost have been called
"the seats of the mighty."[53] Some among them, such as
Brothers Archer, John Sutherland, Rev. William Ross,
Rev. George Gladstone, Brother Rev. J. D. McKinnon and
wife, were already friends of mine and others were
added to my list on that occasion.

Among the prominent members in the American party,
in addition to those mentioned in my last chapter, were
our honored brother, Dr. D. H. Mann, W. Martin Jones
[both of New York], Uriah Copp of Illinois, Mrs. J. R.
Pollard of Maine, Colonel T. B. Demaree of Kentucky,
O. W. Blain, Mr. and Mrs. P. J. Connell, and Mrs.
T. B. Knapp of Michigan, Wm. B. Reed and W. P. Roberts
of Minnesota, Miss Florence Cram of New Hampshire,
J. N. Stearns, Mrs. and Mrs. J. E. West and W. H.
Crampton of New York, Rev. W. G. Lane, P.R.W.G.T.;
J. R. Miller, G.C.T. of Virginia, Captain Davis of

---

53   For the Scottish Good Templars, see Tom Honeyman,
Good Templary in Scotland: Its Work and Workers, 1869-
1894 (Glasgow: Grand Lodge of Scotland, 1894); Tom
Honeyman, Good Templary in Scotland from its Inception
to the Diamond Jubilee, 1869-1929 (Glasgow: Grand Lodge
of Scotland, n.d.); and Robert McKechnie, Good Templary
in Scotland: Its Work and Workers, 1929-1979 (n.p:
Grand Lodge of Scotland, 1980).

Washington, Lou J. Beauchamp and wife, Walter S. Payne and "Mother Stewart" from Ohio, etc. Taken all in all, the Edinburgh session was a goodly gathering.

In conjunction with Brother Thomas Nixon of Manitoba, I had the honor of serving as auditor of this session. A hundred dollars each was voted to us for our services and some dissatisfaction was expressed at the action. Agreeing with those who opposed the appropriation, I was yet obliged to accept what was voted, but I settled the matter with my conscience by turning over $75 of the $100 paid to me, to the European Mission Fund, which had by this time begun to show good results from Sister Gray´s hard and efficient work.

Among the many interesting happenings at this session was an incident which gave our Sister Miss Agnes Sutherland of Edinburgh a chance to distinguish herself. A meeting of the juveniles had been planned for the afternoon of Saturday, but the end of the session was in sight and some of the Americans were anxious to rush things through in order that they might have time to visit places of interest before leaving for home. Consequently it was voted to continue the session during the afternoon and the result was that only a few could go to the children´s demonstration. The session did not close until it was almost midnight, but before the final adjournment Sister Sutherland found opportunity to voice the indignation of the Scottish sisters at the slight which had been put upon "the bairns." She expressed herself fearlessly and effectively and the applause she received showed that she had the sympathy of all the sisters and many of the brothers present.

It was at this session that our Bro. Doctor Oronhyatekha received a triumphant election to the office of Right Worthy Grand Templar, it being understood that our honored Brother Turnbull would not again be a candidate. It must have been a source of much satisfaction to the doctor that some of his warmest supporters were those who had been among his opponents in bygone days and I know he deeply appreciated the fact that the nomination was made by Brother Malins. Brother Wavrinsky of Sweden was elected R.W.G.C. I was nominated by Brother Tom Honeyman of Scotland for R.W.G.V.T., but declined. Sister Miss Schreiner of South Africa was elected to that office.

I was asked to accept a nomination for R.W.G.S.J.T. at this session, but would not stand in opposition to the late Sister Brookbank, who was re-elected to the position in which she had already done such good work. Brother Parker was, of course, re-elected, and Brother G. B. Katzenstein of California was chosen for Treasurer. These officers, with the appointed officers, who represented Ireland, India, Nebraska, England, Virginia, Queensland and Norway, were installed by Hon. S. D. Hastings, P.R.W.G.T., with Brother Brunton of South Africa and myself, acting as marshals.

Some of us desiring to honor our beloved Brother Hastings contributed to a beautiful gift which was presented to him by Dr. Oronhyatekha. I had the privilege of assisting the doctor in selecting the

present, which was a solid silver inkstand, made to
represent the curling stones and broom used in the
Scottish national game. It is hardly necessary to
mention that Brother Hastings was deeply touched and
that he responded to the doctor´s well-chosen words in
a brief speech which evoked many cheers.

At the close of the session came the inevitable
parting; we bade one another good[-]bye, some of us
expecting to meet again on the steamer, but knowing
that many of us would meet no more on earth. I joined
a little party which was to accompany Brother Malins to
hold a special session of his Grand Lodge, in the
Cleveland district. This gave me the opportunity of
being the guest for a while in the beautiful home of
Brother and Sister J. J. Woods at Hartlepool, and of
making the acquaintance of their numerous progeny. I
have made pleasant recollections of their kindly
hospitality and particularly remember with pleasure a
visit to a juvenile Temple of which Brother Woods was
the S.J.T.

The special session was a very interesting and
pleasant experience. I had the honor of filling the
G.V.T.´s chair and of making an address to the members. A public tea followed the session and in the
evening a great public meeting was held, at which I was
one of the speakers. I was entertained in the hospitable home of Brother and Sister Tennett, at Middleboro
and have, as a souvenir of my brief visit, a pictured
group of their charming children.

Before leaving England I visited Birmingham and
attended a session of "Columbia" No. 1, the historic

lodge through which Brother Malins was the means of introducing the Order into England. Visiting another Lodge I was pleased to find there our Brother W. B. Reed of Minnesota. As an example of the vague ideas of the size of the United States held by some British people it may be mentioned that Brother Reed and I, being pleased to meet one another, were talking over things of mutual interest, before the lodge opened, when a young lady reproached us for occupying ourselves with one another and remarked, "You can talk together when you get back to America, we want your company now." She was greatly amazed when we informed her that our respective homes were half as far apart as is England from America.

The date for sailing from the old land came all too soon and yet we who went from America were glad to meet one another once more on board our steamer. A pleasant and prosperous voyage brought us back to American shores with new inspiration for the work of the Order.

Chapter XVI

THE DES MOINES SESSION

In my last chapter I forgot to mention the great meeting in London under the auspices of the Middlesex District Lodge, which occurred shortly before the date of our sailing on the return voyage to America. This meeting was preceded by a tea-party, at which some of the ladies prominent in the district waited upon the guests. A number of the American representatives were present and the lion of the occasion was, of course, our new R.W.G. Templar, Dr. Oronhyatekha. Everyone was cordially welcomed, but he was received by tremendous applause. There were a great many brief speeches delivered, and one of the hits of the evening was made by Sister Anna Schultz, of Iowa, when she told how she had been appointed a special constable during the prohibition campaign in her state, and exhibited a revolver which she had been authorized to carry while she was speaking in behalf of the unpopular measure. Judge Chamberlain of Massachusetts, and Sister Altie Reed, now Mrs. L. B. Walker of Wisconsin, had escaped being seated upon the platform, but were discovered in the gallery and called on by Dr. Oronhyatekha to speak for their respective jurisdictions, which they did in a very effective manner. Middlesex is my old district; it had a membership at the time of this meeting of about five thousand, I think, and I felt very proud of the appearance it made and of the warmth of its welcome.

In 1892 Dr. Oronhyatekha attended the session of the Grand Lodge of Massachusetts at Worcester. Much to my delight he was accompanied by his wife and daughter and I thoroughly enjoyed the time I was able to spend in company with these friends. Dr. Mann, G.C.T. of New York, was also one of the party and the visit of the distinguished guests was much appreciated. On the evening prior to the opening of the Grand Lodge, a banquet was tendered to the R.W.G. Templar in Boston, by The Templar Publication Company. This was an association composed of Brothers Jefferson, [Miguel] Sereque, Hitchins, and Wylie, organized for the purpose of publishing a monthly paper called The Templar. This neat and useful sheet was issued for several years [ca.

1891-95], but finally died for lack of support. In the course of its career, I rendered it some help, both literary and financial, and Sister [Josephine] Leonard and myself were finally added to the company. The banquet was a very brilliant affair and was attended by well-known members from all over the State. Brother Jefferson presided, and the list of speakers included, in addition to the guests of honor, the Grand Lodge officers, Rev. Brother Yeames, and others.

It was in 1892, I think, that I attended the Grand Lodge of New Hampshire for the first time and I well remember the cordial greeting I received. I have been to nearly every session since that date and am as much at home among Granite State members as in my own jurisdiction. Among so many friends as I can count in New Hampshire, it seems almost invidious to mention any names, but I have especial reasons for gratitude to Sister Mrs. Ruslow and to Brother Roswell H. Hassam. Sister Ruslow is well-known in the I.S.L., but Brother Hassam has not attended a session of the body since the famous Louisville one of 1876. He has always been a faithful member of the Order, however, and he is one of the kindest and best of men. He is a former Grand Secretary of New Hampshire and his name is known in connection with some [membership subscription] due cards which he invented and which were widely used. He also originated the membership list published by the famous Stark Lodge of Manchester, which shows at a glance the length of service and the honors won by the individual members.

The Des Moines session of the International Supreme Lodge was in 1893. From Massachusetts went as

representatives Rev. Bro. Yeames, W. O. Wylie, and
Mrs. L. M. Robinson, and I made a fourth of the party.
At Manchester we were joined by the New Hampshire
delegation, Brothers Wilson and Parker, and much to my
surprise they informed me that they had been instructed
to prevail upon me to be a candidate for R.W.G.S.J.T.,
and to do their utmost to secure my election. Our dear
Sister Brookbank was known to be in a very critical
condition of health and it was not supposed that she
would desire to hold the office any longer. After some
urging, I consented on condition of Sister Brookbank's
voluntary retirement to allow my name to be offered as
a candidate for the office. The plan was agreed to by
the representatives of my own State, and by those of
Vermont, and Quebec, who later boarded the train.

We stopped over in Chicago for Good Templars' day
in connection with the World's Fair. Here we met
Brother Malins, Brother Chase, Brother Hastings,
Dr. Oronhyatekha, Sister Gray, our European missionary
and many other well-known members. The late Brother
John N. Stearns of New York, had the management of the
exercises, which were interesting and useful. In the
evening, those of us who were favored with invitations,
attended a magnificent banquet under the auspices of
the Swedish Good Templars of Chicago.

The Des Moines session was a largely attended and
interesting one. It was a pleasure to meet Bro. George
W. E. Hill, Sister Schultz, and other friends again and
to make the acquaintance of Sister Remington, G.S.J.T.,
who has ever since been a faithful and loyal friend.
And it was a delight to meet again with Mrs. and Miss
Oronhyatekha, Brother N. T. Collins of New South Wales,

who was accompanied on this occasion by his wife, an
Australian born and a very sweet woman. Brother Wavrinsky, faithful as ever, against represented Sweden,
and had with him his charming wife. Brother Parker's
wife and daughter were among the well-known members
from Wisconsin. It may be mentioned that Brother
[George F.] Cotterill, who has since won such distinction in the I.S.L., made his first appearance at
this session as a representative from the State of
Washington, and immediately won for himself a large
place in the regard of leading members by his marked
ability and modest bearing. One would like to mention
all who were present, but the list is too long. It is
enough to say the gathering, as usual, did credit to
the Order and the cause.

We were all saddened by the fact that our Sister
A. A. Brookbank, R.W.G.S.J.T., was in a most distress-
ing state of health. It was pitiful to note her
countenance worn with pain, and the feebleness which
made it necessary for her to be lifted to and from the
platform in her chair. To the Juvenile workers,
especially, the condition of our leader was a cause for
deep sorrow. The request which had been made to me
regarding the office was repeated as soon as I arrived
at Des Moines, by representatives from New York and
from the jurisdictions of Great Britain. But when it
was learned that Sister Brookbank desired re-election,
every possible candidate refused to be nominated in
opposition to her. When her lamented death occurred, a
few months later, it was a pleasure to remember that we
had given her the happiness of a unanimous re-election.

Notwithstanding the illness from which she suffered, our dear and honored leader, with the aid of the
beloved Sister Mrs. M. B. O´Donnell, and the late Mrs.
Hewitt, G.S.J.T., of New York, managed to conduct a
very interesting and profitable session of the National
Institute (which was, at that time, changed to the
International Institute) of Juvenile Templar Workers.
It was delightful to witness the interest manifested in
the work among the children and to listen to the
testimonies of such workers as Mrs. Remington,
G.S.J.T., of Iowa; Mrs. Knapp, G.S.J.T., of Michigan;
Miss Agnes E. Safley, G.S.J.T., of Minnesota; Miss
E. Ella Stern, G.S.J.T., of Pennsylvania; Rev. John
Cairns, G.S.J.T., of Scotland; S. W. Russell, G.S.J.T.,
of District of Columbia, and Thomas R. Thompson of
Connecticut, so well-known by reason of his chalk-
talks, etc.

In connection with the Des Moines session of the
I.S.L., the first graduation exercises of the Course of
Study were held. Among those upon whom the honored
Chancellor, S. B. Chase, P.R.W.G.T., bestowed diplomas
were Brother Parker, R.W.G. Secretary; the late Captain
J. F. Cleghorn of Wisconsin; Brother Geo. F. Cotterill,
Sister Kate S. Hosmer of New York, and Sister Florence
Webster of Pennsylvania. I am sure that many others
felt as sorry as I did that they had not made an effort
to prepare for graduation on that occasion. I had been
one of the first to enroll, but after being elected
G.S.J.T. of Massachusetts, I had not been able to spare
the time to fill out the examination papers, which were

then much more lengthy and difficult than they are at present.[54]

It being understood that Dr. Oronhyatekha could on no account accept the office of R.W.G. Templar again, Dr. Mann of New York was nominated by Brother Sutherland of Scotland, and received a triumphant election. Brother Malins of England was elected R.W.G.C., and other officers were Mrs. S. E. Bailey of Virginia, R.W.G.V.T.; Mrs. A. A. Brookbank, R.W.G.S.J.T.; B. F. Parker, (of course) R.W.G. Secretary; George B. Katzenstein, Treasurer. The appointed officers represented Scotland, Ireland, District of Columbia, Australia, South Africa, India. They were installed by Hon. S. B. Chase, Senior P.R.W.G.T.

Among the notable events connected with the session was a very delightful reception tendered by the Ministerial Association of Des Moines, and a reception at the beautiful State House by Governor Boies. A particularly liberal spirit prevailed at this session apparently, for presentations were made to Dr. Oronhyatekha, Bro. Wavrinsky, of Sweden; Col. J. J. Hickman, P.R.W.G.T.; Mrs. A. A. Brookbank, R.W.G.S.J.T., and Bro. Thomas R. Thompson. The gift to Sister Brookbank took the form of a handsome album with

---

54   "The course, as first adopted, was rather too difficult, but quite a few members were enrolled, and the graduation exercises were for several years an interesting feature of the R.W.G.L. and of several Grand Lodges. The writer is rather proud of the possession of the diploma of the International Course, and also of the diploma of the course established by the Grand Lodge of Iowa." Forsyth, "Some Good Templar Memories: Some Outstanding Templars," Australian Temperance World, Dec. 1928, p. 10.

portraits of the G.S.J.T.´s in it. In some way I had
not received a notice of the intended presentation, so
my portrait was not among the rest, and when I took
leave of Sister Brookbank I explained to her how it
happened that my pictured face was absent from the
collection. She replied: "Never mind, dear Sister, I
will keep a place vacant until you send me one." As I
bade her farewell, I realized that I should see her
face no more in this life, and the foreboding was true,
for she only lived until the next October, dying, like
John B. Finch, in harness.

Chapter XVII

I AM APPOINTED TO THE OFFICE OF R.W.G.S.J.T.

On October 20, 1893, our dear Sister Brookbank
passed away after long weeks of suffering, and on
November 11th, upon the nomination of Dr. D. H. Mann,
R.W.G.T., I was appointed by the I.S.L. Executive to
fill out the unexpired term. Only those who have had
such an experience can understand what a difficult
matter it is to gather up the threads of such a work
when the hands which held them and the brain which
controlled them are cold in death. When the news of my
appointment came to me, I received also a large bundle
of letters with nothing to indicate whether they had
been answered or not. It must be remembered that the
condition of Sister Brookbank´s health had interfered
with the prompt and methodical performance of the
duties of the office during the last few weeks of her
life, so it was not surprising that some of the
"threads" above referred to had become a somewhat

"tangled skein." In order to deal with the matter as effectually as possible, I resigned my office of G.S.J.T. of Massachusetts, in which I was filling the fourth term, and also that of Secretary of my own District Lodge, and applied myself to getting the affairs of the Juvenile department of the I.S.L. into order. The circular issued to the membership in my new capacity will give some idea of the way I felt at the time and I quote the following paragraphs:

"I need hardly say to you that I assume the charge with a deep sense of the responsibility which such a trust involves. The ordinary difficulties which confront one who essays to fill an office so long and ably administered by another, are enhanced ten-fold by the sorrowful circumstances under which the position has become vacant."

"During the long illness of my predecessor, and in the interval which has elapsed since her death, it is possible that some matters which should have been attended to may have been overlooked, and that some delays and disappointments may have occurred. In such cases I can only ask that everyone will be patient and forbearing, and ready to forgive any errors arising from the change in the administration. If your last letter has not been answered, kindly write again. If you have failed to receive the information you sought, be so good as to repeat your questions, and rely upon receiving prompt attention and careful consideration."

* * * * *

"In conclusion, I know that you, my brothers and sisters, will pardon a few personal words. I feel that I have yet to earn the love and loyalty which have been so deservedly bestowed upon my predecessor, but you will be ready to credit me with a sincere devotion to the noble purpose for which we are banded together, and will excuse any shortcomings resulting from inexperience."

"We are sharers in a common grief for the loss of our leader, and I need not remind you that we can best honor her memory by a brave and united effort to carry on the work."

"For her sake, then, who was faithful to the end; [sic] for the sake of the little ones whose cause she pleaded, and in the name of the Master she served, let us consecrate ourselves anew to our holy cause."

This letter was sent to all Grand Chief Templars and Grand Secretaries, as well as to all Grand Superintendents, establishing a custom which I have followed ever since, in the hope of interesting the whole of a Grand Lodge Executive in the Juvenile work. The response was most gratifying and encouraging. Letters promising support and assistance came from all over the world and surely no officer ever entered upon his duties with a more cordial and general expression of sympathy. In this case, as in many other events of my Good Templar history, I am almost afraid to mention names for fear of omitting some who merit a recognition, but among the G.S.J.T.'s who rallied to my standard and who were ever most loyal and kind, I especially remember Mrs. E. M. Remington, of Iowa; Mrs.

T. B. Knapp, of Michigan; Miss Agnes E. Safley, of Minnesota; Mrs. M. S. Henry, of Indiana; Miss S. Ella Stern, of Pennsylvania; Miss E. E. Cain, of Maine; Miss Nettie M. Parlette, of Maryland; the late Mrs. Louisa Harris, of Missouri; Mrs. Emma G. Dietrick, of New York; Mrs. R. F. McDowell, of Ohio; Mrs. E. J. Forbes, of Wisconsin. Then among those who were not especially identified with the juvenile work, but who were in full sympathy with it, I gratefully remember the kind words of welcome and encouragement which came from Bro. W. H. Clark, G.C.T. of Wisconsin; Bro. George H. Fullinwider, G.S. of Kansas; Bro. A. P. Walbridge, G.S. of Arizona; Bro. G. W. E. Hill, of Iowa, and others. Dr. Mann was most kind and helpful, as was Bro. Parker and Rev. Bro. Yeames, while letters most highly prized came from Bros. Chase, Hastings, Malins and Sisters Amanda Way and Mrs. M. B. O´Donnell. The last named sister, the founder of our Juvenile work, has always been a true and sympathetic friend. Her words of appreciation have been an inspiration to me, ever since I succeeded to my present office and I am glad to make acknowledgment of the debt I owe to this most beloved and honored woman.

Almost the first duty which demanded by attention as R.W.G.S.J.T. was that of preparing for a special session of the International Institute which had been invited to meet in Washington, D.C., in 1894. I entered immediately into correspondence with the Grand Lodge Executive of that jurisdiction and can never be sufficiently grateful to Brother S. W. Russell, who was then P.G.S.J.T., and to Brother Canfield, the G.C.T., for their co-operation in the effort to make the meeting the great success it undoubtedly was. I shall take the liberty of quoting from the published report of the meetings as follows:

"The session was called to order by the R.W.G.S.J.T. as President, ex-officio, on the morning of Saturday, June 23d, in the lecture-room of the First Presbyterian Church, Washington. Rev. Bro. Yeames, P.R.W.G.T., was appointed Chaplain pro tem, and opened the proceedings with a selection of scripture and prayer. Bro. John R. Mahoney, G.S.J.T. of District of Columbia, spoke some very cordial words of greeting, which were responded to in a graceful and effective manner by S. Ella Stern, G.S.J.T. of Pennsylvania. Bro. S. W. Russell, P.G.S.J.T. of District of Columbia, was appointed Vice-President of the Institute, pro tem, and was given the pleasant duty of escorting the visitors to the platform. Among those who thus graced the session were Dr. D. H. Mann, R.W.G.T.; Mrs. S. E. Bailey, R.W.G.V.T.; Mrs. Annie J. Weichmann, of Pennsylvania, P.R.W.G.V.T; Mrs. H.[arriet] N. K. Goff, of New York, P.R.W.G.V.T.; Mrs. C. Evelyn Gilbert, P.R.W.G.V.T.; John N. Stearns, Secretary, National Temperance Society; Mrs. J. M. Thorne, G.V.T. of Virginia, James B. Morgan, G.S. of West Virginia, etc."

"The memorial service, conducted by Sister T. B. Knapp, G.S.J.T. of Michigan, was made the occasion for some tender tributes to and loving reminiscences of the late Sister Brookbank, R.W.G.S.J.T. At the close of the service, Sister Knapp, on behalf of the Institute, extended a cordial welcome to the present R.W.G.S.J.T., and promised her the co-operation of all the workers."

The following jurisdictions were represented: District of Columbia, Virginia, Maryland, West Virginia, Pennsylvania, New Jersey, New York, Connecticut, Maine, Massachusetts, Ohio, Indiana, Michigan, Wisconsin, Iowa, England. Letters were received from about thirty other jurisdictions.

"'I know something of your work, and I certainly entertain the deepest respect for your organization. The work you are engaged in is worthy of the highest encomium.' This remark was made by Hon. John W. Ross, President of the Board of Commissioners of the District of Columbia, in the course of his address of welcome. In replying to the address, the R.W.G.S.J.T. gave a brief resume of the Juvenile work of the Good Templars throughout the world."

"Children's Day was an occasion never to be forgotten by the Juvenile Templars of the District. It included a Temple Drill of a very high character, given by Undine Temple under the direction of Brother S. W. Russell. At its close, brief addresses were delivered by the following G.S.J.T.'s and P.G.S.J.T.'s, who were introduced by the R.W.G.S.J.T., Sisters Knapp, of Michigan; Forbes, of Wisconsin; Henry, of Indiana; McDowell, of Ohio; Stern, of Pennsylvania; Holmes, of New Jersey; Parlette, of Maryland; Woodhouse, of Virginia; Bros. Sereque, of Massachusetts, and Mahoney, of D.C. Sister E. F. Bishop, the faithful S.J.T. of this Temple for many years, was quite overcome with emotion when she attempted to express the pleasure which the remarks of the visitors had afforded her."

A Medal Contest was held in the afternoon, with Bro. A. N. Canfield, G.C.T., in the chair. Three medals, one of gold, given by the R.W.G.S.J.T., one of silver, by the Institute, and another of silver, by the Grand Lodge of District of Columbia, were awarded. An entertainment in the evening consisted of a short programme of recitations and music by the Juveniles and one of the famous "Chalk Talks" by Brother Thomas Roberts Thompson, of Connecticut. A magnificent bouquet was presented to the R.W.G.S.J.T. by Undine Temple. All of these events attracted large and enthusiastic audiences.

During the business days of the session a number of excellent papers by well-known workers were read and discussed. These included one on "Self Improvement" by Hon. S. B. Chase and another on "Methods of Temple Work" by Rev. James Yeames.

"R.W.G.T., Dr. D. H. Mann, is reported to have said that the time was coming when the sessions of the International Institute would be second in importance only to those of the I.S.L."

These things are very pleasant to recall and it is a pleasure to me to mention with appreciation and affectionate remembrance those workers who made this session the great success it undoubtedly was.

Chapter XVIII

BOSTON, 1895, INTERNATIONAL SUPREME LODGE, AND INSTITUTE SESSIONS

Returning from Washington, after the events related in my last chapter, I stopped over at Baltimore for a day or two for the purpose of organizing the Maryland Institute of Juvenile Templar Workers. Sister Nettie M. Parlette, G.S.J.T., was the moving spirit in the matter and she had many earnest assistants. The organization was successfully effected and the Institute began a useful work which continued through several years. A feature of my visit was a meeting with Drakeley Lodge, which was a very strong and flourishing organization, and which maintained a fine Juvenile Temple. I have appreciative recollections of the cordial hospitality and kindness which was shown to me by the Maryland brethren.

Later in the year, I made a little trip westward, with the Grand Lodge of Iowa as the farthest objective point. My first stop was at Lakeside, Ohio, where the Good Templars were holding some meetings in their own beautiful little building. Dr. Mann, our R.W.G.T., was in attendance. The Good Templar meetings were not very large, owing to those of other organizations, notably the Anti-Saloon League, occurring at the same time, but they were very pleasant and, I think, profitable. Sister McDowell, G.S.J.T., reported good work among the Juveniles, and other friends seemed interested. Our present Legislative Superintendent, Brother Rev. E. C.

Dinwiddie, now of Washington, was with us and rendered
material help in a session of the State Institute.[55]

From Lakeside, I went to Detroit by steamer, and a
chill taken upon the lakes resulted in one of the most
serious illnesses of recent years. I had just arrived
at the hospitable home of Sister Knapp, G.S.J.T., in
Howell, when I was taken ill, and for ten days I was
held fast and was dependent upon the care of Sister
Knapp and the members of her family. I can never
forget the kindness I received and think that, under

---

55   "It was soon after my appointment as [Right
Worthy Grand Superintendent of Juvenile Work] that I
accepted an invitation from the Ohio Good Templars to
attend a meeting to be held in the Temperance Temple
which they had erected at Lakeside, near Cleveland.
The meeting was not a large one, but was very interesting. An important item in the programme was a memorial
service in honor of the late Sis. Brookbank. Many
speakers voiced their appreciation of this good woman
and her work, and some of them added to their testimonies their good wishes for her successors. Oddly
enough most of them hoped that she might `follow in the
footsteps of her predecessor.´ This wish was becoming
rather monotonous and was having a rather depressing
effect on me, when a young brother, who at that time
was unknown to me, rose, and after paying a warm
tribute to the departed, said he was not going to hope
that her successor would `follow in her footsteps,´ as
he felt sure that she was capable of carrying on the
work according to her own ideas, and that she would not
be satisfied with just imitating another´s methods, no
matter how good they might be."

"This young brother was Rev. E. C. Dinwiddie who
has since become world renowned as a Prohibition leader
and now holds an Executive office in the International
Supreme Lodge." Forsyth, "Incidents in a Good Templar
Life," Australian Temperance World, May 1929, p. 3..
Dinwiddie served as national legislative superintendent
of the Anti-Saloon League. Dinwiddie´s mother had
joined the Good Templars in the 1850s, shortly after
the Order had spread to Ohio. International Good
Templar, Feb. 1904, p. 49.

God, it was due to the ministrations of these dear friends that the office of R.W.G.S.J.T. did not become vacant again in a less than a year after my appointment.

Owing to the illness, I was obliged to forego the session of the Grand Lodge of Iowa, but managed to get to that of Michigan, which was held in the great Temple erected by the Order at Hackley Park. I spent a few pleasant days with the members of this jurisdiction, enjoying to the full the healthful location, and the privilege of boarding and lodging right on the premises, which gave one opportunities for social intercourse often lacking on such occasions. In this delightful place I regained my health very quickly and was able to return home in much better condition than I had feared would be the case. Dr. Mann was also a guest, and I, as well as the members of the Michigan Grand Lodge, was enabled to profit by his instructions. During the years that have elapsed since this session the Grand Lodge of Michigan has encountered many vicissitudes, and some of those who were then active have fallen from the ranks. But the labors and interest of Brother Connell, P.G.C.T.; Bro. Blain, P.G.C.T., Sister Whitney, G. Secy., and many others, are still employed in an earnest endeavor to build up the Order.

My first visit to the Grand Lodge of Rhode Island was paid in the spring of 1895. I have met with this little Grand Lodge many times since and have attended other occasions in connection with the Order in Rhode Island. I have counted Sister Allie E. Parker, who for two years was a most efficient G.C.T., among my most loyal friends, and others are included in the list, notably Sister Mrs. Read, P.G.S.J.T.; Brother E. P. Van Doorn, P.G.C.T; Brother Hilton, P.G.C.T., etc.

The Boston session of the International Supreme Lodge was held June 26th to July 3rd, in the hall of the Boston Y.M.C.A. It occupies a conspicuous position in the list of recent sessions for many reasons. It was the last session held in the United States [to the time that she was writing in 1904]; it was largely attended, and it included several exceedingly brilliant public occasions.

The membership throughout the state had been asked to contribute towards a reception fund and the responses were most generous. As secretary of the committee appointed to raise money I was able to acknowledge the receipt of over $900. This was used to defray advertising, printing, hall rents, orchestra, decorations, banquet tickets for representatives and International Supreme Lodge officers, souvenir badges, etc. In addition to the amount named above, Brother Sereque, G.S.J.T., raised a good sum for the Juvenile department, by means of a fair, and in other ways, and this enabled us to provide free lodgings for some of those who attended the International Institute, and to invite the Juvenile workers to a luncheon, and to arrange for a fine rally of the Juvenile Templars.

This rally was the first public occasion. It was held in Berkeley Temple. A fine special programme of vocal music was rendered by a Juvenile choir under the direction of Rev. James Yeames, P.R.W.G.T., who had spent some weeks prior to the event in training the

children. By the request of the G.S.J.T., Brother
Sereque, Brother Malins, our R.W.G.T., presided, and
brief addresses were delivered by myself, Sister Gray,
European missionary, Sister Remington, G.S.J.T. of
Iowa, and other well-known workers.

The public reception meeting was held in Association Hall; it was largely attended and most enthusiastic. Rev. Brother Yeames presided. W. O. Wylie,
G.C.T., delivered the address of welcome, to which
response was made by Dr. Mann, R.W.G.T. The remainder
of the evening was spent in listening to brief remarks
from visiting officers and members. An amusing episode
was the presentation to Brother Malins of an enormous
cake from Joseph Malins Lodge of Boston. The cake was
accompanied by an elegant silver cake knife upon the
blade of which was inscribed the lines:

"If you love us as we love you,
"No knife can cut our love in two."

The cake was built in several tiers and required
the efforts of two or three able-bodied brethren to
lift it to the platform. To satisfy the curiosity of
those who may wonder what Brother Malins could do with
such a cake, I well add that before he sailed home, he
sent all but the top tier to Joseph Malins Lodge, with
the hope that the members would share it with him.
This was an excuse for a festive occasion, and on the
next Lodge night the cake was devoured by a merry
company of Boston Good Templars, to the accompaniment
of ice cream and lemonade. As one who "sampled" the
cake I may say that it was exceedingly good.

A banquet in Copley Hall, which was attended by
700 or 800 persons, was an event of such brilliancy as
has seldom, if ever, been equalled in Massachusetts.
Brother Wm. Leonard, P.G.C.T., was the toastmaster on
this occasion and in addition to the many distinguished
members of the Order present, the veteran Neal Dow as a
guest of honor. The programme included addresses by
W. O. Wylie, G.C.T.; Dr. D. H. Mann, R.W.G.T.; Dr.
Oronhyatekha, P.G.C.T.; Rev. James Yeames, Rev. Geo. F.
Clark, Joseph Malins, ex-Gov. Dingley of Maine, Mrs.
[Othelia] Mhyrmann of Illinois, Miss Agnes Sutherland
of Scotland, and myself.

An excursion to Fort Warren on the invitation of
the City of Boston was an interesting and pleasant
event. A long list of the pulpits in the city and
suburbs were filled acceptably by prominent Good
Templars from all parts of the world on the Sunday
which divided the working days of the session. Apropos
of this fact, I may mention a little joke on Brother
Yeames, who was chairman of the pulpit supply committee. On the evening of the reception Brother Lou
J. Beauchamp of Ohio had been speaking in his usual
witty fashion which had sent his audience into convul-
sions of mirth. When Brother Yeames rose to present
the next speaker, he referred to Brother Beauchamp's
address in complimentary terms and said, "Those of you
who desire to hear some more in the same line, had
better attend the _____ Methodist Episcopal Church on
next Sunday evening, when Brother Beauchamp will occupy
the pulpit." This announcement was followed by another
burst of laughter in which the chairman joined when he
saw the point of his remark.

A banquet tendered to the International Supreme
Lodge by our Swedish Lodges, which somewhat later were
formed into the Scandinavian Grand Lodge, was another
delightful occasion.[56]   Brother C. F. Lybeck, the
present G.C.T. of Massachusetts Junior, delivered the
address of welcome.

The sessions of the International Institute were
numerously attended and full of enthusiasm. The Alumni
banquet and the Course of Study graduation exercises
were both successful and delightful occasions. At this
time I, with W. O. Wylie, G.C.T., Mrs. S. A. Leonard,
G.S., and several other Massachusetts students received
the M.R.T. [Master or Mistress of Royal Templars] diploma from the hands of our honored Chancellor, S. B.
Chase.

The session itself was a good one and many promi-
nent members from all parts attended it. The officers
elected were R.W.G.T., Dr. D. H. Mann; R.W.G.C., Joseph
Malins; R.W.G.V.T., Mrs. Margaret McKinnon;
R.W.G.S.J.T., Jessie Forsyth; R.W.G.S., B. F. Parker;
R.W.G. Treas., Geo. B. Katzenstein. The appointed
officers represented South Africa, Nebraska, Iowa,
Florida, Wales and India.

Presentations were made at this session to Hon.
S. B. Chase, P.R.W.G.T., Mrs. S. E. Bailey, the
retiring R.W.G.V.T., Charlotte A. Gray, our European
missionary, while I received an album quilt from the
Juvenile workers, a beautiful little orange wood gavel

---

56   For the Scandinavian organization, see E. Hjalmar
Nordstrom and others, <u>A Historical Review of Activities
and Decisions Made by the Eastern Grand Lodge</u> (1946).

from California, a basket of flowers from E. M. Thomas Lodge of Boston, and a bouquet from Morning Start Temple of Lowell.

Chapter XIX

VISITS TO SOME GRAND LODGES

It should have been mentioned in my previous chapter that one sad incident marred the otherwise happy week of the Boston session of 1895. This was the sudden death of Mrs. Kate Stevens, wife of P.G.C.T., C. A. Stevens, who passed away during the night following the great reception meeting, which she had attended. The members of the I.S.L. testified to their respect for her and her husband, and to their sorrow for her loss, by subscribing to a beautiful floral tribute and by sending a delegation to the funeral. Mrs. Stevens had been a warm friend of mine during all the years of my association with her husband in the Junior Grand Lodge, and her death was to me a personal loss. Our good Brother Stevens survived his wife only a little more than five years when he himself was suddenly summoned hence.

In the fall of 1895 I visited the Grand Lodges of Connecticut and Vermont, receiving a most cordial greeting from each body. Brother Dr. Mann, the R.W.G.T., was present at both sessions, speaking inspiring words and giving valuable instructions. I may as well say here that Dr. Mann has invariably treated me with the utmost kindness and courtesy and has always been ready to help forward the work of my department in every way possible.

The Grand Lodge of Connecticut had at that time a few loyal workers, some of whom are still connected with the Order. Among them were Brother J. J. Coates, Sister Nettie Bray, the lady who has since become his wife, Mrs. Bishop, G.S.J.T., etc. The Grand Lodge of Vermont has been especially fortunate in being able to retain at its head for many years one of the best Grand Chief Templars known to the Order. Under Brother [C.H.] Hayden's wise and impartial control, this Grand Lodge is one of the most dignified and harmonious bodies I ever visited. And it is especially happy in retaining as active workers a large proportion of its old and honored members.

In April, 1896, I paid my first visit to the Grand Lodge of Maine which held its session at Bangor. It was an enjoyable experience and one which I have only been able to repeat once since, owing to the fact that the Grand Lodge of Maine usually meets on the same date as that of Massachusetts. In addition to Dr. Mann, I had the pleasure of meeting many old friends at this session, especially Brother George E. Brackett, the faithful Secretary for so many years, and his dear wife. An excellent Juvenile meeting, held under the management of Sister Mrs. E. E. Cain, G.S.J.T., made one feel hopeful regarding the future of this branch of our work in the Pine Tree State.

On May 9, 1896, I assisted Dr. Mann in the institution of the Scandinavian Grand Lodge of Mas-sachusetts. This Grand Lodge was formed of lodges which had been given leave to withdraw from the Senior Grand Lodge. It started with a membership of about 800

and with a good staff of officers, and has always
maintained an excellent standing, keeping free from
debt and adding a little to its numbers. I had the
privilege of presiding during the conferring of the
G.L. degree for the first time by this body and have
been present, I think, at every session since. My
relations with our Scandinavian brethren in Massachusetts and elsewhere, have always been of the
pleasantest nature.

In the later part of August, 1896, I attended the
session of the Grand Lodge of Iowa and received a great
inspiration from the various meetings of the Grand
Lodge and of the Training School, or "Good Templar
Normal." The Training School was under the management
of Brother George W. E. Hill and the meetings were of a
really remarkable character. The program included the
reading and discussion of papers by prominent workers;
graduation exercises, medal contest, banquet, juvenile
meetings, public demonstrations, etc., with two
evenings devoted to lectures by John G. Wooley[.] [It]
was a most profitable week and was remarkable for the
fact that the interest of the membership, which was
largely composed of young people, was retained from
start to finish. Although the Grand Lodge of Iowa is
not now in such a flourishing condition, it should be
realized that the instruction received by the members
in connection with such gatherings as I have referred
to, must have made a permanent impression and have had
a lasting influence upon the character of many who are
perhaps not now connected with our Order. Among the
many friends who helped to make this week in Iowa a
happy one for me, was Mrs. E. M. Remington, the

talented lady who was for several years the G.S.J.T.,
and who has always been one of my truest friends.

On my way home from Iowa, I attended by special
invitation a reception, which had been arranged by the
Good Templars of Chicago. This was a very large and
most brilliant affair. The G.C.T., Brother Uriah Copp,
others of the G.L. officers, the district lodge officers, Miss Jessie Ackermann, Deputy Right Worthy
Grand Templar, and other prominent people were present. A pleasant feature of the occasion was the
introduction of a large delegation of the Juvenile
Templars of the State. As the children marched past me
in charge of the G.S.J.T., Mrs. Hannah Stevens, I
recognized in the ranks a little boy who had been an
active member in a Boston Temple and who had recently
removed to Chicago. To this little fellow had been
assigned the duty of presenting to me a beautiful
bouquet of American beauty roses and he was immediately
followed by a little girl who brought me a handsome
Chicago souvenir spoon. Well-remembered among the many
friends who helped to make this occasion a most
successful and enjoyable one, are Brother and Sister
McWhorter, in whose home I was entertained, and
Brother George E. Benson, who was formerly a very
efficient G.S.J.T., in Plymouth, Mass. The next day an
equally large and enthusiastic reception was tendered
by the Scandinavian members in Chicago.

Before leaving Illinois, I spent a day and night
in the pleasant home of Sister Mrs. Genie F. Hazlett,
the former editor of our magazine [the International
Good Templar], and her husband. Brother [R. J.]
Hazlett was at that time and had been for many years

prior to it, the Grand Secretary of Illinois. Stopping over in Michigan, on the way home, I spent a few pleasant days with my friend Mrs. Knapp, P.G.S.J.T., at Howell, and was the guest for a night of her successor, the present efficient Grand Secretary, Mrs. M. E. Whitney, in Grand Rapids, where successful adult and juvenile meetings were held. I also attended a similar meeting in Detroit.

In 1897, taking advantage of the fact that the I.S.L. was to meet in Switzerland, I determined to start upon my European trip a couple of months earlier than was necessary, in order that I might fulfill one of the aspirations of my Good Templar life, by attending a session of the Grand Lodge of England. As my membership began in England, my desire to visit the Grand Lodge of my native land will be readily understood. But prior to having that long anticipated pleasure, I had some important business to transact which required my presence in Ireland. The year before, I had offered a "World's Prize Banner," to be awarded to the Temple making the largest per cent. gain in membership, and this banner had been won by Golden Heather Temple, Belfast, Ireland. In response to an urgent request, I decided to carry the banner to Ireland and make the presentation myself.

Accordingly, I landed at Queenstown, Ireland, instead of proceeding to Liverpool, and found that Brother Robert Semple, the Grand Secretary, had made such excellent arrangements for my reception that, although the steamer arrived some hours ahead of the time she was expected, the friends at the port, and in the near-by city of Cork, were ready to receive me.

And such a cordial welcome as they tendered; not only
were the welcomes planned by the lodges most delightfully warm and cordial, but the courtesies tendered by
individuals were most kind. In this connection, I
remember a visit to Blarney Castle, in company with
Brother and Sister Pulvertaft, and an evening spent in
the delightful home of these good people.[57] A journey
of several hours brought me to Belfast, where I was
given a hearty welcome and installed as a guest in the
home of Brother Semple and his late dear wife. A round
of meetings followed: three lodges were visited in one
evening--a carriage waiting to convey me from place to
place--but naturally, the chief event was the great
meeting at which the presentation was made. It was
held in the City Hall, which was crowded. The audience
mainly consisted of children; the prize winner, Golden
Heather Temple, was out in force with its 400 members.
The <u>other five temples, belonging to the same lodge</u>,
the "James Caithness," were also largely represented,
as were all the other Temples in the city. And what an
enthusiastic audience it was! One wondered whether it
was possible to hear such cheering anywhere but in
Ireland. The guest of the evening was cheered vocifer-
ously, the G.L. officers were cheered, especially the

---

57   During a three-hour stopover in Dublin, Bro.
Maloney, the Grand Marshall, took the opportunity to
ask numerous questions. "He, in fact, proved himself a
veritable interrogation point, and his questions did
not cease with my departure from Ireland." Forsyth
also mentioned that "I had a lady friend with me, who
kept my company from Boston until she joined her
relatives in Belfast. She was not a Good Templar, but
she was taken to the kindly Irish hearts, whose welcome
was warm enough to include my friend as well as myself,
and she shared all the attentions paid to me."
Forsyth, "Incidents in a Good Templar Life", <u>Australian
Temperance World</u>, Dec. 1929, p. 5.

devoted G.S.J.T., Brother William Thompson; the winning
Temple came in for a tremendous round, in which its
members were not prevented by modesty from joining, and
the unrolling of the banner was the signal for an
outburst of applause such as was worth the journey
across the Atlantic to hear. The occasion was probably
one of the most successful ever held in the Grand Lodge
of Ireland.

A few days spent in Ireland, filled as they were
with public events and private hospitalities, ended
with a farewell meeting at the James Caithness Lodge.
Many kind words were said by those who had taken part
in making my visit so pleasant and the guest could not
fail to be gratified at the outspoken appreciation. An
amusing incident, illustrating the difference in the
meaning attached to certain words in the British Isles
and in the United States, occurred in the complimentary
tribute offered by one good Brother. Enumerating the
reasons why the visit of the R.W.G.S.J.T., had given
the membership pleasure, he said, "And among other
things, we like her because she is <u>homely</u>." The guest
knew that the meaning attached to the word in Ireland
had nothing to do with one's personal appearance, but
meant that one was approachable and as some would
express it, "easy to get along with," but in order to
have a little fun with the speaker, she affected to
suppose that the word was intended to apply to her
appearance. In replying to the speeches she said that
she hoped that the editor of the <u>Irish Templar</u> would
not quote the brother's doubtful compliment when
reporting the meeting, as if it were known that she had
been called "homely" by an Irishmen, her reputation for
good looks would be gone for ever. The Brother was

overcome with confusion, but apologized for the "Irish bull" and was, of course, very readily forgiven.

I value much a very pretty shamrock pin, suitably inscribed, as a souvenir of this enjoyable meeting.

Chapter XX

ENGLAND AND SCOTLAND

The Grand Lodge of England held its 1897 session in the Royal Pavilion, at Brighton, which was built for a palace by George the IV. [sic], but has never been used as a royal residence by any of his successors. I arrived on the afternoon of the first day, too late for the civic reception, but in time for the public demonstration in the great dome, formerly King George's riding school, which seated about four thousand persons. In addition to the numerous friends among the English members, including Brother and Sister James J. Woods, the late Brother John B. Collings and wife, the late Brother Sutherland, Brothers Hayler, Insull, Sisters Eliz. Browne, Shipman, Haeffner, Weeks, and many others, I was glad to greet Sister Mrs. McKinnon of Scotland, R.W.G.V.T.; Brother Baillie Wright, of Scotland; Brother John Vautier, G.S. of the Channel Islands; Sister Crispin, P.G.A.S. of Victoria, Australia; Bro. Dr. [Magnus] Jonsson, P.G.S.J.T. of Iceland, and Brother Geo. W. E. Hill, G.C. of Iowa. With the other visitors I was given a place upon the program and appreciated the honor of speaking to such a large and enthusiastic audience. Several other public gatherings took place during the week, including a very pleasant

meeting of the Juveniles, a conversazione of the
Templar Institute (the English Course of Study), and a
concert in aid of the Good Templar Orphanage at Sunbury
on Thames. A feature of this occasion was the presentation of purses by the Juvenile Templars of Sussex
County, who had been collecting for the Orphanage. The
contents of the purses reached the magnificent total of
$178.

But the Grand Lodge session itself interested me
more than the public occasions, splendid as they were.
It was a great delight to me to sit upon the platform
and watch the proceedings, and to see Brother Malins,
for the first time in all my years of acquaintance with
him, presiding over his own Grand Lodge. And how proud
I felt of the appearance and the conduct of that Grand
Lodge, the body to which I had owed allegiance during
the first two years of my membership. As I wrote
regarding it at the time, the impression made upon me
"was due, not so much to the size of the body, as to
the order and method which prevailed.[58] The attendance, which at the recent session was about seven
hundred, is not greatly larger than that of many Grand
Lodges which have a much smaller membership, with a
different basis of representation. But it is emphatically a most dignified and imposing organization."

---

58   "Every member wore the proper regalia of the
degree; there was none of the moving about, the
whispering, the canvassing for officers, of which, I am
sorry to say, I had seen a good deal in America. In
fact, I am afraid that members there regarded the item
as part of the `fun of the session.´" Forsyth,
"Incidents in a Good Templar Life," Australian Temperance World, May 1929, p. 3.

"Those who have known Joseph Malins in the International Supreme Lodge, and have long recognized his great gifts, must be freshly impressed with his rare abilities when they see him in his chair as Grand Chief Templar, controlling and directing, apparently without effort, an assembly which includes many of the ablest men in the country."

"There was little manifestation of authority, the gavel was seldom used, and the presiding officer's voice was never raised above the regular even tones which were audible all over the house. The personality of the head of the Order was not made prominent, but a watchful eye was kept upon the proceedings, and nothing was allowed to escape the notice of the chair. The slightest infraction of a rule of order was checked with a quiet word, which had an instantaneous effect. The result of this was that there was none of that perpetual raising of `points´ [of order] which causes confusion in so many bodies. There was, however, ample opportunity for the frankest and fullest debate upon every question, and a matter was never put to the vote until all who desired had a chance to speak upon it. This privilege was used to an almost unlimited extent, and one felt astonished at the number of able debaters, as well as at the entire candor--unmixed with personal prejudice--of the debates. The reports of officers and committees were often severely handled, but no mali- cious intent was shown, and it was evident that the good of the cause, and that alone, was the controlling motive of all present."

Such was the impression made upon me by the business of this Grand Lodge and I was glad to note that a similar spirit prevailed during the election of officers. The spontaneous outburst of applause which greeted the presentation of Brother Malins' name as Grand Chief Templar, for what was then the twenty-eighth consecutive term, was overwhelming, and one almost marvelled that the subject of it could sit through it as calmly as though the demonstration had nothing to do with him personally. I regard the fact that I was privileged to install the officers of the Grand Lodge of England as one of the pleasantest events of my Good Templar life, and of course, I felt it to be an especial privilege to place the official collar upon the neck of Joseph Malins, the man from whose words I received my first inspiration to earnest Good Templar work and to whom I have always been indebted for kindly encouragement. One can readily believe that the spirit and tone which characterizes the Grand Lodge of England is largely due to this same inspiration, coming as it does from a life devoted to Good Templary and the cause of temperance. I may mention a practice which is usual, I believe, with Brother Malins, and which might well be adopted by other Grand Chief Templars. In making his inaugural address he has little to say about himself, or his plans, but he spoke briefly and kindly of his colleagues individually, mentioning the best qualities of each one, and causing the brethren referred to as well as the Grand Lodge, to feel that an executive had been chosen who would be thoroughly efficient and harmonious supporters of his efforts during the year. This manner of establishing a pleasant understanding may seem hardly worth speaking of, but anyone who has served on a Grand Lodge executive will realize that it means a great deal to an officer to feel that he is serving with a chief who is ready to recognize his best gifts and encourage his endeavors.

Before leaving Boston, I had agreed in response to an invitation from Brother [Tom] Honeyman, Grand Secretary of Scotland, to pay a few visits in that country and soon after the close of the Grand Lodge of England, I started out to fulfill the appointments made for me. This gave me a few very busy days, but they were very happy ones. In every place I was met and entertained according to a program perfectly arranged by Brother Honeyman and I brought away from Scotland the recollection of cordial welcomes, generous hospitality, enthusiastic meetings, and a general air of heartiness and good-fellowship, and of earnestness in work. My trip began with a very pleasant sojourn in the Manse at Dumfries, as the guest of our late dear Brother McKinnon and his wife, at that time our R.W.G.V.T. Perth, Ayr, Glasgow, Dundee were visited, and the last two days were spent in the hospitable home of our present R.W.G.V.T. Sister Mrs. Peter McDonald, whose husband was then Grand Chief Templar of Scotland. Some of the meetings took the form of conferences on Juvenile work, and in nearly every place I attended a gathering of Juveniles as well as one of adults. It was very inspiring to find in the British Isles that this work held such a prominent place and I cannot but believe that the strength and stability of our cause in these countries is due to the fact that every year hundreds of boys and girls are drafted from the Juvenile Temples into the subordinate Lodges, carrying with them a knowledge of the methods and aims of the Order and a strong love of its principles.

It is obviously impossible to mention all of those who helped to make this visit to Scotland so memorable, but I have especially kind memories of Brother Rev. James Strachan, for several years the very efficient G.S.J.T.; Brother D. A. Anderson, and wife, the earnest young couple in whose home I was a guest at Dundee; my old friends, the Sutherland family and the late Sister Herd, in Edinburgh, and others too numerous to mention, but whose kindness is remembered.

Returning to England I attended a fine Juvenile meeting at Leeds on one evening and the next a gathering held under the auspices of the Warwickshire Juvenile Council in Birmingham, at which I was pleasantly surprised by the gift of a most beautifully executed illuminated address of welcome. The presentation was made on behalf of the Council, by Brother Arthur Peters, D.S.J.T.

Going on to London the next day, I had time for two or three enjoyable meetings with Good Templars, before leaving to join Sister Charlotte A. Gray, in Paris, en route for Switzerland.

Chapter XXI

SWITZERLAND. THE ZURICH SESSION

A few pleasant days were spent in Paris with Sister Gray and her sister, Alice, who had accompanied me from London. The incident most pleasing to me was a tea party for the members of "Gallia" Lodge, followed by a good session of that little organization. This Lodge, the only visible fruits of Sister Gray's earnest

labors to establish Good Templary in France, no doubt
did a much greater work than can ever be known by the
influence it exercised on many of those who passed
through it. I am acquainted with one young Swiss
brother, a former member of "Gallia" Lodge, who was
introduced to kind and helpful Good Templar friends in
America by its means. It was my privilege to install
the officers of this Lodge upon the occasion of my
visit and I remember that those elected to fill the
position represented several nationalities. While
referring to Sister Gray and to what is perhaps
regarded by some of the failure of her work in France,
I may mention the fact that the distinguished Dr.
[Paul] Legrain of Paris was won to our ranks by her
devoted efforts, just as Dr. [August] Forel of Switzerland, and many other eminent men.

It lacked several days of the opening of the
International Supreme Lodge when we arrived in Switzerland, but the time was turned to good account, as
Sister Gray had planned a number of meetings in
different parts of the country. Our first stop was at
Bienne, where we were most kindly and hospitably entertained by a charming Swiss family named Courvoisier,
who had long been friends and supporters of Sister
Gray. This family resided in their beautiful home,
"Altersheim," and our stay in Bienne was made very
enjoyable and restful for us. It was also, it is to be
hoped, made profitable for the Order, as we visited
both the French and the German-speaking Lodges and
Temples in the town.

When leaving Bienne, we joined a party of Good
Templars who were on their way to attend the Grand

Lodge of Switzerland at La Chaux de Fonds. Dr. Forel
was with the party and this was my first meeting with a
man who occupies a most distinguished position in the
world of science. I found him very kind and very
interesting and was indebted for many courtesies during
my stay in Switzerland.[59]

It was while in Dr. Forel's company that I had my
first view of the Alps. During our stay at Bienne,
Madame Courvoisier had taken us to various points of
interest from which the snow mountains should have been
visible, but on each occasion they had been hidden by
clouds. So beautiful were the landscapes, however,
that I had not missed the crowning glory, as my
delighted gaze rested upon the rugged rocks and green
hills, lakes and rivers and waterfalls. The train was
hastening through the picturesque scenery and I was
listening to Dr. Forel's animated conversation when he
suddenly exclaimed, "Behold; the Bernese Alps!" and
looking, I beheld a sight to be remembered as long as
life should last--a white glory, glittering in the
sunshine, reminding one of nothing so much as the
pilgrim's view of the heavenly city. But I must not be
tempted to linger over the beauties of Switzerland.

The Grand Lodge of Switzerland, although a
comparatively small body, was an exceedingly

---

59   Forsyth wrote a short account, "How Dr. Forel
Became Interested in Temperance," for Youth's Temperance Banner, reprinted in International Good Templar,
Feb. 1900, pp. 56-57. On Forel see also a memoir of a
visit to Switzerland in 1887 by the son of the Grand
Chief Templar of England. Joseph Malins, M.A., "The
Beginnings of Good Templary in Switzerland," International Good Templar, Jan. and April 1937, pp. 14-15,
34-35. Malins, then aged 16, accompanied his father.

well-ordered one, over which Dr. Forel presided with much ability.[60] A fine banquet was a feature of the occasion and opportunities for social intercourse were numerous. I was entertained at La Chaux de Fonds in another beautiful home and much appreciated the opportunity which this trip gave me of becoming acquainted with some delightful Swiss families. I remember with sincere gratitude the kindness and courtesy shown to me by all with whom I came in contact.

A stay of two or three days at Basle, on the way to Zurich, gave me the opportunity of visiting more Lodges and Temples, all of which were conducted in a most orderly and business-like manner. In this city the Lodges had the privilege of holding their meetings in the handsome school houses, no rent being charged them. I had further opportunity of meeting the Juveniles and the Juvenile workers through attending a picnic in a park near Basle from whence we could see the Black Forest of Germany.

In Zurich I took up my quarters at the Baur au Lac Hotel, although Dr. Forel offered hospitality at [his home] Burgholzli. But I wished to visit Lodges and Temples and had a sadly neglected correspondence to deal with, and so I felt the need of a place where I could control my own time for a while. But I spent one long-to-be-remembered day at Burgholzli and became acquainted with Madame Forel, a most sweet and gracious woman, and with the half dozen bright, happy and well-behaved children, who made the Forel home a very

---

60   French was the language of the Grand Lodge of Switzerland. Forsyth, "Incidents in a Good Templar Life," Australian Temperance World, Nov. 1929, p. 3.

lively and attractive one. Then, too, I had the
privilege of seeing Dr. Forel´s wonderful collection of
ants, for, as many of my readers know, this man of many
talents is one of the greatest of living authorities on
these wonderful little insects. He has thousands of
specimens, gathered from all parts of the world, of all
sorts and sizes, and all properly classified. I may
mention here that when Dr. Forel visited Massachusetts
two years later, he was delighted to find in Franklin
Park, Boston, some ants of a kind not often seen so far
north. I speak of these things to make my readers
realize what manner of man this famous Dr. Forel is,
who amid all his graver duties as a most distinguished
scientist, and as an untiring temperance worker, can
pursue, as a recreation, the study of an insect with
such enthusiasm and thoroughness as to have his
pronouncements regarding the subject received as final.

The session of the I.S.L. in 1897 at Zurich is of
too recent date to render it necessary for me to
describe it at any length. It was well attended and of
great interest and our good Swiss brethren were
delighted to meet those already well[-]known to them by
reputation as honored workers and leaders. Among these
were P.R.W.G. Templars Hastings, Chase, Yeames, and
Oronhyatekha; Dr. Mann, R.W.G.T., who at this session
retired from the office which he had filled with such
acceptance, and was succeeded by Bro. Malins; Bro.
Parker, R.W.G. Secretary, and many others. The social
occasions were most enjoyable; the parade, headed by
the Juvenile Templars, carrying garlands of flowers,
was a most beautiful sight. The garden party and
reception to the Good Templars by the Baroness von

Sulzer-Vart, in her beautiful grounds at Castle Au, was a delightful function.

At the great reception meeting in connection with the I.S.L. the children filled the first part of the program and a feature was the presentation of bouquets to Dr. Mann, R.W.G.T.; to Sister Gray, and to me. The flowers composing the other bouquets were exotics, but mine was formed of edelweis and mountain roses. A card attached to it bore the words, "The flowers of our home for the dear R.W.G. Superintendent." The beautiful thought connecting the children with the flowers was even more prized than the offering itself. One could but pray that the fair "flowers of the home" might never be blighted by the poisonous breath of alcohol, and that the teachings in our Temple might help them ever to retain the "noble whiteness" of the mountain blossom.

Two amusing incidents occurred at this meeting. One when Dr. Forel introduced Dr. Oronhyatekha with the remark that "The Doctor will address you in his own language." Sister Gray stepped forward to act as interpreter and a puzzled expression appeared upon her face when the famous Indian began to speak in what was to her, with all her linguistic accomplishments, an unknown tongue. Asked for an explanation, the Doctor said: "I was told to address you in my own language and I have been speaking Mohawk. But as I find you have not provided an interpreter for that language, I must speak English." He continued his remarks amid much laughter and applause. Mrs. Florence Richards of Ohio delivered an eloquent address, in the course of which she dealt with the question of woman suffrage and used

the illustration of a hen defending her chickens from a
hawk. Bro. Hildebrand of Zurich interpreted for her
and when he reached the point I have referred to in the
speech, he became so excited and enthusiastic that he
moved his arms in imitation of the hen flapping her
wings. His admirable pantomime "brought down the
house."

Of course, before we left beautiful Switzerland we
all did a little sight-seeing and, equally of course,
we gathered upon the summit of Mount Righi to see the
sun rise. This is an oft-described scene, but the experience is ever new. For surely everyone must feel
the same sense of awe as he stands in the dim light,
surrounded by the silent gray peaks. And then comes
the first soft blush of dawn, deepening by slow degrees
to a glowing crimson, which in its turn changes to
vivid gold, until the snow mountains are ablaze in the
sunshine and the beholder is filled with rapture at the
sight.

A large party of Good Templars, representing many
lands, gathered on Mount Righi on that morning of which
I speak. And of those who stood there silently regarding the glory of the sunshine over the Alps, several of
the noblest and the best have since passed on to behold
the greater glory which "eye hath not seen." Among the
departed ones who are linked in our memories with that
dawn on Mount Righi are Hon. S.D. Hastings, P.R.W.G.T.;
Captain J. F. Cleghorn of Wisconsin; W. S. Payne of
Ohio; John B. Collings of England, and John D. McKinnon
of Scotland.

Chapter XXII

A LITTLE TRIP NORTHWESTWARD

I ought to have mentioned the meeting of the International Institute of Juvenile Templar Workers which was held in connection with the Zurich session, for the reason that it was of a particularly interesting, and instructive character. This was due to the fact that Brother Dr. Forel favored us with a most interesting lecture on the "Effects of the Use of Alcohol on the Brain," and Brother Arthur Newell, G.S.J.T., of England, gave one or two of his very useful "Eyegate" lessons. The Course of Study graduation exercises should have been referred to also. They were presided over by our dear and honored Brother, Hon. S. B. Chase, P.R.W.G.T., and were of the usual excellent character.

After leaving Switzerland, I was obliged to hasten back to Great Britain in order to fulfill an engagement in Wales. A couple of days were happily spent in the beautiful town of Swansea and two good meetings were attended. Brother Jenkins who was at that time the successful G.S.J.T,, was most kind in his efforts to make me welcome and he was very cordially helped in this endeavor by all the other members. When I left Wales, I carried with me a beautiful album containing views of Swansea and vicinity, as well as the autographs of many of the members; a bouquet, and, best of all, the recollection of the kind and cordial welcome which had been given to me.

From Swansea to Liverpool was another hurried trip and the evening prior to embarking for my return voyage to America found me at a farewell meeting of the Juvenile Templars of England, over which Brother Arthur Newell presided. The church in which the meeting was held was very prettily decorated and when I rose to speak in acknowledgment of a lovely bouquet presented to me by a dear little girl on behalf of the Juvenile Templars of the District, I spoke of the beauty of the decorations and said that I supposed they were in honor of the good Queen Victoria, whose jubilee had been so recently celebrated. But Brother Newell informed me that the flags and flowers were in my honor and the children were very much amused at my making such a mistake.

After a three months' absence from home, it was pleasant to find that one was not forgotten and it was with much pleasure that I accepted an invitation from Brother Sereque, who at that time was G.S.J.T. of Massachusetts, to a reception tendered by the Juvenile Templars of the State. Many kind words were spoken and the good will expressed in them was emphasized by the gifts of a choice bouquet and a beautiful album containing portraits of some of the workers.

On October 12th, 1897, I celebrated the twenty-fifth anniversary of my initiation in the Order, by tendering a reception to my friends. I did not announce that the occasion was an anniversary, but the fact became known, nevertheless, and again I was overwhelmed with tokens of good will from my friends. A beautiful pair of opera-glasses, an elegant lamp, and a cluster of twenty-five long-stemmed pinks came from different groups of members, and a lovely bouquet, tied with blue and yellow ribbons, the Swedish colors, was an evidence of the good will of my Scandinavian friends.

In 1898 a very urgent request came to me from Dr. E. A. Blakely, G.S.J.T., for me to visit the Province of Manitoba and I arranged to go at a time when I could visit two other jurisdictions en route.

My first stop was in Minneapolis where I attended the Grand Lodge of Minnesota. Here I met many old friends and made several new ones. Our dear Sister Agnes E. Safley, who had served many years as G.S.J.T., was at this session elected Grand Secretary. Although suffering from many discouragements, and with a decreasing membership, a good spirit was shown among the members and a determination to work. At a fine public meeting held at Minnehaha Falls, Brother J. H. Campbell, lecturer for the Grand Lodge of Iowa, and Brother Geo. I. Stratton, one of Wisconsin's most active workers, were among the speakers. After I had delivered a brief address, Brother Campbell suggested that a collection should be taken to pay for the charter of a Juvenile Temple to be named for me. The amount was easily raised.

From Minneapolis, I journeyed on to North Dakota, where, at Jamestown, the Grand Lodge session was held. Here I met a delightful lot of people, earnest and courageous. Among the best of them were Sister Briggs, G.S.J.T., and her worthy husband. Public meetings were held in connection with the session and a banquet was

also a feature of it. A sad incident occurred at the
hotel where I stopped. A fine-looking man sat at
dinner at the same table with me and some of the party
noticed that he acted rather strangely. A few minutes
after he left the table, the report of a pistol was
heard in the room he occupied. The servants hastened
to the chamber and found the man lying shot through the
head, self-slain. An empty bottle lay upon the table
with the words "Whisky did it" scrawled upon a piece of
paper.

The good friends at Jamestown had planned to take
their visitors to visit the Insane Asylum, the chief
place of interest in the city. All the available
vehicles had been chartered to convey the party to the
place and some of them were neither elegant or comfortable. I sat beside the driver of one of the carriages,
having expressed my preference for that seat. As we
journeyed along I noticed that one of the pair of
horses was acting in a rather wild and eccentric manner
and I said to the driver, "What is the matter with that
horse?" The reply took me somewhat by surprise; said
the man, "That is not a horse." I am not very well
informed regarding matters equine, but I thought I knew
a horse when I saw one, so I asked "If that is not a
horse, what is it?" and the driver replied "[I]t´s a
bronco." It was my first experience of the animal, so
my ignorance may be pardoned.

When we arrived at the asylum, I was introduced to
the Superintendent as a visitor from Boston and he
inquired whether I had seen many such institutions. I
replied that I had only seen the one presided over by
Dr. Forel at Zurich, Switzerland. Immediately I became

aware that I had produced a profound impression. The
gentleman summoned the members of the medical staff and
introduced them to "a friend of the celebrated Dr.
Forel." The reflected glory in which I shone caused me
some embarrassment which was increased as they began
to question me regarding Dr. Forel´s way of treating
the insane and I could state frankly that, while I had
an immense respect for Dr. Forel, I knew nothing
whatever about his methods. But the incident proves
how world-wide is the fame of our renowned Swiss
brother, who was at that time R.W.G. Treasurer.

The visit to Manitoba was a very interesting and
enjoyable one, and the few days spent with Brother
Dr. Blakely (who was at that time Minister of Education
for the Province) and his wife, at their pretty home in
Winnipeg, were most pleasant. On one afternoon their
hospitable doors were thrown open to the ladies of the
city, who had been invited to meet me and a large
number came in response to the invitation. Among them
were the wife and daughter of our veteran Brother
Nixon, so well-known to members of the I.S.L. Several
meetings took place during my stay in Winnipeg, including three in the interests of the Juvenile work.
A reception tendered by the Icelandic Lodges was
largely attended and a successful affair and gave me an
opportunity of meeting many representatives of that
nationality, fine, stalwart, earnest young people, who,
while they retain their enthusiastic affection for the
land of their birth, are yet among the most loyal and
exemplary citizens of parts of the United States and
Canada. Many of these brethren joined the Order in
Iceland and to-day it is practically due to their
efforts that the Order continues to exist in Manitoba.

Chapter XXIII

JUBILEE CELEBRATIONS

The session of the International Supreme Lodge for 1899 was held at Toronto, Canada, and this also is of too recent date to make any detailed account of it necessary in these reminiscences. But it will be remembered from the fact that much of its success was due to the efforts of Dr. Oronhyatekha, who spared no pains in making us welcome to his home city. The magnificent Foresters´ Temple was given over to our use and we were made to feel that we were welcome guests in this fine structure for the sake of the renowned head of the great Foresters´ Order. The doctor himself did the honors of the place with all his well-known kindness and hospitality. The reception and banquet tendered by Temple Lodge was a most brilliant affair and many of the members of the I.S.L. were guests of the doctor on other and less numerously attended occasions.

At this session Brother George F. Cotterill, of Seattle, was elected R.W.G. Counselor by a large majority. Brother Cotterill, of Seattle, had been a much esteemed member of the I.S.L. from the time of his joining it at the Des Moines session, and his popularity had been secured by his unselfish devotion to the interests of the Order, his ability and his modesty. These traits had brought him to the notice of our late revered Brother Hastings, P.R.W.G.T., and it was the nomination by this honored man which helped to place Brother Cotterill in the second place so early in his history as an I.S.L. member. Brother Cotterill´s subsequent career has proved that "Father" Hastings had made no mistake. Brother Cotterill was a most useful and able member of the Executive during the two years he served and he has always retained the good-will and the unqualified respect of his colleagues.

The Toronto session was the last one attended by Brother Hastings. When it was voted to hold the next one in Sweden, the beloved veteran knew that it was very unlikely that he would be able to make the trip at his advanced age. And he told us that he never expected to meet with us again in I.S.L. session. His farewell words were most touching and impressive, as he committed to us the interests of the Order which he had toiled for and loved so many years. Surely all who heard him must have been inspired to greater zeal than ever before, so that the cause for which so many good men had labored might not be allowed to suffer when they were called upon to enter into rest.

Brother Theodore D. Kanouse, of California, P.R.W.G.T, and Brother Colonel John Sobieski, lineal descendant of the last king of Poland, were in attendance at this session, and I had the privilege of meeting for the first time two men whose names had been very familiar to me for many years.[61]

One incident in this session has always been a pleasant one for me, at least, to recall. It was the fact that for a half a day I had the honor of presiding

---

61   See John Sobieski, Life-Story and Personal Reminiscences of Col. John Sobieski (Los Angeles: L. G. Sobieski, [ca. 1907]).

over the I.S.L. while the Juvenile work was discussed. This privilege, which was due to the courtesy of Brother Malins, R.W.G.T., is one which has been given to very few of my sex, I think.

From this session our R.W.G. Templar, Brother Joseph Malins, started upon his famous tour around the world, which occupied almost a year and which resulted in so much good for the Order in the places he visited. The prolonged absence of the head of the Order left additional responsibilities in the hands of the R.W.G. Counselor, but Brother Cotterill proved himself equal to all the demands upon him.

During the summer of 1900 I attended the sessions of the Grand Lodges of Nova Scotia, Prince Edward Island and New Brunswick. That of the first-named was held in Yarmouth, and I made one of a party from Massachusetts which included our late Brother Chisholm, a P.G.C. of Massachusetts and a P.G.C.T. of Nova Scotia; Mrs. Chisholm, Brother Herbert E. Phinney, P.G.C., a faithful member for many years in Massachusetts, although still a comparatively young man, and others. We had a pleasant time with our Nova Scotia brethren and hoped that we did them good.

I went on alone to Prince Edward Island and found a very earnest company of Good Templars at the Grand Lodge of this province, which was held in the beautiful little village of Pownall. Brother Martin, Brother Frazier, Sister Horton and many others were doing their best to promote the work of the Order in the face of many difficulties. In New Brunswick the same devotion was shown by another set of workers, and Brother Dodge,

225

Lawson and Rev. Thomas Marshall were making an earnest fight. The session was held in the fine capital city of Fredericton. In each of the jurisdictions I met with the kindest reception and the warmest of welcomes and could only hope that some good resulted from my visit to them.

The jubilee of the Order was celebrated at Utica, N.Y., in 1901. The preparations for the event were made by Hon. W. Martin Jones, and some very interesting meetings were held. The occasion was graced by the presence of Mrs. M. B. O´Donnell, P.R.W.G.S.J.T., and Mrs. Mattie McClellan Brown, P.R.W.G.V.T., two of the most eminent women in the Order and both very kind friends of mine. Bro. Hon. S. B. Chase was with us, as were many other good and true members, such as Bro. Parker, Bro. Yeames, etc.

Following the Utica meetings some of us enjoyed a visit to East Rochester Lodge, a very large and successful organization, the home Lodge of Brother Harry Greensmith, then G.C.T. of New York. Later we were guests of members in Buffalo at an anniversary banquet. On the way to Utica I stopped over at Schenectady, where a fine public meeting was held under the auspices of Ancient City Lodge.

In company with the Right Worthy Grand Templar, Brother Preece of England, and Brother [William] and Sister [Clara] Crowhurst of California, I visited the Grand Lodge of Pennsylvania at Coudersport. The occasion was of special interest to Brother Malins, because it was in this State that he had first joined the Order in connection with which he was destined to

do such a noble work. Needless to say that the members
of the Grand Lodge were delighted to welcome the
distinguished guest and were proud of the fact that he
began his career in the jurisdiction. But the lesser
lights among the guests were not less cordially
received and I have very kindly recollections of the
hours spent in Coudersport. I was very glad to meet
here, for the first time since the Boston session of
the I.S.L., with the old friend and time-honored
worker, Sister Mrs. Annie J. Weichmann, D.R.W.G.T.;
also with Mrs. Belle Jones, G.S.J.T., who had been for
several years one of my most loyal co-workers. The
session was a very pleasant and profitable one; some
good public meetings were held in connection with it
and some attention was given to the Juvenile work.

A hurried trip to Massachusetts was taken, so as
to reach Boston in time for various events which had
been planned for the proper reception of the R.W.G.
Templar. These included a banquet by the Scandinavian
Grand Lodge, in charge of J. T. Engdoll, G.C.T.; a
public meeting under the same auspices; a fine Juvenile
Templar rally under the joint management of Mrs. Robin-
son, G.S.J.T. of the Senior, and Brother Anders Nilson,
G.S.J.T. of the Junior Grand Lodge; a meeting of the
Veteran Good Templar Association; a banquet in Faneuil
Hall, tendered by the Good Templar Woman's Auxiliary
Society, with Mrs. Grace V. Bourcy presiding, and a
great public meeting in the same hall on the following
evening under the management of J. Sydney Hitchins,
G.C.T., with Hon. L. E. Chamberlain in the chair.
These events were all of a very high character, with
large attendance and fine programs. The guest of honor
was received with tremendous enthusiasm and the story

of his "Round the World" trip was eagerly listened to. Everyone felt that it was indeed a privilege to belong to an Order which "belts the globe," and which extends its blessings to all without regard to race or nationality, sex or creed.[62]

Chapter XXIV

SWEDEN REVISITED

My thirty years' membership terminated in 1902 and it was during this year that the famous Stockholm session of the International Supreme Lodge was held. I made one of a party of Good Templars who sailed for Scandinavia on the "Oscar II.," [sic] and I have some very pleasant recollections of the delightful voyage and the social times enjoyed. The party included Rev. Brother Yeames, P.R.W.G.T.; Brother George F. Cotterill, R.W.G.C., who was accompanied by his wife; Brother Colonel B. F. Parker, R.W.G.S.; Bro. Hon. W. Martin Jones, R.W.G. Treasurer, and many other well-known members from all parts of the United States.

Many of our party were great fun-makers and the tedium of the voyage was relieved by various forms of amateur entertainments, the most ambitious one being a mock trial, in which Brother Gowan of Maine acted as the defendant, with Bro. Cotterill as counsel for the prosecution, and Brother W. Martin Jones as counsel for the defense. Brother Yeames impersonated the judge and he rendered some very unique decisions. Sisters

---

62   Forsyth omits mentioning her appointment, effective January 1901, as editor of the International Good Templar, with the title honorary literary editor.

Cotterill, Fisher, [Laura D.] Rudy (of Pennsylvania) and myself were witnesses, and Brothers Parker, W. H. Clark, Fullinwider of Kansas, Sister Whitney of Michigan, and some others occupied the jury box. Fourth of July was celebrated with all due ceremony, with Brother Yeames for the orator. Our fun had the effect of recommending our total abstinence principles to many of the passengers, who were not teetotallers, and as we neared the end of the voyage they thanked us for the pleasure we had afforded and expressed their surprise that so much mirth could exist without wine to inspire it.

Two of the merry party who travelled on the "Oscar II." have since then journeyed to the "Silent Land"; one was Brother Samuel Osborne, the remarkable colored man who was an old member of the Grand Lodge of Maine and who made many friends during the trip. The other was Brother I. B. Buason of Manitoba, a fine young Icelander, who was no less a credit to his adopted country than to his native "land of ice and fire."

The voyage occupied nine days and during the latter part of it we were delighted with the scenery of the north coast of Scotland, the south coast of Norway, and later the shores of Sweden and of Denmark. We landed in Copenhagen, where we were cordially welcomed by many of the local members, including Brother Victor Holmes and his wife, who entertained a large company at a garden party in the grounds of their beautiful home. A large number of the British representatives were [sic] already arrived in Copenhagen, and very early the next morning we all started to Stockholm. In addition to the Americans our company included our honored

R.W.G. Templar, Joseph Malins, and many other prominent members from the British Isles, besides Rev. S. J. Chowrryappah, a native Hindoo, from Madras, and Chief [William] Zecheus Coker, a native African prince from the Gold Coast. The latter was clothed in handsome European dress; he spoke fine English and was exceedingly courteous in manner. Brother Chowrryappah wore the Hindoo garb and with his turban and his long beard presented a striking and venerable appearance.

The journey to Stockholm was a series of wonderful receptions. At every station along the route the members of the local Lodge and Temple came out with banners and flags and music to greet us. They sang and cheered and gathered around the train doors to shake hands with us and sometimes the children offered flowers. Long before we reached Stockholm we realized that we were welcome guests and that our coming had been prepared for from one end of the kingdom to the other.

It seemed impossible to realize, as I stepped from the train at Stockholm and again beheld the great square filled with thousands of Good Templars, that seventeen years had elapsed since I was there before. The songs, the cheers, the banners were all in evidence, and the welcome was as cordial as that which had greeted me upon my previous visit. Only some of the familiar faces were lacking; many of the true and the tried ones who were in the forefront in 1885 had laid down their arms, but it was good to know that their places had been filled by others as brave and as loyal. There were, nevertheless, many old friends to greet; Brother Wavrinsky and his dear wife; Brother

Oscar Eklund, Brother [Johann] Ahlen, G.S.J.T., who has since been called up higher, and many others.

The session opened on the morning after our arrival in the Rigsdaghuset (the Parliament House) in which the session of 1885 was held, and which was beautifully decorated with plants and flowers for the occasion.[63] It was a remarkable gathering and one could not look around the assembly without getting a thrill of pride at knowing oneself a part of it. For the first time it was necessary to have the business translated into German as well as Swedish, owing to the fact that our German Grand Lodges were fully and ably represented. The session is so recent that it is not necessary to refer to the business transacted except to mention that Brother Malins, R.W.G.T., Brother Parker, R.W.G.S., and I were honored with unanimous re-elections to our respective offices, while Brother Prof. Johan[n] Bergmann of Sweden was chosen R.W.G.C., and Brother Herman[n] Blume, G.C.T. of Germany,

---

63   "The morning after the close of the Session Bro. Malins asked me to go with him to the Parliament House and help him to collect books and papers, etc. which he had left. Among the articles was the famous gavel [presented to Malins in 1885], which he handed to me. I left the building first, carrying [the gavel] in full view, but outside stood the custodian of the House, who regarded me very suspiciously. He touched the gavel and said: `Rigsdag Klubba,´ as a gentle admonition to me, but I replied: `Na, Na. Vorlds Storlogen Klubba,´ which was about as much of the language as I could manage in an emergency. But the old gentleman had evidently not heard of the duplication, and was not willing to allow me to pass. I called Bro. Malins, who was highly amused at my predicament, but soon settled the matter by taking the faithful officer back into the Chamber and showing him the original Klubba." "Incidents in a Good Templar Life," Australian Temperance World, July 1929, p. 6.

R.W.C. Treasurer. Rev. Bro. Yeames had the novel
experience of being the only P.R.W.G.T. present at the
session and upon him devolved the pleasant duty of
installing the officers. He was assisted by
Mrs. Margaret McKinnon, of Scotland, P.R.W.G.V.T., and
Mrs. Cora Cotterill of Washington, as Marshals.

The public and social events connected with the
session excelled anything ever attempted in any jurisdiction. The great reception meeting was held in the
Royal Opera House, a beautiful building, with a seating
capacity of over 2,000, which was taxed to the utmost.
The audience included people prominent in the government of the nation and of the city, in art, literature,
science, commerce, etc., and, with the Good Templars--
who represented many lands and all sorts and condi-
tions--it was certainly a wonderful gathering. The
royal box was occupied by the Crown Prince of Sweden,
the Princess Ingeborg, wife of Prince Carl of Sweden,
and her sister, Princess Thyra of Denmark. The
Minister of Foreign Affairs, Count Lagerheim, presided
over the meeting and welcomed the Good Templars in
behalf of the King. A magnificent band, a fine choir
of male voices, and one of the most famous soloists of
Sweden, Herr C. F. Lundquist, rendered selections
between the addresses, which were delivered in seven
different languages, English, French, German, Danish,
Norwegian, Icelandic, and Swedish, of course. Brother
W. Styrlander, the G.C.T. of Sweden, welcomed the
members on behalf of the Grand Lodge, and a fine poem
in Latin, written by Prof. [Johann] Bergmann, was
distributed among the audience. I had the honor to be
the only lady speaker on this great occasion.

There were several other notable occasions,
including a splendid banquet at Salsjobaden; an excursion to Drottingholm, where the Crown Princess of
Sweden received many of the guests, including Mrs. Cotterill, to whom was assigned the honor of presenting a
bouquet to Her Highness; the great parade of about
twenty-five thousand members to Skansen, etc. Other
pleasant incidents were the carriage drive about
Stockholm, and visits to the Scandinavian Temperance
Congress, and to the Grand Lodge of Sweden. In the
latter body, I was privileged to speak for a few
moments and I referred to the fact that when I had
visited the Grand Lodge in 1885, there were few sisters
in the membership, but now I had learned that thirty-
three per cent. were of my sex. I congratulated the
Grand Lodge upon having so large a proportion of the
"better half of the Good Templar Order."

The deputation to the King was a great event and I
was the only lady included in the list of seven persons
to which the deputation was restricted. I had the
honor of representing the United States and of replying
to His Majesty's complimentary references to our "great
country." The other members of the deputation were
Brother Malins, representing Great Britain; Brother
Blume, Germany; Brother Professor Lars O. Jensen,
Norway; Brother P.[eter] Aarseth, Denmark; Brother
Coker, Gold Coast, and Brother Chowrryappah, India.
Each one of us was greeted by King Oscar with a cordial
grasp of the hand and a few personal words. The King
commended very warmly the great work our Order was
doing in his dominions.

An excellent session of the International Institute, at which our good Sister Charlotte Gray was a
wonderful help, and graduation exercises of the Course
of Study were events of interest during our ten days in
Stockholm. On the latter occasion I presented the
diplomas to the graduates, in the absence of our
beloved Chancellor, Hon. S. B. Chase. At a meeting of
the Alumni a little later, we voted to present a gold
veteran badge to Brother Chase. A delightful luncheon
party tendered to the officers of the International
Supreme Lodge by Brother and Sister Wavrinsky was
another pleasing incident.

All too soon came the time for saying farewell to
the kind Swedish brethren who had made our sojourn with
them so pleasant. We little thought, when we said our
last "good byes" that Brother Eriksson, the one who as
chairman of the committee had been chief in caring for
our comfort during our stay, would meet with us no more
on earth. But in very few months the news came to us
that he had been taken away from the work, leaving a
place it would be very hard to fill.

A fine meeting of a lodge in Copenhagen was
attended en route to Kiel, where a few of us, including
Brother Malins, R.W.G.T., Brother J. W. Hopkins, the
excellent G.S.J.T. of England, and Sister Mrs. Ruslow,
of New Hampshire, attended the session of the Grand
Lodge of Germany. This was a delightful experience and
I could devote many paragraphs to the occasion did
space permit. But it must suffice to say that the
order and dignity of the proceedings of the Grand Lodge
were most impressive, while the great public meeting
with over 2,000 persons present was a sight to gladden

one´s heart. It was an especial pleasure to me to meet
Brother Koopman, G.S.J.T., who for several years had
been a most successful and valued co-laborer.

And here I close the story of my thirty years in
the Order. In relating it I have tried to give due
honor to those with whom I have been associated, but I
have only been able to make the briefest possible
mention of their labors, and many who have deserved
mention have not been spoken of at all. I look around
the world and count among our members some of the
noblest and best in almost every land, and I rejoice to
be able to claim many of them as valued personal
friends. To their kindly help and counsel and encouragement I owe more than I can ever express. I have
said little about the work which for several years
past has been my especial care, but I cannot close
these reminiscences without referring to the true men
and women everywhere who are devoting themselves to
this most difficult task of caring for the children.
If one thing more than another calls for gratitude as I
review my connection with the Order, it is that I have
been blessed with the unfaltering loyalty of these
noble souls, whose zeal and fidelity have made it
possible for me to render a creditable report to the
International Supreme Lodge.

My work for our great organization has filled with
interest what might otherwise have been a dull and
colorless life. The reward of an honest endeavor to
perform whatever task has been assigned to me to the
best of my ability, has come not alone, and not
chiefly, in the recognition which my efforts have
received, but in the development of my own gifts. And

I am only placing the credit where it is due when I say that whatever there may be in me worthy of the affection and the respect of my friends is owing, in a great measure, to my thirty years of Good Templary.

1905--SOME NOTES OF TRAVEL

[International Good Templar, Nov. and Dec. 1905, Jan. and Feb. 1906; there is also a briefer account in an installment in Forsyth´s series, "Incidents in a Good Templar Life," subtitled "A European Anti-Alcohol Congress," Australian Temperance World, Sept. 1929]

I

I promised my co-workers [in the Juvenile Temples] that I would give them some account of my travels during my absence from home and, as most of the journeys were taken in the interest of our Order, I am sure that all my readers will enjoy hearing of the many pleasant experiences I enjoyed.

On July 20th [1905] I made one of a little party which had been gathered together by Brother Willard O. Wylie, P.G.C.T. of Massachusetts, and which sailed for Ireland on the White Star Steamer "Arabic." The party included, besides Brother Wylie and myself, Brother Rev. James Yeames, P.R.W.G.T., and Sister Robbins of Westfield, Mass; Brother P. J. Connell, P.G.C.T. of Michigan; Brother Macauley, G. Treas. of Minnesota; Brother A. H. Bisbee, G.C. and Brother Gowen, G.E.S. of Maine; Brother McQuaid, G.C. of Quebec, and his daughter, Sister Mrs. Jackson, G.S.J.T. of New Brunswick; Rev. Brother Proude of Rhode

Island; Brother Chas. N. Hall, G.S. of New Hampshire,
and Brother [Bruno] Hockert of Connecticut, our able
Associate Editor [of the International Good Templar].
On the evening prior to sailing, Wylie Lodge of Boston
tendered to us a great farewell reception and Brothers
Yeames, Wylie, and myself were presented with beautiful
bouquets. The G.C.T., Brother [Albert] Sutcliffe, also
received a bouquet. When I reached my quarters on
board the steamer I found another magnificent bouquet
from the Good Templar Woman's Auxiliary Society, as
well as a quantity of other flowers, and candy, fruit,
daily letters, etc., from other friends. All of these
things were enjoyed on the voyage.

We had a pleasant passage and we were a very
harmonious party. We discussed I.S.L. matters when we
felt disposed for serious business, and between whiles,
we sang and read, and talked and told stories. Brother
Connell proved himself a master in the art of organizing little entertainments and he was the moving spirit
in planning a concert given in aid of the Seaman's
Charities of Liverpool and Boston.

We landed in Queenstown on July 28th and went on
immediately to Cork, where we spent the night. Rising
very early the next morning, we paid a flying visit to
Blarney Castle, enjoying very much the drive in the
fresh morning air. Then we took train for Killarney
and spent the remainder of the day at this lovely spot,
surely one of the fairest places in the world. We were
rowed over the beautiful lakes and walked back through
the Gap of Dunloe. It was a long walk--seven Irish
miles, which are said to be equal to nine English
ones--but one could not think of being fatigued [at age

58] when such wild and romantic scenery met the eye at every turn. Truly our day at Killarney will be long remembered.

The next day our pleasant little party divided, some of the friends going to other places of interest and others hastening to Belfast to be ready for the duties which awaited them there. We arrived in Belfast after midnight on Saturday, and were met by Brother Haveron, the Grand Secretary of Ireland. Brother Yeames learned then for the first time that he was advertised to preach a Good Templar sermon in the Belfast Cathedral on the next morning. It was very short notice, but Brother Yeames proved himself equal to the occasion. His sermon showed no signs of hasty preparation but was universally spoken of as a fine effort. Our brother preached in the historic Cathedral at Londonderry on the following Sunday, as the Grand Lodge of Ireland had accomplished what was certainly a unique feat, that of securing permission to use both cathedrals for services in connection with the session of the I.S.L.

I shall refrain from mentioning the business of the session, as it has already been reported in our columns. But I want to make my acknowledgments to our brave Irish brethren for their kindness and hospitality. They were most lavish in their expenditure and most cordial in their welcome. Brother and Sister Gray, Brother and Sister Yule, Brother Semple and others were unfailing in their efforts to make the visitors happy. A feature of the social occasions was the excursion to the world-famed Giant's Causeway. A party of 200 accepted the invitation to see this great

natural wonder, and the train which bore them to
Portrush was made up entirely of first-class carriages. At Portrush a fine dinner was served and when
the guests returned from the Causeway a substantial tea
awaited them. The menu cards were in the shape of a
shamrock and were intended to be kept as souvenirs of
the occasion.

Another delightful event was a drive around the
beautiful city of Belfast and its environs, in the
famous Irish jaunting cars. This was on the invitation
of the Belfast District Lodge and it took more than
sixty cars, each holding four, to accommodate the
party. The reception by the Lord Mayor in the Exhibition Hall, Botanical Gardens, was a very brilliant
function. It was reported in the society papers of the
city and the portraits of some of the guests with
description of the ladies' gowns occupied several
columns.

The Grand Lodge of Ireland held its session in
another hall during the first days of the I.S.L. meetings. On one evening the I.S.L. Executive paid the
Grand Lodge a visit, and in speaking to the body, I
recalled the fact that I installed the officers of the
Grand Lodge of Ireland twenty years ago.

The members of the Executive stayed at the hotel
where the Scottish representatives and many of the
German brethren were quartered. The latter proved to
be very genial and companionable, and as for the Scotch
they took me to their hearts in their usual kindly
fashion. My good old name is always a passport among

our Scottish brethren. They regard me as one of their own and I am quite willing to be so regarded.

I left Ireland in company with Brother Malins and Brothers Jepson, Grand Secretary, and Hahnell, Grand Vice Templar of Germany, and I had the pleasure of accompanying our German friends on a visit to the home of Shakespeare at Stratford-on-Avon. Spending a few days in Birmingham, I was able to accompany a large number of the Birmingham Juvenile Templars and their adult friends, including the active and genial Bro. James J. Woods, P.G.C., the business manager of the Grand Lodge Publication House, on an outing to Bourneville. It was a beautiful afternoon and the little folks thoroughly enjoyed themselves as, I think, did their elders; at least I can speak for one of them.

A few days in Newcastle-on-Tyne followed and here I received many courtesies from Brother Guy Hayler, our new International Electoral Superintendent, and Brother Thomas King, the indefatigable District Chief Templar, concerning whom I shall have more to say later. In company with one or both of these brethren I visited three Temples and three Lodges. A few hours' journey on August 21st, took me to Glasgow, Scotland, where was held the first of a series of meetings which had been planned for me by Brother Honeyman, the able and genial Grand Secretary.[64]

I stayed in the hospitable home of Brother Rev. M. Bruce Meikleham, G.C.T., and was very glad of

---

64 For a contemporary account of the visit, August 21-27, 1905, see (Glasgow) Good Templar, Oct. 1905, p. 339.

the opportunity to become better acquainted with him
and his good wife, who is one of our Past Right Worthy
Vice Templars.   The meeting took the form of a
reception to me by the great Glasgow Lodge which has
over six hundred members, and it was one of the
greatest gatherings I ever saw in connection with the
Order.   The City Hall was filled to overflowing (it
holds about 4,000 persons, I believe), and a most
excellent musical programme was presented.   Brother
Walter Freer, the leading spirit of Glasgow Lodge,
presided in the most happy fashion and the G.L.
officers and other dignitaries kept me in countenance
on the platform.   It was a sight to gladden the eyes to
see such a company assembled under the auspices of a
temperance organization in a great busy city like
Glasgow.

The next day Brother and Sister Meikleham took me
to Rothesay Bay, a beautiful summer seaport upon the
Clyde, and we returned in time to go to Airdrie and
take tea in the home of Brother Hendry, who had invited
Brother and Sister [Elsie] Honeyman, Sister Jane
K. Ford, P.G.V.T., and some other members to meet us.
Airdrie is the town in which flourish the largest Lodge
and the largest Juvenile Lodge in the world.   Between
them they count a membership of over 3,000.   The work
of our Order in the town has been as greatly blessed as
it was badly needed.   During last year no fewer than
twenty-seven liquor saloons were closed through the
efforts of the Good Templars.   On the evening of my
visit the Juvenile Lodge held a session and I had the
pleasure (and it was a great one) of speaking to about
1,000 bright, lively lads and lasses.   Various educational efforts are carried on in connection with this

Juvenile Lodge. Among the most successful are the physical drills for boys, and I had much pleasure in witnessing an exhibition by some of the teams. In addition I was presented with three pictures, two of them showing the Physical Drill teams in their most effective poses and the third showing a group of the officers of the Lodge.

II

Another night was spent in Brother Meikleham's home and very sorry I was when the time came to say "good bye" to these kind friends. After leaving them I traveled to Dundee and was met by Sister Mrs. Peter McDonald, P.R.W.G.V.T. I was the guest of Brother and Sister McDonald some years ago when they were residing in Edinburgh and it was a pleasure to be again under their hospitable roof. I had only a few hours with them, but as many good things as possible were crowded into the time. Some friends were invited to meet at tea and others came to late supper after the meeting. The evening Conference was well attended and was a very enjoyable occasion to me and, I hope, not less to others. Among many other worthy members, I was glad to meet a former Chief Templar of Joseph Malins Lodge, Boston, in the person of Brother Simpson, who is now residing at Dundee.

On Thursday I went on to Aberdeen, the far-famed "Granite City," and my only regret regarding it was that I had not time to see much of it. But if I was unable to see the sights, I met a great many earnest and true brothers and sisters and the short time I spent with them was sufficient to prove that Good Templary is a very real serious business among the

Aberdonians. The members were nearly all strangers to
me, but I soon felt that I was among friends and the
kindly greeting I received will not soon be forgotten.
A fine juvenile meeting in the afternoon was followed
by a tea-party and conference in the evening. At the
former meeting I was given a beautiful bouquet by the
members of Grampian Juvenile Lodge. I was quartered
for the night in the home of another Brother and Sister
Macdonald and although there was a difference in the
spelling of the names of these and the Dundee friends,
there was none in the warmth of the welcome.

Friday found me at Elgin. This was my grandfather's birthplace and I felt a more than common interest
in the beautiful "Royal Burgh" because of this fact.
Sister Marjorie Edwards, a very bright and earnest
young lady, is one of the leaders of the Good Templar
work in this place. She accompanied me in a drive
which enabled me to see as much as possible of the town
and I found her a very interesting companion. The
latter part of the afternoon was given to a juvenile
gathering and later came a tea and public meeting over
which Rev. Brother Woodside, Grand Chaplain of Scotland, presided.

On Saturday I journeyed to Edinburgh over the
Highland Railway and saw more of the Scottish Highlands
than I had ever seen before. A beautiful sight were
those heather-covered hills. Noting the names of the
places through which we passed--many of them famous in
song and story--one could live over again the legends
of former days and I felt a thrill of pride in the fact
that I could claim kinship with a people whose national

characteristics include much of the strength and
stability of their native hills.

The bright sunshine which had crowned the mountains with glory in the early forenoon faded away as
the afternoon approached and when I reach Edinburgh the
rain was falling in a steady downpour. But I was soon
safely housed and kindly welcomed by Brother and Sister
Linkie and remained in their pleasant home until
Monday. The Saturday meeting--preceded by a tea in the
genial Scottish fashion--was fairly well-attended
considering the weather and on Sunday afternoon a
goodly number of the bairns, under the charge of Sister
Wiseman, D.S.J.W., greeted me. I met many friends,
including our excellent Brother Sutherland, with his
wife and daughter, Brother Herd, and others.

My visit to Bonnie Scotland was a rare treat and I
can only hope that I gave to those I met a tithe of the
pleasure and inspiration which I received.

But my pleasant experiences did not end when I
left Scotland. I had long looked forward to an
opportunity to visit the famous "Spring Blossom" Temple
of Newcastle-on-Tyne and August 28th had been fixed for
some weeks as the date of my visit. It was "Flower
Night" in the Temple and when I entered the hall, I
found it a perfect bower of beauty. There were
blossoms everywhere, all contributed by the members and
ranging from the tiny nosegay, which had perhaps been
gathered from a window garden, to the garlands, and
baskets, and large bouquets of wealthier donors. One
young lady, a former member of the Temple, had come
with her father all the way from Leeds, Yorkshire, to

bring her floral tribute. She, like many others, bore testimony to the love and respect felt for Brother [Thomas] King, the S.J.W., whose efforts and enthusiasm have made Spring Blossom Temple one of the most wonderful Juvenile organizations in the world.[65]

Brother King is a most devoted worker. He is the D.C.T. of his district and not a day passes but he visits either a Lodge or a Temple and usually it is both. He is of such frail physique that one fears he is overdoing, but it is easy to see that it would be impossible for him to cease, or even to lessen his labors.[66] Unlike many workers, Brother King manages to keep other people also to work and he has a staff of very loyal helpers. One of those best-known to me is Sister Mrs. Clarke, but there are many others worthy of mention.

The programme presented on the evening in question was a good one and the children acquitted themselves well. A particularly attractive feature was the tambourine drill presented by a company of little girls. Brother Guy Hayler, I.E.S., and myself were

---

65 Four members of Parliament had been members of this juvenile temple, including Thomas Burt and Arthur Henderson. "Notable Lodges, No. 2, The `Light-on-the-Hill,´ Newcastle-on-Tyne, England," International Good Templar, Jan. 1914, p. 9. Spring Blossom Temple was affiliated with Light-on-the-Hill Lodge. At the end of the nineteenth century the Temple had nearly 250 members, 85% of whom attended any particular meeting, and had an excellent choir. "`Spring Blossom´ Temple," United Temperance Gazette, Sept. 1899, pp. 108-11.

66 Despite his frail health, King, who had joined the Order in 1872, lived till 1934. International Good Templar, April 1934, pp. 35-36.

accorded a place on the programme and I was given a
souvenir of the occasion in the shape of a very pretty
album of photographs showing the children in some of
their exercises and on some of the numerous "rambles"
which keep them interested during the summer. I have
the plates of some of the pictures and shall hope to
publish them in future issues of the International Good
Templar.

From Newcastle I hurried to London, (for no visit
to Europe would be complete without a few days in the
dear old city of my birth), there to spend a few days
in quiet with an old friend before leaving for the continent to attend the great Anti-Alcohol Congress.

III

On September 6th, in company with Sister Charlotte
A. Gray and Brother Joseph Malins, Past International
Chief Templar, I started from London and travelled by
way of Holland and Belgium to Dresden to attend the
meetings of the German Temperance Federation. Brother
Malins has given an excellent account of the European
Congresses in the article which appears in this issue
[January, 1906] and it does not seem wise for me to
repeat the details.

But speaking from a personal standpoint, I wish to
say that I was amazed and delighted with the evidences
of the wonderful progress which the temperance movement
is making in Germany. The exhibition alone was worth
the journey to see and there were besides the largely
attended meetings, the intense interest noticeable in
the debates and the strong enthusiasm. To a Good
Templar it was delightful to recognize the fact that

our Order has played a large part in the great work
which is being carried on in Germany. Good Templars
were to the front in all the gatherings, our Brother
Hahnel especially, whose numerous gifts are given so
freely to the Cause, was indefatigable in his efforts
to make the congress the success ,it undoubtedly was.
The temperance movement in Germany is no mere child´s
play; it is a tremendous force which is advancing with
giant´s strides towards the end in view.

And second only to my satisfaction at the success
of Good Templary, was the pride which, as a woman, I
felt in the advancement of my sex in the Fatherland.
One has been accustomed to think of the German woman as
the model hausfrau, devoted to her home and her children and taking little interest in the movements outside
of the domestic circle. But perhaps the strong mother-
love has helped the women there as elsewhere to realize
that they must take a part in the fight against the
great foe of the family and the home. At any rate
they are rallying to the temperance standard in great
numbers and the remarkable meeting of the German
Woman´s Total Abstinence Society, under the leadership
of the veteran Miss Ottilia Hoffman[n] was something to
rejoice one´s heart. An audience made up of 2000
people, including many of the most eminent scientific
men of the country listened and applauded the always
thoughtful and often vigorous addresses delivered by a
number of ladies. Among the speakers were our Sister
Gray, and Sister Mrs. Helenius, of Finland.

The Good Templars were very much in evidence at
the excursion up the Elbe to the Saxon Switzerland

which took place the last day of the Congress. The
invitation was given by the District Lodge of Saxony
and numerous bannerettes bearing the names of local
Lodges and Juvenile Temples testified to the fact that
one was among a cordial people in whom a mere difference in language could not hinder the expression of
fraternal fellowship. The excursion was a delightful
one; the weather, the scenery and the companionship
making it a pleasant thing to remember.

Dresden was a particularly pleasant city to
sojourn in, clean and beautiful and interesting. Here
as elsewhere one could only take a brief time to see
something of the local features, including, of course,
the world-famous picture galleries.

The long journey to Vienna and thence to Budapest
was made in distinguished and agreeable company,
several of the German notables and those of other
countries who had attended the Congress being of the
party. We reached the Hungarian capital only just in
time for the first meetings and, as it was my fortune
to be the only one from America present for the first
four days until Brother Dinwiddie of Washington
arrived, I had to bear all the honors which were
bestowed in recognition of the United States as well as
those which were given to the representative of the
Juvenile work of the Good Templars. I need not say
that the attentions received were very gratifying and
that in responding in behalf of the "land of the stars
and stripes" I took care to mention what that land had
done for the temperance cause, not forgetting the fact
that it was the birth-place of Good Templary.

And this reminds me that the Good Templars of
Hungary, although not yet as numerous as we hope they
will be in the future, were conspicuous in the arrangements for the Congress. Brother Dr. Philip Stein was
chief in all the affairs which depended upon local
management and he was assisted by a staff of young
brothers who cared for the comfort and convenience of
those who attended the Congress in a most cordial and
kindly as well as a most business-like manner. I for
one was very favorably impressed with the Hungarian
people and can bear most grateful testimony to their
courtesy and hospitality.

Good Templars were also very much in evidence
among those who attended the Congress. Our International Chief Templar Brother Wavrinsky, with his
charming wife and daughter; the International Counsellor, Brother Prof. Jensen of Norway; the Past International Chief Templar Brother Malins; the Treasurer
Brother Blume, of Germany; Sister Charlotte A. Gray,
who received much recognition as one of the originators
of the Anti-Alcohol Congresses [in 1885 at Antwerp];
Brother Hahnel, Grand Electoral Superintendent, of
Germany; Brother Dr. Forel, of Switzerland, who was one
of the most distinguished men at the Congress; Sister
Mrs. Allie Trygg Helenius, of Finland; Brother E. C.
Dinwiddie of Washington, D.C., (who arrived in time for
the great banquet given on the evening of the fourth
day by the municipality of Budapest,) and many others.
Nearly all of those I have mentioned took part in the
proceedings; Brother Malins spoke in his usual convinc-
ing manner in opposition to the advocates of the
Gothenburg system [of non-commercial management of the
sale of alcohol drink for on-premises consumption] and

Brother Dinwiddie ably defended the local option laws of the United States against an attempt to prove them futile.

There were fourteen languages spoken at the Congress and, naturally it was not possible for one who only understands some French and a very little German, in addition to her own tongue, to keep up very closely with the numerous topics discussed. But it was interesting to observe the manners of the different speakers who represented nearly every country in Europe, some even coming from Siberia, and who were many of them men who ranked high in the world of science. It was most inspiring to realize that these men were giving an honest and serious consideration to a subject which they have come to recognize as a very important one in its relation to the well-being of the race. One must rejoice in the spread of temperance ideas in the old world and look forward to the time when those who come from Southern and Central Europe to make their homes in America, will be as well-trained to help us in our fight against the Drink as are so many of our brethren who come here from Scandinavia.

IV

Buda-Pesth is a most beautiful city and the weather during our stay there was ideal, bright and warm but not oppressive.[67] We were able to take our meals out of doors and a banquet tendered to the Congress by the temperance societies of the city was held in an open pavilion in a garden on the banks of the Danube. The American custom of serving water with

---

67 Forsyth spelled Budapest in several ways which have been left unedited

the meals was followed everywhere and it was a comfort
to be able to get all one desired of this most necessary beverage without being compelled to ask for it, or
taking the chance of being regarded as harmlessly
insane while drinking it.

Another custom which gladdened the heart of the
American member of our little party was the fact that
ice cream was served in generous portions, as in
America. One could believe that Richard Harding Davis
was not far wrong when he said that Buda-Pesth is the
most American city on the continent.

On account of the fact that I was representing the
United States as well as the Juvenile work of the Good
Templars, I had the honor to be included in the limited
list of invitations issued to members of the Congress
by the Royal Hungarian Minister of Education, M. de
Lukacs and the Baroness, his wife. This reception was
a most informal and delightful affair.[68] The host and
hostess were very cordial and kind, the Baroness
especially showed a lively interest in the United
States and both she and her husband expressed their
sympathy with our work for the children. M. de Lukacs
has done much to promote the teaching of temperance in
the public schools of his country and one could see
that the interest was genuine.

---

68   Among the people Forsyth met was the Hon. and
Very Rev. J. W. Leigh, Dean of Hereford, a leader in
the National Temperance League and the Church of
England Temperance Society, who "had a long talk with
me about America." Forsyth, "Incidents in a Good
Templar Life," Australian Temperance World, Sept. 1929.
Forsyth misreported the Dean's name as John Lee.

But the occasions already mentioned did not cover everything which was done to welcome the Congress. The chief social event was the great banquet tendered by the Municipality of Buda-Pest and this was one of the most magnificent functions I ever witnessed. The beautiful building magnificently lighted, the tables glittering with china and glass and silverware, the flowers, the music, the brilliant company of over 1000 guests, to say nothing of the list of dainties which made up the menu all combined to make the occasion a most delightful one.

I must not forget an event which gave some of us a much-prized opportunity of visiting in a real Hungarian home. Brother Professor Weixelgartner and his good wife entertained a few of us to dinner in his home in Buda, the older section of the city. Our brother's house is built on the side of a mountain, and after enjoying a most appetizing vegetarian repast composed of a large variety of delicate vegetables and choice fruits all grown in his own grounds, we were invited to take our coffee in the garden. We climbed a long flight of steps and when we reached the arbor in which our coffee was served we were able to look down upon the roof of the house. Our host and his wife are faithful members of our Order and we were glad to meet them and others in the Lodge sessions which were convened during our stay in Buda-pest.

We left this beautiful city with much regret on the Saturday evening and reached Vienna the same night. Sunday was passed quietly and our journey resumed at night through the Austrian Tyrol to Switzerland. The delay occasioned by a landslide somewhat interfered with our plans, but we were repaid for the annoyance by being able to spend a short time in In[n]sbruck, a most beautiful and interesting place.

A night and part of a day were spent in Zurich where we were reminded of the session of 1897 and of the entertainment provided for us by our Swiss brethren, many of whom we would have gladly met again had there been time to seek them out. But we had to hasten to Basle for the conference which Brother Malins desired to hold with our translator, printer and publisher. An afternoon was profitably spent in discussing the revisions of our rituals, etc. We had tea with Brother Rheinhart in his house overlooking the Rhine and later we shared the evening meal of our Brother Vockroth and his charming little wife in their pleasant home. At midnight we were on the way again and we made all possible haste to London.

The date when I must sail for home was rapidly approaching and the time for parting with my old London friends came all too soon. I reached Liverpool on the afternoon of September 23rd, in time for the meeting of the National Juvenile Templar Council but too late to attend the magnificent reception tendered to the Good Templars by the Mayor of Liverpool. However, I learned that this was a most delightful function and I noted that one of the local papers, published, no doubt, in the interests of the liquor traffic, said some very harsh things of the Lord Mayor because he had entertained a company of temperance people. It was pleasant to find, however, that the criticism did not prevent the Mayor from appearing on our platform on the Monday evening following when he spoke some strong words in behalf of the cause in which we were engaged.

The National Juvenile Council included a most interesting and enjoyable series of meetings. They began with a tea-party at which I renewed some old acquaintances and made some new ones. Then came a finely attended session of the Grand Lodge presided over by the G.C.T. Brother Malins. A crowded public meeting followed and here a beautiful bouquet testified to the warmth of welcome accorded to me. A similar tribute was given to Brother Hopkins, G.S.J.W., and the presentations were gracefully made by Miss May, the young daughter of Brother Walker, the Secretary of the Reception.

Sunday afternoon was devoted to a church parade and a service in St. Mary Magdeline's church at which Brother Malins read the lessons and the Vicar, Brother Rev. G. H. Lunn, preached a most excellent Good Templar sermon. In the evening a Gospel Temperance meeting was held in Wesley Hall, with Brother Malins for the speaker.

Monday was spent in transacting business for the Council and discussing plans for promoting the welfare of the Juvenile branch of the Order. Brother J. W. Hopkins, the popular and efficient head of the Juvenile work in England presided with much tact and ability and many of the members debated the various questions with keen interest. A ritual which had been prepared for the use of the Council by Brother Hopkins was adopted and it fell to my lot, by the courtesy of this same good Brother, to install the officers and so be the first one to use the new form.

Altogether I found the meetings of the Council most profitable and inspiring and was glad that I had extended my stay so as to be present with them. In addition to the pleasure which it gave me to observe the interest felt in the Juvenile work by so many of the adults, I appreciated the kindness and hospitality shown to me. When I sailed away next day on the "Saxonia" for Boston I carried with me many pleasant memories of the members and the work of the National Juvenile Council.

1907--SOME NOTES OF TRAVEL

[International Good Templar, December 1907]

I am intending to give my readers a little account of my European trip [in 1907] as I am sure they will be interested in what I saw of the work of the Order in the different countries I visited.

I sailed this time from Quebec on the great Canadian Pacific Line Steamer "Empress of Ireland"; Dr. [T. D.] Crothers, of Hartford, Connecticut, and Dr. [V. A.] Ellsworth, Superintendent of the Boston Washingtonian Home, the oldest institution in the world for the care of inebriates, were among my fellow passengers. These two gentlemen went over to attend the Anti-Alcohol Congress in Stockholm, they having been appointed by President Roosevelt to represent the United States Government at the Congress. Our

[<u>International Good Templar</u>] Associate Editor, Brother B. E. Hockert had also been appointed but was prevented from going by serious illness.

The voyage was pleasant and interesting from the fact that the steamer travelled a route which was new to me, going through the Straits of Belle Isle and passing the shores of Quebec, Nova Scotia, Cape Breton, Prince Edward Island, the Island of Anticosti, and Labrador. We made a quick passage and landed in Liverpool early in the forenoon of July 19th. Here we were met by Mrs. Walker, P.G.V.T. of England who showed us every courtesy and kindness. On the same evening Dr. Crothers and I attended a Lodge meeting, receiving a cordial welcome. Dr. Crothers gave a very instruc- tive talk on scientific lines which was listened to with marked attention and was much appreciated. On the next evening, Saturday, I attended another Lodge meeting in company with Sister Walker and her excellent husband and on Sunday I spent most of the day with these hospitable friends, attending the morning service in the Cathedral and the evening meeting in the great Charles Garrett Memorial Church.

On Monday I started for the Continent. On the way to Harwich I met Brother Joseph Malins, P.I.G.T. and Brother Guy Hayler, I.E.S. We crossed from Harwich to the Hook of Holland, giving a thought, as we landed on Tuesday morning to the terrible wreck which had occurred there a few months previously. Tuesday was spent in railroad travel through parts of Holland and Germany and we reached Flensburg, a beautiful city, situated in the Danish part of Germany, on Tuesday night. Here we were met by German brethren and conducted to our hotel.

The next day we attended a gathering of the Juvenile Templars in the hall of the fine Lodge building in Flensburg, which is owned by the Good Templars. This building contains, in addition to the lecture hall, three handsomely appointed rooms, ante-rooms, a cafe and a garden restaurant. The exterior was finely decorated in honor of the Good Templars, the appropriation having been made by the municipal authorities for the purpose. I need not dwell upon these matters, however, as they have already been referred to by Brother Hayler in the October [1907] issue [of the International Good Templar].

The Juvenile meeting was intensely interesting even to one who did not know the language. Brother Lund, the D.S.J.W., a most earnest worker, conducted an examination of the children and it was pleasing to note the readiness with which they answered the questions and the eagerness they showed. Later the excellent G.S.J.W., Brother J. Koopmann, who has done such good work for the children of Germany, addressed the children and the I.S.J.W. also made a little talk with the aid of an interpreter.

In the evening we attended a Lodge meeting, and a meeting of the new Youth´s Lodge. This is an organization for young people who, by reason of having to go to work, are unable to attend the Juvenile Lodge and who are below the age of seventeen, which they must reach before they can be admitted to the adult Lodge. It will be seen that the Good Templars of Germany are making provision for people of all ages in their work.

The annual session of the Grand Lodge of Germany is the rallying point for all the other temperance societies in the country and the week was filled with the meetings of the various bodies. Chief in interest to me were the meetings of the German Women´s Abstinence Union and I was glad to renew my acquaintance with Miss Ottilie Hoffman[n], the President; the Baroness Von Hausen, Miss Marie Stucker, Miss Julie Kassovitz, and others whom I had met on previous occasions.

Saturday evening was given up to a tremendous public meeting, held in the largest hall in the city, into which the people crowded until the police came in to forbid the admission of any more. Brother George Asmussen, P.G.C.T., was the principal speaker and his address dealt with the scientific side of the temperance question. A number of brief speeches followed, including a few words from myself to whom fell the honor of representing the International Supreme Lodge at this Grand Lodge, the two brothers, Malins and Hayler, having been obliged to leave for Stockholm the day before.

The Grand Lodge session was attended by about 1100 members. The degree was conferred on 450 candidates and later in the day, a special session of the International Supreme Lodge was convened and 94 persons admitted to membership in the Supreme body. The business of the Grand Lodge was quickly dispatched under the able leadership of Brother Blume, our International

258

Treasurer, who was again elected Grand Chief Templar.[69] During the noon recess about 1000 members paraded through the principal streets of the city to the music of a fine band. They presented a fine appearance and the banners of the various Lodges, carried in the procession, were very handsome. Germany now has about 30,000 adult and nearly 9000 juvenile members and it is probable that in the course of time the Grand Lodge will rival Sweden in numbers and influence.

The pleasure which it gave me to see this great Grand Lodge at work was purchased at the expense of the loss of the first three days at the Anti-Alcohol Congress in Stockholm. I missed the Royal Garden Party and some other of the social occasions. But I was in time for the special session of the International Supreme Lodge and for the great welcome meeting of the Grand Lodge of Sweden which followed it. This was a noteworthy gathering, presided over by Brother Oskar Eklund, G.C.T., and addressed by the representatives of a great many jurisdictions. Brother Malins, P.I.C.T., spoke for England; Brother Councillor Nielson, of Glasgow, G.E.S., for Scotland; Brother Lars O. Jensen, Int. Counselor, for Norway; Brother Blume, Int. Treas., for Germany; I represented the United States, and others, whom at this time I am unable to name, brought the greetings from several other countries. Our International Chief Templar, Brother Wavrinsky, was a prominent figure on this as on other occasions. The addresses were interspersed with the magnificent

---

69 Forsyth quarrelled with Blume at this meeting. See the memoirs of the Danish journalist and Templar, Lars Larsen-Ledet, <u>Mit Livs Karrusel</u> (10 vols., Copenhagen: Gyldendalske Boghandel, Nordisk Forlag, 1945-57) 9: 206.

singing which seems to be a matter of course in
Sweden. Our Brother Eklund had good reason to feel
happy, as he welcomed his guests in the name of the
190,000 Good Templars of Sweden. And I felt happy in
the thought that 52,000 of the great total are Juveniles. Sweden now has the largest Juvenile membership,
as well as the largest adult membership in the
world.[70] And this in a country with only about
5,000,000 population.

I shall not refer to the Congress, as Brother
Hayler has already given such a good account of it,
except just to mention that the attendance was very
large, about 1200 members being enrolled. Almost every
country in Europe was represented, most of them by
delegates officially appointed by their respective
governments. Then there were the representatives from
the learned societies, teachers, doctors, etc., as well
as those who came from temperance organizations. I
represented the Massachusetts Total Abstinence Society
and bore a credential signed by its president, Hon.
John D. Long, former Governor of Massachusetts and
former Secretary of the United States Navy.

---

70   In fact, England had the largest juvenile membership, as Forsyth´s states in her report in 1908 as
International Superintendent of Juvenile Work.

REPORT OF THE INTERNATIONAL SUPERINTENDENT
OF JUVENILE WORK

[International Supreme Lodge session held in Washington, DC, 1908, reported in International Good Templar, July 1908; omits details on individual Grand Lodges, particularly the small North American ones, provided in International Supreme Lodge, Proceedings (1908)]

I rejoice to be able to tell you of another large gain in our membership. The present statistics show a total of 239,586 members in 3,487 branches, as compared with 207,902 members in 3,045 branches reported in 1905. This is a net increase of 31,684 members and 439 branches.

It is proper, however, that I should call your attention to the fact that nearly the whole of this gain has been made on the Continent of Europe, chiefly in Scandinavia and Germany. And while we have good reason to congratulate these countries upon the triumphs achieved and to express our gratitude for the blessings which have attended their labors, it is necessary for us to face the fact that the numbers quoted do not indicate a universal prosperity.

* * * * *

THE NATIONAL GRAND LODGE

I am one of those possessing firm faith in the mission of this organization [the National Grand Lodge, organized in 1905] to uplift the Order in the United States from the discouraging conditions of the past few years. Already there are signs of improvement in some

261

of the jurisdictions, although it is too soon yet to look for much fruition from effort which must be scattered over so wide a territory. But the sessions of the body cannot have failed to send those who attended them back to their homes with renewed hope and enthusiasm. And the officers have, without exception, toiled most earnestly and unselfishly. I am glad to pay a tribute to the labors of Dr. Elsie R. Schmitz, N.G.S.J.W., who has labored amid much discouragement and with a fidelity which must surely, in time, awaken a response. Dr. Schmitz has issued leaflets, pledge cards, wall-sheets and numerous other helps for workers and has never wearied of making appeals to Grand Lodges by means of her active pen.

TO ACCOUNT FOR THE PRESENT SITUATION

The work in the United States has been for several years the most discouraging part of my report. This fact has been a matter of profound grief to me and I have hoped and prayed each year for a change. But, as I have mentioned on previous occasions, there are many extenuating circumstances to be considered. In the first place, the Juvenile work has never taken the prominent position, in many of the states, which it holds in the British Isles and in other parts of the world. That this fact may account, in a great measure, for the decline of the Order in the United States, I firmly believe. We have not been "growing Good Templars," and our boys and girls have come up without the love for the Order which has been inculcated in the young people of other countries.

A second consideration is that as soon as the Order has begun to decline, the Juvenile work has been

the first to be cut off from financial assistance and
the Grand Superintendents have been left to "make
bricks without straw."

In the third place, with a decreasing adult
membership there has been less material for good and
efficient superintendents. And where Lodges have given
up, it has been impossible, except in a very few
instances, to continue a Temple, and for this reason
alone, many useful Juvenile organizations have been
lost to the Order.

And in addition to all these difficulties there is
the tremendous extent of our country which is not
always understood by those who live in smaller and more
thickly settled jurisdictions. The size of the territory; the small and scattered population in some
states; the constant influx of people from other
countries; the occupations of the inhabitants in many
sections--farming, mining, logging, etc.--all render
the work of an Order such as ours difficult beyond the
understanding of people in the older civilizations.

And in the more settled portions of the country
there are the numerous and ever[-]increasing organizations to hinder our work. Many of these Juvenile
Societies are carried on in connection with the
churches and the pastors are not apt to look with favor
upon a work which may divert attention from their own.

Taking all these matters into consideration, it is
perhaps not surprising that the recovery of our Order
from its depressed condition should be slow, but I
believe it will come in time.

THE BRITISH ISLES

In the British Isles the Juvenile section is healthy and flourishing, each Grand Lodge giving much time and attention to the Juvenile department. The Channel Islands have 506 members in eight Temples; England 61,694 members in 866 Temples; Ireland 2,424 members in 54 Temples; Scotland 47,584 members and 491 branches; Wales (English) gives 5,251 members and 68 Temples and Wales (Welsh) report 23 Temples and 1691 members.

THE CONTINENT OF EUROPE

Here advancement has been made all over the field--Denmark has now 64 Juvenile Lodges with 3,907 members; Germany I [Danish-speaking] has made a start with Juvenile work and has one Juvenile Lodge with 55 members. Germany II reports 12,409 members in 229 branches. The new Grand Lodge of Hungary returns two Temples and 69 members. In Iceland 39 Temples are at work and report 2195 members. The little Grand Lodge of the Netherlands has eight Temples and 300 members to its credit. The figures from Norway are full of encouragement; they tell of 20,198 members and 297 Lodges. Roumania appears on our roll for the first time with one Temple and 25 members. The great Grand Lodge of Sweden will soon be the greatest in Juvenile work as it is in adult work. The latest returns show a membership of 52,433 in 720 Juvenile Lodges. Troubles in Switzerland have hindered the work but the Juvenile section is still represented although only by two Temples with a small membership.

AUSTRALASIA

The Grand Lodges under the Southern Cross tell of "something attempted, something done" on behalf of the young. New South Wales heads with 56 Temples and 2,420 members; New Zealand follows with 40 Temples and 1,510 members. Queensland reports 1020 members with twenty Temples; South Australia 80 members and two Temples; Tasmania 291 members in eight Temples; Victoria shows well, 49 Temples and 1503 members; Western Australia has 450 members in eight Temples.

ASIA

The Juvenile work in this vast continent labors under many difficulties. They have, however, five Temples and 136 members in Burmah; three Temples and 131 members in Ceylon; 33 Temples and 1,114 members in India; 18 Temples and 490 members in Madras; and one Temple with thirty members in Palestine.

AFRICA

Central South Africa has a goodly record of 2,302 members in 43 Temples; Eastern South Africa reports 1,073 members in 13 Temples; Natal has 503 members in eight Temples; Western South Africa is doing splendidly and now reports 28 Temples and 2,077 members. The Gold Coast has twenty Temples and 1,508 members, and Southern Nigeria retains its one Temple with an increased membership of 96.

A SENIOR JUVENILE LODGE IN GERMANY

I have approved the idea of such an organization [for working youths under age 17] and it was understood

that the Ritual for it would be prepared by Brother
Koopmann, G.S.J.W.

THE WORLD´S PRIZE BANNER

Offered by me during the previous term was won by
a Temple in Rochester, New York. I have decided that
the offer of such a prize has not been of much value,
and have, therefore not renewed it during the present
term.

THE INTERNATIONAL INSTITUTE

Of Juvenile Temple Workers has been almost crowded
out of existence at recent sessions of the I.S.L. A
meeting of the Institute was arranged in connection
with the session of the National Grand Lodge of the
United States, held in Boston, July, 1906. The session
was largely attended and full of interest. In the
course of it, I suggested that the Institute revert to
its original form of a National Institute, to meet each
year at the time and place of the National Grand Lodge
session. The suggestion was adopted and the change
effected. I hope and believe that it will be for the
advantage of the cause.

IN MEMORIAM

The roll of our honored dead is a long one and, as
usual, I offer my tribute to the memory of those who
were either personal friends, or known to me by reason
of their interest in, or labors for the Juvenile branch
of our Order. First in the list are the two Past
International Chief Templars, Dr. D. H. Mann and
Dr. Oronhyatekha, both of whom were very kind to me and
both of whom were in strong sympathy with the department I represent. Mrs. Margaret McKinnon of Scotland,

P.I.V.T. was another dear friend. Brother J. S. Vorley, P.G.S.J.W. of England; Mrs. Susan Isabel Cullen, P.G.S.J.W. of India; Mrs. Emily E. Cain, P.G.S.J.W. of Maine; W. V. Lambert, P.G.S.J.W. of Victoria; John Hylander, P.G.S.J.W. of Sweden, and Mrs. Esther R. Hockert, P.G.S.J.W. of Connecticut had all been active and successful leaders. Brother Daniel A. E. Ocran, Special Deputy I.S.J.W. for the Gold Coast was taken away suddenly from a work which he had toiled and sacrificed for. Sister Mrs. F. C. Stuart, one of the oldest members of the Order, was for many years a faithful worker for the children of Michigan. Brother G. H. Graham of England had rendered good service for many years by the publication of his <u>Temperance Worker and Wide Awake Reciter</u>. Brother Captain Thomas, the veteran Grand Treasurer of Wales; Brother Rev. D. C. Machellar, P.G.C.T. of Scotland; Brother John Sutherland, P.G.C.T. of Scotland; Brother F. W. Dimbleby, G.C. of England; Mrs. Haefner, P.G.V.T. of England, and Sisters Mrs. M. H. Thomas, and Mrs. H. R. Bailey of Massachusetts were all devoted Good Templars and friends of long standing.

"But life and death with God are one,
   Unchanged by seeming change, His care
   And love are round us here and there
   He breaks no thread His hand hath spun."

ACKNOWLEDGEMENTS

I have to acknowledge as heretofore the kindness of those with whom I have been associated upon the I.S.L. Executive Committee. Brother Wavrinsky, I.C.T., has been most kind and helpful and Brother Malins is always ready to assist or advise. Brother Parker,

International Secretary, has co-operated in the work to the best of his ability, and my relations with the whole Executive have been of a most harmonious character. Sister Mrs. M. B. O´Donnell, P.R.W.G.S.J.T., has given me many words of kindly encouragement, as have many other leaders in all parts of the world.

I feel that words are inadequate to express my sense of the splendid loyalty, self-sacrifice and zeal shown by the workers for the children in a large number of our jurisdictions. In many of them the results bear testimony to their devoted labors, but there are other places in which the fruition is small and in which the laborer fails of the inspiration given to the brother in the larger and more fertile field. I have much sympathy for these faithful ones and, whether the labor be productive or not, I am grateful to the willing toiler.

PERSONAL WORK

I have given prompt attention to the correspondence of my work, writing thousands of letters, as well as many papers for special meetings--including one for the Institute of Juvenile Workers--articles for newspapers, etc. I have also continued the work of editing the <u>International Good Templar</u>.

Before returning to America after the Belfast session [in 1905], I spent a few days in Scotland, attending a number of meetings; visited several Lodges and Temples in the North of England and, later, some in London; was present at the meetings of the German Temperance Federation in Dresden and at the great Anti-Alcohol Congress in Budapest, Hungary. Before leaving England I attended the session of the National Juvenile Council at Liverpool.

I crossed the Atlantic again last year to be present at the meeting of the I.S.L. Executive Committee in Stockholm and this gave me the opportunity of attending the Anti-Alcohol Congress which was held in that city last August [in 1907]. During this trip I was present at the session of the Grand Lodge of Germany and at the Grand Lodge of the Netherlands, and with Sister Gray I visited the Temple in Antwerp carried on by Sister Mrs. Esselbach and was at a little conference of Good Templars convened by Sister Gray with a view to securing a Lodge in Antwerp. I also went to several Lodges and Temples in England. On my own side of the Atlantic I have visited the jurisdictions of New Hampshire, Vermont, New Brunswick, Rhode Island, and New York, American and Scandinavian.

CONCLUDING WORDS

I was appointed to this office nearly fifteen years ago on the decease of my predecessor. The membership on the books at that time was 169,981 in 2,879 branches. The membership at the present time, compiled as carefully as possible, with no padded statistics, is 239,586 in 3,487 branches. And this advance has been made in spite of the constantly declining membership in America.

During my incumbency of the office, I have visited many of the jurisdictions in the United States, Canada and Europe, using in that manner the greater part of the financial appropriation made for my office. In saying this I am not unmindful of the fact that this appropriation has enabled me to have the pleasure and privilege of going to places which I could not otherwise have reached. I have issued several leaflets, etc., at my own expense and have used my pen constantly for the cause.

I have arranged at considerable personal expense for several successful sessions of the International Institute; prepared an exhibit in the shape of a beautiful little model of a Juvenile Temple, for the World's Fair at St. Louis; offered five World's Prize Banners (paying for three of them myself) which have gone to the jurisdictions of Scotland, Ireland, Wales, South Dakota and New York; have contributed to numerous enterprises, and have represented the Order in various places.

I have made many friends, whose regard I hope to retain throughout my life. It is possible that I may have slighted or offended some, but it has been unwittingly. I have met with much sympathy, kindness and hospitality, and I lay down the work with feelings of gratitude to all who have helped me in any way, and of thankfulness to our Heavenly Father who has so abundantly blessed the efforts put forth. May His blessings continue with the cause as long as such work shall be needed.

[Forsyth had not intended to stand for re-election at the International Supreme Lodge session in 1908. Scandinavian members, from European and American Grand Lodges, such as Oskar Eklund of Sweden, persuaded her to change her mind. On the first ballot she received

62 votes, while the head of the English Juvenile organization, the largest in the Order, J. W. Hopkins, received 58, and a third candidate got four votes; 63 votes had been needed for election. On the second ballot Forsyth got only 60 votes, while Hopkins received 64 and was elected. Forsyth´s defeat was part of a transfer of power between North America and Europe. It was not a generational change, as Hopkins was the same age as Forsyth. Women had occupied the international office for Juvenile Temples since 1874, when it was given a seat on the Executive.

At the same International session, B. F. Parker, for twenty-three years International Secretary, was defeated for re-election by Tom Honeyman, Grand Secretary of Scotland, on the first ballot by a vote of 64 to 59. Ironically in 1908 the International Supreme Lodge session was held in the United States, at Washington, DC. When the Secretaryship moved to Glasgow, so did the editorial offices of the Interna-tional Good Templar. Forsyth had been editor since the January 1901 number. She ended her service as editor with the December 1908 number.

Perhaps because she had planned to retire as International Superintendent of Juvenile Templar Work, Forsyth had been a candidate in April 1908 for the office of Grand Secretary of Massachusetts. In a rehearsal for the defeat in Washington, she had led on the first ballot with 143 of the 151 votes needed for election, but on the second and decisive ballot received only 134 votes.

During S. B. Chase's final illness in late 1908 and early 1909, Forsyth briefly had responsibility for the Course of Study, but she was not appointed Chancellor when he died. She was appointed to a few committees in the National Grand Lodge of the United States and contributed to its new paper, the <u>National Good Templar</u>. But she never again held high office in the International Supreme Lodge or in an American Grand Lodge. Suffering from poor health, she closed her printing business in Boston late in 1911 and emigrated to Western Australia, where her only relatives lived.]

INCIDENTS IN A GOOD TEMPLAR LIFE
A WONDERFUL JOURNEY

[<u>Australian Temperance World</u>, March 1929]

It has been my lot to make a good many wonderful journeys, but perhaps the most wonderful was nearly the last one--that which brought me from America to this vast and beautiful land of Australia at the close of 1911. Although personally a stranger, I was allied to Australia by the ties of kinship, the only relatives I possessed having settled in Western Australia many years before.

But ties of blood are sometimes not any dearer than those we form with true and faithful friends, and during my long residence in America I had formed many such. I scarcely realised what it would cost to leave them until on November 17 I was actually on the train for Chicago, which was to be the first stage of my journey. The little group which assembled at the platform at Boston to see me off (consisting of

Bro. Rev. James Yeames and members of his family, Brother Sereque and his wife, and others) all showed signs of grief at parting from an old friend, who managed to withhold her tears until the train had borne her out of sight of the waving handkerchiefs.

In about twenty-six hours the first thousand miles of the trip was accomplished, and at Chicago Bro. [J. Martin] Skinner was waiting to escort me to the Washingtonian Home, the great institution for the care and cure of inebriates, which happily, [because of National Prohibition] has now ceased to be the necessary institution it was at that time. Here I had tea and spent the interval before starting on the next stage of the journey. The same good brother saw me safely on the train, and another fifteen hours found me in St. Paul, the fine capital of Minnesota. And there, to my joy, I found Bro. G. H. Hazzard, Sis. [Lizzie P.] Cole (who is now Mrs. Hazzard) and Etta Schmidt, Good Templar friends who rode with me to the next stop, Minneapolis, the twin city.[71] The cheery and affectionate company of these dear friends formed a delightful prelude to the dreary journey across snow-covered plains, which ended when I arrived in Seattle three days later. Here I was met by Hon. George F. Cotterill, our Int. Coun., and taken by him to his beautiful home, where I spent five comfortable and happy days with him and his pretty wife, with whom I had formed a strong friendship when we had met at several I.S.L. sessions.

---

71   Forsyth had to turn down an invitation to stop over in St. Paul. Jessie Forsyth to George H. Hazzard, Nov. 1, 1911. A.H.431, Hazzard (George Henry) papers, Minnesota Historical Society.

I visited Baltic Lodge (Scandinavian) in its fine building, enjoyed meeting a number of friends at a reception tendered by Bro. and Sis. Cotterill, dined with Sis. [Emily M.] Peters, G.W.J.W., had an auto ride to view the city with Bro. [John R.] Bowdish, and left by steamer early on the 27th in company with my kind host and hostess. The steamer took us to Victoria, the beautiful capital of British Columbia, where we were met by Bros. Rev. C. M. Tate and Rev. Thomas Gladstone. We were taken about the city by Miss Spencer in her auto, and taken to her home to afternoon tea and evening dinner, where we were waited upon by Chinese servants in evening dress. Later we were driven to a splendid meeting of adult and juvenile Templars, who expressed their goodwill to me in a bouquet of choice flowers and a book of views of beautiful Victoria. A night´s sail by steamer brought us to Vancouver and here a group of members met us and took us to a hotel. After breakfast the Mayor of Vancouver took us in his auto about the wonderful city and surroundings of Vancouver. In the afternoon a company of women assembled to listen to me, and in the evening Vancouver District Lodge got out a large gathering of members and friends to hear Bro. Cotterill and me talk on the Order and its work. The next morning, November 29, a number of Good Templars came to the wharf to see me on board the S.S. Marama, bound for Sydney.

The next four weeks, although full of interest to a traveller, yet contained nothing interesting to me as a Good Templar. I was charmed, as everyone must be, with Honolulu, and equally so with Suva [in the Fiji Islands] and its wonderful people. And the few hours

spent in Auckland made me wish that I could spare time
to meet some of the New Zealand Good Templars. We
arrived in Sydney on Christmas Day. I had written to
Bro. [G. D.] Clark notifying him of my coming, but I
hardly expected that anyone would leave their homes to
meet me on such a day, so when the steward called my
name and I went ashore I was agreeably surprised to
find Bro. and Sis. Clark, Sis. Marion Hall, Bro. Sherar
and Bro. Hampton awaiting to give me a hearty welcome.
But I learned that New South Wales Good Templars were
not behind those of other parts of the world in
remembering to "entertain strangers."

I spent nearly a fortnight in Sydney. It was
filled with all manner of delightful experiences,
visits to the Blue Mountains, the famous beaches, a
trip down the harbor, which I had always heard of as
"the most beautiful in the world," besides visits to
Lodges and Juvenile Temples, etc. And besides these
there were a number of private entertainments, dinners
and teas in the homes of various members, including a
day at the home of Bro. N. T. Collins and his wife. I
cannot remember the names of all the dear friends whose
generous hospitality I shared, but I do not forget
their kindness. And I remember that my first Communion
service in Australia was partaken of in the Church at
Redfern, at which Bro. the Ven. Archdeacon [Francis B.]
Boyce, whom I had met in America, was the rector. And
chief among these pleasant memories are the days spent
in the home of the late dear Sis. Hall, whom I had
learned to love for her work's sake during the years
she held my commission as G.S.J.W. My happy days in
Sydney came to an end, and I sailed for the West on the
Kanowna on January 6 and arrived in Melbourne on the

8th. [I] was met by Mrs. Martin who took me to her home to tea. Our late Bro. Martin and his family were all earnest Good Templars, and for a long time their Lodge and Temple held their meetings in a pleasant hall provided by Bro. Martin on premises connected with his own house. In Melbourne I attended a good Lodge meeting, and I met Bro. Berglund and others, whose names I do not remember. But everyone greeted me very kindly.

The stay in Adelaide was too short to enable me to look up members of the Order, and I was only able to obtain a passing glimpse of a beautiful city.

January 18 [1912] brought me to Fremantle, exactly two months and one day from the time I left Boston. Here I met and was warmly welcomed by all my relatives, most of whom I had never seen. But among them were my dear sister and her good husband, whom she had met in the London Good Templar Lodge. My brother-in-law, Thomas Smith, was a staunch Good Templar. He had successfully filled the office of G.C.T. in Western Australia as well as Mayor of Fremantle. Very much to my regret he departed this life soon after my arrival.

This little story of my journey from America to Australia is written to show that it is a good thing to travel as a Good Templar and to show how wonderfully the spirit of the Order prevails among its members in every part of the world.

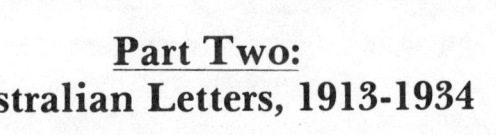

Part Two:
Australian Letters, 1913-1934

I have just received, through the kindness of Brother Sereque, a copy of the <u>Proceedings</u> of the Ninth Annual Session of the National Grand Lodge of the United States which must have been issued in a surprisingly short time after the session. I have read it with much interest and congratulate the members upon what must have been a very successful session.

But the part that most appeals to me is the report of the Obituary Committee, and looking over the list of departed members, I am impressed with the fact that it includes the names of several with whom I have been intimately associated in past years. Chief among these is, of course, our dear veteran sister, L. C. Partington. It was my privilege to know Sister Partington very intimately for many years and like all who knew her well, I honored her for her steadfastness and her unflinching courage. She always had the courage of her convictions and was never afraid to say what she thought, even when by doing so, she endangered her popularity.

Only a few months before Sister Partington died, she wrote me a long letter. It was soon after she had learned that it would be necessary for her to undergo an operation for cataract. She was naturally feeling anxious about the result, but her cheery courage had not deserted her. She spoke of her "pleasant memories of happy yesterdays and hopes of still happier tomorrows" and ended her letter with the following verse:

> "To walk by faith and not by sight
> Makes me secure.
> 'Tis sweet while on the Heavenward way,
> To hold His hand, to hear Him say
> `My help is sure.'"

Another old friend, although much younger in years, was Sister Mrs. Belle Odenatt Jones, who as G.S.J.W. of Pennsylvania, worked under my commission for several years. The last letter I received from this true and loyal sister was written soon after the death of her husband and I was able to realize from it how great was the bereavement she had sustained. But the Christian courage which had enabled her to do such good service for the cause, upheld her in her grief and loneliness. Knowing how devoted she was to her husband, her friends must rejoice that she was so soon called to join him.

Sister Mrs. Emma F. Bishop was another untiring worker for the children with whom I came frequently into touch. Surely her influence must indeed be far-reaching as the boys and girls who were trained in her wonderful Temple, have taken up their duties in the world.

Rev. C. H. Mead I knew well and greatly admired and honored. Brother Dexter, Brother Campbell, Brother Munsell, Sister Mrs. Doe and others I counted among my many friends. Rev. John Russell [who had headed the Order, 1871-73] I never had the privilege of meeting, but his name has ever been an honored one to me.

Since I left Boston [in November 1911], nearly every mail has brought me news of the passing of some old associate. The last which told me of the death of Sister Jefferson was quite a shock and most unexpected. But while the tidings in each case, caused a pang of regret and sympathy for the dear ones left behind, one must not forget to thank God for the noble lives and work of those who have gone before. Those who have grown old in the work must look forward to soon receiving the call to lay down their arms. But the younger ones must take fresh courage from the example which these departed ones have set and "highly resolve that these dead shall not have lived in vain."

FORSYTH TO GEORGE H. HAZZARD, FEBRUARY 25, 1915

[A.H431, Hazzard (George Henry) papers, Minnesota Historical Society, Archives/Manuscripts Division.]

I feel that I owe you a hundred apologies for my delay in replying to several kind letters of yours.[1]

---

1   Hazzard commented elsewhere that "Sister Forsyth is six or seven weeks to the west." They were regular correspondents. G. H. Hazzard, "Memories, Records, Suggestions," International Good Templar, Feb. 1915,

But I know you will give me credit for the fact that the delay has not been caused by indifference but by the numerous demands upon my time. I get a tremendous number of letters, for old friends do not forget me, but I never seem able to answer them as promptly as I should. So you must please forgive me and believe that I never forget my Minnesota friends and am always grateful for a line from any of them.

I was very sorry to hear of your wife´s illness and trust she is well again by this time. I am glad that Lizzie [P. Cole, later Hazzard´s second wife] and Etta [Schmidt] are together and hope they are keeping well and that Etta is doing well in her store. You say that while we have many acquaintances we have very few that we can reckon as true and tried friends. But I have been blessed with many kind and true friends, almost beyond my deserving, I sometimes think, although I try to do my part towards them. Thank you all very much for the Christmas cards recently received with their messages of cheer and of remembrance.

People are very good to me here. The ladies of the W.C.T.U. (of which I am still State President, in my second year) are exceedingly kind and loyal and I enjoy working with them very much, although nothing will ever take the place of the I.O.G.T. in my heart. We have a very good little Lodge now at the Sailors Rest. It is called "Sailors Rest" Lodge and I think it is doing very good work. I am D.I.C.T. [Deputy International Chief Templar] for Western Australia and could have been elected G.C.T. at the last G.L. ses-

---

p. 35. Hazzard died at age 83 in 1929.

sion, if I had not declined. I could not do justice to two organizations and I think I can do the best work in connection with the W.C.T.U.

I am afraid that this terrible war will make a great difference to the Order and it will take a long time to restore its International character again. How thankful we shall all be when the conflict is ended. I understand that the next I.S.L. session will be held in Minneapolis. I should like very much to attend it, but fear that it is hardly probable that I shall.

Besides working a little in the IOGT and more in the WCTU, I am a member of the Executive of the West Australian Alliance.[2] This organization is composed of representatives from Temperance organizations, Churches, etc. and it is supposed to look after the political work of temperance. Just now we are making an effort to secure a reduction of the hours of sale and I hope we may succeed even if only in a slight degree. They have done considerable in that line in England, more in France and the action of Russia in prohibiting the sale of vodka has astonished the whole world.

I think you will like to see the last report of the WCTU so I am sending you a copy. You may like to read the address of the President and also the report of the Sailors Rest.

I think I may have written to you since I made my two little trips last June in the interests of the

---

2   In these instances Forsyth wrote the IOGT and WCTU, not I.O.G.T. and W.C.T.U.

W.C.T.U. I travelled fifteen hundred miles, all in one
State, and made about fifteen addresses. My experiences in America and my knowledge of the working of
Local Option and Prohibition come in very useful
here. Of course, the newspapers are against the
temperance movement, as they are in many places and
they try to discredit the stories about the work in the
United States, so I am glad to be able to prove them in
the wrong. The editor of a newspaper in Albany, a
small port on our South-West coast and a very beautiful
place, asked for an interview with me and asked me
whether I could vouch for the statements I had made
regarding the results of prohibition in Kansas. I
replied "I am simply quoting the exact words of the
Attorney General of Kansas." At this the editor agreed
to publish my address and did so. His paper goes all
over that part of our big State, among the farming
population and I hope that my statements will do good.

Our rains have begun very early this year. Last
night we had some of the heaviest rain I ever saw, and
the wind blew great guns.[3] But this morning we have a
lovely clear sky and brilliant sunshine. Our bad
weather never lasts long.

The war has caused a great deal of excitement here
and we have all manners of funds started. It is really
wonderful what amounts of money such a small population
can raise. But Australians are very generous and, as a
rule, everyone has something to spare. The pressure of
real poverty has never touched our people yet although

---

3   Printing errors, and in this case obvious mental
slips, have been silently corrected. (Forsyth typed
"blue" for "blew.")

they are complaining now of hard times because some
have experienced a cut-down in wages, or are on short
time. They do not know what it is to be for weeks out
of work, with the thermometer down below zero. They
need to spend very little here for warm clothing or for
heat in their houses and those are about the heaviest
items in American housekeeping. Meat has gone up in
price here but we can get splendid roasting beef for
eighteen cents a pound and although bread is three
cents dearer than it was, it is only now the price it
was in Boston and is much better bread.

I trust that the war will soon end and things
become normal again and I am sure you will echo that
wish. I close with best regards to you and all friends
and best wishes for all.

FORSYTH TO GEORGE H. HIGBIE, OCT. 7, 1915, NEW YORK TEMPLAR, DEC. 1915

I wonder whether you would like to publish the
enclosed which is a portion of my report to the annual
Convention of the W.C.T.U. of Western Australia, in
which organization I am serving my third year as State
President. You will note that I give Good Templary
credit for its good work in the direction of the
advancement of the cause of woman.

I am very grateful for the New York Templar and
find it exceedingly interesting. It gives me pleasure
to read of old friends.

We have a very excellent Good Templars´ Lodge at the Sailors Rest here. I enclose copy of its quarterly program.

[The presidential address appears in the section, "Representative Writings."]

FORSYTH TO LAURA D. RUDY, <u>NEW YORK TEMPLAR</u>, JUNE 1916

You will be surprised to hear that I have left the Sailors´ Rest. The work of the Institution was always very trying, but since the outbreak of the war there has been the additional worry of devising new methods of raising funds for the work, as all the old sources of revenue failed, or nearly so. People here are very generous, but they have been so heavily taxed with the various funds, Belgian Relief, Serbian Relief, Red Cross, etc., that all the local institutions have suffered. This extra worry wore me out. I had several little bouts of illness and, finally my relatives insisted upon my sending in my resignation. My nieces organized a very fine fete for the benefit of the Rest last November and it was so successful that I was able to pay everything up and leave a fair balance in hand for my successor. I was fortunate enough to secure Lady Barron, the wife of the Governor of Western Australia, to open the fete. I had met her on several previous occasions and she agreed to come immediately upon my request. She was so nice and pleasant, really jolly, and she was very generous in patronizing the stalls. People tell me that this was the finest affair ever held in connection with the Sailors´ Rest, but my nieces know a great many people and they went into the affair with great enthusiasm.

At present I am staying with my sister, but in the course of a month I am intending to move out to Palmyra, a beautiful suburb of Fremantle, and start a little drygoods business. I could not endure to be idle and think I shall like this. A nice store and house is being built for me and my brother's widow is coming to keep house for me. I have bought new furniture for my rooms and think I shall be very comfortable.

Although we are so far from the scene of the war we see a good deal of its effects. You will have heard what a very heavy toll has been taken of our Australian youth, but we feel very proud of our boys and of their readiness to go to the help of their country, as well as of their achievements. But it is sad to see those who went forth in the glory and pride of their young manhood coming back crippled and maimed and to know that many will never come back. There is hardly a family in Fremantle which has not lost some relative. We have very few males in our family and no single young men. But my niece's husband has several relatives at the front and one nephew of his was killed in the first charge at the Dardanelles. It is all very sad and it is difficult to believe that some good purpose is behind it all, but we must believe that. If we refuse to believe that we must doubt the wisdom and goodness of God. And, after all, there is much to be thankful for and proud of; the noble sacrifices, the heroic deaths and all the other glorious things which make one feel that there is much that is noble still in our poor, weak, human nature.

FORSYTH TO CORA R. COTTERILL, MARCH 17, 1917

[Box 26, Folder 9, George F. Cotterill papers, University of Washington Libraries]

I think you and your husband will be surprised to hear that I am now living in Melbourne, nearly 2000 miles nearer to you and the same distance away from my dear ones in Fremantle. I will tell you how it happens:--This [Australian National Prohibition] League was organized on January 31st and a wire was sent to me on that day to ask me whether I would accept the position of Secretary, if elected. I did not suppose there would be much chance of being elected but I wired back to say that I would accept and on what terms. Two days later I was notified by wire of my election and as soon as possible I started for Melbourne to assume my duties. The voyage by Steamer took just a week from Fremantle to Melbourne and I arrived here on the 3rd instant. So I am in active work again for the temperance cause. It seems that even when I am put "on the shelf" I cannot stay there and now I hope to "die in harness."

Under another cover, I am sending Brother Cotterill some of our literature.[4] We are planning big

---

4   George F. Cotterill served the Good Templars as International Counsellor, 1899-1902 and 1908-30, and as National Chief Templar, 1905-13. An English-born engineer, he was mayor of Seattle, 1912-14, and active

things and hope to enroll the prohibitionists of all
Australia. I daresay Brother Cotterill will remember
Bro. [W. F.] Finlayson who represented Queensland at
the Des Moines session [in 1893]. He has been for
several years a representative to the Commonwealth
Parliament and he has always been a very strong and
unswerving advocate of all temperance measures. This
Prohibition League is the realization of a plan he has
cherished for years.

I was very much surprised at having the offer of
the Secretaryship and it is due to my regard in Good
Templary chiefly that it came to me. And the members
of the League seem to think themselves very fortunate
in securing my services, while Bro. Finlayson appears
to think I am equal to anything. Everyone is very kind
to one here and I feel encouraged to do my very best.

They arranged a fine farewell meeting to [for] me
in Fremantle at which all the temperance organizations
were represented. The local W.C.T.U. gave me a
handsome album and the Sailors Rest Lodge of Good
Templars, which I founded, gave me a beautiful gold hat
pin with the letters "I.O.G.T." engraved upon it. The
next evening the Woman´s National Movement, at a large
gathering, presented me with a lovely bouquet of roses.
On my arriving in Melbourne there was a big reception
arranged in the Temperance Hall. My people did not
much like my coming away but they realized that I was
not really in my element trying to "keep store" in
Palmyra and shut out from all temperance activities,
although I tried to make the best of things and not

---

in Democratic politics. He died in 1958 at 92.

grumble. So when this opportunity came they all turned
to and helped to get me off and I came away in style
laden with fruit, candy, flowers, books and magazines
enough to last me for a trip to America.

We have a very nice office which is my sanctuary
and I am beginning now to get the work in hand. Mr.
Finlayson is kindness itself and so wise and strong.
When I first started other members of the Executive
Committee overwhelmed me with advice and suggestions,
all kindly meant, of course. I told Mr. Finlayson that
while the "good book" says "in a multitude of counsel-
lors there is wisdom," there is also confusion. His
reply was "Well, you just listen to all they say and
then do as you please. I'll trust you." So, I have a
free hand but shall take care to be guided by Mr.
Finlayson's knowledge and experience just the same.

Well, dear Cora, how are you and your husband and
all the family? I should be glad of a line or so when
you can find time to write. Meanwhile, with love and
every good wish, I am [signed]

FORSYTH TO LAURA D. RUDY, <u>NEW YORK TEMPLAR</u>, DEC. 1917

The executive of our National Prohibition League,
at least those who are near enough to Melbourne to
attend its meetings, are all men. One who is very
congenial is our president W. F. Finlayson. Were you
at the Des Moines session of the I.S.L. in 1893? If so
you will perhaps remember the two splendid brothers who
represented Queensland. Mr. Finlayson was one of these
and for several years he has represented Brisbane,

Queensland, in the Federal Parliament, and has been the best fighter for all temperance measures that we have ever had. He is a true Good Templar, a very clever speaker, and a ready debater. He is also kind-hearted and appreciative, which makes my work as secretary a pleasure.

FORSYTH TO WILLARD O. WYLIE, <u>NEW YORK TEMPLAR</u>, ### APRIL 1918

I have recently had the news of the passing of a brother who was for many years identified with the Good Templar Order in New Hampshire. I refer to Mr. Roswell H. Hassam, a former Grand Secretary, who, although physically disabled from taking active part in the work of late years, never lost his love for the Order and never failed to render financial assistance to the cause of temperance and Prohibition.

It was my good fortune to have an intimate acquaintance with Brother Hassam for several years before I left America. On my frequent visits to Manchester I was always a guest in his home and I have grateful recollections of the many kindnesses received from him. It was always a great pleasure to talk to Brother Hassam about the Order and to note his keen interest in all that related to it.

Some old members may recall the fact that Brother Hassam was exceedingly methodical in his secretarial work and it is probable that his book for the use of Financial Secretaries which he originated and had printed, is still in use in some Lodges. The Record of Membership which he delighted in preparing for Stark

Lodge, Manchester, was unique in the fact that it showed at a glance the status in the Order of every one of the numerous members on the roll. I am only able to mention a very few of the helpful deeds of Brother Hassam but no doubt other old members may recall other kindly and generous things for which his memory deserves to be honored.

Another member who recently died in New Hampshire was also an old friend of mine. This was Miss Florence Cram, a P.C.V.T. and P.G.S.J.T. Sister Cram represented her Grand Lodge, in company with Sister Rachel Reid at the Edinburgh session of the I.S.L. in 1891, and again in 1897, with the late Miss Eliza Westover, at Zurich, Switzerland. She was an exceedingly able and faithful member both in Grand Lodge and in I.S.L.

Sisters Cram and Westover, with the late Sister Mrs. Bailey, P.R.W.G.V.T., Mrs. Ruslow, P.G.V.T. and her sister Mrs. Wilson formed a group of congenial friends whose company always helped to make my visits to New Hampshire enjoyable. Sister Bailey and I became acquainted through serving as members of the historic Boston Conference on Union, in 1886. At that time we were each filling the office of R.W.G.V.T. in our respective R.W.G. Lodges, but it fell to my lot to receive the honor of election to that office in the united body at Saratoga the following year. Sister Mrs. Ruslow was my companion on the trip to Stockholm in 1902 when she represented her Grand Lodge at the I.S.L. session. After the meetings in Stockholm we together attended the Grand Lodge of Germany at Kiel, where Sister Ruslow acted as International Deputy Marshal during the installation.

It will not hurt our younger members to be
reminded sometimes of the work of those who have passed
away, or who have reached the point where they are
unable to render further service. They played a noble
part in carrying on the Order in the past. The strong
sentiment in the United States in favor of total
Prohibition today is largely due to the steadfast
example of those who advocated it when it was by no
means as easy or as popular a purpose to work for as it
is today.

In addition to these New Hampshire friends, I have
noted with sorrow the passing of several Massachusetts
Veterans, among them Bros. George E. Bowen and
A.P. Wilson. And I would especial mention a sister who
was for many years one of my kindest and most intimate
friends, Mrs. Mary Mountford of Lowell, Mass. For
upwards of thirty years Mount Zion Lodge of Lowell was
one of the best Lodges in Massachusetts and the Mountford family were notable figures in that Lodge and in
the Grand Lodge [and] the Mountford home always had a
ready welcome for members of the Order. Now Mr. and
Mrs. Mountford, who were conspicuous among the original
founders of the Lodge, have passed on to their reward,
but I hope and believe that the members of their family
are still Good Templars. It will be remembered that
Sister Mrs. Bessie (Mountford) Santesson, who had
filled several offices in District or Grand Lodge in
Massachusetts, removed to Australia with her husband
and son between three and four years ago. They are all
members of the Sailors Rest Lodge of Fremantle and
Mrs. Santesson has been prominently identified with the

I.O.G.T. and the W.C.T.U. ever since she settled in
Western Australia.

FORSYTH TO LAURA D. RUDY, <u>NEW YORK TEMPLAR</u>, MARCH 1919

[Response to news about Sister Annie Weichmann of
Philadelphia:] What a wonderful woman Sister Weichmann
is.[5] Indeed it is fine to hear of the splendid work
that is being done by Quaker City Lodge. While our
beloved Order has fallen numerically there is much to
be admired in what is being done throughout the world.
I am told and I believe there is good reason for the
statement that a larger proportion of Good Templars
have enlisted [sic] for the war in Australia than any
other organization. One-third of the whole membership
in Western Australia and Victoria have gone to the
front and many have made the supreme sacrifice. A
lodge in Midland Junction (a few miles from Perth) had
25 brothers on its roll and of this number 23 enlisted. A lodge I belong to in Melbourne had hardly a
brother left and the work was carried on by the
sisters. Several Good Templars have won their medals
or other decorations for valor and the first Victoria
Cross to the credit of Western Australia was worn by
Victor Throssell of Northam, whose father, now deceased, was a former G.C.T. of Western Australia.

I spent a year and a half very happily in Melbourne, busy all the time with the work of the Australian National Prohibition League. During July a great
movement was started called the Strength of Empire
[analogous to the Strength of Britain movement in the

---

5   Annie Weichman died aged 85 in 1920.

United Kingdom], which having for its purpose War-Time
Prohibition, instead of permanent prohibition, was more
acceptable to many people, including the churches. It
absorbed a good many of the societies and a majority of
our members felt that it would be wise for us to unite
with it. The idea was adopted, and our League as an
independent organization, came to an end. Personally I
was very sorry and I think still that we made a mistake. But the majority ruled, as was right, of course,
and our membership, which had grown to considerable
proportions, was transferred to the Strength of Empire
movement. I was offered a position with the new
movement but I had planned to have a vacation and go
over to the West with the delegates to the W.C.T.U.-
Australasian Convention, and now my relatives do not
wish me to return. They say Melbourne is too far away,
so for the present, I am located in Fremantle again.

There were ninety ladies from the other States who
travelled to Western Australia to attend the Convention. We filled the train and were a very happy and
harmonious party during the three and a half days'
journey. You may remember that I attended the Australasian Convention three years ago when it met in
Adelaide, South Australia. On that occasion I invited
the convention to hold its next session in Perth and
the vote was carried. Some of the ladies objected to
coming so far; the convention had never been held in
W.A. and members in the other States doubted whether
proper accommodation could be found. They seemed to
think that we were very much behind in most matters,
but instead, they found that we were quite up-to-date.
The convention was the largest and the best which has
ever been held. The State Government took the ladies

by train to Mundaring Weir to see the great Goldfields
Water Scheme and treated them to afternoon tea, the
city gave them an official reception in the Perth Town
Hall, with the mayor presiding, and with flowers, music
and refreshments in abundance, and various other
smaller functions were held, showing that W.A. knew how
to do the proper things. And the weather was simply
ideal; bright sunshine, blue skies, gorgeous sunsets,
etc. The wild flowers were growing in great profusion
everywhere and the visitors were charmed with their
beauty and luxuriance. It is claimed that Western
Australia has the largest and most varied natural
flowers of any place in the world. Some naturalists
have claimed that there are 2,000 varieties of wild
flowers to be found, and when one sees them growing and
notes a different kind at every step, one can well
believe the statement.

Unfortunately, I was out of the enjoyment of most
of the convention for almost immediately upon my
arrival in Fremantle [I contracted] Grippe. It was
fortunate that I was at home and able to have the good
care given me by my sister and nieces. And I am
alright again now. At the few functions I did attend,
I was given due honor as the one who secured the
holding of the convention in Perth and I had the
pleasure of meeting several good friends.

FORSYTH TO WILLARD O. WYLIE, <u>NEW YORK TEMPLAR</u>, SEPT. 1921

I have managed by taking things as easily as
possible and resting a good deal to keep things going

at the office, but have not yet attempted anything
else. I am very much better but still ache a good
deal. Although I am mercifully relieved of that awful
pain in my head I have frequent spells of facial
neuralgia, but these I think are passing off by
degrees. I was about as sick as I could be. They had
a consultation of doctors and for several days I was on
the danger list. I quite thought my time had come, but
I suppose there is still something for me to do. I
have grown thin and do not weigh a hundred pounds. I
do not mind losing the flesh, but I would rather have
it than to have what it has cost me to lose it.

I am not able to walk properly yet and can go only
very slowly but I have reason to be thankful that I am
as well as I am.

FORSYTH TO THE MEMBERS OF THE WOMAN´S CHRISTIAN TEMPERANCE UNION OF WESTERN AUSTRALIA, [JANUARY 1922]

[<u>West Australian White Ribbon</u>, Feb. 1922; the letter
was accepted by the Executive of the WCTU of Western
Australia at its January 10, 1922 meeting.]

Dear Sisters,--
    For the little more than two years I have filled
the office of Corresponding Secretary to your State
Executive, I have tried to do all that was possible for
the advancement of our work and of the Temperance
cause. But during the last few months the weakness
consequent upon my severe illness has rendered it
difficult to keep up with the duties, although I think
my efforts have prevented any lapse or failure in them.

But my strength has not returned, and I have at last decided that it will be the part of wisdom to resign the office. That I do this with extreme regret I need hardly say. I have become attached to our workers, both among the adult and juvenile branches, and it is hard to bid them farewell. My life has been filled with active work for the Temperance movement; it will be difficult for me to reconcile myself to inactivity. But if health permits I may still find something to do for the cause.

In bidding my friends good-bye I wish to thank them for all their kind words and many helpful deeds. I wish for members and branches God-speed in all their endeavours. That His blessings "without which we labour in vain," may be yours in richest measure is the prayer of--

Yours in White Ribbon bonds.

FORSYTH TO WILLARD O. WYLIE, <u>NEW YORK TEMPLAR</u>, JUNE 1923

You may have heard that I have been very ill and have been obliged to give up active work. This is rather a trial to me, as my brain is as active as ever and my memory as good, but having rounded out my fifty years of active service I must not complain at being compelled to be still.

You will be interested to heard that the Grand Lodge of Western Australia has just closed its annual session in a suburb of Perth, and as it was one of my good days I was able to attend for a few hours. The session was a very good one but the Grand Lodge is a very small body. Some of the best of the old members continue faithful to the Order and carry on the work in spite of many discouraging circumstances. Our state is a very large one, covering nearly a million square miles, and we have a population of less than 350,000. The towns are small for the most part and widely scattered, so you will realize that it is difficult to run an organization of any kind.

We are overloaded with organizations, religious, social, political, and reform. The joke which I have heard that when a half-dozen Americans meet they immediately organize a society and elect a board of officers might well be applied to Australia. However, these organizations are all formed with a good purpose and are more or less educational. While I have been in very much larger bodies, the little Grand Lodge here would compare more than favorably with some of them. The reports were full of interest, the debates keen but temperate, and the ceremonial work carefully executed. I had the pleasure of meeting many old friends and was given a most cordial reception. The entertaining lodge furnished dinner, afternoon tea and supper, and the social features of the meals were enjoyed no less than the good things provided.

Good Templary will always stand first in my affections and my greatest regret now is that I cannot now attend the subordinate lodge very often. The condition of my health will not permit this.

Greetings to all old friends.

FORSYTH TO GEORGE F. AND CORA R. COTTERILL,
NOVEMBER 24, 1925

[Box 23, Folder 27, George F. Cotterill, University of
Washington Libraries]

I hope that you have not quite ceased to feel an
interest in me, although it is so long since I heard
from you that I am almost inclined to fear that you
have. I wrote last, a long time ago, and I sent a card
last Christmas.

However, I do not forget you and all your kindness. I have very pleasant recollections of my stay at
your home in Seattle, and of other occasions when we
have been together. I hope that you are both keeping
well. I have heard of Brother Cotterill's various
successes and have felt very glad for his sake.

Perhaps you may have heard of my total break down
in health more than four years ago which obliged me to
resign the Secretaryship of the W.C.T.U.? I spent
several weeks in a private hospital and for a time was
on the "danger list." However, my time had not come to
depart, but I have been obliged to give up active work
and the enforced rest has done me so much good that I
am feeling pretty well now, although I cannot walk very
far or very fast. But my brain is as clear as ever and
my memory wonderful and I sometimes feel inclined to
envy those who are called always in the midst of their
activities. Now I am sharing with Bros. Malins, Yeames
and a very few others, the distinction of being a last
survivor of some of the remarkable events of the Order.
The recent death of Brother Turnbull of Scotland leaves

me the last survivor of the executive elected at the union session of the I.S.L. held at Saratoga in 1887. Well, I have many happy memories of the events in which I have taken part and of the dear friends I have met in connection with Good Templary.

I have learned of the "carryings on" of Mr. [Albert] Sutcliffe [of Massachusetts] in the National Grand Lodge and was not surprised, but felt sorry for the annoyance he must have caused to those who were active in that organisation. Since then I have learned that Sutcliffe has been in trouble over some of his bogus money-making schemes. It was about time that his career was stopped, although even now it seems that he has managed to come out without the punishment he has deserved for years.

One of my nieces [Marion Smith] has taken up the study of Christian Science and has been for several months in America studying with professors of the cult. She got to Boston and was very hospitably treated by some of my friends, especially the Yeames and Sereque families. You may be sure that I could not help envying her and she wrote that they asked why she had not brought her aunt with her.

Good Templary is almost dead in Western Australia. The membership is now composed of a few of the old workers and it does not seem possible to add to the numbers. Ours is such a tremendous territory, nearly a million square miles, with a population of about 370,000. And we are done to death with organizations of all kinds. We had a Prohibition Poll a few months ago, but it was not wisely managed and we were badly beaten.

I am only able to get to a Good Templar Lodge very occasionally as the nearest one is in Perth and I am not able to be out after nightfall alone. I give a talk occasionally at a W.C.T.U. meeting as they are usually held in the afternoon, and I am sometimes able to say a few words of cheer in writing.

Now I must conclude with love to Mrs. Cotterill and regards to her husband. I should be glad to have a word from you, if you find time to write and, meantime, I am very fraternally and sincerely yours.

FORSYTH TO WILLARD O. WYLIE, NEW YORK TEMPLAR, FEB. 1928

I have heard of the death of Bro. [Theodore D.] Kanouse and unless Bro. W. G. Lane is still in the order, Bro. Yeames is probably the only surviving P.I.C.T. I believe also that I am the oldest sister of the I.S.L. My membership began in 1883 at Halifax, N.S., where I was elected I.V.T.

It is interesting to recall some of the many noble men and women with whom we have been associated, and many of whom have preceded us to the land beyond. These memories are very pleasant and I can never cease to be grateful for all that I have experienced in my connection with Good Templary. So, now in the eighty-first year of my age, and the fifty-fifth of my

membership in the Order, I have nothing but good will
and good wishes for the cause and its members.

Good Templary has dwindled down to a very few
lodges in this state, but we have some very faithful
members who will not give up and I think there are
indications of a reviving interest. I hear similar
hopeful statements from other jurisdictions; New South
Wales especially seems to be making good progress. I
am not able to do much active work now, but I occasionally speak at a meeting, and more often for he
W.C.T.U. as their meetings are held in the afternoon,
and I cannot often go out in the evening, unless my
nieces can make it convenient to take me in their auto.

FORSYTH TO G. D. CLARK, AUSTRALIAN TEMPERANCE WORLD,
MAY 1928

[When G. D. Clark, the editor of the Australian Temperance World, published his history of the Order, Forsyth
wrote in her congratulatory letter:]

Your History is exceedingly valuable, I consider,
and the chronology is a **gift worth preserving** by any
good temperance man or woman.[6] Of course Bro. [N. T.]
Collins would be interested in the History articles as

---

6   At first published as a serial in the Australian
Temperance World, Clark's history then appeared as a
book, The Good Templar Movement: Its History and Work.
A World View of the Liquor Problem. Handbook for Tem-
perance Workers (Sydney: Grand Lodge of New South
Wales, 1928).

his memory goes back a long way, like mine and yours.[7] It is surprising how much there is in Good Templary, to those who know its history, to make one feel proud and glad of belonging to it. A friend said to me the other day that it was a wonder I had continued in membership so long. I replied that it would be a greater wonder if, knowing the Order as I do, I had **not** continued.

I note that the [G. W.] Sherars [of New South Wales] are doing good work still. Their experience of the workings of the prohibitory law in America must surely convince some of the doubters.

I am enclosing a little item regarding Bro. [John] Sobieski. He was a most interesting character.[8]

FORSYTH TO WILLARD O. WYLIE, NEW YORK TEMPLAR, MAY 1928

I am now in my eighty-first year. I get tired physically but my brain is as clear as ever and my memory wonderful. I give an occasional talk before a Good Templar or W.C.T.U. meeting and only this week I went to Maylands, a suburb of Perth, and addressed both lodge and temple. It is always a pleasure for me to

---

7   An American-born Australian, Collins was one of the representatives of the Right Worthy Grand Lodge of the World at the Boston union conference in 1886.

8   The Polish-born Sobieski spent much of his life as a Templar organizer in the Middle West. He spent his old age in California. See his autobiography, Life-Story and Personal Reminiscences of Col. John Sobieski, published around 1907.

get to a lodge meeting and to meet a fine company of Juvenile Templars is an additional delight.

It was very thoughtful of your grand lodge [of New York] to pass the resolution of greetings to Bro. Yeames. He certainly is a wonder. He writes to me every month and his letters are full of matters of timely interest. There is no doubt that total abstainers are more likely to retain their faculties into old age than the so-called moderate drinkers. [Yeames died in 1931.]

FORSYTH TO G. D. CLARK, AUSTRALIAN TEMPERANCE WORLD, JULY 1928

[G. D. Clark, the editor of the Australian Temperance World, had opposed a prohibition referendum in New South Wales which would have provided compensation for the drinksellers. Most of the N.S.W. temperance party, in contrast, had supported the referendum as the best prospect for obtaining State prohibition.][9]

I am glad of your attitude on the compensation proposals. I cannot understand how any sincere Prohibitionist can entertain them. Certainly true Good Templars cannot.

---

9   See Gar Dillon, A Delusion of the Australian Culture: A Brief History of the Clash with Alcohol in New South Wales, 1788-1983 ((Sydney: New South Wales Temperance Alliance, 1985), pp. 141-42; David Bollen, "George David Clark," Australian Dictionary of Biography, vol. 8, 1891-1939 (Melbourne University Press, 1981).

FORSYTH TO CORA R. COTTERILL, JULY 13, 1929

[Box 4, Folder 5, George F. Cotterill papers, University of Washington Libraries]

Your letter was indeed a great surprise, but a very pleasant one. I have thought of you very much and very often, and have wished that I could hear from you. I have always remembered your and your husband's kindness and that we were always the best of friends when we met on many very happy occasions.

I am very sorry to hear that your health is not good and hope that, if you make the trip to Australia, that it may have the same effect on you as it did on me. You know I was in very poor health when I left America. It was that fact that decided me to accept the urgent invitation of my relatives. But the long voyage did me so much good that I felt really ashamed of meeting my sister and her family when I arrived in Fremantle. They were expecting to see a semi-invalid and I was the picture of health. And so, much to my surprise, I am still alive, aged 82, and in good health. My brain and my memory are just as clear as ever and my sight good. But my hearing is impaired and I cannot walk without a stick. But I feel that I have much reason for thankfulness, when I think of all the dear friends who have gone before me. I believe Brother Yeames and I are the oldest surviving members of the I.S.L.

I am not surprised to hear that Seattle has improved although I thought it a very fine city when I

saw it. Our State is celebrating its Centenary this
year and it´s really surprising to note what has been
accomplished in a hundred years by such a small population. Not much over 400,000 now and with a territory
of almost a million square miles. When my brother came
to Fremantle in 1865 there was no Harbour, no railroads
and very few houses. My brother became Harbour Master
a year or so after his arrival and he had a much harder
time of it than the present one has, for there has
since been built a fine little Harbour, which needs to
be enlarged. When my sister and her husband came in
1881 there was a railroad running from Fremantle to
Perth, twelve miles, and my sister says that when she
first travelled on it, she could only see one house
between the two towns. Now all the space is thickly
settled with about a dozen thriving towns. And of
course there are railroads over a good many parts of
the State, besides the Trans-Australian road, which
enables us to go from west to the Eastern States.
Before 1915, we had to travel by water; I came down
from Sydney to Fremantle in a fine comfortable steam-
boat and the journey took twelve days. Now by rail it
takes five.

There are lots of other things I could say about
this very progressive State, but they would take too
long, and I hope you will come and see them for yourself.

I am glad to hear about Sister [Emily M.] Peters.
Please give my love to her. And with best love to
yourself, trusting that this will find you well, or I
should say, better, I am your affectionate friend.

FORSYTH TO GEORGE F. COTTERILL, JULY 19, 1929

[Box 4, Folder 5, George F. Cotterill papers, University of Washington Libraries]

I am very glad to get your letter and to learn that you are really planning to visit Australia. But I am really afraid that you are making the same mistake as Brother Malins did in allowing far too little time for the trip. If you are to do any good to the Order, you will have to allow at least six or seven <u>months</u> instead of six or seven <u>weeks</u> for the visit. Do you realise that Australia is as big as the United States, that Adelaide, the nearest Capital to Perth is about 1500 miles away and Melbourne, the Capital of the State of Victoria over 500 miles from Adelaide, Sydney another 500 miles, and Brisbane yet another 500 miles, while Hobart, the Capital of the island of Tasmania is 628 miles from Sydney. I am giving you the distances by water. Fremantle to Sydney is about 2400 miles and takes about ten days to make the voyage. As to seeing New Zealand in two weeks, well you might get a glimpse of it but you would not have time for many meetings. Sydney to Auckland, N.Z., or to Wellington, N.Z., is between 1,200 and 1,300 miles. I suppose that your idea and that of I.S.L. Executive in suggesting this trip is to do the Australian Grand Lodges some good, but I think you will see that seven weeks will not be much good for the purpose. I hope you will reconstruct your plans and allow enough time to make the visit of some use.

I am writing in a hurry to get this letter posted as I find there is a mail [ship] leaving tomorrow morning. I will write to Bro. Honeyman and give him my opinion.

I think that the Grand Lodge of W.A. has had the matter of an I.S.L. visitor in contemplation and I have no doubt it will do its part. We are small but excepting for N.S.W. I think we are as much alive as any of the other G.L.'s.

FORSYTH TO GEORGE F. COTTERILL, OCTOBER 22, 1929

[Box 23, Folder 27, George F. Cotterill papers, University of Washington Libraries]

I have delayed fulfilling the promise to write to you again because I have been hoping to have something more to tell you. But until last Saturday I have heard no mention of your trip to Australia from any of the Grand Lodges. But on Saturday, I went to a fine Juvenile Rally in Perth and there I met Brother Hitchcock, the G.C.T. of Western Australia. I wrote to him after hearing from you but had received no reply to my letter. I asked him the reason and he said that he had been waiting to hear from Sydney. He had only heard one thing, that was that the idea had come to a stop because [the Grand Lodge of] Queensland Good Templars had said that they would prefer that Brother [E. C.] Dinwiddie should come instead of you.[10] I don't know

---

10 Dinwiddie was best known as national legislative superintendent of the Anti-Saloon League of America, 1899-1907 and 1911-20.

who was responsible for the suggestion. It would not
be W. F. Finlayson because he is busy in South Australia, lecturing for the Prohibition League.

Brother Hitchcock said he had heard nothing from
Brother Sherar [of the Grand Lodge of New South Wales].
I have not written to him because a letter which I sent
to him regarding another matter has never been replied
to.

I am still of the same opinion that the time you
propose to give to such a trip is far too little. A
niece of mine has just returned from a visit to Java.
She was gone six weeks and only spent two of them in
Java. She went by steamer from Fremantle and it took
just a fortnight for her to get away from West Australia, calling for a few hours at all the West coast (or
North West) Ports until she got to Port Hedland and
sailed from there to Batavia. I daresay you remember
Brother Eugene Chafin's visit to Australia [in 1919].[11]
He wrote to me when he first landed and promised that
he would be in W.A. shortly. I was disappointed when I
heard that he had returned to America without getting
near our State. I suppose his courage, or his
finances, gave out when he got to Melbourne. When
Tennyson Smith visited Australia the last time, he
found plenty to occupy him for two years.[12] The Bishop
of London visited Australia two or three years ago. He

---

11   Chafin (1852-1920), at one time a leader in the
Grand Lodge of Wisconsin, was the presidential candidate of the Prohibition Party in 1908 and 1912.

12   Edward Tennyson Smith, a prominent figure in the
Grand Lodge of England, lectured in a number of
English-speaking countries. E. Tennyson Smith, From
Memory's Storehouse (2nd ed., London: R. J. James, 1925).

got to Sydney first and by the time he reached Perth, he had only two days left of his time before he sailed from Fremantle. The Anglicans here were dreadfully disappointed as they had been counting on something more than a glimpse of him. The fact of it is that people do not realise the size of Australia. I think I told you Brother Malins´ experience [during his trip around the world, 1899-1900]. I remember how dreadfully disappointed my late brother in law [sic] and my sister were. They had known him in England and had planned to entertain him in their beautiful Fremantle home and he barely had time to take a meal with them. If you came to Fremantle first, you could find plenty to do in our big State which comprises one third of Australia. But if you landed in Sydney, I am afraid you would never reach us.

I am sure you know that I should be very glad to see you and especially Cora, but I am not able to do much now, except write. I cannot walk very far, and have to use a stick, and when I occasionally attend a meeting, I get so dreadfully tired that I am no good next day. Of course, this is not surprising considering my age, (82) and I have reason to feel very thankful for the measure of health which I enjoy, and for my excellent memory and clear brain.

We have been celebrating the Centenary of our State and the celebrations have been very interesting. A pageant was shown at Fremantle, representing the landing of Captain Fremantle and the raising of the Union Jack. The scene was enacted on the identical spot where the original landing took place. A company of British soldiers, sailors and marines, dressed in

the uniforms of a hundred years ago, came ashore. We
had seats on the balcony of the Sailors Rest, which
was just opposite the landing place, so we had a fine
sight of everything. I enjoyed it very much and could
almost have fancied that I was really looking on the
actual happening of a hundred years ago. Captain
Fremantle named the new possession the "Swan River
Colony" but later it took the name of Western Australia.

I must close now, with love to Cora and best
regards to yourself, hoping to hear from you again. I
trust this will find you both well and that Cora is
stronger than when she wrote. If you come to Australia, I hope I may live to see you, but one cannot count
on anything in the future when one gets to be my age.
But whether I ever see you again or not, you may be
sure that I never forget the old pleasant times we have
enjoyed together.

FORSYTH TO CORA R. COTTERILL, AUGUST 22, 1930

[Box 23, Folder 27, George F. Cotterill papers, University of Washington Libraries]

I suppose you will have returned from your
European tour by this time and so I venture to reply to
your letter of long ago. I was very glad to hear from
such old friends after so long a silence but sorry to
know of your failing health. I trust this will find
you quite restored. And I hope that Bro. Cotterill
continues to retain his good health.

I have not had any news from the I.S.L. session yet, although I have had several letters and cards from Swedish members including Sister Wavrinsky and Bro. Eklund. But a letter from Bro. Yeames says he has received copies of the new Rituals and that he does not approve of some of the changes. Has there been any change in the officers? I have hoped, at every session, that Bro. Cotterill would be I.C.T. [International Chief Templar]. I learn that Bro. Wylie has had a serious illness and was prevented from going to Stockholm, I am sorry [to hear]. I get the New York Templar and have been pleased to read about the National Grand Lodge. It seems to have recovered from the attack Sutcliffe made upon it.

I suppose Bro. Cotterill has abandoned his idea of visiting Australia.[13] It would be a big job and a costly one and the Grand Lodges do not seem at all enthusiastic about it. They are all very weak, although improving somewhat in the last two or three years. In this State and in N.S.W. some good old members hold on to the work, but they cannot enlist many new ones. And we have such a number of other societies and novelty attracts the people. In the meantime the liquor traffic gains ground and Australia's drink bill is enormous when compared with its population.

---

13   An officer in the Grand Lodge of New South Wales said that it was fortunate that Cotterill could not come to Australia because massive unemployment had impoverished the Grand Lodges. George W. Sherar to George F. Cotterill, March 25, 1930. Box 23, Folder 27, George F. Cotterill papers, University of Washington libraries.

My niece Marion, my sister´s second daughter, is now in the United States. She is to attend a course of lectures on "Christian Science" in Aurora, Illinois. She went over about four years ago and attended a Class in Oakland, California, and has practiced here since her return. She visited the Yeameses and some other of my friends in the east. I wish she could give you a call. Perhaps you might be disposed to send her a line. Address Miss Marion E. Smith, c/o Mr. W. W. Walter, 564 New York Street, Aurora, Illinois.

I am thankful to say that I am keeping very well, but I am not able to walk without a stick. But my mind and memory are wonderfully good and I keep up a large correspondence, much of it international, and do some other writing. My niece Edith has an automobile and I get a good many Sun[day]s in that. We have some lovely drives around Perth and our King´s Park is very large and very fine. We have had a great quantity of rain this winter which has been good for the country but has not been pleasant in the towns, but it has made the grass very green and our wildflowers are coming out in great abundance and variety.

Well, dear friend, I must close, hoping that this will find you much better. I shall be glad to hear from you again. I am ashamed of my writing; my typewriter is out of order and a long course of writing on the machine has spoiled my handwriting, but you will pardon the scribble. Give my kindest regards to Bro. Cotterill, remember me to Mrs. Peters and any other friends, and accept best love yourself from your affectionate friend.

P.S.

I am sorry the Australian trip is off. It would have been a joy to see you.

FORSYTH TO GEORGE F. COTTERILL, NOVEMBER 6, 1930

[Box 23, Folder 27, George F. Cotterill papers, University of Washington Libraries]

I have written to Sister Cotterill and acknowledged her share in the kind message which reached me from Stockholm but, after reading the list of officers, I feel I must write and tell you how sorry I feel that you are no longer included in it, and that the United States has no longer an officer on the Executive. You have been very faithful and I daresay you are glad to be free from the responsibility, but it is a question whether the loss of a U.S.A. Executive officer will not add to the decline in interest there. However, I hope not, I love the Order, and believe in it, and should rejoice to see it regain its old-time strength and glory.

I know that you and others of the few remaining faithful ones, will still continue your efforts for its welfare and I wish you all success. We have a few faithful old members in this State, but the immense territory and small population makes propaganda work very difficult and, now we have come to a crisis in our domestic affairs and, for the first time, Australians are feeling poor, I might say, panic-stricken. There is trouble between the States and the Federal Government, and this State is talking of seceding. However,

I hope it will not come to that, for I believe in the American motto: "United we stand, Divided we fall," and I have always felt proud of the title, the "Commonwealth of Australia." There is much talk of retrenchment but in all the suggested plans for economy, the abolition of the liquor traffic does not appear!

I must close with best regards and wishes to you and Cora. I trust the European trip has benefited her health and that you are quite well. For myself, I am in very good health considering my age. I often think of old times and old friends and am, as ever, yours very fraternally.

FORSYTH TO MINNIE B. VIEROW, MARCH 2, 1931, NEW YORK TEMPLAR, MAY 1931

I have again to thank you for your kindness and courtesy in sending me the Journal of your Grand Lodge [of New York]. I found it very interesting and, after reading, have passed it on to the Grand Secretary of our Grand Lodge. I am sure he will appreciate the news, as I do. The Grand Lodge of New York is the only one of the U.S.A. ones that I get direct news from and you cannot imagine how much I appreciate the New York Templar. Although so far away from America, where I spent so many active and happy years, I have never lost my love for it, nor my interest in its welfare.

Some dear old friends in Massachusetts keep me informed regarding affairs in that State, but they have not an official organ, and I occasionally get a few lines from some of the other jurisdictions. Still, as far as American news is concerned, I depend chiefly upon what comes to me from New York.

I supposed Brother [Harry] Greensmith has had much of interest to tell you about the I.S.L. session. It was evidently a very interesting one and the order has made great advance in some of the foreign countries. I recently had a most charming letter from Miss Arriens [of the Netherlands], the I.V.T.[14] I visited the Grand Lodge of the Netherlands in 1907 and there has evidently been an advance there since that time.

I am very pleased that the I.S.L. has again a sister on its Executive [with the election of Arriens as International Vice Templar]. I served on that Executive for twenty-one years, six as Vice Templar and fifteen as I.S.J.W. I served with John B. Finch, Joseph Malins, Doctor Oronhyatekha, Dr. D. H. Mann, Edward Wavrinsky, as heads of the order, and with many other noble and worthy brothers and sisters, whose memories will always be precious to me.

Well, dear sister, I must not forget that I am writing to a very busy woman, who can scarcely spare the time to read long, gossipy letters, so I must close with kindest regards and sincere appreciation of all your good work.

---

14   After a three-year term as International Vice Templar, A. Arriens served as International Superintendent of Juvenile Work, 1933-52. A teacher by occupation, she edited the weekly Dutch paper, Die Tempeleir, 1925-40. She died at age 86. International Good Templar, Jan. 1966, p. 13.

FORSYTH TO GEORGE F. AND CORA R. COTTERILL, JANUARY 18, 1932

[Box 23, Folder 27, George F. Cotterill papers, University of Washington Libraries]

I have just received your "glowing" Christmas greeting and am feeling a corresponding glow of pleasure, quite equal to the color of the envelope. I am indeed very glad to be remembered by such dear old friends with "the same old wish, in the same old way." I take it for granted that all is well with you, although you not give me any particulars.

I miss your name from the list of I.S.L. officers and am sorry that the U.S. is not now represented. Of course you heard of the death of Brother Yeames. I had letters from him almost up to the last and now his wife and daughter are trying to feel the gap which the loss of his monthly budget has made in my life. But he had lived a long and useful life; he was in his 89th year when he died. His decease leaves me the oldest surviving past officer of the I.S.L. Bro. Oskar Eklund ranks the same in point of membership (we were both elected to office at the Halifax Session in 1883) but I am considerably the elder in years. Bro. Eklund writes to me some times and so does dear Mrs. Wavrinsky and so do other Swedish friends, and a good brother in Norway writes frequently and recently sent me a letter from his District Lodge signed by forty members, headed by old friend, Pedar Jansen [Jensen]. And I have letters from other parts showing that I am still remembered. This last Christmas I had letters from New York State, Pennsylvania, Minnesota and Tennessee, besides a number from Massachusetts, and from all over this country. In fact, the receiving and replying to letters is now my chief occupation, for I cannot do much active work. I keep in touch with the Good Templars here by paying my dues, but cannot often attend a meeting. The members here are very good sending me messages at Christmas and on my birthday. The[y] are quite proud of the fact that I am in my sixtieth year as a Good Templar. I joined the Order October 14th, 1872. Our little Grand Lodge here had a sad loss a few months ago in the death of Bro. Macreadie, the G. Sec´y. A most excellent man and faithful worker. A little over a year ago, our family had a sad loss in the death of my niece Mrs. Jessie Forsyth Waugh who left a devoted husband and two daughters and a son. She was my sister´s eldest daughter and was my favorite niece and I feel her loss very keenly.

The other day I was looking through the volumes of the International Good Templar which I have bound, covering from the first number up to 1908. I found much to remind me of old friends, including you and Sister Cotterill, and I came across a sketch of myself written by you. By the way, I have arranged for these volumes to go to the Public Library at my decease. The Trustees have assured me that they "will be very glad to receive them."

I am afraid you will be tired of my long letter and you must not be too critical about the penmanship as I cannot write as well as I used [to] and I get very tired if I use my typewriter much.

Let me assure you again that I am more glad than I
can say, to hear from you again. I have never forgotten your kindness when I was leaving America and the
happy visit I had in your lovely home. I trust this
will find you both well and prospering. God bless you
both is the wish of

> Your affectionate old friend
> (signed) Jessie Forsyth
> (in her 85th year)

P.S.: There is no need for you to be so careful in
locating "Claremont" as it is a town of considerable
size. Some time ago a letter was delivered to me which
was sent from Tennessee and was addressed Miss Jessie
Forsyth [at]

> (47 Victoria Avenue)   where I was living then
> Western Australia

Western Australia has an area of nearly a million
square miles. Don´t you think our P.O. officials are
pretty smart?

FORSYTH TO GEORGE F. AND CORA R. COTTERILL, MARCH 23, 1934

[Box 29, Folder 24, George F. Cotterill papers, University of Washington Libraries]

You have probably learned from the _International
Good Templar_ that I am _hors de combat_. I had a fall
some weeks ago and hurt my right leg quite badly. I
have been in bed ever since and this accounts for my

dreadful scribble which is the best I can do under the circumstances.

I was pleased to get your card and glad to be reminded of our many happy meetings and journeyings together. I was sorry you could not be at the I.S.L. George must have been greatly missed on the Executive. I am glad they had a good session and particularly glad that they have a woman again on the Executive.

I have been much touched by the kindness of the Good Templars here. Our small membership have been most good. They are proud of the fact that I have been [more than] sixty years a member. I have callers, flowers and gifts from them and with the International correspondence I keep in touch with the Order. I send greetings to all members and love to you both and all good wishes.[15]

---

15   Cora R. Cotterill died in 1936.

Part Three:
Representative Writings, 1882-1932

Only a few examples of Forsyth´s short stories and official reports have been reprinted in this section, which consists mostly of didactic essays. In addition memoirs of European travel published in <u>Temperance Brotherhood</u> during the 1880s appear in Part Three.

GRAND LODGE OF MASSACHUSETTS
REPORT OF THE GRAND WORTHY SECRETARY AT
THE SEMI-ANNUAL SESSION HELD IN LOWELL, MARCH 8, 1882

[<u>Good Templars´ Watchword</u>, April 10, 1882]

To Officers and Members of the Grand Lodge of Mass.,--I have the honour to come before you once more with a report of our doings during the past six months, and our present condition.

The present number of Lodges under our jurisdiction is eight, as follows:-

Favourite, No. 2, Boston	15	members
Mount Zion, No. 3, Lowell	66	"
Seaside, No. 4, Winthrop	34	"
Charity, No. 6, Watertown	32	"
E. M. Thomas, No. 11, Boston	83	"

Perseverance, No. 12, Lowell   40 "
W. L. Garrison, No. 13, Boston   12 "
Onward, No. 14, Lowell   40 "

With reference to these Lodges, I would say that, with the exception of Favourite and William Lloyd Garrison, they are all in a healthy and flourishing condition and actively engaged in carrying on the good work of "raising the fallen" and "saving others from falling." Edward M. Thomas Lodge, as usual, heads the list in point of number, and it is not in number alone that its strength lies. The sisters composing it are "zealous in good works," and the influence of such a Lodge must be far-reaching. Our Lodges in Lowell are worthy of all praise for the earnest efforts they are making in the cause of Temperance; among other things I would especially call attention to the Sunday prayer meeting held under the auspices of the Lodges. All who believed in the answer promised to the "two or three gathered together," must see in this, an active agency for extending our cause. Great credit is due also to Charity Lodge, of Watertown, which, in spite of its somewhat isolated position, and the many difficulties it had to encounter, is steadily doing a good work and making a good report. I am sorry to say that Favourite Lodge and Wm. Lloyd Garrison are both in a very weak condition. The latter has not made any report, and it is feared will have to surrender, but the few faithful members remaining in Favourite Lodge are still holding on to their charter, and will make one more special effort to revive the Lodge before giving up. Notwithstanding the great need for Temperance work in Boston, it seems of all places the hardest in which to carry it on. With so many amusements at hand to attract the young people, a Temperance organiser stands very little chance, and we learn that some of the Lodges under the Hickmanite branch of the Order have adopted the plan of having dances and other similar amusements to induce young people to join.

Since our last meeting, Equal Rights Lodge, of Waltham, has left us. This Lodge, which we always regarded as steadfast, had a member who was disappointed of an office in the Grand Lodge to which he aspired, and after plunging his Lodge into great financial difficulties, he took advantage of the absence of a number of the best members to induce the Lodge to surrender its charter and go into another Order whose name I forget. Our G. W. Councillor will be able to tell you more particulars as he was a member of Equal Rights Lodge. We have today to give the right hand of fellowship to the representative of our new Lodge, Seaside No. 4, of Winthrop. This Lodge was instituted by Special Deputy P. E. C. Bower and myself, on February 15, and started, with good prospects of success. Like many another little craft which has set sail in fair weather it was soon to encounter a storm. The Hickmanite branch of the Order in this State is just now very much on the alert, owing to the fact that their R.W.G.L. is expected to meet in Boston shortly, and as soon as it became known that a Lodge had been instituted in Winthrop, the G.W.C.T. of that Order wrote to the Lodge saying that they had been duped into joining a "bogus" Order; that your G.W. Sec. and Special Deputy were impostors; and that he himself would (very kindly) go down and form them into a genuine Lodge. Our Sister Kate Hardie (late a member of Favourite Lodge) had been too long a member

of the Order to be deluded by any such story as that,
and she immediately notified Dr. [William Wells] Brown
and myself. At Dr. Brown's suggestion I telegraphed
for our G.W.C.T., and upon his arrival we started for
Winthrop, where a meeting had been called. Dr. Brown
soon demonstrated to the satisfaction of everyone
concerned that we, being incorporated under the laws of
the State of Massachusetts, and working under a
charter granted by the R.W.G.L. of the World, are not
by any means a bogus Order. His remarks were received
with much enthusiasm. Your G.W.C.T. then initiated six
new members, and we left the Lodge working harmoniously, and not likely to be affected by any of the slander
that our enemies may invent. If the Hickmanite G.L. of
Mass. has not been sufficiently disgraced by the stand
it has taken upon the negro question, its present
G.W.C.T. will bring it still further into contempt, if
instead of using such influence as he possesses to
promote the cause of Temperance, he employs himself in
trying to undo our work. It is to be hoped that its
failure in this instance will give him a lesson not to
interfere again. It will be remembered that at our
last session it was voted that such means as we possess
should be employed in extending the Order in this
State. Unfortunately for our plans the agent whom we
had elected disappointed us, and while we were waiting
for him to be at liberty the winter (our harvest time)
was passing away. At last we put Bro. P. E. C. Bower
in the field, but it was so late in the season that his
efforts were not attended with the success we hoped
for. However, he planted the Order in Winthrop, and
opened the negotiations in other places, where we hope
for some results. Bro. Bower is not able to be with us
to-day, but I have his report which I will read if

desired. I would say that our R.W.G.S. keeps me well
supplied with reports, and I learn from them that our
Order is constantly extending and increasing. We of
the G.L. of Mass. are a link, if a small one, in a
chain which encircles the globe, a chain of brotherly
love which binds us together to work for the elevation
of mankind without regard to race or colour, country or
creed. Let us then be more faithful and earnest in the
cause, let us live--

> "For the wrong that needs resistance,
> For the cause that lacks assistance,
> For the victory in the distance,
> For the good that we can do."

Respectfully submitted in Faith, Hope and Charity.

SISTER FORSYTH, R.W.G.V.T., ON EMIGRATION

[Letter to the editor, n.d., Good Templars´ Watchword,
January 28, 1884]

The very sensible letter from Bro. Dunlop, of
Queensland, in one of your recent numbers has reminded
me that I have for some time entertained the idea of
writing to you on a similar subject.

I have learned that a great many people who leave
England for another country, seeking, as they say, "to
better" themselves, are the very ones who are least
likely to do so, and I am often forced to conclude that
they have rushed into the scheme of emigration without

taking proper thought upon the subject or asking the advice of those better posted than themselves.

Truly, <u>Punch</u>´s advice to those about to marry would often be well[-]applied if addressed to those about to emigrate, and I have often wished that some judicious friend had been at hand to say "don´t," when first the idea of emigration had been mooted by some of the "innocents abroad" whom I have met during my nine years´ residence in Boston.

It would seem that any person composed of an ordinary amount of common sense, would, when he first conceived the idea of emigrating, endeavour to make himself acquainted with the nature of the place to which he thought of going: but so far from that I often meet with English people, just arrived, who have only the vaguest idea about the climate and none at all regarding the business prospects, etc. "Perhaps you can recommend me to something to do?" is, very often, the first remark, after a newly arrived brother has introduced himself. "What is your trade?" I ask, only to be told, in nine cases out of ten, "Oh, I haven´t any trade, but I am handy at anything."

Now, Mr. Editor, let me say most emphatically, that such persons are not the ones most likely to do well here. In the first place, all Yankees are "handy men," consequently the market is overstocked with men who can turn their hands to anything, while, on the other hand, the proportion of American boys who thoroughly learn a trade is very small, and so a skilful intelligent workman who is perfectly master of a trade, and who is sober and industrious stands a good chance, and such men are the ones who should come here.

The next consideration should be as regards the climate (indeed, I almost think it should be the first thing considered), and I would lay it down as a safe rule that persons troubled with weak lungs or liable to throat or chest diseases had better avoid this part of the country, although the Southern and some of the Western States are not, of course, open to the same objection. Still, I am of opinion that one of the first requisites for the intending emigrant is good health, for I can assure you, from personal experience, that under the most favourable circumstances, anyone who has left his own country will know many homesick days, full of longings for the old scenes and the familiar faces, and if to these natural and generally transitory feelings be added bodily pain and sickness one can imagine the condition of the "sojourner in a strange land" to be sad indeed.

We will suppose, however, that the intending emigrant has good health, and a good trade at his finger ends. The next essential is a little money over and above his expenses, with which to support himself in case he should fail to find immediate employment, and then, if he be fully prepared to work hard for every dollar he earns, and to pay a much higher price for most things than he did at home, I see no reason why he should not do well. But those who come expected to find in this country an El Dorado, where great wages are paid for small work, and where good situations are to be had for the asking, are only rendering themselves liable to severe disappointment.

I have only spoken of men in all I have said but the same advice may be even more forcibly addressed to women, because a young girl runs more risk in leaving home than a young man does.

There are often cases where the older and more experienced members of Lodges might prevent their younger brothers or sisters from some rash proceeding, by a few words of kindly advice: in this, as in many other matters, much good may be done by the word spoken in season.

SOME NOTES OF TRAVEL

[Temperance Brotherhood, October 1885-April 1886. This is the first extensive piece of writing which Forsyth published. The section on Scandinavia was reprinted with minor changes in International Good Templar, March-April 1902, on the eve of another meeting of the Order in Stockholm. In 1903 Forsyth borrowed extensively from these reports for her memoirs.]

[October 1885]

The rain was falling in a steady downpour as the good ship "Scythia," bearing me on board, steamed out of her dock at East Boston, May 23 [1885]; and, in spite of the fact that I had `crossed before,´ and of all my bright anticipations of the pleasant experiences which awaited me, I must acknowledge that I felt a little lonely and homesick when the faces of the friends who had gathered to see me off faded from view, and I realized that we were fairly started, and that three thousand miles of ocean were to be travelled

before I set foot on solid land again. However the
bright sunshine which greeted us next morning banished
all gloomy thoughts, and, notwithstanding some rather
severe attacks of seasickness and a little rough
weather, the voyage was not unpleasant.

A prosperous voyage, like a happy life, is apt to
be uneventful; and, excepting a magnificent display of
icebergs which kept us interested and charmed during
nearly the whole of one day, there was little to
relieve the tedium of the passage, and all seemed glad
when we came in sight of land.

The word "glad" hardly expresses the emotion with
which, after long years of absence, I gazed on the
shores of dear old England. Those who have been
"exiles from home" will understand the feeling which
makes one´s own country still seem the dearest land of
all, although it may have ceased to be one´s home, and
although none but strangers are to be found in the old
familiar places. The love of country is a pure and
sacred feeling, and even when one has learned that
"higher patriotism" which teaches that "the world is
our country," one need not feel ashamed if the heart
should throb and the eye kindle at the sight of the
well-remembered shores.

So exceedingly fair and peaceful did England´s
shores look in the bright sunlight, that the exclamations of delight and admiration which came from all
on board seemed only a well-deserved tribute. The
"beautiful isle of the sea" appeared full worthy of all
that has been said and sung in her praise.

I landed in Liverpool, June 2d [1885], and received a hearty welcome from Sister Green, P.R.S. [sic] of Juvenile Templars, whose comely presence and gracious manners will be favorably remembered by those of our American readers who attended the Halifax session [in 1883]. I spent a day very happily with her, and saw something of the fine buildings, for which Liverpool is famous.

The next stage was Birmingham, where I met Bro. Joseph Malins, G.W.C.T., Bro. Collings, G.W.S., and others of the executive of the G.L. of England, and was shown over the G.L. offices. Sister Townsend of Birmingham then took me in charge, and in her company I visited Aston Hall, a very interesting place, which was once an old family mansion, but is now the property of the people of Birmingham, and is used as a museum, while its beautiful grounds are a public park. The old hall is a very fine specimen of Elizabethan architecture, and, of course, has its history. During the Civil Wars in England it was besieged, and the ball from Cromwell's cannon, as well as the hole which it made in the oaken balustrade of the staircase, are shown to curious visitors. Birmingham, though not as large as Liverpool, is a busy, bustling city, and has many handsome buildings. I enjoyed a ride in the steam street-cars very much.

From Birmingham I went down into Somersetshire, and spent ten delightful days in Sister Impey's lovely home.

The line of Lowell's regarding the month of June, that "Then, if ever, come perfect days," is true of Old

England as of New England, and I regard it as a great
privilege to have seen this lovely part of England in
its early summer beauty, while the hedges were still
white with the hawthorn, the English "may," and the
laburnum trees were a mass of golden bloom. So much
has been written of rural England that any attempt of
mine to describe its beauties will seem a clumsy effort
to do what others have done so much better, but I do
wish I could bring to the sense of my readers something
of the soothing and refreshing influence of the fair
sights, sweet sounds, and fragrance which surrounded me
during my stay in Street. To a wearied toiler from a
busy city, it seemed a perfect heaven of rest and calm.

Still, the calm restful feeling which pervades the
place is not by any means the dolce far niente [plea-
sant idleness] [about] which poets sing, nor are the
dwellers in this delightful home at all inclined to the
doctrines of the Lotus-eaters. On the contrary,
ceaseless activity in good works goes on; only, after
the manner of the Quakers, all is done without fuss or
bustle, and the earnest thinking and praying which bear
their fruit in the earnest living and working, are a
matter of course.

Our readers, in the South particularly, will like
to know something of the place in which Sister Catherine Impey lives, and where she finds time, amidst all
her immediate cares and duties, to plan and work for
the welfare of the colored people. Nor is it only to
those at a distance that her sympathy goes out. The
hospitable doors of her home have been open to more
than one representative of the [black] race. Upon the
pages of the visitors' book are inscribed the names of

Rev. E. M. Pinckney, of South Carolina, and our late brother, Dr. Wm. Wells Brown, while a poem describing the beauties of Street stands over the signature of Dr. [B. T.] Tanner of Philadelphia.

This visitors´ book, by the way, is somewhat of a curiosity, and much amusement can be gathered from its pages. It dates back to beyond the period of the separation in our Order, and near the beginning of the book we find Sister Isabella Metford´s name appended to the assertion that the

"Negro
Question
Spoiled
Digestion."

The institution of "Who is My Neighbor" Lodge is thus "done into verse" by Bro. Macmillan, of Castle Cary, who says:-

"The occasion of your visit?
Let me see, what is it?
To aid in Sister Katie´s labor
In seeking out "Who is My Neighbor?"

Sister Jane Metford celebrates the Temperance work in Street as follows:--
"In big, little Street
Two societies meet,--
The Temperance League and I.O.G.T.;
May each act like a brother
And honor the other,
And the fruit of their work may we joyfully see."

A distinguished member of the Order [very likely Joseph Malins], whose name I withhold, but whose style may perhaps be recognized, thus "drops into poetry":--

"Folks good!
Nice food!
Home Clean!
All serene!"

I could give many more abstracts, if space permitted; but, after all, perhaps, the sentiment written by Bro. James J. Woods, P.G.W. Sec. of England, though not original, would best express the feelings of all who have had the pleasure of visiting Askew House.

"I have been there and still would go;
'Tis like a little Heaven below."

While at Street I had the privilege of meeting with several earnest workers in our cause, amongst them Bro. John Morland, Treasurer of the [Negro] Mission Fund, and Bro. T. Bevan Clark, both of whom have contributed letters to The Temperance Brotherhood.

In addition to the rural beauty of this part of England, there are many places of historic interest in the neighborhood. Not far off is the town of Wells, with its beautiful Cathedral, which I had the pleasure of visiting. Still nearer is Glastonbury, with the ruins of the grand old Abbey, which was built upon the site of the first church in England, and a fourteen-mile drive takes one to Bridgewater, where there is a

fine old church to be seen, and also the house in which
Admiral Blake lived.

Besides the <u>bona fide</u> historical places, there are
several spots which have traditions connecting them
with Roman, Saxon, Danish, or Norman periods, and which
one can accept or reject according as one has a
believing or sceptical mind. Chief among these is the
spot where King Alfred burned the cakes, according to
the story which every child remembers, as one of the
oases in the dreary desert of English history.

A VISIT TO BRISTOL.

On the Monday after my arrival in Street, I went
in company with Sister Impey to Bristol, where a
meeting had been called by the district executive.
Here I was the guest of Bro. and Sister Osborn, two
loyal and earnest workers in Good Templary, who were
present at the Halifax session in 1883, and who will be
remembered by friends in Massachusetts, New Jersey, and
Pennsylvania, in which places they attended meetings
and made addresses before returning to England. The
meeting in Bristol was very enthusiastic, and all
present listened with interest and attention to all
that I was able to tell them regarding the work among
the colored people. The D.C.T., Bro. Padfield, who is
one of the rare people who understand the art of making
things go smoothly, and who therefore, as a chairman,
is the "right man in the right place," presided.

The next morning, before returning to Street,
through the kindness of Bro. and Sister Osborn, I had a
delightful drive to Clifton Downs and the Suspension

Bridge, and afterwards visited the fine old church of St. Mary Redclyffe.

After staying as long at Street as my other engagements permitted, I went to London, where my time was pretty well taken up in looking for a few old friends. However, I managed to get a glimpse of the some of the improvements in the "world´s metropolis," and to visit the Doré Gallery and the "Inventions" exhibition. After living so long in a smaller city, the size of London seemed perfectly overwhelming, and I rather grudged the time which I was obliged to spend in getting about from one quarter to another. However, London has excellent facilities for travelling, and the fares are perhaps cheaper than in any other city. For instance, during one day, I rode in six different conveyances--three omnibuses, two horse-cars, and on the Metropolitan (or underground) Railroad, at a total expense of eighteen cents, or an average of three cents each ride. The custom in London is to regulate the charge according to the distance travelled, so that the man who rides one mile only has to pay his fair proportion of the fare demanded of the man who travels ten.

[December 1885]

While I was in London, I paid a visit to the "Henry Ansell" Lodge, at Islington. In this Lodge, thirteen years ago, I began my Good Templar career. At that time Henry Ansell himself was presiding officer, and it was a great pleasure to meet this veteran worker again, and find him still earnest and zealous in the cause. Some few old friends came from a distance to greet me; but the majority of the members present were strangers. However, this did not hinder them from

giving me a very hearty welcome. The Lodge is flourishing, and doing good service. The hall was filled
upon the occasion of my visit, and the members
manifested much interest in what I was able to tell
them regarding the work in America.

I noticed, during my stay in London, many little
things which served to convince me that there has been
a great growth of Temperance sentiment during the past
few years. It is true that the Gin Palaces still
flaunt their gilded splendor at every corner, and that
even the sanctity of the Sabbath is little restriction
upon the dreadful traffic; but there is an under-cur-
rent of popular feeling which is growing daily, and,
although the indications of it are small, still, as
"straws show which way the wind blows," so I believe
that these little indications may be accepted as good
omens for the future and that Temperance workers may
"thank God and take courage."

On June 23d, I left London for Hull, en route for
Stockholm, and was met upon my arrival by Bro. Woodall,
who already had Bro. Cooke, G.W. Sec., of Wales, in
charge. A few minutes later came the train from the
North, bringing four Scottish brethren,--Messrs. Archer, Turnbull, Hamilton, and Craig. Four of the representatives of the Grand Lodge of England--Sister Impey,
and Bros. Rev. E. Franks, Scott, and Dodgson--arrived
still a little later, and then our good Brother Woodall
conducted us to his home (called Nephalism House, in
honor of the Temperance principles of its owner) [the
word nephalism is a Greek-derived synonym for teetotal-
ism], where Sister Woodall and her daughters gave us a
warm welcome, and we were entertained to tea in real

Yorkshire style,--the table literally groaning with the
weight of the good things upon it. It was pleasant to
meet old acquaintances again, and this helped to make
us a very merry party as we did justice to the fare.

After tea we were conducted to "Paragon" Lodge,
where a large company of the Hull Good Templars were
assembled, and where we received a most enthusiastic
welcome.

Short addresses from all the guests and some of
the hosts, with some more Yorkshire hospitality displayed by what is called a "Coffee Supper," kept us
entertained until nearly midnight, when a number of
friends escorted us on board the S.S. "Albania," and
before morning dawned we were well out to sea.

The voyage to Hamburg occupied two days, and was
very smooth and bright and pleasant. It was after
midnight when we got into port, but our good Bro.
Harvey was on the lookout for us, and he came on board
and made arrangements with Bro. Turnbull (who throughout the journey acted as our guide) to meet us in the
morning, and assist us in our endeavor to see what we
could of the city.

We had nearly a day in Hamburg, and found it
extremely interesting. In some parts it is very old
and quaint; but new quarters are handsome, especially
we noticed some fine buildings on the banks of the
river Alster. A particular object of interest to our
brethren from north of the Tweed was the beautiful
church of Saint Nicolai, which was designed by a
Scotsman, Gilbert Scott.

We spent some time at the Zoological Gardens,
which are reckoned among the finest in Europe, and some
of us visited the "Battle of Wurms,"--a cyclorama
similar to the "Battle of Gettysburg," in Boston.

We noticed a number of peasants wearing their
picturesque national dress. The Vierlanderins, especially with their brocaded stomachers and the enormous
stiff, black bows at the back of their heads, were
object of much attention. Before leaving Hamburg we
paid a visit to Bro. and Sister Jones, at the Seaman's
Bethel, and, after having tea with them, we took the
train for Kiel.

At Kiel we embarked on a Danish steamer, which
landed us next morning at Korsoer, a town in Zealand,
where we had time only for a hasty breakfast, and then
proceeded to Copenhagen, where we arrived about 11 a.m.
and were met by Bro. Jacobsen. Here, too, our party
was augmented by Sister Gray of Antwerp, whom we found
awaiting us at the Hotel Leopold. The few hours spent
in Copenhagen were among the pleasantest incidents of
the journey. The city of itself is clean and bright
and lively, but chiefly modern,--the old portions
having been destroyed by fires in 1728 and 1795, and by
bombardment by the English in 1807. There are a number
of nice little parks and gardens; in one of them, the
Rosenborg, we saw the statue to Hans Christian Ander-
sen, and were glad to realize that we had been treading
the very streets in which this well-beloved writer of
fairy lore had played as a boy before it was known that
the "Ugly Duckling" had "been hatched from a swan's
egg."

339

We remembered, too, that other boy who made his
first models of the clay in the streets of Copenhagen,
and who afterwards became the world-renowned sculptor,
Thorwaldsen,--"our Bertel," as the Danes proudly call
him.

Our time permitted only a hasty run through the
Museum, which is filled with the creations of this
prolific genius, and which also contains his tomb, and
I am afraid, that as far as I am concerned, I should
have brought away a very imperfect idea of his works,
if a visit to the "Frue Kyrke" had not given me
something to remember with delight as long as I live.
This church contains the beautiful colossal statues of
Christ and the Apostles, by Thorwaldsen, which have
become famous throughout the world. It is impossible
to describe the effect which the sight of these
exquisite statues produced upon one. All ordinary
terms of admiration seemed poor and trifling when
applied to them, and one could only gaze in silence,
and come away feeling somehow better and happier for
having seen them. During a drive, which we took
through the city, Bro. Jacobsen pointed out to us the
Good Templar Hall. It appeared to be a very fine
building, but we could not spare time to go over it,
and we regretted being obliged to leave Copenhagen
without attending a Lodge meeting, and seeing something
more of our Danish brethren. However, some of us hoped
to take in Copenhagen on the return journey, and this
consoled us for being obliged to hurry away.

From Copenhagen we went, by steamer, to Malmo,
arriving there about eight o´clock in the evening. We

were met, on landing, by a party of brethren who
invited us to visit the Good Templar Hall, and, having
an hour to spare before the departure of the train for
Stockholm, we concluded that it would be a good way to
spend the time.

The Good Templar Hall is a fine building, with the
emblems of the Order carved upon its front, and containing a cafe, Lodge-rooms, etc. In one of the rooms
we found a party of young people who appeared to be a
Good Templar choir at practice, and who very kindly
sang some pieces for us. This answered instead of
conversation, which the lack of a knowledge of each
other´s language prevented, and we bowed and smiled our
thanks, and shook hands with as many friends as we
could, before we hurried to catch the train, which was
to bear us on the last stage of our journey, to
Stockholm. A fourteen hours´ railroad ride carried us
to Stockholm, where we arrived about noon, June 28th.
The railroad carriages were very comfortable, and we
were not crowded, so that we managed to sleep through a
good part of the night.

Upon arriving in Stockholm, we were met by a
delegation of Good Templars, and greeted with an ode of
welcome, very finely sung by male voices. We were then
conducted to our rooms at the Grand Hotel, where we
were very glad to refresh ourselves after our long
journey.

[January 1886]
We were not long in Stockholm before we discovered
that we had fallen into the hands of a generous and
hospitable people. The greatest kindness and attention

were shown to us and everything done to prove that our
Swedish brethren were full of the fraternal spirit
which is one of the chief characteristics of our Order.
We soon felt at home and as the members of the reception committee all spoke English well, we had no
difficulty in becoming acquainted with them. Our party
was almost the first to arrive, but a little later in
the day came Joseph Malins, who had been lecturing for
two or three weeks in Sweden, and whom about one
thousand Good Templars had gone to meet and escort on
the last stages of his journey. With him came Rev.
Burford and Mrs. Hooke, from Wales, and from that time
there were arrivals on every train, of delegates who
had come by various routes, until on Monday evening we
were summoned to meet the last detachment. This consisted of Brother and Sister Collings, of Liverpool;
Sir William Fox, of New Zealand; Sister Brown, of
London; and others. On reaching the station we found
about two thousand Good Templars, with banners flying,
who greeted the newcomers with odes of welcome, very
beautifully rendered by male voices. At the close of
the singing a hearty "Rah, rah!" was indulged in by the
Swedes, while the visitors responded by a ringing
English cheer, and there were enough Britishers present
to do it well.

Rooms had been secured for all the visitors at the
Grand Hotel, which made it very pleasant, as we were
able to see more of one another than if we had been
scattered in different parts of the city. The Grand is
considered the best hotel in Stockholm, and is a fine
five-story building, situated on the opposite side of
the river from and commanding a good view of the King´s
Palace. In all its appointments the hotel is elegant

and comfortable and every convenience which is common
to an American hotel is to be found within it; the only
things lacking being the hurry and confusion which
prevails upon this side of the Atlantic, and one could
soon see that life is lived at a less rapid pace in
Sweden than with us. During the eight or nine days
which we spent in Stockholm we managed to see a great
deal of the city, and were delighted with its fine
buildings and with its beautiful situation and surroundings. Built upon several islands, the city is
extremely picturesque and well deserves the name
bestowed upon it of the "Venice of the North." By
means of a steam elevator which carried us to the
highest point of view, at no labor to ourselves, we
were enabled to reach the Mossbacke (Mose Hill), which
commands the best prospect to be obtained of the city
and its environs. Looking down from the elevation to
which we had so rapidly and easily attained, we found
that the objects below looked very small indeed, and as
we waited with interest the moving panorama beneath us
we were able to form a good deal of the size and
importance of this northern capital.

Some of our party found time to take a look
through the magnificent royal palace; others went over
the National Museum, which is a fine specimen of
architecture and is full of curious and beautiful
things. There are a number of fine churches in Stockholm, some of them very ancient. Chief among these is
the Riddarholms Church,--the royal mausoleum of
Sweden,--which contains the tombs of Gustavus Adolphus
and other great heroes whose names are "famous in
story." This church dates back to about the end of
the thirteenth century, but many alterations and

repairs have been made at different periods. In 1835 its tower was destroyed by lightning, and its present spire of perforated iron, three hundred feet high, was erected.

Scarcely less interesting is the Storkyrkan (St. Nicolai church) which was originally built by Birger Jarl--the founder of Stockholm--in 1264, and contains many beautiful monuments, as well as an altar piece which is regarded as an exquisite specimen of sculpture.

Many fine statues adorn the city; that of Birger Jarl, cast in bronze, stands in the square near the Riddarholmskyrkan, and that of Gustavus Vasa, also in bronze, in front of the Riddarshuset (House of Nobles). In the King's Park is a beautiful statue, by Molin, of the brave young warrior king, Charles XII, and representations of some of his successors are to be seen in different parts of the city. A statue of Jacob Berzelius, the famous chemist, stands in the Berzelii Park, while in the garden known as Hasselbacken, a beautiful bronze statue of the national bard Bellmann is placed under the oak tree, where, nearly one hundred years ago, the poet used to sing his compositions to admiring listeners.

The Technical College, the Carolian Medical Academy, the Academy of Science, the Ethnology Museum, the Art Union, the Academy of Music, and other similar institutions, show us that Stockholm is not behind other cities in the arts and sciences; while the numerous hospitals, asylums for the blind and insane and orphan institutions, prove that the spirit of philanthropy is not lacking.

But time would fail if we were to attempt to describe all that we found to admire in Stockholm, and we can only mention in passing that the streets are clean and well-ordered, the bridges handsome, the numerous little parks shady and cool, the stores tasteful and full of beautiful wares, and the people, from the highest to the lowest, delightfully courteous and kindly.

The politeness of the Swede, while it equals that of the Frenchman, yet differs from it. The simple dignity of bearing which characterizes the former gives him an appearance of sincerity which the more volatile Frenchman lacks. To one accustomed to the free and easy manners in vogue among the lower grades of the population of the United States, the stately courtesy which prevails in even the lowest ranks of Stockholm is very striking. What should we say if we saw the ashmen and scavengers of Boston doffing their caps to one another?

Another thing which impressed us in Stockholm, and in Scandinavia generally, was the healthy, cleanly and tidy appearance of the poorer people. Of course, we had not time to investigate very thoroughly, but during our short stay we saw none of the squalor and misery which is so apparent in most English cities, and unfortunately, in many American cities also. As in Hamburg a national characteristic dress is worn by many of the peasantry. One costume frequently seen in Stockholm is that of the Dalecarlian peasant whose dress is very

bright and striking. Many of the Dalecarlian girls
whom we saw were very pretty and they appear to be very
strong, doing men's work, and--what is better--
receiving men's wages. We were glad to notice some of
these peasants wearing our badge and taking part in
some of the gatherings held under the auspices of the
Order.

It must not be supposed, however, that because we
found time to observe so much we had nothing else to
do. Our R.W.G. Lodge session occupied the greater part
of four days and two evenings, while two others
evenings were given to a reception meeting in the
Bethel Church, and to a visit to Welcome Lodge. Our
session was held in the Riksdaghuset (Parliament
Building), which, although not an imposing building,
was very comfortable and well adapted for our purpose.
The session was well attended, and everybody showed a
lively interest in the proceedings. Many of the
prominent Swedish brethren spoke English fluently, as
did also the delegates from Norway and Denmark, but for
the benefit of those who were not linguists it was
thought advisable to have an interpreter, and Brother
Thorelli, a professor of languages at Stockholm,
acquitted himself adroitly in that capacity. At the
reception meeting all the R.W.G.L. officers and many
others had an opportunity of trying how it seemed to
talk through an interpreter, and it was rather an
ordeal to some, especially to those who found that
their little jokes would not bear translating into
another language. However, if some of the jokes fell
flat, the speeches as a whole gave great satisfaction,
and were received with much enthusiasm. We had the
pleasure of seeing ourselves reported <u>verbatim</u> in all

the next day´s papers; and of amusing ourselves with conjecturing how are poor, little innocent words could have been twisted into the alarming polysyllables which adorned our speeches when "done into Swedish."

The visit to Welcome Lodge was interesting. Over one thousand members were present, and an initiation was finely performed. The proceedings did not terminate until a late hour, and it seemed very strange to go out and find that it midnight it was light enough to see to read. It made it seem almost absurd to go to bed, and in view of the late hours in which the meetings we attended were continued we felt inclined to think that our good Swedish brethren must get all their sleep in the winter time.

[February 1886]]
Three particularly pleasant incidents connected with our visit to Stockholm were a trip to Upsala, a dinner at Ulricsdal, and the Sunday service in Djurgarten. I shall relate them in the order in which they occurred. "Upsala is the most interesting place in Sweden," said one of our "brither Scots," and, as this famous old university town is only about forty miles from Stockholm, a half dozen of us decided that we must see it. The one day which we had at our disposal before the opening of the R.W.G. Lodge was therefore devoted to that purpose, and soon after breakfast we boarded an express train, which carried us to Upsala in a little over an hour.

Almost the first thing which greeted our eyes as we alighted from the train was a poster, upon which the name of Joseph Malins figured in large letters; and as

the poster was headed Good Templarorden, we judged it
to be an announcement of our R.W.G. Templar´s lectures.
We saw many copies of this poster in conspicuous places
in the town, and concluded that our Swedish brethren
knew how to advertise their meetings.   While walking
about the town, we encountered a student who was
wearing our Blue Ribbon Badge, and who, recognizing us
by our badges, came and introduced himself, and
volunteered his services as a guide.

We spent some time in the Cathedral, which is very
large and imposing, and is said to have been built upon
the site of the old heathen temple of Upsala.   It dates
back to the year 1260, but is greatly disfigured by two
modern towers built to replace the original towers,
which were destroyed by lightning in 1702.

The interior of the Cathedral is wonderfully
interesting.   A pretty, modest Swedish maiden, who
acted as guide, did her best, with the aid of a very
few English words which she had probably picked up from
travellers, to point out the many remarkable things
which it contained.   One of the chief objects of
interest in the silver shrine containing the bones of
St. Erik, the patron saint of Stockholm; but we were
more impressed with the tomb of Gustavus Adolphus, upon
which the recumbent figure of the famous monarch is
represented, and also those of his two wives.   The
walls of the chapel which contains the tomb have seven
of the principal events in the life of Gustavus
Adolphus painted in fresco upon them.   We were also
shown the tomb and monument of Linné, the famous
botanist (better known to English-speaking people by

his latinized name of Linnaeus), who was a student and professor at Upsala University.

The University was founded in 1477. It has about one hundred professors, lecturers, and tutors, and 1,500 students. The famous library known as the Carolina Rediviva contains about 200,000 volumes and 7,000 manuscripts. The most noted of these is the Codex Argentus, a copy of the four Gospels in silver letters on parchment. This was the work of Bishop Ulphilas, one thousand years before Gutenberg was born.

From Upsala we drove to Gamla (or Old) Upsala to see the famous Kungshogar, or Tumuli of the Kings. These are three large mounds, each about sixty feet high, and are said to have been the burial-places of the Scandinavian Gods Odin, Thor, and Frey. Close by the mounds is a very old church, into which is built part of the wall of a still older structure, supposed to be the remains of a Druid Temple. The interior of the church is very bare, with brick floor, whitewashed walls, and rough wooden pews. There is little save its age and primitive condition to make it remarkable. We noted only one tablet, which is in memory of Celsius, the inventor of the thermometer in use in Sweden. Around the church is a peaceful little village church-yard, where I suppose the "forefathers of the hamlet sleep," and where we noticed some very old tombstones almost hidden in the long grass.

Gamla Upsala, whatever it may have been in the past, is a very small village now. Some little white cottages stand near the churchyard, and two or three pretty, fair-haired children, who were playing near,

came and gazed at the strangers, and made their bows
with that gentle gravity which seems to be a Swedish
characteristic.

The dinner at Ulricsdal took place on Friday
afternoon, and was a part of the programme arranged by
our Swedish brethren for our entertainment. The
R.W.G.L. session closed at about 4 o'clock on that day;
and we went by special steamer to Ulricsdal, a most
delightful sail. The scenery on both sides of the
river is lovely, and I can recall now the calm enjoyment which I experienced as our boat glided along past
woods and gardens and parks, all green and refreshing
to the eyes, while a choir of our student brethren
delighted our ears with their songs. Arrived at
Ulricsdal, we sat down to a sumptuous dinner, which was
served in the Pavilion [of the Queen's Summer Palace],
and after the numerous courses were disposed of a
number of toasts were drunk in water, milk, or seltzer.
Complimentary speeches were made in honor of our new
R.W.G.T., Rev. W. G. Lane, and of Joseph Malins; both
of whom responded very happily. The "ladies" were
toasted by Lieut. Wavrinsky, and response made by Sir
William Fox. Two or three original poems were read;
one of them written in English by Hon. Erik Nystrom,
professor of philosophy, and member of Parliament, was
as follows:--

    We give you hearty welcome,
    Ye friends from foreign lands,
    Who made this toilsome journey
    Unto our northern strands,
    From kingdoms and republics,
    From islands of the sea,--

From England and America,
We greet you all with glee.

What made you spread your pinions
For such a weary flight?
What made you leave your home nests,
And on our shores alight?
Was it to burn and plunder
And win a bloody spoil,
As when our northern Vikings
Made inroads on your soil?

A double answer given,
Its meaning we may trace:
"No, no, for we are brethren
Spite language, name and race."
Yes, yes we come for plunder,
And victory and fame;
But we´ll make war together,
Our enemy the same.

God bless you all: we thank you
For friendship and for love,
God bless you in future;
And may we meet above.
God bless your homes, your children,
Your people and your land.
And lead us on to victory
By His Almighty Hand.

After dinner we were conducted over the Palace of
Ulricsdal, where some beautiful pictures and other
interesting things are to be seen, and then in the

cool, pleasant evening we made the return trip, arriving at the pier in Stockholm at about 11 o´clock, P.M., in broad daylight.

It had been arranged to hold a Good Templar Service in the Djurgarten (Deer Park), and on the Sunday morning following the R.W.G.L. session, the Lodges of Stockholm and vicinity assembled in one of the squares, and formed in procession. Every Lodge had its banner, upon which was painted or embroidered the name and number of the Lodge, as well as various devices and emblems. We counted eighty-four of these banners as the procession filed past us, and they made a most imposing display.

When we arrived at the Djurgarten we found a large company assembled, all wearing the Good Templar badge, and all seated as decorously and quietly as if in a church. A rostrum had been erected for the preacher, and an organ placed near it, and soon all voices blended in a hymn sung to a grand old psalm tune, in the rather slow measure which seems to be the rule in the Lutheran church; it sounded very sweet and solemn in the open air. Then followed a prayer, which was listened to in reverent silence. And then [there came] a sermon by a Swedish minister, and one in English by Rev. Enoch Franks.

During the day the platform was occupied by various speakers, chiefly representatives of the R.W. Lodge, who made Temperance addresses. We had tea with Bro. Thorelli and his wife that day, and afterwards attended service, which was conducted in Bro. Thorelli´s lecture-room by Rev. W. G. Lane and Rev. Wm. Ross.

The close of the Sabbath day brought us to the hour of parting. Some of our friends left that night; but those of us who were going to Christiania remained until Monday evening. It was with much regret that we said farewell to Stockholm, and to the many kind friends who had made our visit so pleasant. Everybody was so good to us that it seems invidious to mention some, and not all; but I have a grateful recollection of Bros. Lundin, Berg, Wavrinsky, Sahlin, Stromberg, Thorelli, and many others; not forgetting our good Bro. Oskar Eklund, who made so many friends when in America two years ago. Then there were Bro. Lundin's wife and fair young daughters, Mrs. Thorelli, and other ladies, and Bro. Eklund's father and little sisters. Nor must I forget the Danish friends who were at the session-- particularly Dr. Selmer and his wife, who made us think that the qualities which have made the Princess of Wales so beloved in England, must be a natural heritage of Danish ladies.

I feel it a great privilege to have made the acquaintance of these people, and to have seen something of their country and customs. I honor them for their earnest work they are doing in the Temperance field, and say with the poet:

> "Not chance nor place of birth hath made us
> friends
> (For are we not of different tongue
> and nations?);
> But the endeavor for the self-same ends,
> With the same hopes and fears and aspirations."

[March 1886]

In order to meet the engagements made with the Grand Lodges of Norway and Denmark, it was found necessary to divide the R.W.G.L. Executive into two parties to attend the special sessions to be held in those jurisdictions. Bros. Rev. W. G. Lane, Malins, and Allen, accompanied by Brother and Sister Collings, Sister Gray, and others, returned with Dr. and Mrs. Selmer to Copenhagen; and Bros. Turnbull, Rev. Wm. Ross, and myself went with two of our Norwegian brethren, [M.] Laumann and Jansen [Lars O. Jensen], to Christiania [later known as Oslo]. Our party also included Sister Impey, Sir Wm. Fox and niece, Bros. Osborn, Derrington, Potter, and others. The journey occupied seventeen hours, and although we did not travel as comfortably as on our other long railroad ride from Malmo to Stockholm, we were greatly delighted by the beauty and variety of the scenery through which we passed. We had daylight throughout the whole of the night, and at 3:15 in the morning we saw the sun rise over the magnificent Lake Wenern, and it was a sight to be remembered. After we got into Norwegian territory, the scenery became wilder and more rugged. For a long distance we skirted the banks of the Glommen--a large and beautiful river, where there is apparently an extensive lumber trade carried on, for we could see the logs being whirled along in the rapids. It was nearly noon when we reached Christiania, where we found a large company waiting to give us a most cordial reception. Our kind-hearted brethren of Gamle Norge (Old Norway) showed themselves no less anxious to make us welcome and to do us honor than their Swedish neighbors had been. We were escorted to the Royal

Hotel, and, after an interval to enable us to remove
the dust of travel, we were entertained to a dinner,
with toasts and speeches and everything in order. We
found Bros. [Lauritus] Balle and Henriksen, who had
left Stockholm before us, awaiting us in Christiania;
and we made the acquaintance of many more Good Templar
friends--many of them already known to us by name, and
honored for "their work´s sake."

The R.W.G..L. session was held in the same afternoon in the Good. Templar Hall, and the degree was
conferred upon forty-three candidates. The session was
well-attended, and a great deal of enthusiasm displayed. It is evident that a good work is being
accomplished by the Order in Norway. In the evening a
public meeting was held in the Drill Hall, in which
four thousand persons--including many of the city
dignitaries--were assembled. An address of welcome was
delivered by Bro. Tolnaes, who translated his own
speech into excellent English. Then followed addresses
by Rev. Wm. Ross, Sir Wm. Fox, and others of the
visitors (who were interpreted by Bro. Jansen [Jensen]
and Captain Reynolds), and a rousing speech from Bro.
Torjuss Hansen [Hanssen], the present G.W.C.T. of
Norway. A student choir rendered many of the national
airs very finely; and some solo singing, and good music
by a band, helped to make up an excellent programme,
which did not reach its last number until nearly
midnight, and by that time we were ready for our long-
delayed repose.

Christiania is a much smaller and less imposing
city than Stockholm, and must of course suffer by
comparison. The Carl Johan Gaden, the principal street

of the city, is a fine, wide thoroughfare, and some of
the public buildings are quite handsome. It is the
only university town in Norway, and is quiet, orderly,
and thrifty-looking, and very clean. The wooden houses
make it look almost like an American town, and the iron
stoves, instead of the elaborate porcelain ones which
we saw everywhere in Stockholm, would make a Yankee
feel quite at home.

Christiania is beautifully situated, as we were
able to see for ourselves the next day, when through
the courtesy of some of our kind Norwegian friends, we
went for a drive of five miles to the Frognersoeter,--a
chalet on a hill 1,400 feet above the sea-level. The
way was through a forest

"Of tall and sombrous pines;
And where the sunshine darted through
Spread a vapor soft and blue,
In long and sloping lines."

When we reached the chalet we had to walk about
another mile to the top of the hill, and then ascend a
wooden scaffolding thirty feet in height. From the top
of this tower, which is over nineteen hundred feet above
sea-level, and is called Tryvanshoide, we looked upon a
scene of indescribable loveliness made up of mountains
and valleys and lakes, with the city of Christiania and
the glittering waters of the Christiania Fjord as the
central features. This little excursion was a great
pleasure, and we felt grateful to the kind friends who
had planned it for us. In Christiania, as in Stockholm,
we experienced the greatest kindness and courtesy, and

brought away nothing but pleasant memories,--only
tempered with regret that we could not stay longer, and
see more of this wild and beautiful north-land and her
brave people.

We left Christiania at noon the following day on
the North Cape steamer, and enjoyed a never-to-be-
forgotten sail down the Christiania Fjord, through
scenery which for picturesque beauty is probably
unsurpassed by anything in the world. At an early hour
next morning we landed at Christiansand, and spent a day
in this quaint little town, where we soon found some
Good Templar brethren, who arranged a public meeting for
the evening. During the day we went to a service in the
handsome Lutheran Church,--the only building of any size
in the place,--and afterwards drove to Ravnedal, a
beautiful little park, which lies at the foot of a great
rock (called in Norway a fjeld), and contains a miniature lake, with rustic bridges and shaded walks. Here
we found wild-flowers in abundance,--amongst them
specimens of the Scottish blue-bell and heather, as well
as many blossoms common in England.

The meeting in the evening was small, but the
audience showed much interest in what we were able to
tell regarding the progress of the cause in other
places. This was the last gathering in which we took
place in Scandinavia, and when we sailed from Norway I
felt that we had all learned something from what we had
seen in these countries, and that, apart from its
Temperance teachings, our Order is doing a grand work in
helping to bring about the day when

"Man to be man the world o´er
Shall brithers be and a´ that."

We had a delightful voyage of about thirty-six hours´ duration on a exceedingly comfortable and well-appointed Scottish steamer; and in the bright sunshine of the Sabbath afternoon, I first saw Scotland. A wonderful sail was that up the Firth of Forth, with the bonny blue hills and the lovely landscape on each side; and when we came in sight of Edinburgh, I marvelled not that the Scotsman is proud of "Auld Reekie."

A city most "beautiful for situation" it is, and no less beautiful upon nearer view. It was only a glimpse which I had of it on that day, and indeed it was only a glimpse of Scotland which I had altogether; for my time was growing short, and it was in Scotland, unfortunately, that I encountered almost the first bad weather which I had experienced in Europe. However, I had one bright and beautiful day in Glasgow, where I was most hospitably entertained by Bro. Hamilton´s wife and daughter.

Glasgow is a fine, thriving city; but it is not beautiful. After the Scandinavian cities, the hurry and bustle of this busy place seemed rather confusing. I spent a pleasant hour or two in the Cathedral, and was much interested in some of the old tombs in the Necropolis.

On the Monday evening I sailed for Belfast en route to Londonderry, where I was due at the annual session of the G.L. of Ireland.

[April 1886]

The visit to Ireland, although nearly the last of my experiences, was not by any means the least pleasant one. I landed in Belfast quite early in the morning of July 14th, and had my first ride in an Irish jaunting-car. If I may be allowed a free expression of opinion with regard to this famous vehicle, I must say that the novelty of it is the best thing about it to a stranger, although some friends in Ireland told me that it is "quite comfortable to ride in <u>when you get used to it</u>." I did not get used to it; but I directed all my energies to "houlding [sic] on," in obedience to the driver´s recommendation to that effect, and so escaped disaster. I had some time to wait for a train, and employed it in looking about Belfast, which is a bright and busy city, and was on that day decorated very gaily in honor of the Anniversary of the Battle of the Boyne. The railroad journey was tedious and uncomfortable, and when passing through the rural districts, which, in their bare and desolate aspect, presented such a contrast to the thrifty, well-tilled fields in England and Scotland, one could realize something of the woes of Ireland and wish for her more prosperous days.

I reached Londonderry early in the afternoon, and at the Temperance Hotel found a number of the Grand Lodge officers, who greeted me very kindly. I was soon rested and refreshed. The Grand Lodge was in session, and when I was introduced by Bro. Caithness, G.W.C.T., I had no reason to complain of my reception. I had heard of the warmth of the Irish heart, and I learned something of the warmth of an Irish welcome.

The Grand Lodge of Ireland is much smaller than the G.L. of Scotland; but it has to contend with innumerable difficulties, and it speaks well for the membership, that, in the face of such opposition, it is still a flourishing and growing organization.[1] It was easy to tell that the interest shown in the questions that came up for debate that the members were zealous and enterprising, and anxious to push forward the good cause.

Amongst those whose acquaintance, I made were the earnest G.W.C.T., Bro. Caithness, who was unanimously re-elected to the office which he so worthily fills; his son, who was re-elected to the office of G.W. Sec.; another son, who is a clergyman of the Established Church; and a daughter. Then there were Bro. and Sister Wilkinson, Rev. John Pyper, Bro. Robt. Semple (formerly of Scotland), and his wife; and also Mrs. Crawford, a lady well[-]known for her literary as well as her Temperance work; and many others. Among the visitors were Bro. Rev. J. Mottram from England, Bro. Sutherland and his daughter, and Bro. Hill from Scotland, and Bro. Cooke, the G.W. Sec. of Wales, who was one of my travelling companions from Hull to Stockholm, and whom I was therefore very glad to see again.

The session continued through the whole of Wednesday, 15th, and in the evening there was a rousing public meeting, when each of the visitors had a chance

---

1   The hostility of the Roman Catholic Church toward secret societies kept Catholics, with rare exceptions, from joining the Order. Moreover, during the "Negro Question" schism the Hickmanites had much greater success in Ireland than in England or Scotland.

to make a short address to a very appreciative audience. There was also some good singing by a choir, and
one or two solos by Bro. Semple, and altogether the
evening was a most enjoyable one.

Apart from the enjoyment which the meeting with
our Irish brethren gave me, there was the pleasure
which I found in being in the historic city of Londonderry, and in being able actually to walk on the old
walls, and picture the scene of the famous siege, so
vividly described by Macaulay. A new town has grown up
in the two hundred years which have elapsed since the
city was so bravely held for over eight months by the
gallant men of Derry; and, looking at the peaceful
homes which now surround the old walls, it is hard to
realize that an invading army could ever have been
encamped there.

On the morning of the 16th I joined the members
and visitors of the Grand Lodge in an excursion to "The
Giant's Causeway," and spent several very delightful
hours in examining this wonderful natural formation.
Before leaving we formed a group in the Wishing Chair,
and were photographed. We were able to make the return
journey all together as far as Coleraine, where I had
to say farewell to the party, and in company with
Brother Cooke and two or three other Good Templars I
took the train for Belfast. We arrived in Belfast in
time to pay an unexpected visit to a nice little Lodge,
where we received a warm greeting, and were able to
give some pleasure in return for it, by relating some
of our foreign experiences. I have a hearty sympathy
for a little struggling lodge, and feel glad to know
that our "surprise" was an encouragement to this one.

I had a few hours in Belfast next morning, and saw many beautiful specimens of Irish manufactures in the stores. The lovely laces, linen, and poplins, the bog-oak and Wicklow-spar jewelry, but above all the beautiful Beleek china, made one wish for a much longer purse than I possessed.

About noon I went on board the boat, and had a delightful sail back to Scotland, arriving in Glasgow that night, where I again shared the hospitality of our good Sister Hamilton. The next day, my last in Scotland, was a very rainy one, and I was only able to ride about Edinburgh, and see what I could of the exterior of the buildings. It was a great disappointment to be obliged to leave without seeing more of Scotland; but my time was drawing too near its close to admit of a longer stay in the "land of Burns," and so with much regret I turned my face towards London again.

The few remaining days of my trip were spent in London, where I had still some friends to see, and some business to attend to; and I found that this left me no time for sight-seeing; so that with the exception of a delightful visit to Westminster Abbey, where I heard some fine singing, and an excellent sermon from the Bishop of Bedford, I have nothing of importance to record. However, the time was very pleasantly spent, and when the hour for leaving came, the sorrow which my friends were kind enough to express was echoed in my own heart.

I spent one night in Liverpool at the home of Brother Collings, and, in company with Sister Collings, attended a public meeting in Garston, where I met our R.W.G.T., Bro. Lane, who with myself had been advertised to address the meeting. We were listened to with attention and evident appreciation, and I was glad to learn later that the meeting resulted in a substantial increase to the Lodge.

My steamer, the "Pavonia," sailed the next morning, July 20th [1885], and I was obliged to leave without attending an Executive meeting, and a public farewell meeting to Bro. Lane and myself, which had been arranged for that day. However, I had the pleasure of seeing and saying farewell to the members of the Executive, and also to Sister Impey, who with Brother and Sister Collings waited on the wharf to see the last of me as I left Old England's shores.

The homeward voyage was pleasant, very calm, and rather slow. We had a very agreeable party of passengers, and managed to pass the time fairly well with the aid of music and other amusements; but I was not sorry when we came in sight of dear old Boston again.

The three months of my absence had passed quickly and happily. I had brought back a store of pleasant memories and fair pictures "in the mind's gallery." Remembering all the kindness which I had received, all the pleasure I had experienced, and the freedom from accident with which my numerous journeys had been accomplished, my heart was filled with gratitude to

"Him whose hand
Led me o'er sea and land,"

back to the every-day duties and cares of life, with renewed health and strength, and with fresh courage to work for our cause, and hope of its ultimate victory.

DEBATE ON REUNION IN R.W.G. LODGE OF THE WORLD, SARATOGA, NEW YORK, MAY 25, 1887

[Good Templars´ Watchword, June 27, 1887; third-person outline]

[Forsyth´s friend, Catherine Impey, the English Quaker who had been in charge of the Mission committee, led the fight against the terms of reunion adopted at the Saratoga session of the Right Worthy Grand Lodge of the World. Her American supporters included two black editors, Dr. B. T. Tanner and T. Thomas Fortune. Tanner, who was a bishop in the A.M.E. Church, edited the (Philadelphia) Christian Recorder until 1884 and then the A.M.E. Church Review. Fortune edited the (New York) Globe until 1884 and then the (New York) Freeman; he supported the Prohibitionist Party in 1885-87. During the debate Tanner argued that by allowing parallel Senior and Junior Grand Lodges on the basis of race the Boston terms of union "branded the coloured man as an inferior being."[2] If parallel Grand Lodges were to be created, "let [the basis of membership] not be race, but of condition," so that people such as

---

2   According to Catherine Impey "Bro. Dr. Tanner had intended presenting to the R.W.G.L. a memorial, adopted on the previous Sunday night by a meeting composed of 2,000 coloured people assembled in one of the principal coloured churches of New York," but did not because of his chilly reception in Saratoga. Catherine Impey, "Supplementary Report," Grand Lodge of England, Proceedings (1888), p. 61.

himself would not be "put off with the ignorant and uncultured of his race."]

Sister Jessie Forsyth, R.W.G.V.T. (Massachusetts), said she could not allow the debate to close without expressing her feeling with regard to two references which had been made. Originally an English Good Templar, she had, on behalf of our battle for the coloured people, worked for 11 years amongst them in Boston, her Lodge, the Joseph Malins Lodge there being a mixed Lodge, and its chief a coloured brother [the Rev. S. C. Gooseley (sometimes spelled Goosely), Past Grand Worthy Chief Templar of South Carolina]. She protested against any implication that by reunion we were retrograding. By it we were opening to our coloured members hundreds of the white Lodges of the other section. She was shocked at Dr. Tanner's suggestion of Lodges based upon "condition."

[Tanner protested that he had been misinterpreted.]

Sister Forsyth (continuing): If Bro. Tanner had stood by us during these 11 years of our struggling in behalf of his race, instead of dropping out of the Order three times and remaining out for years, we might regard him as competent to tell us to go in disunion. And now we are told to hear Mr. Fortune, who is coming to tell us our duty to his people. When I remember that, though repeatedly solicited to join us, Mr. Fortune has never done so, but has, during our struggle in years past, backed our opponents in attacking us through his paper, I feel indignant at the thought of our seeking guidance at his hands, and I hope we shall not entertain it for a moment. While we have fought and suffered for their race, such men have not helped us, and it is not for them to affect to teach us our duty.

DUAL GRAND LODGE DEBATE

FORSYTH TO EDITOR, <u>GOOD TEMPLARS´ WATCHWORD</u>, MAY 1, 1888

[<u>International Good Templar</u>, May 1888]

Dear Sir and Brother,--In reading the report of the "Dual Grand Lodge Debate," in the <u>Watchword</u> of 16th April [1888], I observe that a reference is made to my visit to Virginia. It occurs in Sister [Catherine] Impey´s address, and reads as follows:

"Sister Forsyth goes south, and, <u>as the result</u>, an amalgamation of ours and the Dual [or black Hickmanite] Order takes place, and all is peace, peace."

I understand the imputation to be that I brought an undue influence to bear upon these Grand Lodges, which causes them to unite in opposition to the judgment and wishes of the members.

It is not my purpose to endeavor to convince Sister Impey that the imputation is an injustice, not only to me, but to the intelligence of the colored Virginians themselves, and I forbear to offer any comments of my own upon this and other statements made by her. I consider, however, that is due to the membership in England that they should know the facts, and a plain statement of facts is all that I shall present.

The union between the two Junior Grand Lodges of Virginia had been arranged for some months before the Richmond [union] session occurred, as the following extracts from letters now in my possession will prove. I will begin with a paragraph from the much-quoted Brother [W. S.] Wilson, whose letter, dated 27th July, 1887, says: "The R.W.G.C. Templar, Brother Finch, learning that I could not possibly arrange to meet on the 9th of August, submitted this proposition, which I accepted: `That, as the Senior [or white] Grand Lodge of Virginia is to meet in Richmond on 5th December, the two Colored Grand Lodges to meet on the same date, preparatory to forming one Grand Lodge, which will be the Junior Grand Lodge of Virginia.´"

The closing paragraph in this letter, while it does not actually bear upon the matter may be interesting in view of other of Brother Wilson´s utterances, which have been quoted to prove his opposition to union. The paragraph reads: "I firmly believe the Order will advance much faster under the present administration than it could ever have done otherwise. I trust that God will spare our dear Sister Impey to realize this view of mine."[3]

---

3   W. S. Wilson had seconded Catherine Impey´s amendment at Saratoga to omit any reference to separation of the races and had rejected the notion that separate Grand Lodges "could or would bring the races nearer to each other." Paraphrased in Catherine Impey, "Supplementary Report," Grand Lodge of England, Proceedings (1888), p. 62.

A letter from Sister Lucy Wooden, G.Supt.J.T., of Virginia, dated 14 September, 1887, says: "I had a letter from Brother J. B. Finch this morning, saying that he would meet us at Richmond on 5th December."

A letter, dated 12 September, 1887, from R.W.G. Templar Finch, has this paragraph: "I shall meet the Grand Lodges of Virginia early in December."

When [after the death of Finch] the request came from the R.W.G. Counselor to go to Richmond to represent the R.W.G. Lodge at the union session of the two Junior Grand Lodges of Virginia, I wrote to Brother Wilson, and to Brother Prof. Vassar, as G.C. Templars of the two Junior Grand Lodges, and also to Sister Wooden, the G.Supt.J.T., of the Grand Lodge (World) who, for several years, has been my valued correspondent and friend. Brother Vassar's reply was prompt and cordial: "Come, by all means; Brother Finch would have been with us; come in his place." Referring to the contemplated union, he says: "Both Lodges are weak, and a union will undoubtedly strengthen us."

Sister Wooden's reply, dated 14th November, 1887, was: "Yes, our session will take place in Richmond on 5th December. I am not yet prepared to state at what place we will hold our session, but we want to get as near to the place where the Dual Grand Lodge Session will be held as we can."

A postal from Brother Wilson, dated 23rd November, says: "Have arranged to meet in Richmond, 5th December."

The above will prove that the union session had been planned without reference to my visit. Now for the facts regarding the session itself. I find Brother Wilson quoted in Sister Impey's address as having written "It was the earnest wish of the majority of our delegates to remain as they were, that is not favoring the union, but after a long debate they decided to accept the terms as a half loaf."

I understand this to mean that a long debate occurred in the Grand Lodge at Richmond, and I am able to state that this is not the truth. I entered the Grand Lodge within an hour after it was opened and was invited to preside. Upon asking for the order of business I was surprised to learn that they were already engaged in drawing up resolutions to present to the "Dual" Grand Lodge as to terms of union. There was no debate and the idea seemed to be general that union was desirable. I will say here that I found, and was glad to find, our colored members excellently well able to manage their own affairs. I offered an occasional suggestion with reference to the wording of the resolutions (which, by the way, were written by Brother Wilson) but I certainly brought no pressure to bear and had no occasion to do so.

After the resolutions had been drawn up they were unanimously adopted.

They were submitted to the "Dual" Grand Lodge at the evening session, and were adopted by that body unanimously. The union took place immediately, with much rejoicing and enthusiasm. I heard not a single word of dissatisfaction until after the election of officers when Brother Wilson found fault because, as he claimed, all the most important offices had been given to the "Dual" Grand Lodge. In this complaint Brother Wilson received no countenance from the members of his Grand Lodge, and the offer generously made by Brother Vassar to exchange the office of G.C. Templar to which he had been unanimously elected, for that of G. Counsellor, held by Brother Wilson, was not entertained by anybody. Before I left the United Junior Grand Lodge of Virginia, I was assured by many of the members that they were well[-]satisfied. Later in the week, I met a large representation of what was our membership in Norfolk, and I found them jubilant over the union.

I spent several hours in the home of Sister Wooden, in Norfolk, where many of the leading members called upon me. I heard no expression of dissatisfaction, and I may add, that neither by letter [n]or by word of mouth, has Brother Wilson ever expressed to me any desire or intention to apply for admission to the Senior Grand Lodge.

The assertion made by Brother Wilson, in a letter to Sister Impey, dated 15 March, 1888, that "our part of the Order that was are greatly dissatisfied" is not borne out by the statements of other members. Sister Wooden, dated 10th April, says, "we are working very harmoniously here."

It will be apparent to all that Brother Wilson´s statements contradicted one another again and again. His testimony, therefore, must be regarded as unreliable, and the wonder is that Sister Impey should be willing to use such testimony to discredit those who are as truly the friends of the [black] race as herself.

ORONHYATEKHA, THE RIGHT WORTHY GRAND COUNSELOR

[<u>International Good Templar</u>, Aug. 1888; reprinted from <u>Eastern Good Templar</u>. Oronhyatekha has been translated as "it (is a) burning sky"]

The subject of this sketch may well take rank among the most eminent members of the Order. He is a full-blooded Indian of the Mohawk Nation, the head tribe of the celebrated Confederacy of the Six Nations, and was born on the Indian Reservation, near Brantford, Ontario, Aug. 10, 1841. He is a large man, with a full rounded figure, fully six feet in height and of very imposing presence. He has the traditional black hair and piercing black eye of his race, and a very pleasant and genial expression.

His childhood days were spent among his own people, and at ten years of age he began his English education in the Industrial School, near Brantford, established for the training of young Indians. Here he remained four years and a half, and was taught the shoemaker´s trade in addition to the rudiments of English. Upon his leaving this institution his parents wished him to work the trade which he had been taught, but anxious for more learning, he ran away from home and became a pupil in the Wesleyan Academy at Wilbraham, Mass. In order to support himself--as he was without means and would not apply to his family for help--he worked at any odd job he could find to do after school hours. He related that he once sawed a cord of wood, twice in two, split it and piled it up for a kind-hearted Methodist minister, for which service he received the goodly sum of forty cents. He is of the opinion that he was just as happy then as when, some years later, he received a fee of two hundred dollars for a surgical operation which took him about a half hour to perform. By dint of hard work and the severest economy, living as he expresses it "on bread, salt and water for breakfast, salt, water and bread for dinner, and water, salt and bread for supper," he was enabled not only to remain at school for two years, but to keep clear of dyspepsia. During his last year at the academy he received the maximum number of marks in all his classes.

At the end of two years he returned to his home, taught school among the Indians for a year and then entered the preparatory department of Kenyon College, at Gambier, Ohio. In this institution he succeeded in taking the two years' preparation course in one, and matriculated into college at the end of the first year, where he remained as a student three years. He afterwards studied at Toronto University and was also for some time a student at St. Edmund's, Oxford University, England.

When the Prince of Wales visited Canada in 1860 Oronhyatekha was selected by the chiefs of the Six Nations to present an address to the Son of their "Great Mother." It was owing to the impression he made on this occasion that he received the invitation to go to Oxford to continue his studies. On his arrival at that ancient seat of learning he was placed under the care of Dr. Acland, the Prince's Physician and Regius Professor of Medicine in Oxford University.

He began his career as a physician at Frankford, Canada, where he soon acquired a large practice, and at the organization of the Hastings County Medical Association, was elected its first secretary, a post which he held until he removed to Stratford. On his leaving Frankford he was presented by his friends with an address and a gold watch.

During his residence in Stratford he took a prominent part in politics, and in 1872 took the stump for the Conservative candidate, and by his organizing powers secured the success of his party and defeated the sitting member. Shortly afterward he was appointed Consulting Physician to the Mohawk Indians, but resigned the position in 1874. In 1875 he took up his abode in London, Canada, where he now resides and practices his profession. He was then appointed Consulting Physician to the Oneida Indians, a post which he still holds in addition to an extensive private practice.

He married Miss Ellen Hill, of the Mohawk tribe, a great-grand-daughter of the celebrated Mohawk Chief, Capt. Joseph Brant. They have a son and daughter; the boy is named Acland after his father's old friend and tutor, Dr. Acland, of Oxford, and is a student in Toronto University.

Dr. Oronhyatekha is a true Indian and is very proud of his race. He has never allowed his connection with his tribe to be impaired, and at home in his own

family the Mohawk language is always used. He was
elected president of the Grand Council of Chiefs, of
Canada, in 1874. The Canadian Indians are thoroughly
loyal, and Oronhyatekha, while in the Toronto University, joined the volunteer force and was on active duty
in the University Rifle Co. of the Queen's Own during
the Fenian Raid of 1866. He was also a member of the
first Wimbledon team, where he won nine prizes.

The Doctor's connection with Good Templary has
extended over thirty years. During that period he has
been Grand Chief Templar of his Grand Lodge four times,
and is now filling for the third time the post of Right
Worthy Grand Counselor, and in addition to that office
he is Superintendent of Missions for North America.

He is prominently associated with other societies,
notably the Loyal Orange Association. He was one of
the Canadian delegates to the Imperial Triennial
Council, when it met in Glasgow, Scotland, and addressed a number of mass meetings in different towns of
the United Kingdom. He was made a "Prentice Boy" in
Derry, and was for some days at Florence Court, as a
guest of the Earl of Enniskillen. He is a
thirty-third-degree Mason and a Past Grand Master
General and Grand Lecturer of the Royal and Oriental
Masonry. At the head of the Independent Order of
Foresters, he has, by his energy and perseverance, made
that society one of the strongest in the Dominion of
Canada, financially speaking. When it was reorganized,
six and a half years ago, the membership was less than
four hundred, while the debt was over $4,000. On the
first of July last there was in the treasury over
$100,000, with all claims paid.

The members of Order of Foresters have not been slow to recognize his services. They have repeatedly elected him unanimously to the highest office in their gift, and at the last annual session of the Supreme Court the representatives voted $2,000 as some recognition of his services for the past year, and placed his salary for the next two years at $2,500.

With such a record we have no doubt that the new Good Templar Benefit Association in which Dr. Oronhyatekha takes a deep interest, will soon occupy a leading position among successful benefit societies, as its constitution and laws are a transcript of the I.O.F.

As a debater the Doctor has few equals in the Order, and the Right Worthy Grand Lodge appointed him one of its representatives to Great Britain when the great split in the Order occurred in 1876. He was also appointed by our late Brother Finch one of the commissioners to represent the R.W.G. Lodge at the session of the Boston conference, and at Saratoga took an important part in the debates and negotiations that finally resulted in reunion.

He and Brother Malins were chosen by the Boston conference to reduce the systems and constitutions of the two Right Worthy Grand Lodges into one. That they succeeded pretty well with their work is proved by the fact that the united body accepted their report and embodied it in the new constitutions, substantially as agreed to by these two Brothers.

Between Brother Finch our late R.W.G. Templar and Brother Oronhyatekha, there existed the strongest possible friendship, and so when the sudden death of Brother Finch was flashed over the country, and Brother Turnbull succeeded to the leadership of the Order and created a vacancy in the office of R.W.G. Counselor, the Executive Committee by unanimous vote called upon the Brother, who probably knew more [than anyone else] of the plans and intentions of Brother Finch as affecting Good Templary, to fill the office of R.W.G. Counsellor. Since then the Executive Committee have [sic] perfected the plans for the Good Templar Course of Study, and the Benefit Society which Brother Finch had in contemplation has been put into operation.

As head of the Independent Order of Foresters a large correspondence is entailed upon Brother Oron-hyatekha, but when we add to this the work in connec-tion with the editorship of The Independent Forester and the managing editorship of The International Good Templar, and the correspondence in connection with his position as Superintendent of Missions for North America, it makes Brother Oronhyatekha one of the busiest of men. [He served as Right Worthy Grand Templar, 1891-93, and died in 1907.]

FORSYTH TO ORONHYATEKHA, APRIL 30, 1889

[International Good Templar, June 1889]

Will you be so good as to send me that letter from Brother [C. A.] Lundberg regarding a Scandinavian Grand Lodge for this country, immediately.

A Swedish Lodge in Lowell, which was working under Junior Grand Lodge prior to the union [in 1887], has just withdrawn from the Order, with the avowed intention of joining the Swedish Grand Order [an organization formed in Sweden by persons who had seceded from the IOGT]. I think if I had known of the intention I could have persuaded the members to remain with us by holding out the hope of a Scandinavian Grand Lodge; but it was too late when I heard about it. However, I instituted a Swedish Lodge two or three weeks ago and I don´t want that to follow the example set by the seceding one.

You heard, of course, how badly we were beaten over the Constitutional Amendment [in Massachusetts].

I spent the day at a polling place in one of the worst wards of the city [of Boston]. A number of saloon keepers and their bartenders were on duty all day. It was dreadful to see some of their voters; two were quite tipsy and several had been drinking. It was humiliating to a woman to see the kind of men who are intrusted with the ballot which is too great a responsibility for our sex. However, I feel quite sure that there will not be much done in the way of temperance legislation until the women are allowed to vote--in Massachusetts at any rate.

Some of the liquor men entered into an argument once in a while with me and the lady who was with me. One man very frankly told me that we temperance people had no chance against "the trade." "Whip," said he, "have you any idea of the amount of money we have put into this campaign?" As an example of their resources, he wrote down the names of three Boston brewers who between them had contributed $24,000.

A respectable looking man came in during the day and I offered him a "yes" ballot. He glared at me and said in a withering tone, "Certainly, Madam, I'll vote yes; by all means let us put the saloon down in the kitchen or cellar." I thought I was equal to the occasion when I rejoined, "The lower you put it, sir, the nearer it will be to the place it came from." The man gave a grim smile and passed on to deposit his "no." I learned afterwards that he was a rumseller.

I think if the ministers who have opposed the amendment could have heard their names bandied about and their words quoted by those liquor men they would have felt ashamed of their position. There was no middle ground, they had to be on the side of temperance or on the side of the saloon. It was sad to know that some of the honored names of Boston pulpits were counted on the side of the traffic. Still, I am glad to say that the large majority of the ministers were with us: only 87, I think, out of near 1,100 declared themselves opposed to a prohibitory law. We have "failed in the fight" this time, but we are not discouraged. I believe that victory will be ours in God's good time.

THE DUTY OF THE SUBORDINATE LODGE
TO THE JUVENILE TEMPLE

[<u>International Good Templar</u>, Sept. 1890. Also reprinted there, Jan. 1891.]

It is time that true Good Templars everywhere realized that to them, no less than to the Christian Church, comes the divine injunction, "Feed my Lambs!" They need to be reminded that the whole duty of a Good Templar is not performed until some provision is made for the "little ones."

A place for the children has been found in our Order almost from its earliest days. In some jurisdiction the Juvenile work has for years received equal attention with that of the adult branch, and has met with equal success. But there are other places in which but little has been done in this direction, and where the members have not yet learned that the training of the children is a duty which cannot be shirked without injury to the cause.

If we are to carry out the full purpose of our Order, that of "saving the young, pure and virtuous from ever falling into the shares of the tempter," we must begin with the children. It is not enough to wait until they are old enough to enter our Lodge rooms, because before that age, in too many cases, habits are formed which will influence the whole life. We have surely learned by long and painful experience that it is easier to prevent than to cure; that it is better to save than to reclaim.

In establishing itself in a town or village the
Good Templars' Lodge practically makes a demand upon
the inhabitants for support and encouragement, and
pledges itself to advance the cause of temperance by
every means in its power. Unless it is making due
provision for the temperance training of the young, the
Order is not fully living up to its pretensions. A
sufficient excuse for neglect is not found in the claim
that the children should be taught at home, because in
many homes such teaching is absolutely unknown. Nor is
it any excuse for a Lodge in a quiet country place to
claim that because no temptation exists in that place,
special work is unnecessary. The children will become
men and women, and will probably go out into the world
to meet its many temptations. It is well, therefore,
that they should go around at all points to resist the
foe.

Then, too, Good Templars looking into the future,
longing and working and praying for the ultimate
triumph of our principle of total prohibition, know
that our hope lies in the rising generation, in the
boys (and the girls too, as we trust) who will be our
voters by and by. Is it not worth a little toil and
pains now to help these children grow up strong,
staunch temperance men and women, whose influence will
be on the side of right?

The wisdom of the R.W.G. Lodge in providing for
the election and installation of a Superintendent of
Juvenile Templars with the other officers of a Lodge
has been proved with an increased interest in the
Juvenile work generally. But in too many cases the
post is looked upon as merely an honorary one, and the

incumbent feels no responsibility regarding it. The
Lodge should in the first place use great judgment, and
care in the selection of such an officer, and should
then insist upon the faithful performance of the duties
devolving upon him. Having done this the Lodge should
stand ready to assist the Superintendent, first by
helping to gather in the children, next by furnishing
as many adult members to the Temple as possible, and
last, though not least, by contributing such financial
support as it can afford, at least until the Temple is
strong enough to be self-supporting. The idea that the
responsibility of the Lodge ceases when the Superintendent is installed is one which cannot be too strongly
condemned. While there are instances of live Temples
which exist without any help or countenance from the
Lodge, it too often happens that Superintendents who
would be willing and faithful workers, are discouraged
and dismayed by the apathy or indifference of the
Lodge. Another idea which prevails in many places must
also be discouraged. It is that if a Juvenile organization of any kind exists in a town, the Lodge is
relieved from the responsibility. Without desiring to
be selfish or narrow, I think that we, as Good Templars, are bound to advance the interests of our own
Order. If our juvenile branch were inferior to other
societies for children, we might reasonably be excused
for neglecting to push it. But we have an organization
as nearly perfect as possible; its pledge four-fold
[against alcoholic drink, tobacco, gambling, and bad
language], its ritual at once simple and impressive,
its teachings pure and lofty. Having this admirable
machinery ready to our hands, we are certainly to blame
if we do not make use of it.

I have presented the matter so far from the lofty
stand point of duty, but I think it can be proved that
in this, as in other matters, it <u>pays</u> to do one´s duty.
It is an advantage to a Lodge to have a Temple affiliated with it for the following reasons:

1. An active Temple will add to the popularity and
prestige of a Lodge. A community will take more
interest in, and have more respect for the organization
which is doing a work for the children.

2. It will insure the permanency of a Lodge,
because, from time to time, members will be drafted
into it from the Juvenile Temple, bringing in new life
and vigor.

3. It will add, also, to its efficiency, because
these members will come ready trained for the work,
able as well as willing, to take a share of the burdens
and responsibilities.

4. It will continue and increase the true spirit
of the Order, because the members drafted in from the
Juvenile Temple will be true Good Templars who, trained
in the Order, believing in it and loving it, will be
full of zeal for its success. And so the beneficent
influences of Good Templary will spread over the world,
until instead of six hundred thousand members, we shall
have ten times that number linked together by one tie
of universal brotherhood, all doing battle for our
principles of total abstinence for the individual and
prohibition for the state.

Brothers and sisters, the "cry of the children" comes to us. Let us see that we fail not in our response, for there is truth in their words;

"We shall be what you will make us--
Make us wise and make us good;
Make us strong for time of trial;
Teach us temperance, self-denial,
Patience, kindness, fortitude.

We are willing, we are ready;
We would learn if you would teach
We have hearts that yearn towards duty;
We have minds alive to beauty.
Souls that any height can reach.

Raise us by your Christian knowledge;
Consecrate to man our powers,
Let us take our proper station;
We, the rising generation,
Let us stamp this age as ours."

SOME OF OUR DIFFICULTIES AND HOW TO DEAL WITH THEM: A FEW WORDS FOR THE WORKERS

[written for the National Institute of Juvenile Workers, held at Findlay, Ohio, Nov. 1892; International Good Templar, Feb. 1893]

In our work for the children, as in every good cause, we are obliged to admit that there are some discouraging features. It is well for us to face this fact at the outset, so that we may learn to regard

every obstacle, when it presents itself, as something
to be overcome.

There is no royal road to the attainment of any
purpose, and it is only by patient, persistent effort,
and unselfish devotion, that we hope to achieve
success.

In advocating the claims of the children before a
lodge of Good Templars, we have sometimes been met with
the objection, "A Juvenile Temple will be a great deal
of trouble and work." The reply to such a plea is, "We
are in the Order to work, and let us be glad if we can
find something to do."

We need to educate our members to the point where
they will realize that connection with the Order means
a great deal more than the mere keeping of one's own
pledge of total abstinence. To any one who should ask
the reason why we are banded together in our lodges, I
think we should find ourselves replying in the familiar
language of our ritual, that our purpose is to "raise
the fallen and save others from falling."

It must be apparent, to even the least thoughtful,
that an object so noble as this involves a great deal
of hard work. We are certainly to blame if those who
join us are not soon made aware of their responsibilities to the Order, to the temperance cause, and
to the community. When we shall have made the nature
of the obligation resting upon us fully understood, we
shall have disposed, I think, of one of our duties.

We are sometimes embarrassed in our attempts to induce a lodge to form a temple, by the lack of the right person to undertake the charge of such an organization. There are numberless children running wild in the streets, learning the wild manners and rough words of their surroundings. We desire to have them gathered into our fold, that they may be taught gentler speech and purer ways before it is too late. "The fields are white unto the harvest," but where are the laborers? Too often comes the message, "There is nobody in our lodge able to take charge of a temple." And yet the communities must be few in which there are not some persons fitted for such a task, and anxious that an opportunity for useful work should be opened before them.

It is clearly, then, the duty of the lodge to look around the locality in which it is situated, and when a desirable person is found, to induce him or her, as the case may be, to join the Order, with a view to doing this special work. The individual who is thus approached will see that the lodge is in earnest, and will not refuse to lend a hand to such a thorough-going organization. The result would probably be--

(1) A good member for the lodge;
(2) A good temple, ably managed;
(3) A decided increase in the respect felt by the community for the Order.

In another case, the perplexity may be caused, not by the lack of a competent and willing worker, but by the fact that he is already so overwhelmed with duties that he cannot undertake the burden of carrying on a temple.

A practical solution of this problem is for the lodge to appoint a committee of thirteen members, each to be responsible for one meeting of the temple during the quarter. This will insure the attendance of at least one adult at every session, and will be a great help and support to the Superintendent without unduly taxing any one.

Instances have been known where temples have disbanded on account of the unruly conduct of the children. I do not regard this as, in any sense, a sufficient cause. I never heard of a Sunday-school closing its doors for such a reason, and, to my mind, the more unruly the children, the greater the need for the discipline and instruction afforded by a juvenile temple. It is quite possible, too, for a temple to be kept in proper order under good management. A really earnest Superintendent will endeavor to prepare himself for his work; it will then be easy for him to keep the children so entirely interested that there will be no opportunity for disorder or insubordination. A few hints under this head will suffice:

(1) Avoid making the sessions of the temple too long.
(2) Keep every moment occupied.
(3) Give the children themselves plenty to do.
(4) Have plenty of singing.
(5) Make the talks brief and bright.
(6) Have a <u>very short</u> intermission, if any.

In cases of very large temples, a plan might be adopted which I heard suggested by the late Jonathan H. Orne, P.R.W.G.T. The idea was as follows:- After the necessary business is ended, form the children into classes as in Sunday-school. Let each class have a teacher, who will be responsible for its behavior. Some of the elder children might act as teachers, a simple plan of lessons might be adopted, and the sessions of the temple made both pleasant and profitable.

The question of a suitable meeting place is sometimes difficult. It is an unfortunate fact that in some localities where there are numerous churches, whose vestries are closed from Sabbath to Sabbath, it is impossible to find a place in which a juvenile temple may meet. I have often thought, that if the authorities of these churches were approached, and the objects and methods of our juvenile branch properly presented to them, they would recognize the value of our work and be willing to allow the use of a room in the church building for one afternoon of each week. There should be no antagonism between a church and a Good Templar's Lodge. If any but good feelings exist between the two organizations, the cause for such a state of things should be sought out and removed. The well-conducted Good Templars' Lodge will be a valuable adjunct to all Christian effort in a town, and the countenance and support of the ministers and other Christian people is needed to make the Order what it is intended to be. So let us not be afraid to ask the churches to give us their sanction and help in our work among the children.

The indifference of the lodge is a frequent excuse for refraining from an attempt at juvenile work, or for discontinuing the work when once begun. It is too often the fact that the members of a lodge are not in sympathy with the Superintendent, but I would advise that officer to go on cheerfully and unselfishly until he can awaken the desire interest, or <u>grow</u> his own helpers in the Temple. To do this requires patience and tact. Let him avoid scolding or complaint, but watch for the opportunity to say the right word in a kindly persuasive manner. If thoroughly in earnest, his zeal will not fail to inspire others.

There is one other means of dealing with the difficulties which best us in our labors, and that is to cultivate the spirit of the Master "who went about doing good." To consecrate ourselves to the work; to do earnestly and faithfully "what our hand finds to do" and to leave the results to God; this will give us strength and courage under all our trials. In our work for the children, as in all other effort, "let us look to God for His blessing."

DES MOINES DRIFTWOOD

[<u>International Good Templar</u>, August 1893, reprinted from (Massachusetts) <u>Templar</u>, July 1893]

At the public reception tendered by the Grand Lodge of Iowa to the International Supreme Lodge [when the latter met at Des Moines], and equally so at that given by the Ministerial Association of Des Moines the excellence of the addresses made to those who were

chosen to represent the Order was noticeable. Every
speech was a gem of its kind, and the committee in
charge deserve credit for their [sic] skill in making
selection from what must have been an "embarrassment of
riches." Any one of the listeners, however, who
happened to be well acquainted with the delegates
present, could look around and pick out scores of men
and women from different parts of the world who could
have done equally well upon the platform. As a matter
of fact, the meeting might have gone on for a week or
two, with a different set of speakers for each evening
and the supply would not have been exhausted. The
Order has no reason to be ashamed of its orators.

An increased membership, an excellent financial
condition, and the fact that the Order has entered new
territory in this country and Europe, these are some of
the reasons for gratitude and rejoicing which the
reports of officers made manifest.

"The session was a harmonious one." We say the
words with little thought perhaps regarding their
significance. And yet is it not wonderful that people
born and reared in such widely differing climes, used
to different customs and, in some cases, speaking
different tongues, should be able to meet under the one
world-wide banner of Good Templary to discuss the best
methods of work for "God and Home and Every Land." The
International Lodge is not a Peace Congress but it is
doing much to bring about the time

"When man to man the world o´er
    Shall brithers be and a´ that."

"Nothing to find fault with?" Oh, of course if one were looking for flaws one could find a few. There are spots on the sun, you know. Some of the good brothers, and sisters, too, would like to have seen a more strict observance of the rules of the Order. It was hardly possible to find fault with a Chieftain [Dr. Oronhyatekha] who presided with such admirable tact and courtesy and such unfailing good nature as our P.R.W.G.T. did, but a good many of us would have been pleased to have seen the regalia of the office adorning his stately form while he occupied the chair.

Another thing, we <u>should</u> like to see the sisters recognized a little more. In an Order which was the first to give woman an equal place with man, and in whose ranks the sisters are doing a large part of the work, there should surely not be any discrimination against the sex. It was observed that very few sisters were appointed on committees (the writer is not finding fault on her own account, [as] she was chairman of a committee [on the <u>International Good Templar</u>]), and some were heard to wonder whether the omission was due to the lack of gallantry on the part of the appointing power or to an excess of the commodity. In any case we are sure that the sisters do not desire that it shall be made a question of gallantry at all, but simply one of justice.

And speaking of the sisters, there were some grand women and grand workers present. There were Amanda Way, the only member at the session who was present at the organization of the Supreme Lodge [in 1855]; Mrs. O'Donnell, to whom belongs the honor of inaugurating the Juvenile Work of the Order; Mrs. Margaret

Parker of Scotland, the founder of the British Women's
Temperance Association; Charlotte Gray, who has done so
much for the cause of temperance on the continent of
Europe, and many others who deserve to be honored for
their work's sake. Among those of a younger generation
Sister Agnes Sutherland of Scotland, deserves especial
mention for her speech, which contained some well
deserved home thrusts, and was well received.

We should like to say something about the brothers, too, but space will not permit. Let it suffice
that the brothers were worthy of the sisters, and that
all must be impressed with the fact that an organization in which men and women can meet upon equal terms
in the best kind of an organization in the world.

Take it for all in all the International Supreme
Lodge was a success, and we are glad we went.

FORSYTH TO GEORGE W. E. HILL, DEC. 30, 1893

["For Correspondence Week," in <u>International Good
Templar</u>, Feb. 1894]

I fear I am somewhat late in making a response to
your request for a letter to be read in the Iowa
Lodges. But you will understand that my new office [as
R.W.G. Superintendent of Juvenile Templars] has brought
me a great increase of work and I have not yet caught
up with the arrears of correspondence which accumulated
in consequence of our late dear Sister Brookbank's long
illness. I like your plan of obtaining letters from
individuals and lodges to be used as a part of the

programme of lodges in Iowa. The more closely we come in touch with one another and the more we learn about one another's conditions and difficulties, the greater and stronger will be that fraternal bond which unites us.

I often think that our members would value our Order more if they all understood, as some of us do, what a wonderful, worldwide fraternity it is. I was speaking at a public meeting held in connection with our State Institute of Juvenile Templars recently, and I found it necessary to refer to some remarks which had been made on a recent occasion by a lady connected with some other organization. Her remarks had been aimed at our Juvenile work and she had ridiculed our rituals and badges. I said: "Our little badge is not only a reminder to our boys and girls of the pledge they have taken, but is also a sign to them of membership in a worldwide brotherhood. Our ritual is not simply for use in Massachusetts or in these United States or even in the English speaking countries of the world." I then told of the countries where our Order was to be found; of the Temples in Scandinavia, in Germany and Switzerland, of the soldier brethren of India gathering the children of the regiments together and teaching them; of the Temples in Africa, on the Gold Coast, composed of black children. And I said that in telling them of this work I was not relating a fairy story but only saying what I could prove by facts and figures in the documents which have come to me as R.W. Supt. I trust that all brothers and sisters who read this letter will make themselves acquainted with the history and work of our Order and will learn to love it and value it as it deserves.

THE VALUE OF THE COURSE OF STUDY

[written for the Iowa Training School; <u>International
Good Templar</u>, January 1895]

It may be taken for granted that the large
majority of Good Templars have learned what they know
of the temperance question as a result, directly or
indirectly, of their connection with the Order. If
they have made use of their opportunities they will
have acquired, almost unconsciously, and at very little
cost, some knowledge of the dangers of the drink habit
and of the traffic; some idea of the enormous proportions of the evil, and some belief in the necessity for
earnest effort in opposition to its encroachments.
These acquirements, with an ever-growing conviction as
to their own individual responsibilities in the matter,
should be a natural consequence of their membership in
our progressive and aggressive organization.

But the true Good Templar who has reached this
point will not stop there. His eyes once opened to the
evil, his soul will be filled with a desire to "be a
hero in the strife," and he will look around for some
means by which he may **help the good cause.** Then is the
time when he will realize his lack of knowledge and
feel himself as many a great and good man has felt
himself, in past days, to be "fettered and hampered by
his own ignorance." It is not enough to know that we
are right, we must have the knowledge which will enable
us to demonstrate our position. We say to a man "there
is no strengthening property in beer," and the beer

drinker laughs at us. We prove our assertion by the quotation of an analysis of the beverage in question and we, perhaps, set the beer drinker to thinking. We speak vaguely and in general terms of the evils of the drink traffic. The audience listens respectfully and retires unconverted. It is an old story. We bring forward an array of facts and figures; we present the "Nation's Curse" in all its hideousness, as proved by indisputable statistics, and these, like "the handwriting on the wall," will startle and shock our hearers, and give food for thought to many an earnest mind.

It must be understood that I do not put mere book knowledge in the place of earnest conviction of duty and sincere desire to do good. These must always come first. The most feeble utterance, which is the outcome of **a man's own honest thought** is more weighty than the brilliantly turned phrases which voice sentiments having no foundation in the speaker's heart. But, given the earnest conviction and sincere desire to do good--and they are indispensable--the lack of knowledge is found to be the great drawback to the success of our workers. I think the most earnest and zealous worker will be the readiest to admit this. It was the understanding of this fact and the desire to furnish a remedy which, doubtless, led to the formation of the Course of Study. It is the increasing realization of its truth which will lead our workers to avail themselves of the opportunity offered them to supply their deficiencies.

All the arguments in favor of the education of temperance workers apply with peculiar force to those who labor for the young. They gave special

opportunities, and have especial need of the knowledge,
which is power. Everyone who has filled the office of
G.S.J.T. will agree with me when I say that one of the
greatest hindrances to the success of the Juvenile work
is **the lack of competent workers.** There are persons in
every community who would gladly take up such work if
they were not so painfully conscious of their own
shortcomings. Said one S.J.T. to me, when resigning
her office, "I don´t know enough to teach those
children."

It is a fact that the boys and girls of the
present generation have advantages and opportunities
such as their parents never dreamed of. Educational
methods have been changed, improved and adapted to such
a degree that we find the little folks acquiring
knowledge with what appears to us a lightning rapid-
ity. The difficulties which dismayed our youthful days
have vanished from the path trodden by the young
student of to-day. The awful problems over which we
toiled and wept are to him little more than amusing
conundrums. This is as it should be; it is a part of
the change which the march of time is bringing. But it
goes to prove that the plea made by the good sister
referred to above is a true one. Too many of our adult
Good Templars <u>do not</u> know enough to teach the young.
Children are very **keen to detect a fraud.** Their bright
eyes look into the face of the would[-]be instructor as
if, instinctively, they were "taking his measure." Woe
betide the unprepared teacher when he meets that clear
gaze. All pretence of knowledge will crumble away and
leave behind nothing but a sense of defeat and humilia-
tion.

But while the truth of the plea must be admitted
it does not therefore prove that those who realize
their lack of knowledge should, because of it, be
satisfied to abandon all attempt to work.

The changes which have simplified the methods of
education for the children have given facilities for
supplying that which is lacking in that of the adult.
There may be many reasons which make ignorance ex-
cusable, but, as a general rule, few persons, in the
present day, are **compelled to remain ignorant.** While
it is true that our children have advantages such as we
never knew, it is, nevertheless, true that we can avail
ourselves of opportunities for improvement which are
offered to the adult and thus keep pace with the rising
generation.

This is especially true of Good Templars, because,
within our own Order, we have these facilities for self
improvement and mental culture. Therefore, let no one
say "I do not know enough to teach" but, let him
rather, realizing his need, turn to the means by which
this need may be supplied.

The Course of Study is of value in itself. The
books are carefully chosen and one who reads them
diligently will acquire an amount of information which
will go far to entitle him to be considered **an educated
man.** Besides the knowledge of the temperance question
which he will gain, he will learn something of physiology and hygiene and become possessed of numberless
facts of history, geography and other matters.

The value of the Course to the student cannot be overestimated. In the first place the discipline to the mind which is the result of a well[-]arranged and connected plan of study, is a consideration. No amount of desultory reading, even of good books, will produce the same effect.

A result of the reading will be, naturally, to make him think, and his studies being of a methodical character he will find his **thoughts shaping themselves** in the same manner. In this way his reasoning faculties will be developed and strengthened.

A further result of the reading and thinking will be the development of an ability to express himself with tongue and pen. A well-stored mind will insure a ready utterance, but you cannot draw water from an empty well.

Beside the cultivation which is given to his intellectual faculties, the student will find his moral perceptions sharpened and his convictions strengthened. What were formerly vague ideas will become solid principles, which will influence his own life and the lives of others.

His desire to help his fellow creatures will grow in proportion as he realizes the **blight which the drink curse** upon so many lives, and he will be inspired anew with a desire to work for its overthrow.

His ambition will be awakened and he will not be satisfied to stop when he has graduated and obtained his diploma. His appetite for knowledge will only be whetted and he will go on reading and thinking and keeping up with the times.

The total result of all this will be that he will find himself armed and equipped for the fight. With a zeal born of his convictions and a self reliance based upon the knowledge of his powers he will be prepared to face the foe.

OUR MONTHLY LETTER TO THE BOYS AND GIRLS

[<u>International Good Templar</u>, Jan. 1895.]

There was once a little girl whom we will call Agnes. She wished very earnestly to be called pretty, but a long sickness had wasted her plump little form, and had driven the color from the small, sunken cheek, which used to be so round and rosy. Because she was thin, and sallow, and pale, people would turn from her to the fair, dimpled face of her little sister, and would sometimes say to one another, "What a difference!"

This little girl (She was very young or perhaps she would have been so foolish) thought so much about her looks that she learned to fancy that beauty was the thing most to be desired of all things. So when she said her prayers she asked God to make her pretty.

The years passed on, and Agnes, in pursuing her studies, almost forgot her childish desire for beauty. By and by, while she was still a very young girl, a great many sorrows came into her life. Those who were nearest and dearest were taken from her, and she found herself almost alone in the world. In her loneliness she began to think that the best thing which could come to her was a loving friend who would sympathise with her. So just as she began to pray for beauty, she began to pray for love.

The time flew by, and Agnes learned that there were many other mourning hearts and many other lonely lives. She began to long to help the sorrowful ones, and then her prayer to God was that He would make her useful. No doubt it was because this petition was the right one that Agnes found her eyes opened immediately, and she saw many ways of being helpful to those around.

She was poor and could not give money, but she gave of her time and effort, and her sympathy. She had no more time to be sad or lonely, for she was always busy and useful. The sunshine which she made for other people warmed and cheered her own heart. And a wonderful thing happened. The answer which came to her last prayer seemed to bring with it a response to the other two. Only the beauty manifested itself in her character, and the love was given to her by those whom she helped and cheered. People would say "What a dear girl Agnes is," and little children would look in her face and say "I love you, Agnes." A glad greeting awaited her wherever she went, and all who came in contact with her felt the influence of her bright, cheerful spirit.

There are many girls, and some boys too, I think, who spend their time wishing for some good thing for themselves. I have written this story of little girl's experience because I want you to learn that the best way to be happy is to try to make others happy. When

you read these words we shall have entered upon the New
Year, which, I trust, will be a year of usefulness,
and, therefore, of happiness, to every reader of The
International Juvenile Templar.

Make up your minds that you will--

"Do all the good you can,
In all the ways you can,
To all the people you can,
As long as ever you can."

and then ask God to help you in all your good resolutions.

That "His love may be shed abroad in your hearts,"
making you helpful and happy, is the earnest desire of

Your friend,
Jessie Forsyth,
R.W.G.S.J.T.

SOME SIDE ISSUES OF GOOD TEMPLARY

[International Good Templar, April 1895, reprinted from
the (Massachusetts) Templar; also appeared in (Glasgow)
Good Templar, Jan. 1895]

The Good Templar Order was organized primarily for
the promotion of the principle of total abstinence from
all that can intoxicate. Its work was intended to be
twofold; first, that of reclaiming those who had become
slaves to the drink habit; second, that of "saving the

young, pure and virtuous from falling into the snares of the tempter." The records of the organization, during its more than forty years of existence, prove that it has faithfully adhered to its original purpose. Thousands of rescued ones in every land bear grateful testimony to the Order, and many thousands of noble lives credit their first impulse towards right living to its teachings.

But aside from its legitimate purpose a number of other movements have either been originated or have received material help, as an incidental result of Good Templary.

The process has been, in many cases, unnoticed. The Order has never swerved from its original intention. It has not branched out into multitudinous departments, but gradually, quietly, often times unconsciously, the weight of its influence has been lent to various other phases of social reform, and, as a consequence, these movements have been greatly aided.

It is hardly necessary in this connection to speak of the movements to secure the prohibition of the liquor traffic. That has become so distinctly a part of the Order's work that it cannot be dealt with as a side issue. It is well, however, that our members should be reminded sometimes that the idea of constitutional prohibition originated in the Order, and that its conception is to be credited to our honored R.W.G. Secretary, B. F. Parker.

First among the side issues of Good Templary we must place its recognition of the equality of sexes.

The Order has not always had the credit which belongs to it, for its part in helping woman to attain to her rightful place. It was the first organization in the world to admit woman on equal terms with man, and from its formation until the present time all rights and privileges of the Order have been common to both sexes.

If this equality had not extended beyond the pale of the Order, much would have been gained for the sex. But it was impossible to prevent the idea from spreading. The ambition of woman herself was awakened. When she realized her capacity for assuming the responsibilities and enjoying the privileges which had been monopolized by the stronger sex, the thought would naturally come to her that these responsibilities and privileges need not be limited to one organization. That woman can bear this equality worthily is proved by the fact that the host of woman who are enrolled in our great Order rank among the noblest, purest and best of their sex.

The growth and prosperity of the Order demonstrate that woman´s work has been an advantage to it. Her latent abilities, in debate, upon the public platform, with her pen, as an organizer, as a presiding officer, as a secretary, upon committees, and in various other ways have been called forth and are recognized wherever Good Templary is known. The talents which have been developed in the Order have been used for the advancement of many other movements until it is a common thing to hear the remark made of a prominent woman that she began in the Good Templars´ Lodge-room. She has gained the respect of her brothers, so that it is hardly possible to find an intelligent male Good Templar who is not a woman suffragist.

Hardly less noticeable is the influence of the Order in the promotion of socialistic ideas, though here again the work has been done quietly.[4] No blatant demagogues have been employed to advocate the rights of man, but the principle of human equality has been recognized. In the lodge-room are to be found "all sorts and conditions" meeting together as one family. The teachings of the Order are distinctly socialistic, as an examination of its rituals will prove. It knows no rank save that which it bestows, and it honors the true worker without regard to the length of his pedigree or the depth of his purse.

Good Templary avows, as a fundamental principle, its belief in the "Fatherhood of God, and the Brotherhood of Man." Its attitude thus practically proclaiming "There are no classes or races, but one human brotherhood," the abolition of race distinctions would be naturally only another step forward. In no other organization is the principle that "God hath made of one blood all nations to dwell upon the earth," so truly recognized.

The North American Indian, the Hindoo, the African, the Mongolian, the native New Zealander, and the Polynesian, stand side by side with the Caucasian in our world-wide chain of fraternity. We have united to do honor to the noble red man [Oronhyatekha] whose

---

4   Jessie Forsyth had been an advocate of Edward Bellamy's utopian socialism and secretary of the Second Boston Nationalist Club in 1889-91.

abilities have won for him a place at the head of the
Order, and we stand ready to show approval of the
fidelity and zeal of all our workers regardless of
race.

One of the greatest living Good Templars has said
that in our Order "we meet, not as Englishmen nor as
Americans, but as Good Templars." This sentiment is
exemplified in almost any Good Templar gathering.
There are grand lodges whose list of officers sometimes
includes representatives of more than one race and of
two or three other nationalities.

It is not surprising that the Supreme Lodge of an
Order whose rituals have been translated into nearly
twenty different languages and dialects should be a
very cosmopolitan body. The surprising feature is that
the representatives of the various countries, educated
under different customs and conditions, living under
widely diverse laws, and speaking various tongues,
should be able to meet together in amity and plan for
the destruction of a common enemy.

It must be an education for the narrow, conservative man who has not learned the higher patriotism
which teaches that "our country is the world," to
attend a session of the International Supreme Lodge.
He cannot fail to realize that "mankind is one in its
rights and wrongs," and as he clasps hands with
representatives which he has hitherto regarded with
prejudice or even aversion, his heart must echo the
words of Abraham to Lot: "we be brethren."

A natural result of this is that Good Templary is playing no mean part in bringing about the day when "nation shall no more rise against nation," and in this we are aiding the work of the Peace Societies. Nothing will so quickly or so closely unite people as "the endeavor for the self same ends, with the same hopes and fears and aspirations."

"Drink, the only terrible enemy which England has to fear" is the foe no less of every other land and the one against which Good Templars of all "nations and people and languages" are united. In fighting this mighty foe they learn to overcome all distinctions of race or nationality, sex or creed.

FORSYTH TO JUVENILE TEMPLARS, MAY 1, 1895

["Our Monthly Letter," in International Good Templar, June 1895]

I want to say a few words to you about THE THINGS WHICH HOLD US DOWN.

I believe that all boys and girls have ambition, and want to make something of their lives. It is a common thing to hear children planning what they will do when they grow up, and, as a general rule, they desire to be good and noble.

The things which hold us down are bad habits, and the boys and girls who wish to succeed in life must guard against these hindrances to progress.

I wonder if any of you have read the story of
"Gulliver's Travels"? If you have, you will remember
that when Gulliver was cast ashore in the country of
the little people, called Lilliputians, he found
himself lying upon the beach unable to move hand or
foot. He soon discovered that he was firmly bound by a
multitude of tiny ropes, each no thicker than a fine
thread, but each doing its part to <u>hold him down.</u>

This illustrates the manner in which many people
are kept from getting on in life. The bad habits,
which seem but trifles when acquired, and which could
be so easily broken, one at a time, united are strong
enough to find men and women in slavery to their own
evil natures.

Suppose an employer has a good position made
vacant in his business. He will, perhaps, look among
his employés for one who deserves promotion. "There is
John," he says to himself, "he is a smart fellow, but I
cannot believe all he says. A liar is apt to be a
thief; I cannot trust him in that position. Harry
would do for it if he had not that foolish habit of
giving <u>smart</u> answers. He would rather offend a
customer than lose the chance to make a pun. I see
that Tom has learned to chew tobacco, and I can't put a
dirty fellow like that in such a place." And so he
goes through the list, and the young man who is honest
and truthful, civil and obliging, steady and neat, will
be the one who will get ahead.

If this is so in worldly matters, how much more is
it true in spiritual things. Every evil propensity
yielded to blunts the conscience, and hinders the

soul´s growth, while each victory over temptation makes us stronger for the fight.

Now, it is because we want you to become successful men and women, as regards your worldly affairs, and because, above all things, we desire you to become earnest Christian men and women; having, as Canon [F. W.] Farrar puts it, "Natures strong, sweet and simple, hating selfishness, and loving all things pure and good," that we try to teach you in our temples to avoid bad habits. May God bless our Juvenile Templars, and lead them all "to covet earnestly the best gifts."

BEGIN AT THE BEGINNING

[(Glasgow) <u>Good Templar</u>, March 1896; also printed as a pamphlet]

The Good Templar Order is based upon practical principles. It is organised in such a manner as will enable it to do the greatest good to the greatest number. It is ever ready to lend a hand to lift up those who have fallen, and "to restore them to family, friends, and society," and it is constant in its endeavour "to save others from falling."

Because of the practical character of the organisation, the workers in it have long realised that their efforts, to be effective, must begin at the beginning. And so it has come to pass that, while the original methods of the Order have never been abandoned, and its Lodge room still represents a haven of safety and peace, in which the weak ones may gain strength to resist temptation, and the strong may learn sympathy and charity for the weak, it has added to its usefulness by the formation of a Juvenile Branch.

It is a glorious thing to be the instrument of saving a soul, and our Order will not come short of the blessing promised to those "who turn many to righteousness." But although we may reclaim the fallen one; may induce him to give up the fatal cup; and may surround him with helpful and inspiring influences, yet we cannot restore to him what he has lost. His years of recklessness have doubtless brought their accompaniment of ruin. Too often the reclaimed man "comes to himself" only to find himself a wreck. Health, reputation, fortune, friends--all gone! We may if we believe him to be truly penitent, venture to assure him of God´s forgiveness, but we cannot prevent him from suffering the penalty of his misspent life, and realising the truth of the inevitable law that

"WHAT A MAN SOWS, HE REAPS."

And even when such a man has been mercifully spared the worst consequences of his wrong doing; if wife and children remain with him to rejoice over his reclamation; if his forfeited character be restored; he will yet be haunted by the remorseful memories of his wasted years and opportunities. It was these memories which led John B. Gough to wish that he could blot out the past, when he exclaimed: "Young man, keep your record clean." It was this thought which inspired the poet when he wrote:

Wounds of the soul, though healed will ache;
The reddening scars remain, and make Confession;

Lost innocence returns no more;
We are not what we were before Transgression.

Because we desire that the rising generation shall
be spared these "wounds of the soul," we endeavour to
gather them into our Lodges and teach them that the
only safety lies in total abstinence from all that can
intoxicate.

You will ask us, perhaps, whether we find our
efforts in this direction prove successful. For
answer, we can point you to thousands of young men and
women among the noblest workers in our Order, who began
their career in the Juvenile Lodge; and who have
faithfully lived up to the principles taught them. We
find them everywhere--in our Lodges, in our District
Lodges, even in our Grand Lodges--and they are rarely
found wanting in the qualities which make good citizens
and true Christians.

The future of the temperance cause depends upon
the boys and girls of to-day:--

For, be sure, the new things grow
  As the old things fade.
As we train the children, so
  Is the future made
That shall reign when we are low.

All the good we would have wrought
  Must by them be done;
We shall pass, but not our thought,
  While in every one
Lives the lesson we have taught.

This being so, it is no less the duty than the privilege of our Order to do its part well and faithfully in this important work of training the young. One of the most encouraging signs of progress is found in the rapidly growing conviction which is inspiring temperance workers everywhere to labour for the young. The time when victory shall crown our efforts cannot be foretold, but the longed-for triumph will be hastened when all shall realise that it is the part of wisdom to

BEGIN AT THE BEGINNING.

QUESTIONS ABOUT THE ORDER

[International Good Templar, March 1896]

[Its editor had sent leading members of the Order the following questions:
(1) What do you regard as the strongest characteristics of our Order?
(2) What is our Order´s greatest need to-day?
(3) What do you regard as the greatest hindrances to the cause of temperance as a whole?]

[In her reply Jessie Forsyth wrote:]

(1) That it is self-supporting and therefore truly independent; its uncompromising attitude towards the liquor traffic; its educational facilities; its work for the children; the absence of distinctions of sex, race, nationality or creed.
(2) Consecrated, educated workers.

(3) The fact that its lofty purpose and high ideals are not fully understood and maintained by its membership.

A PRACTICAL TALK TO GRAND SUPERINTENDENTS

[International Good Templar, Aug. 1896]

In a letter from a newly elected Grand Superintendent [of Juvenile Work], the writer says: "I know very little about my duties; please send me instructions and tell me what are the qualifications of a good G.S.J.T., as I want to cultivate them." This has suggested a topic for a practical talk to my co-workers, and first I will deal with the qualifications which may be developed, in a greater or less degree, by all who have a desire to do faithful work. The most important quality is that of sincerity, the foundation-stone of all that is noble in any character. In these days, when it is customary for certain people to pose as possessors of gifts and graces greater than nature has bestowed, it may happen that a shallow and insincere person will sometimes attempt to fill an office without having the true spirit to inspire the work. The influence of such an officer is especially harmful to our branch of effort, because there is need for the utmost simplicity and straightforwardness when dealing with children. So, while our workers should cultivate earnestly "the gift which is in them," they must avoid posing for effect, or pretending to be what they are not. The man of one talent was not expected to pretend that he possessed ten; he was simply required to use the one gift faithfully. The experience of single-hearted and simple-minded workers proves that the

small gifts, earnestly and faithfully used, may be
made greater powers for good than the more brilliant
endowments, whose use is prompted by self-interest or
the desire for applause. Therefore sincerity is a
grace much to be desired, and earnestly to be cultivated by those who would do wise and effective work.

Christian courtesy is the term by which, after
some thought, I have decided to designate the qualities
which include all that is admirable in the demeanor of
any Good Templar, and are therefore necessary to that
of the successful G.S.J.T. The code may be found in
the thirteenth of First Corinthians, where the Apostle
bids us cultivate that love which "suffereth long and
is kind;" which "vaunteth not itself, is not puffed up,
does not behave itself unseemly;" which "is not easily
provoked;" which "beareth all things, believeth all
things, hopeth all things, endureth all things."

Kindness, patience, courage, cheerfulness, are all
qualities especially valuable to the one who must
inspire and direct the work of others, while a proper
sense of the dignity of the office will prevent the
office from either becoming "puffed up," or from
indulging in frivolous or "unseemly" behavior which
would bring reproach upon the cause.

Another essential for a successful officer is
executive ability. Let it be understood in the first
place that an office in any organization should be
regarded as a position to be filled in a business-like
manner. Sentiment is a very good thing in its way and
in its place, but something more is needed to insure
the successful administration of affairs. A Grand

Superintendent who aspires to fill his office acceptably and with a view to practical results, must avoid
the mistake of considering it a sort of amateur
position. He must cultivate business ability and adopt
business methods.

The office of G.S.J.T. was created and is sustained for the purpose of securing certain desired
ends, viz., the education of the young in the principles of temperance; the advancement of the temperance
cause, and the strengthening and perpetuating of the
Order, The causes suffers when officers are lacking in
the executive ability and business knowledge which are
so necessary to effective work. Such persons look at
matters from an emotional standpoint and are apt to
spend their time in talking aimlessly, or what is
commonly called "gushing," instead of making an attempt
to conduct their affairs upon common-sense principles.
I therefore urge all officers to cultivate practical
methods of speech and action; to be prompt, accurate
and energetic, and to avoid "gush."

Knowledge of the temperance question and of the
Order is a very necessary qualification. The person
who assumes the office of G.S.J.T. will often find
himself hampered by his own ignorance. It should be
borne in mind that an important part of his labors will
be advising and instructing the local workers. He will
be subject to constant appeals for help and guidance,
and he must see to it that he has something more
practical to offer than the pretty little platitudes
which look well upon paper, but which are of about as
much service to one who is seeking real help and
information as a sugar-plum would be to a hungry man.

The Good Templars´ Course of Study offers to the
worker a means of acquiring the necessary knowledge and
of cultivating his mind. He will be better qualified,
after reading the books, to instruct others, and will
be earnest in directing them to obtain the needed
education themselves.

He will have a fuller understanding of the evil of
intemperance and a consequently stronger purpose to
work for its overthrow. Let no one be deterred from
accepting the responsible position of G.S.J.T. because
of the thought that his lack of knowledge disqualifies
him. A very slight expenditure of time and money will
enable him to fit himself for the duties which devolve
upon him.

Enthusiasm? Oh, yes; notwithstanding all that I
have said to the cultivation of practical ideas and the
avoidance of "gush," I believe very heartily in enthusiasm. And it is only those who have an amount of
good, sturdy, practical common sense who can be
genuinely enthusiastic. A real enthusiasm must be
based upon a belief in the work; a realization of the
need for it; a cheery faith in the success which must
come; an unfailing patience; an unflagging industry and
a sincere consecration. Given all these and the
enthusiasm will be of a kind which will never wear out.

Now, in regard to the duties of the G.S.J.T. aside
from those which are defined in the Constitutions and
Rituals of the Order. It is, of course, understood
that this is addressed especially to those who have
recently taken up the work. Officers who have been

414

many times elected will have adopted their own methods
and will probably have no use for the following hints:

The first thing to be done by the newly elected
officer is to open communication with the local
Superintendents. In small jurisdictions this may be
accomplished by a personal letter, but in the majority
of cases it will be found more practical to have a good
circular printed and sent to each local officer, with
his commission. The circular should call attention to
the importance of the work and should include some
helpful suggestions. The following quotations, from a
circular issued by one G.S.J.T., are given as a sample
of what is required:

"If there is no Temple existing in connection with
your Lodge, it will be your first duty to endeavor to
form one. To this end I shall be glad to render you
assistance, by giving you assistance, by giving you
information or advice; or, if necessary, by sending you
a speaker to present the aims and methods of Juvenile
Good Templary to the public."

"Under our present constitution, it will be
possible for you to begin by getting members of the
your Lodge, or persons outside the Lodge, who are
willing to take the Juvenile Templar's pledge, to form
the nucleus of a Temple. This will give you a number
of interested adult helpers in the work of gathering in
the children."

"If you find it impossible to organize a Temple in
the immediate vicinity of your Lodge, you might seek
for an opportunity to form one in some other part of

the town or village in which you reside. A Temple may
be organized in a place where no adult Lodge exists,
and, in many cases, the formation of the one would open
the way for the other."

This same circular contains some practical hints
to S.J.T.´s of active Temples, with regard to regalia,
music, temperance teaching, etc. Superintendents were
fraternally advised to read the <u>International Good
Templar</u> and to take the Course of Study.

Among the duties of a G.S.J.T. is especially the
endeavor to inspire, instruct and encourage local
workers. It will be seen that the qualifications
referred to in the first part of this paper are all
very necessary ones. Let the G.S.J.T. accustom himself
to sympathizing with the conditions of each one, let
him be gentle when reproof is necessary, patient when
mistakes are made, and ready to give deserved commenda-
tion.

Another task devolving upon a Grand Superintendent
is that of addressing the Lodges with a view to
arousing an interest and securing their co-operation.
Here, again, will be found a use for all the gifts
which have been mentioned. There is especial need for
the exercise of forbearance in this connection, for it
is always a misfortune when a Grand Superintendent
loses patience and scolds a Lodge for the lack of
interest displayed by many of its members. So much
more may be gained by "keeping sweet" and using tact.

Wherever possible, the G.S.J.T. should prevail
upon members of the Lodges to take the Juvenile

416

Templars´ pledge [including a pledge against the use of tobacco] and so make them feel that they are a part of the junior branch of the Order. A good plan is to organize juvenile conventions and invite the adults to attend. Another way is to induce a Lodge, here and there, to invite a Temple occasionally to take part in its Good of the Order [section of the program, often including entertainment]. There are numerous methods by which the G.S.J.T.´s can interest the Lodges, popularize the work, and secure the sympathy and co-operation of many of the members.

If the officer is in earnest there will be some faithful ones everywhere who will come forward and help.

Still another duty is for the G.S.J.T. to inform himself thoroughly regarding the actual condition of the work in his jurisdiction, and then devise means of strengthening the weak spots, rebuilding where it has been overthrown, and planting in new places. He must be careful to build worthily and do a work which shall last, rather than for showy and less enduring results.

The work of planning, inspiring, instructing and encouraging, is one which will tax heart and hand and brain. You, my co-workers, will realize that it is no light labor to which you are called. But the reward will be found in the knowledge of duty faithfully performed, and in the upward impulse given to your own nature by the sincere and devoted effort to help others.

"Then do they work; it shall succeed

In this, or in another's day;
And, if denied the victor's meed,
Thou shalt not lack the toiler's pay."

BITS OF HISTORY: HOW THE ORDER WAS INTRODUCED INTO THE ARGENTINE REPUBLIC

[International Good Templar, June 1897]

About the year 1875, Mr. George H. C. Viney, an Englishman, was holding a responsible situation at Rosario de Santa Fe, in the Argentine Republic. He being an earnest Christian temperance man, was impressed with the need for some active temperance work among his fellow employes [sic], both native and European. He called together a few good men who shared his sentiments with regard to the matter, and it was proposed to organize a temperance society.

One of the men had belonged for a short time to a Good Templars' Lodge in England, and he cherished the recollection of it as a very excellent and efficient instrumentality for "raising the fallen, and saving others from falling." He suggested that the proposed organization should take the form of a Good Templars' Lodge. He was ignorant regarding the need for a charter or for any authority, and, of course, he had no books. But he could remember some portions of the ritual and some of the ceremonial work. Such paragraphs as he was able to quote from memory found favor with his associates, and a ritual was compiled from these passages with the gaps filled in with original matter written by Brother Viney.

The so-called Good Templar Lodge was organized and began its good work in blissful ignorance of the fact that it had not a legal title to live and labor.

Some time after the formation of the Lodge, Brother Viney was sent to England on business, and his companions charged him to find out all about the Good Templars when he was in the old country, and bring back with him all the necessary books and paraphernalia. Upon reaching Great Britain, one of the first things which met his eyes, when he landed in Southampton was a large poster, advertising a public meeting to be held that evening under auspices of a Good Templar Lodge. Brother Viney attended the meeting and found it very inspiring. At its close he introduced himself to some of the members and told his story. He heard with delighted surprise, that the Order which had been introduced into South America in such an informal and unpretending manner, was a very large and powerful one, and he was ready immediately to join a Lodge in proper form and receive all the required instruction.

When this was accomplished, the next step was to communicate with the G.C.T. of England, Brother Joseph Malins. A correspondence with him resulted, Brother Viney receiving a commission as Special Deputy for the Argentine Republic. When he returned to Rosario, armed with this authority, and bearing the charter, rituals, etc., Alpha Lodge No. 1 was duly instituted and continued the career upon which it had already en- tered--a career of usefulness and beneficence which terminated only about a year ago after twenty years of active work.

Other Lodges sprung from this one and the work of
the Order has gone on steadily, if slowly, in the
Republic. At present there are five active working
Lodges and a Juvenile Temple. Brother Henry J. King of
Buenos Ayres, is now the very efficient deputy. There
is also a Lodge in the Republic of Uruguay.

Brother Viney, whose love for the Order and
fidelity to the cause are worthy to be held in remembrance, died recently in Westfield, Massachusetts, in
which city he had made his home for the past few years.

WHAT I CAN DO FOR THE ORDER
AND WHAT THE ORDER CAN DO FOR ME

[Written for the District Convention, No. 1, Suffolk
District, Grand Lodge of Massachusetts; first published
in International Good Templar, December 1897; slightly
altered, reprinted with subtitle, "A Little Talk to Our
Young Members," New York Templar, January 1910, mis-
printed as 1909]

Every one who joins a Good Templar Lodge pledges
himself to "do all in his power to promote the good of
the Order and to advance the cause of temperance."
Assuming that this obligation is taken in a sincere
spirit, the question must naturally arise in each mind,
"What can I do?" We may possibly have those among us
who overrate their own powers, and who, in the endeavor
to accomplish great things, may neglect the little
things and come short of the high mark which they have
set themselves to attain, but a huge majority--

realizing that they cannot do much--are often afraid to attempt anything, and it is to such members that this paper is addressed.

"I am not much use to the Lodge, but I count one on the right side," some humble-minded brother or sister will say, not realizing that the strength of the Order is found in the quiet, faithful members whose voices are seldom heard, but whose faces we learn to look for, and love to see, as we assemble every week in the Lodge room. It is doing much for the Order to be willing to be counted upon the right side.

I intend to briefly indicate some of the things which all can do for the Order, and which, if faithfully performed by _every_ member, would make our organization the greatest power ever known.

In the first place, we can attend the Lodge regularly. The best Good Templars are those who keep the Lodge night sacred to the Lodge, and whose presence may always be depended upon when the night of meeting arrives. What could be a higher tribute to the fidelity of a man than to find his unwonted absence a source of surprise and anxiety to his fellow-members, and to hear them exclaim, "Why, where is Brother So-and-So? He must be ill; he never stays away from Lodge."

The same credit is due to the punctual brother or sister. Those who are always in their places when the hour for opening arrives are among the most valuable of our members.

421

Prompt payment of dues is a duty which should never be neglected. In an organization where the quarterly assessments are so small, it is strange to find that in many of our Lodge delinquents are numerous. The explanation must be that it is considered such a trifle that it is not worth troubling about, but our Financial Secretaries know that an accumulation of these trifles makes all the difference between solvency and insolvency. Someone must find the wherewith to pay the necessary expenses of the Lodge; let us all see that we faithfully do our part.

A full share of the work should be taken by each member. In this respect our Lodges are sometimes in an unfortunate position between the over-zealous ones who aspire to offices for which they are not qualified and the timid ones who lack confidence in their own abilities and refuse all official service. A good rule is to let the office seek the man, and, if it is found that a majority of our brothers and sisters desire to place us in some position of trust, to believe in their good judgment and accept the proffered honor with a determination to do the very best we can in the office. There are many other ways, of course, in which one can render service besides that of holding office. There is the doing duty upon committees, and the taking part in the business of the Lodge in the way of making motions and voting. Have we not all seen Lodge meetings where the members would sit around, listless and indifferent, or inattentive, and perhaps even disorderly, paying no heed to the business transacted and scarcely taking the trouble to vote? And yet it has been often noticed that the very members who will let important motions be adopted without saying a word

for or against the proposed measure, are the ones who
will make the loudest complaint if the action taken
should prove to be unwise.

The Order has a claim upon our time, our talents
and our labors, and the prosperity and usefulness of
the organization will be in exact proportion to the
readiness with which the claim is honored. The "Good
of the Order" [section of the Lodge program] furnishes
many opportunities for service to members, and it is
the duty of every one to help to make the meetings
interesting. All have not the same gifts; one member
can play the piano, another can sing, a third read or
recite, and a fourth, perhaps, speak in an acceptable
manner. Let each one feel bound to give of his best,
be it much or little. The true Good Templar will take
an interest in the cause which the Order represents,
and this can be acquired and increased by reading,
observation and study. Let us all remember that we are
enlisted in the fight against intemperance, and let us
qualify ourselves for the warfare by storing our minds
with useful knowledge. I will suggest, in passing,
that temperance and Good Templar papers, particularly
the <u>International Good Templar</u>, the <u>National Temperance
Advocate</u>, the <u>Temperance Cause</u>, the <u>Voice</u> and your own
local Good Templar paper, if the jurisdiction possesses
one, should be regarded as a necessary part of the
equipment of the really earnest member. The Good
Templars´ Course of Study should be taken, and the mind
improved and cultivated in every way. In this, as in
our services, the Order demands our very best.

Besides cultivating the intellect we should
endeavor to render ourselves worthy of the Order in

other ways. Let us bear in mind that nothing is too good for the Order, and study to make ourselves acceptable members by cultivating integrity and uprightness; purity of life and propriety of conduct; patience and forbearance; kindliness and courtesy, and, in fact, the whole category of Christian graces, for a true Good Templar is only another name for a true Christian.

The interests of the Order are committed to each one of its members, and it will be prosperous and honored, or the reverse, according as we each do our part, well or ill. When we each have a full sense of our individual responsibility, the really active, working Good Templar will be a far more common sight that he is at present. In the words of one of our eminent members, "Good Templary is what its members make it by their earnest, faithful lives."

The second part of my paper, what the Order can do for me, need be but brief. The Order, unlike many other organizations, promises no material benefit to its members, but one cannot have been connected with it for even a short time without learning that, if he has been sincere in his efforts to promote its interests, he must have received unlooked-for reward. For instance, if we glance at the points mentioned in the first part of my paper, we can see that the observance of all (or even of part) of them will have benefited the member no less than the Lodge.

The fidelity which enables a member to be regular and prompt in his attendance is a characteristic which is of the highest value in all the relations of life, and which is therefore worth cultivating. The words of

Holy Writ, quoted in our ritual, tell us that "He that
is faithful in that which is least, is faithful also in
much."

The conscientious discharge of our financial
obligations to the Lodge will promote the growth of a
habit which will tend to make us reliable and trust-
worthy in our business dealings.

The readiness to serve the Lodge in any capacity
will develop our business abilities, train us to be
prompt in thought and action, ready in speech, and
capable of thinking, judging and acting for ourselves
in any emergency. If we make mistakes we shall learn
wisdom which will enable us to avoid similar mistakes
in the future. Our efforts to become useful members of
the Order will call out our best gifts and endow us
with that self-knowledge and self-control which will
qualify us for any position in life.

The information which we acquire as temperance
workers will but increase our thirst for knowledge.
Almost unconsciously the habit of study and reflection
will grow upon us, and we shall continue to read, to
think, to learn and to observe. It needs no words of
mine to prove the value of this habit. Those who have
overcome the hindrance which a defective education has
been, can understand what a boon to a man is the thing
which first inspires him to cultivate the gift which is
in him. Who will seek to deny that the Order has been
the means of thus inspiring thousands of people?

And if we do not stop at the cultivation of our
intellectual gifts, but endeavor, by the development of

our moral and spiritual natures, to "walk worthily, unto all the pleasing, being fruitful in every good work," shall we not gain far more than we give? The graces of character which will render us acceptable members of the Order will make us useful and honored in any walk of life. And as we look back in later years we shall realize that in giving ourselves to a worthy cause we have been well repaid by the growth and unfoldment of all that is noblest in our own natures.

Just one more thought before I close. I have sometimes said that one of the best features of the Order is the fact that it offers to very humble people the opportunity for useful work, which is all who love their fellow-creatures must desire. To do effective work in a Good Templar Lodge, one does not need to be rich, or famous, or talented above one's fellows. But such gifts as we have may be used to good advantage, and very often the efforts of the lowliest toiler may secure results far beyond his expectations. Think for a moment of the homes which have been brightened and blessed by the influence of the Order; of the men and women whose feet have turned into paths of sobriety as they were hastening towards drunkards' graves; of the little ones who have been taught to hate the poisonous cup; of the young men and maidens who have been trained to avoid the snares of the tempter. And remember that much of this blessing and saving, teaching and training has been done by the comparatively unknown workers who have found in the Good Templar Order the opportunity for useful labor in behalf of humanity.

"A nameless man, amid the crowd which filled
        a busy mart,

Let fall a word of hope and love, unstudied
    from the heart.
A whisper on the tumult thrown, a transitory
    breath--
It raised a brother from the dust, it saved a
    soul from death.
Oh germ of life! Oh word of love! Oh thought
    at noonday cast!
Ye were but little at the first, but mighty
    at the last."

SUGGESTED PLANS OF WORK FOR 1898

[International Good Templar, Jan. 1898]

[The editor had asked about a hundred members the question: "What would you suggest as the best plans of work for our Subordinate Lodges during 1898?"; Jessie Forsyth contributed this reply.]

1. A steadfast endeavor to live up to the purpose of the Order, that of "raising the fallen and saving others from falling."

2. A systematic effort to educate the members by means of the Course of Study and the literature of the Order.

3. A determined attempt to reach the outside public by means of temperance meetings, distributing temperance literature, etc.

Or to sum up these suggestions in brief, I would say let each Lodge take as its watchword for the year, "Consecration, Education, Agitation."

THE TRACKS ON THE CARPET

[Short Story in <u>International Good Templar</u>, May 1898]

Chapter I

It was a red-letter night in Light in Darkness Lodge. A committee which had been appointed some weeks before to raise funds for furnishing the Lodge-room was ready to make its final report, and the fruits of its labors were visible in the shape of a handsome new carpet, some richly embroidered covers for pedestals and tables, and various other matters which tended to make the place look homelike and attractive. As the members entered there were exclamations of delighted surprise to be heard, and the brothers and sisters who constituted the committee were warmly thanked and congratulated.

An additional reason for satisfaction was found in the report which circulated among the early comers to the effect that Laurence Brown would bring two candidates for initiation that evening, and that he asked for particular kindness to be shown to them as persons who sadly needed the influence of the Order. Light in Darkness Lodge counted several rescued ones among its members and was willing to add to the number of its trophies. The members felt a justifiable pride in their prosperous and useful condition, and when the call to order came, it was not surprising that the line in the welcome ode, "Cheerful are our hearts to-day," was sung with especial gusto.

The time for initiation arrived, and Brother Brown´s candidates were introduced. They were two rough-looking men, unwashed and unshaven. Apparently they were brick-makers, for the clay of the brick fields still clung to their boots and, to the horror of the sisters, as they were conducted round the room, they left their tracks all over the beautiful new carpet.

There was too strong a regard for order and decorum in the Lodge to permit of any manifestation of feeling during the ceremony, but when a recess was declared a little indignation meeting was held in a corner of the hall. "It´s a shame!" exclaimed Miss Clayton, who had been a member of the Furniture Committee, and might be pardoned for feeling a little vexation. "It´s a shame! Brother Brown ought not to bring such people here." Her words caught the ear of Edward Taylor, who had his own reasons for liking and respecting Laurence Brown, and he asked quickly, "What has Brother Brown been doing to displease you, Sister Clayton?" "Bringing in people with dirty boots to spoil our carpet," was the pettish response. "It is too bad," said Mrs. Jenkins, another member of the committee, "it will take hours to clean that clay off the carpet. Besides," she added, apologetically, "I am afraid those poor men will never come again. It would have been better to take them into one of the Lodges where they have bare floors and where things are not so nice as we have them here." (The carpet and other "nice things" had only been in the room a few hours and already the pride of possession filled the good woman´s heart.) Mr. Taylor was not a man of many words, and he only said gravely: "Don´t you think we had better take up our carpet and go back to bare floors if our fine things are to prevent us from doing our duty as Templars in endeavouring to raise the fallen?" No one answered, and just then the two new members were escorted by Laurence Brown to seats near the little group. They gazed around the Lodge-room and were evidently aware that they were hardly in keeping with their surroundings, for one remarked, "I say, Jim, they've got things pretty fine here." "Almost too fine for the likes of us, Bill," was the response, "just look at the mess our boots made on the carpet."

Sisters Jenkins and Clayton regarded Brother Taylor with a sort of "I told you so" expression, but the signal for the resumption of business prevented any further conversation.

Contrary to the expectations of some of the members the two new brothers, William Cook and James Martin, appeared just before the time for opening the next meeting. The handsome Lodge-room had produced a different effect upon the men from that prophesied by Sister Jenkins, for they had evidently made an attempt to improve their appearance. The most noticeable change for the better was seen in their boots, which had been polished in the most approved style. As the weeks went by, each Lodge night found the men in their accustomed seats, taking an evident interest in the business of the Order and gained the regard of their fellow members. Before three months had passed the change in their looks was so marked that one would hardly have recognized in them the two rough-looking initiates who had left their tracks on the carpet.

Chapter II

For three or four years prior to the opening of our story, the abode of James Martin had been a mean little house in a mean little court in one of the poorest parts of the town. There was not much that was homelike about the place, for poor Mrs. Martin had become demoralized by her surroundings and discouraged with her lot, so that even the scanty measure of comfort which a little energy might have secured was lacking. The poor woman, ill-fed, scantily clothed, always neglected and sometimes abused, had long lost heart and hope and bore little resemblance to the pretty, dressy Mollie Thompson who had married James Martin less than a dozen years ago. She had slunk into a slatternly, dawdling creature who spent her time scolding her children and bewailing her hard lot to her neighbors.

Mrs. Martin had not much faith at first in the amendment of her husband and had done nothing to encourage him in the fight he had been waging against habit and appetite. But as the days wore on and he still kept his pledge, a glimmer of hope began to dawn in her discouraged soul.

It was a Saturday evening, just four weeks since James Martin had joined the Good Templars. He had been making ready to go to the Lodge and he now stepped into the untidy little kitchen, and coming to his wife's side he placed some money in her hand. "Mollie," he said, "I have settled up the last of my drinking debts to-day and now I'm a free man. Please God, what I earn in the future shall go to make you and the children comfortable." Mollie could not speak; there was a note

in his voice and a look in his eyes which made her
think of the gay young workingman who had won her
girlish heart, and her own eyes filled with tears as
she gazed at him. Perhaps some old memories were
awakened in Martin's mind also as he regarded her thin
and faded face, for he kissed her tenderly and bade her
"good-bye" in a husky tone.

The poor wife was left in a bewildered condition,
almost afraid to believe in the vision of happiness
which had opened before her. But the money in her
hand--a larger sum than she had handled at one time for
years--was certainly real and the touch of husband's
kiss still burned upon her lips. "Oh, if it would only
last," she said to herself, if only her husband could
be again as he used to be before he took to drink.

She was interrupted in her musings by the entrance
of her three children, who had joined the Juvenile
Temple that afternoon and had been to tea at the home
of the Superintendent, Laurence Brown. The little ones
were full of delight and ready to tell of their experiences. "Me had some take," [sic] cried Jamie, a
wee laddie of four years. "So did I," said little
Bessie, aged six, "and we had some jam, too." Mary, a
tall, pretty girl of ten, who had acquired a wisdom
beyond her years as a result of the hardships of her
lot, had been less impressed with the good things upon
the table than with the order and neatness which
prevailed in the Browns' home. "Oh, mother," she said,
"I wish you could see how clean everything is there.
And Mrs. Brown had her hair done so nicely and such a
pretty dress on. Oh, I wish we could have things nice

like that." "<u>We will</u>," said the mother in a determined
tone, "we will, Mary, and we will begin now."

Mary soon understood that a happier condition of
things was about to begin in her home and was ready to
co-operate with her mother in her efforts to put the
dingy little place into something like order. When the
younger children had gone to bed, Mollie and her little
daughter went to work, and before it was time for the
father to come home the little kitchen had assumed a
really comfortable appearance. Mollie was a very tired
woman when she sought her bed late that night, but the
bodily fatigue was nothing in the light of the new hope
and joy which filled her heart.

It was Martin´s turn to be surprised when he came
down stairs next morning and found, instead of the
disorder to which he was only too well[-]accustomed, a
clean-swept hearth, a bright fire, a snowy cloth upon
the table and a simple but well-cooked breakfast
awaiting him. Nor was this all; the children were as
clean as soap and water could make them, and Mollie
herself looked almost young again in a gown which,
though shabby, was neat, in a clean apron, and with her
pretty hair neatly coiled around her shapely head. The
husband´s pleased eyes took in everything at a glance,
and he exclaimed, "Why, Mollie, this almost comes up to
our Lodge-room, barring the carpet, and we´ll have that
before long."

As he ate his breakfast Martin looked again and
again at his wife, and at last said, "Mollie, as soon
as you can get a new gown and bonnet you must join the
Lodge. The other men take their wives, and why

shouldn´t I? You wouldn´t mind giving up your drop of
beer, would you, Mollie?" "Mind it," replied Mollie,
"why, Jim, I would give up everything in the world to
have you keep as you are now." "Then that´s settled,"
said her husband, "and before you know where you are
they will be electing you Vice Templar or something."

Later in the day came Carrie Thompson, and her
surprise at the changed condition of affairs can hardly
be imagined. Carrie was sister to Mrs. Martin, and was
a nice-looking, bright young woman. She lived out as a
domestic and was highly respected by her employers.
Her sister´s family had long been a heavy drain upon
Carrie´s sympathy and savings. To-day she came laden
as usual with things to supply the more pressing needs
of the children. She had not much respect for her
brother-in-law and she greeted him coldly. But she
could not help noticing the alteration in his appearance, and when he stepped out she was eager to know
what had happened. "Jim has joined the Templars," said
Mollie, "and, oh Carrie, you can´t think what a
difference it has made already."

Carrie was at first somewhat sceptical regarding
the possibility of Jim keeping such a pledge, but when
she had heard the whole of her sister´s story, she was
ready to thank God and believe that brighter days were
in store for them all.

Mollie had blushed like a girl when she told of
her husband´s kiss of the evening before, but it was
Carrie´s turn to change color when her sister mentioned
that William Cook had also become a Good Templar and
was sticking to his pledge like a man. Mrs. Martin was

in Carrie´s confidence and knew that she, warned by her sister´s sad experience, had refused two years ago to marry William Cook because she found that he was getting to be too fond of the drink. So now she whispered: "Who knows what may happen, Carrie, if Will keeps his pledge? You may soon be in a home of your own, and what a wife you will make!"

***

A year had passed. The Lodge was still prospering and doing good. James Martin and William Cook had kept their obligations steadfastly, although they had not been without their trials and temptations. Mollie had learned to feel quite at home in the Lodge, and was, so her friends said, growing younger every day. She and her husband had taken a comfortable house near the Browns´ and she was becoming a notable housewife. The children were well and happy and were receiving sound temperance teaching in the Temple.

The good minister, Rev. Arthur Matthews, who belonged to the Lodge, had persuaded Mr. and Mrs. Martin to come and hear him some months ago with the result that they had continued to attend and had recently joined the church. In their case, as in that of many others, the Lodge had proved the stepping stone to the church, and the man and woman who had already been influenced in the direction of right living, were now publicly pledged to the service of God.

It was Lodge night once more and again there was an initiation which caused a ripple of excitement among the members. The candidate was the bride of William

Cook, and she proved to be our old friend, Carrie Thompson. During the Good of the Order a little presentation was made by members of the Lodge to the happy couple. The newly-made husband, in expressing his thanks for the gift, closed by saying that he and his friend Martin both had reason to bless the evening when they entered Light in Darkness Lodge and made those "tracks on the carpet."

RIGHT WORTHY GRAND SUPERINTENDENT JUVENILE TEMPLARS´ DEPARTMENT

[International Good Templar, May 1898]

SHALL WE HAVE A SUMMER VACATION?

In my recent circular letter to G.S.J.T.´s I made an especial reference to what I cannot but consider the unwise custom of suspending the meetings of the Temples during the warm weather. I reproduce the paragraph here for the benefit of those of the workers who read the magazine but do not see the circular:

"In view of the approach of the warm weather, I ask Grand Superintendents to discourage the practice which prevails in so many jurisdictions of closing the Temples during the summer months. I think that the experience of all workers will agree with my own that it is a matter of extreme difficulty to get the scattered membership of a Temple together again after a recess of several weeks. I renew the suggestions made a couple of years ago to the effect that outdoor meetings, country rambles, picnics, or garden parties

might take the place of regular Temple sessions.
Flower missions might be organized in connection with
Temples. I know of a Temple, a few miles from Boston,
the members of which, during the whole of last summer,
brought in once a week a number of little bouquets for
the children and old people in one of the poorest parts
of the city. Other Temples have carried flowers to
hospitals and other places. Where sessions are held in
halls, they might be made shorter than at other
seasons, but a strong effort should be made to get the
children to attend and to maintain their interest."

ARIZONA.

I have frequently said that there is nothing
[which] gives me greater pleasure or renders me more
hopeful for the success of our branch of the Order in
any jurisdiction than to know that the other Grand
Lodge officers are in sympathy with it and are giving
their support to the G.S.J.T. It was therefore a
source of much encouragement to receive from Brother A.
P. Walbridge, G.C.T., a very pleasant and interesting
letter, showing that the keen interest which he has
always felt is not abated. Our brother says, "We are
making an effort to revive the interest in juvenile
work here, but the great obstacle is the scarcity of
competent and suitable Superintendents. While visiting
a Lodge at Congress recently I did some preliminary
work for a Temple and will return to complete the
organization as soon as a Superintendent can be
secured. Ours is a hard field to work successfully;
our 60,000 population is scattered over 115,000 square
miles, and traveling by rail is six cents per mile."
Brother Walbridge adds that the Temple in Phoenix is
being revived and that one was instituted "down the

valley" with Brother S. S. Green, P.G.C.T., to superintend it.

GOLD COAST.

When sending the returns for Star of Beauty and
Prospect Temples, Brother J. S. Hutton, S.J.T., wrote:
"We are all working hard for the `World´s Prize Banner´
and hope to succeed in our enterprise. I am happy to
say that we are all united, working together to drive
intemperance from our land."

KENTUCKY.

This was a jurisdiction from which I had almost
despaired of hearing, but a recent letter from the
G.S.J.T., Sister Mrs. Carrie V. Demaree, says: "The
I.O.G.T. is being revived in our state. I have
received an application for a Juvenile Temple."
Evidently the work is reviving at the right end and
Kentucky is going to "begin at the beginning."

MARYLAND, SENIOR.

Sister Cummings, G.S.J.T., sends the annual
returns, which show a membership of 479 in nine
Temples. She gives a very interesting account of a
Juvenile convention recently arranged by her, at which
about three hundred children were in attendance and a
delightful time was spent. A collation was served at
the close by a committee consisting of the Superintendents. Our sister is anxious to have the children
supplied with pure literature and is endeavoring to
have the Youth´s Temperance Banner or the Water-Lily
distributed in her Temples.

MONTANA.

Sister Clara N. Belcher was re-elected to her important office at her last Grand Lodge session and she is doing all that she can with small means and a large territory. Concerning the methods of Temple work which she has found successful our sister writes: "Sister W. G. Bennett and I have introduced into our Temple a drill similar to Dr. Mann's Marshal's Drill. The children take great pleasure and pains to be accurate in the march and it adds very much to the dignity of the initiation. We also urge the committing to memory of the ritual and find it very much better than reading the parts. I use pictures in various ways, especially such ones as Neal Dow, John Wanamaker and other leaders in reform movements. I find that very good impressions can be made by temperance posters, especially those sent out by the National Temperance Society. Julia Coleman's Manual has suggested many things which have been interesting and instructive. I try to vary my entertainment and instruction each meeting, and the children always want to know what we shall have next time. I use the stories from <u>The International Good Templar</u> and other papers and books. We pay strict attention to parliamentary usage, committee reports, etc. I know of no place where children can be so thoroughly taught, and it is well to bear in mind that little people like to do the same as `big folks'."

NEW JERSEY.

Brother Eugene De La Roi, of Florence, has shown so much interest in the juvenile work that it seemed to me to be the part of wisdom to commission him as a

Special Deputy. In reply he wrote: "I thank you for the confidence and honor thus shown, and while I may not be able to promise much, I shall at all times do what may be in my power to advance the cause of the children. In our Temple we are initiating every evening and the children are in love with the work. Some of the worst boys in town--those who formerly swore the loudest--are now peaceful and orderly. Of course, it takes constant time and work, but it is work which will tell in Eternity."

NEW ZEALAND.

Sister Mrs. C. Cameron, G.S.J.T., wrote recently that "The work under my charge is steadily progressing, although the adult members do not take as much interest as I should like to see. But it will not be my fault if I do not rouse them to a sense of their duty."

VERMONT.

Sister Mrs. O. S. Willey, G.S.J.T., has taken up the work of her department in real earnest and wrote recently that she was able to report three new Temples, situated at Lincoln, Warren and South Barre respectively. Of the Temple organized by her at Barre last September, our sister writes:

"It now has forty members, thirteen of whom are over twelve years of age. We have literary exercises each week and I require them to have a Bible lesson each week. I feel that no Superintendent can successfully teach the true principles of our Order without first asking God to bless our work. I teach the children to ask God to help them to keep the pledge."

WESTERN AUSTRALIA.

Sister Jessie Forsyth-Smith, G.S.J.T., in a very practical circular addressed to the Lodges of her jurisdiction says: "It has often happened that a Lodge has been saved from collapse by having young Templars in the Temples ready to transfer to the adult Lodge at the needed moment. And these, be it remembered, are well-trained and ready to take up the work at once. Members trained in our Temples are less likely to leave or to take offense at every little tiff. They have been disciplined and love the Order and will prove stickers." Brother Thomas Smith, the father of this energetic young officer, has offered a set of regalia to the Temple reporting the largest proportional increase in membership. The Grand Lodge has voted the sum of one pound to each Temple to be expended in literature. With these aids I am inclined to think that our sister will make a good record.

FORSYTH TO H. A. LAWSON, OCT. 19, 1899

[Wis/Mss/JT, General Correspondence, Grand Lodge of Wisconsin, I.O.G.T., State Historical Society of Wisconsin, Madison. A dozen or more of Forsyth's letters to H. A. Lawson, are preserved in this collection. In 1899 he was Grand Superintendent of Juvenile Templars for Wisconsin.]

I have two letters of yours awaiting reply and am happy to have this opportunity of acknowledging them. It was a pleasure to hear from you after so long a silence.

I am sorry to hear of the loss of membership and should not have felt it a "burden" to read anything which it might relieve you to say upon the matter. I am somewhat accustomed to such burdens and am always glad to feel that the G.S.J.T.´s are free to tell me of the failures--or what they may regard as such--as well as of the successes.

But I am quite sure that you have done all that you could do and I believe that the bright hopes you express for this year´s work will be realized. I am very glad to hear of your re-election and trust a great blessing will attend your efforts.

I think I am to blame for the delay in your receiving those Secretary´s books of the International Institute [for juvenile workers]. I have scarcely seen Mr. Yeames since the Toronto session and have forgotten to tell him who was elected Secretary [namely, H. A. Lawson, succeeding James Yeames]. However, I wrote to him immediately after I received your letter of the 6th, and asked him to send the books to you. He has been very dangerously ill since then and is still far from recovery, but as soon as he is about again, I am sure he will attend to the matter.

Yes, there is a change in the G.S.J.T. of New York State and I regret it very much. Mrs. Dietrick was eminently fitted for the position. But I trust that her successor will prove equal to the task she has undertaken. There have been a great many such changes within the last few weeks. I can only hope that some may be for the better and none for the worse. But I am always sorry to cross the name of a worker with whom I

have become well[-]acquainted off my list; it is like
losing a friend.

It is a little too soon, I think, to be making
plans for the Jubilee demonstration [at Utica, New
York, in 1901]; about a year from the time of holding
it will be sufficiently early, as people are apt to
lose interest if matter is talked about too long before
the event. But I shall be glad for you to make any
suggestions you can think of in the meantime. I
suppose that we shall have to depend upon the workers
in N.Y. State for all the children who will attend.

Thanking you for your promptitude in sending the
returns and with best wishes for the cause in Wisconsin, I am Yours Very Fraternally.

ELSIE´S DOLL´S HOUSE

[International Good Templar, March 1900; one in a
series of Elsie Foster stories which appear to have
autobiographical details]

It was not a real doll´s house, because at this
period of Elsie´s history there was not much money in
the family to spend upon toys and a doll´s house is a
rather costly article. But Elsie was not strong and
she could not run about and jump rope and play games
like other children, and she had been charmed by a
beautiful doll´s house in the home of a little girl she
had visited. She and her mother talked over the matter
and Mrs. Foster decided to give Elsie a small cupboard
in the sitting-room and to help her fit it up for a
doll´s house. The cupboard had three shelves and each

shelf was partitioned off into three rooms with walls
made of stiff cardboard and covered with pretty wall
paper. For windows Elsie cut window scenes out of a
real estate agent´s advertisement book and pasted them
on the back of the cupboard. These looked very natural
when they were draped with lace curtain and some of
them made it appear that there was a garden outside.

What a delightful task it was to plan and contrive
pretty and useful things to furnish the doll´s house.
Mrs. Foster was full of ideas and she and Elsie worked
hard to put them into effect. They covered the kitchen
floor with the marbled paper from an old account book
and it looked like a gay-colored oilcloth. The other
floors had for carpets either some thick wall paper or
flowered damask which was pasted on smoothly. Little
cheap articles of furniture were bought from time to
time which did very well for the common rooms, but the
parlor was a problem, as it required something more
stylish than Elsie´s limited purse could command.
However, with her mother´s help she fashioned a couch
and some chairs out of cardboard and covered them with
damask and they did very well for a makeshift.

The occupants of this house were a family of
cheap-jointed wooden dolls to whom Elsie gave names.
They were Mr. and Mrs. Douglas and several sons and
daughters whose lives were made quite eventful by
Elsie´s busy little imaginative brain. They attended
church, went to the opera, and gave parties, and were
always properly dressed for each of these important
functions. The guests who came to the parties were cut
out of cardboard and painted to represent ladies and
gentlemen in evening attire. Elsie named these people

for the characters in the books which she read and she
avoided getting one confused with another by the simple
process of writing the name on the back of each doll.
So long as these miniature ladies and gentlemen
remained seated or standing against the walls of the
rooms, they looked very nice indeed, and perhaps were
just as interesting and useful as a great many real
people who serve as "wallflowers" in society.

Elsie got a great deal of pleasure out of her
doll´s house and no doubt the contrivances she had to
make helped to keep her interested and amused.

One day a French gentleman visited Elsie´s home.
He was very nice and kind and soon became great friends
with the little girl. Upon his promising "not to
laugh," Elsie allowed "Monsieur," as she called him to
see her doll´s house. The gentleman did not laugh, but
was greatly interested in the doings of the Douglas
family and the various unique inventions which helped
to furnish their home. A few weeks after "Monsieur´s"
visit, when he had returned to his own country, a
parcel came to Elsie from Paris. You can picture her
delight when she opened it and found some beautiful
little articles of furniture with a note from "Monsieur" asking her to accept them from him and use them
in her doll´s house. There were six elegant chairs and
a sofa, with gilt frames and green velvet cushions; a
miniature piano, and a sideboard with shelves and glass
doors. Packed very carefully in one of the drawers of
the sideboard were two little decanters and a half
dozen of the tiniest wine glasses you could possibly
imagine. Elsie felt very rich indeed and the Douglas
family gave a dinner party immediately to show off

their new furniture "from Paris." Some cold tea was put into the decanters to look like wine and every guest was supposed to drink some and to enjoy the occasion very much.

Soon after this Elsie went away into the country to pay a long visit to some Quaker friends. While she was with these good people she heard her first temperance lecture and signed the pledge.

When she came back to her London home she joined a Band of Hope and soon became a very earnest little worker. By and by her conscience began to be troubled about the Douglas family and the wine glasses. It did not seem right for her dolls to take wine when she had left off drinking it, but she did not like to leave off using those "darling little glasses," so she went to her mother for advice and the result was that the inmates of Elsie's doll's house all signed a temperance pledge and agreed to give water to their guests. After that when the Douglas family gave a dinner party the little decanters were filled with water and Elsie always spoke of her glasses as "water glasses."

So you see Elsie was quite a consistent little temperance worker, and I hope all the children who read about her will try to be so too.

RIGHT WORTHY GRAND SUPERINTENDENT JUVENILE TEMPLARS' DEPARTMENT

[International Good Templar, April 1900]

BUENOS AYRES.--A letter received a long time ago from Bro. H. J. King gave some very interesting news of the Temple "Southern Cross." Bro. King wrote as follows: "Owing to the completion of the dock and port works in this city, the workmen and their families have left the place and become scattered, some of them leaving the country. Amongst these was the S.J.T., Sister Hayward. In consequence, the Juvenile Temple was temporarily closed. I, however, have never ceased to urge the need of a Temple among the English boys and girls, and at least succeeded in resuscitating Southern Cross Temple and affiliating it with Progress Lodge at Barracas. The Temple was reopened with twenty-six members, and at my last visit there were 102 on the roll. It is a great pleasure to see the little ones stand up and recite in English or Spanish (for there are many who speak the latter language), and great praise must be accorded to Bro. Gray, the Superintendent, and his assistants, for the careful training which the youngsters receive." Bro. King mentions that the Grand Chaplain of England, Rev. James Sturdee, is an own cousin of his. He was not aware of his connection with the Order until he saw his portrait in the Good Templars' Watchword, as he had not heard from him for over thirty years. It was a very pleasant thing to hear of him in this manner.

COLORADO.--The present G.C.T. of Colorado is Bro. Henry H. Roser, a former well-known worker of Illinois.

Bro. Roser acknowledged the receipt of my last quarterly circular by a kindly and courteous letter, in which he says: "I trust that the New Year will bring prosperity to our beloved Order in this jurisdiction, both adult and juvenile. I have not, as yet, become familiar with the conditions and prospects here, but our executive committee is laying plans for the coming year. As you know, our jurisdiction extended over Colorado, Wyoming and New Mexico. The field is wide, and, on account of the conditions in this Western country, quite difficult to work. For the last few months we have had as our organizer, Miss Anna M. Saunders, P.G.C.T. of Nebraska, and P.R.W.G.C. She has organized several Lodges and has proved herself truly an indomitable worker. We hope that you will favor us with suggestions from time to time." Bro. Roser adds that Mrs. Lena Hollaway is the G.S.J.T., and I have commissioned the sister and hope to find in her an efficient worker.

GOLD COAST.--Victoria Temple is making splendid progress under the charge of Bro. Daniel Sackey, whose latest reports shows a membership of 62, as compared with 32 at the beginning of the quarter. Bro. Sackey says the attendance is good and that the membership has been divided into two companies, with captains. The duty of each captain is to register the company´s attendance, to secure new members, to provide entertainment on alternate nights, etc. The S.J.T., of course, has the oversight of all these matters. Bro. Sackey gives great praise to Bros. Moore, Wilson and Christian for their co-operation with him in his efforts. Bro. D. A. E. Ocram writes in a similar strain regarding Victoria Temple and praises Bro. Sackey´s work.

HOLLAND.--The third Temple in this country was instituted by our European Missionary, Sister Gray, at Den Helder. It started with eleven children and six adults. "Four of these," writes Sister Gray, "are members of Waterloo Lodge. One of them is an old man whose little grand-daughter is the Chaplain in the Temple. Another is the husband of the Superintendent, and although he was a great smoker, he has given up his tobacco in order to help his wife and set a good example to his two little boys. I think this was splendid. Besides these, four mothers joined, two of them Good Templars and the others not yet. Five or six more children were proposed for membership. Much interest was evinced and I feel sure that the Temple will grow and prosper and be a great help to the Lodge." As an offset to this good news, however, Sister Gray informed me that Samuel Temple, at Rotterdam, is not working at present, because no suitable person can be found to superintend it. And the Temple at Amsterdam is also resting just at present. But a very earnest and capable Sister has been elected as S.J.T., and she is looking for a suitable room and preparing to gather the children together again."

IOWA.--"There seems to be a new interest in the Juvenile branch of our Order this year, for which I am truly glad. In less than two months I have organized or re-organized ten Temples." Such is the cheery message sent by Sister Maggie Munson, who is taking a course of scientific Temperance instruction at Battle Creek, to render herself better fitted for her important work. When writing of a Juvenile meeting at Jewel Junction, in a recent number of the Iowa [Temperance] Magazine, Sister Munson makes very kindly reference to Sister Rev. E. M. Remington, P.G.S.J.T. Evidently there is good feeling between Sister Munson and her predecessor, for a recent letter from Sister Remington commends Sister Munson to me in very warm terms.

MASSACHUSETTS, JUNIOR GRAND LODGE.--Bro. Martin Johanson, G.S.J.T., has forwarded one dollar as a contribution to the "Million Dollar Fund" from his Temple at Worcester, "Varblommen." He writes that he has hopes of another Temple soon.

PENNSYLVANIA.--A letter from Sister Belle Jones is always pleasant and encouraging, even when she is not able to give any especial piece of good news. She is always cheery and anxious to do her best. Bro. Wm. G. Hohmann, G.C.T., in a recent letter, reports two new Temples this year in his own district. In addition to being G.C.T., and at the same time holding office in Sub-Lodge and District Lodge, Bro. Hohmann is Treasurer of Triumph Temple.

A good letter from Bro. Mark Norman, D.S.J.T., shows his continued interest in the Juvenile work.

PRINCE EDWARD ISLAND.--After a long silence, a letter from Miss Adelia E. Horton, the faithful G.S.J.T., was very welcome. She is somewhat discouraged over the condition of affairs in her jurisdiction, but is "doing her best and leaving results with God."

SWEDEN.--The last returns show a net increase of twenty-three Temples and 1,729 members, making a total of 12,993 in 218 Temples. In a recent letter, the energetic G.S.J.T., Bro. Johan Ahlen, says: "The Juvenile work in Sweden continues successful, and I hope to be able to report another increase this year." The Grand Lodge has adopted a set of pictures for Juvenile Temples, and Bro. Ahlen has very kindly sent a set for my information. The set only consists of four pictures, but a very complete story is told by them. Bro. Ahlen says: "If you think they can be used in other jurisdictions, we shall be very glad to sell these pictures at one dollar per set, if fifty sets are required. One set may be had for one dollar and fifteen cents. Orders may be sent to me."

WALES (ENGLISH).--I learn from the returns kindly sent me by Bro. Jenkins, P.G.S.J.T., that a total membership of 7,439 in seventy-six Temples was reported at the last session of the Grand Lodge. The National Competitive Examination of the past year was the most successful ever held. The subjects for the competition were taken from the Handbook of Juvenile Templary, prepared by the G.C.T., Bro. Stanford. The prizes were all given by Bro. A. E. Eccles of England, whose generosity to the Juveniles is known all over Great Britain and Ireland. Bro. J. W. Hopkins, G.S.J.T. of England, selected the questions for the examination, and also undertook the adjudication. A beautifully illuminated address was presented to Bro. Eccles in recognition of his generous help.

In 1899 the total membership was 3,320 in twenty-eight Temples, and the great advance made in ten years speaks well for the workers in gallant little Wales. Bro. Jenkins says that the adult membership is worked up to such a pitch of enthusiasm that the deepest interest is taken in the Juvenile work and the last Juvenile Conference was the largest and most successful ever held. Our good brother pays a high tribute to his successor, Bro. Edward Jones, and says that the work will go on all right under his charge.

HOW ELSIE LOST THE PRIZE

[<u>International Good Templar</u>, October 1900]

Elsie was in the habit of paying long visits to the home of her uncle James and aunt Elsie, who were always ready to do anything to make it pleasant for her. Very often they would invite the little daughter of an old friend to stay with them at the same time, and the two girls had nice times together. Kathleen Wilson was a very pretty child with blue eyes and flaxen curls. She was not so nervous and impulsive as Elsie and she had the name of being very sweet and good. But sometimes when Elsie got into trouble on account of her restless, fidgety ways, and her aunt advised her to try and be quiet and gentle like Kathleen, she would rebel a little and say, "It is all very well for Kathleen to sit still and look pretty; she can't help it."

The little girls got along together very nicely because Kathleen was usually willing to let Elsie to do the planning and take the lead. Sometimes they would

have a fancy for making dolls' clothes and would sit
and sew as though their living depended upon their
needles. Or they would play games and read books
together and quite often they would do fancy work. At
one time they became very fond of making crochet lace
and would try which could work the fastest.

One day they had been showing their work to Uncle
James and he offered a prize of half a crown to the one
who should invent the prettiest original pattern for
some crochet lace. The terms of the contest were that
the girls were to remain in separate rooms for two
hours to invent the pattern, and that at the end of the
time Uncle James was to see the work and decide which
one was entitled to the prize.

Elsie went up to her room and sat down to work
with the thought that it would not be a very difficult
matter to be the winner. But, oh dear, it was one
thing to copy a pattern which someone else had invented
and quite another to make one "out of your own head."
No matter how hard she tried to make something she had
never seen before, it seemed as if some pattern she
knew would keep coming out on the crochet needle. She
had to begin over and over again before she could be
quite sure that the pattern was really her own. Then
she sat and looked at the queer production and said to
herself, "Elsie Foster, you will never win that half
crown unless Kathleen has been a great deal more stupid
than you are. I expect Uncle James will make lots of
fun when he sees this thing." But the time was up and
Elsie's patience was exhausted; there was nothing to be
done but turn over the funny and not too clean sample

of her inventive powers for her uncle to pass judgment upon.

Uncle James had quite a solemn and dignified appearance as he sat at the table with the two specimens of lace before him, and the contest appeared quite a serious matter. He made a little address to the girls, when they appeared before him, and said that one of the contestants had evidently taken a great deal more pains than the other and that he should be obliged to award the prize to the maker of the beautiful clean piece of lace which he now help up. "This is ever so much better than the other," he said, and when Kathleen stepped forward with a blushing face, he handed her the half-crown with many words of praise. Then he told poor Elsie that she ought to be ashamed to show him such a ridiculous pattern as hers and that he was sorry she was so idle and so lacking in ambition.

Elise looked at Kathleen´s pattern and walked away feeling very angry indeed, for she saw, what her uncle had failed to see, that it was very like one of the patterns in a book she owned. She wanted to cry out that Kathleen had cheated, but was afraid that her uncle would think she was jealous. So she controlled her temper and held her tongue. After a while she became calmer and in place of being angry with Kathleen she felt sorry for her and did not envy her the money or the praise which had not been honestly gained.

I think Aunt Elsie understand about the matter [of Kathleen having copied from a pattern book] and that she told Uncle James, who did not know as much about crochet work as he did some other things. At any rate, when Elsie was going back to her home a week or two later, her uncle gave her a half-crown and said to her, with a quizzical smile, that "I like honest folks, Elsie, even if they can't always win prizes."

ELSIE'S HAPPY EASTER

[<u>International Good Templar</u>, April 1901]

It was a warm, sunny Easter morning and Elsie was allowed to go to church for the first time since that long illness of which you have heard. Elsie liked to go to church, and while she lay in bed all those weary weeks of sickness she used to listen to the bells of Holy Trinity ringing: "Come to church, come to church" (which was what they always seemed to say) and long to obey the call. Her minister, Rev. David Laing, had been to see her very often and had told how he had missed her from his little flock. Her teacher, Miss Young, had visited her also and had brought messages from her classmates. And she felt very happy at the thought of taking her place in church and Sunday school again and became so excited that mamma felt almost afraid to let her go. But her brother George, who was eleven (four years older than Elsie) and a very manly boy, promised to take great care of her and when they started he kept fast hold of her hand.

How delightful it seemed to be out in the street once more and how beautiful everything appeared to the little girl that bright Easter morning. She was obliged to walk very slowly and sometimes stop to rest, although the way was not long. People hurrying along in their new spring dresses cast pitying glances at the

pale little girl in the mourning which she was wearing
for her little brother Walter, but Elsie did not feel
that she needed pity. She hoped soon to be able to
walk as fast as anyone, and although she missed her
little brother, she liked to think of him as waiting
for her in the heavenly home. Then, too, she was very
fond and proud of her big brother George, who was very
gentle and tender to her. So her little white face
looked very bright as she stepped into church and went
to the place where she knew she would find her dear Mr.
Laing.

The Vicar of Holy Trinity used always to stand by
the font, near the doors, on a Sunday morning and the
children who were early at church were always sure of a
word or a smile from him as they entered. Elsie
thought a great deal of these Sunday morning greetings
and was careful never to miss them by being late. On
this morning Mr. Laing's hands were full of white
flowers and he gave one to each of the boys and girls
as they entered. When he saw Elsie the smile on his
kind face seemed brighter than usual and he said: "Here
is a beautiful white lily for my little old woman."
This was a playful name he had given to Elsie, because
since her illness she had become what is called "old-
fashioned," and she thought a great deal and asked
strange questions.

What a beautiful service it was that morning;
Elsie sat with her lily in her hand almost in a dream.
From her seat she could see the choir boys in their
gowns; her brother George was among them and she was
quite sure she could distinguish his voice when they
sang "Jesus Christ is risen to-day, Alleluia." Then

somewhat [sic] the white gowns made her think of the
children who were "around the throne of God in heaven"
and her little brother Walter did not seem very far
away, but he and George and herself all seemed to be
singing "Alleluia" together.

Then came the sermon and Elsie listened attentively to her dear minister´s words, although she could not
understand all he said. But she knew what it meant
when he spoke of people coming out after a long
illness, "walking in newness of life," and in a vague
way she understood that the life which God had spared
to her when He had called her little brother home to
heaven, was intended to be used for His service. And
all these beautiful things together made this Easter
Day a very happy one and one to be remembered by Elsie
as long as she lived.

URGE THE PLEDGE

[Read at the May 1901 Directors´ Meeting of the Massachusetts Total Abstinence Society, (Boston) Temperance Cause, Sept. 1901]

My reply to the question "Can there be in this
State a campaign for signing the pledge of Total
Abstinence from the use of Intoxicating Liquors as a
Beverage?" cannot be a positive one, because I am aware
that to carry on such a campaign would require the
united endeavor of all the temperance societies in the
State, and I am not sure whether such unity of action
would be assured. But I am quite certain that there is
great need for such a movement, and perhaps one way to

assist in initiating it will be to set forth my reasons
for holding this view.

LACK OF PRINCIPLE.

The earnest person who maintains a radical
attitude with reference to the temperance question is
often astonished at the very light manner in which what
is to him such a serious problem, is regarded by many
good Christian people. It is disappointing sometimes,
after all the years of temperance effort, to find so
large a number of the respectable people with whom one
comes in contact who have really no principle in the
matter. They do not drink alcoholic liquors habit-
ually; perhaps they never place them upon their own
tables; but if they happen to be in society where wine
is passed around, they will take a little without
compunction, and feel affronted if one should blame
them for what they consider a harmless indulgence.
This sort of person is frequently found among the
"Americans abroad," and upon the ocean steamships. "We
never drink beer when we are at home, of course," said
two young ladies, typical Bostonians, who were among my
fellow-passengers upon one occasion, but in London we
often took a glass, and thought it very nice and
refreshing." On an outward voyage I was once very much
astonished to see a prominent Congregationalist pastor,
well-known in the vicinity of Boston, sharing a bottle
of ale with the ladies of his party; and I had a
distinct feeling of surprise when I found that among
forty persons, nearly all Americans, at the dining-
table, the only one beside myself who did not order
something from the wine list, was a Roman Catholic
Priest. I became acquainted during the voyage with
several of these persons, and some of them, when they

learned that I was going over to attend a temperance convention, expressed interest in and sympathy with the movement, but did not seem to realize that their personal example could have any effect upon it. Some of these people told me that they never used intoxicating liquors at home, but "at sea and in Europe it was different." And the flimsy, old excuse about the "bad water" which made it necessary that one should drink something else, was put forward in nearly every case. As I have known many total abstainers who have travelled a great deal, and who have suffered no ill effects from the much-abused water, I have not much confidence in the temperance principles of those who will use such a pretext.

POWER OF A PLEDGE.

In addition to the weak-kneed people just referred to there are those who have been brought up total abstainers, as a matter of course, but who have had no temperance teaching and have never signed a pledge. Lacking this safeguard many a promising young Christian has fallen into the snares of the tempter. His religious principles will yield sometimes to the temptation offered amid delightful and congenial surroundings. The excuse "Is it not a little one?" soothes the conscience, and in many cases the appetite is aroused and the habit formed almost unconsciously. To such people the pledge is a necessary protection. It is not enough to be able to say, "I am a Christian, a church member, therefore I ought not to drink," because one can be pointed to many well-known professors of religion who <u>do</u> drink. But when one can say, "I am a total abstainer; I have signed the pledge," the mere fact of making the avowal has sustaining influence, and it is seldom, in respectable company at least, that the solicitation is renewed when once that declaration has been made. The pledged total abstainer may be considered a fanatic, but he will be respected and let alone as far as any further urging is concerned.

TENDENCIES.

There is not time to refer to the hereditary appetite which predisposes so many to drink. We all know that the liquor habit is one of the strongest proofs in the world of the awful truth that the sins of the fathers are visited upon the children "unto the third and fourth generation." And because this is so, and because we cannot discriminate between those who inherit this dreadful taint and those are free from it, it is for the best interests of the race that all children should be pledged to total abstinence from their earliest years.

WEAK SENTIMENT.

Looking at the matter from another point of view one is obliged to realize the fact that the temperance legislation which has been secured in many places has been weakened or nullified, because of the lack of temperance sentiment in the communities. And this, too, points to the need of a campaign of education.

A CAMPAIGN WELCOMED.

Therefore, I am in favor of a pledge-signing campaign, and am willing to do anything in my power to promote it. But I hardly feel able to make any recommendations other than will doubtless have already been advanced. The work of this Society among the children of the schools is a good one and should be extended

among the Sunday schools and the young people´s religious societies. The work of the various temperance
organizations, reaching as they do so many of the young
people of the State, should be encouraged and promoted.
And in addition to these, there might be some sort of
concerted action, something in the nature of a great
revival, conducted by the temperance societies working
in harmony together, and each gleaning from the harvest
of pledge signers numerous additions to their respective organizations.

FORSYTH TO GEORGE F. COTTERILL, SEPTEMBER 2, 1903

[Box 23, Folder 4, George F. Cotterill papers, University of Washington Libraries]

I was very glad to receive your letter and
intensely interested in its contents. I rejoice to
know that you have reached our shores again in safety
and trust you may be safe and well at home ere this.

You are to be congratulated upon the success of
your mission and your going was certainly providential.
The Europeans will have more respect for American Good
Templary now that they know we still possess members
willing to sacrifice themselves for their principles.

I can well believe that our <u>distinguished</u> R.W.G.
Counselor [Professor Johan Bergman, Sweden] might make
himself tolerably disagreeable upon occasion. I heard
rumors at Stockholm which made me fear that he would
prove a difficult person to get along with. His
assertion regarding the lack of a belief in God among
people of intelligence and culture is a beautiful

specimen of the bigotry which rivals and outdoes religious bigotry. Let us hope that as time passes these men may be led to see something above and beyond their own small selves. I never can imagine how people who do not believe in God can endure life. I dislike very much the frothy and wordy religion professed by some people, and which has so little influence upon their lives, but I regard it as something to be devoutly thankful for that I can look, with the faith of [a] child, up to the Father of all and trust my hopes and plans, and wishes in His hand.

You will have received my previous letter with remittance; let me know how you come out financially as we must see to it that you get enough to fully cover your expenses. With kindest regards to yourself and wife, I am, Your Very Fraternally (signed).

P. S.
Brother Malins wrote me that he was delighted to see you and you had rendered valuable service.

THE AMERICAN TEMPERANCE MOVEMENT IN 1905

[untitled, in <u>Scottish Temperance Annual</u> (1905)]

The present aspect of the Temperance movement in the United States is considered by those who have good opportunities for judging to be a hopeful one. Notwithstanding the constant influx of foreigners, who bring their drinking habits and customs with them, the per capita consumption of alcohol shows only a very slight increase. The consumption of beer has greatly increased during recent years, but, on the other hand, there is a decline in the use of spirits and, basing the calculation upon the actual amount of alcohol consumed, the increase is found to be very small.

Concerning temperance legislation, it is generally conceded that the United States stands in the van, although we are unfortunately open to the charge, in many places, of failure to enforce the good laws we have enacted. In this direction the Anti-Saloon League and other organizations are doing good work.

Laws providing for scientific temperance instruction in public schools have now been enacted in every State of the Union, and every child who passes through our schools must receive some definite teaching regarding the nature and effects of alcohol.

The attitude of the Church, as a whole, is steadily improving. Temperance Societies are organised in connection with even the more conservative religious bodies. The advance among Roman Catholics is especially noticeable; the Father Mathew and the Catholic Total Abstinence Societies are growing in numbers, and it is becoming a very usual thing for children to be pledged to total abstinence until they reach the age of twenty-one, or at the time they make their first communion.

The most discouraging feature at the present time is the decline in membership and influence of the various temperance organizations. But there are many reasons for their decline, one important one being the formation of Church Temperance Societies referred to above. These, with the Christian Endeavour Society, the Epworth League, and other such bodies, have made heavy drafts upon the membership of the so-called secret temperance societies. Another reason is the large number of fraternal Insurance Orders which have come into being during the past twenty-five years. These Societies offer to their members the social features which were formerly seldom found outside of the Good Templar Lodge or the Sons of Temperance Division, and, with the additional attraction of financial benefit in case of sickness or death, they have wrought havoc among the temperance organizations. To offset this it must be said that, while these Societies do not use a temperance pledge, the most of them are distinctly in favour of total abstinence for their members. A rapidly growing sentiment in this direction is also to be observed among the larger and older organizations, such as the Freemasons, Oddfellows, etc.; and there are indications of revival among the temperance organizations which lead one to hope that they may again become the educational, influential, and aggressive bodies of former days.

FORSYTH TO GEORGE F. COTTERILL, NOVEMBER 11, 1905

[Box 23, Folder 4, George F. Cotterill papers, University of Washington Libraries]

I have been anxious to write a few lines to you ever since I received the glad news from Chicago. I was delighted to hear that you were chosen the head of the new organization [the National Grand Lodge]; I fully expected that you would be, as I knew it was the desire of so many, but one never knows what may happen

when it comes to election of officers and it was a
relief to know that all went well. I consider the
whole board a most efficient one and believe that the
new organization is bound to be a great success under
such able management.

Of course, I still entertain the hope that you may
some day be at the head of the International organization because I know no one deserves it better than you
do. I hope and believe that there are many honors yet
in store for you in Good Templary as well as outside
it.

I was sorry, although not surprised to learn that
Massachusetts did not cut a very pretty figure at Chicago. You may be sure that I have not learned this
from those who represented our State at the organization of the N.G.L. According to their story they were
the biggest fellows (I do not mean physically, of
course,) in the whole gathering and they did about
everything that was done. We are used to that kind of
talk here, but I wish we had not so much of it. The
G.C.T. [Albert Sutcliffe] has done a good work in getting the debt paid, (although much of the credit belongs to the G.S. [Miguel Sereque]) and he has a great
deal of "hustle" to him, but he is never without a
fight on his hands and that is not good for the cause.

But my purpose in writing is to ask you to let us
have that cut of yourself which was published in the
New Voice for publication in the magazine. Please send
it to Brother Parker, with a line to me telling me that
you have done so. I am intending to publish portraits

of all the N.G.L. Executive officers [in the <u>Interna-</u>
<u>tional Good Templar</u>].

With love to Sister Cotterill, trusting that she
is well, and best regards to yourself, I am, Yours very
fraternally, [signed]

P.S.:-If there is anything, I can ever do to represent
the N.G.L. at this end of the territory, please command
me. I shall be glad to be of service. I shall look
for you to come to Boston next year with Sister C. [for
the National Grand Lodge session] and will see that
your stay in our city does not cost you much.

FORSYTH TO GEORGE F. COTTERILL, FEBRUARY 14, 1906

[Box 23, Folder 4, George F. Cotterill papers, University of Washington Libraries]

Our International Chief Templar, Herr Wavrinsky
has forwarded to me a copy of the National Grand Lodge
by-laws relating to the duties of the N.G.S.J.W.
[National Grand Superintendent of the Juvenile Work]
These he asks me to use my judgment with regard to
approving and to send the result of my deliberations to
you.

I note that the duties outlined for the N.G.S.J.W.
are identical with those of the G.S.J.W.´s and that the
powers given are similar. This makes it possible for
me to approve the suggested by-laws on the understanding that N.G.S.J.W. bears the same relation to the
I.S.J.W. as that existing between the I.S.J.W. and the

G.S.J.W.'s. That is to say that the powers and duties
of the I.S.J.W. cannot, of course, be affected by any
legislation of the N.G.L.

I just mention this so that there may be no
misunderstanding. There is hardly likely to be any
friction between myself and the present N.G.L. Executive and, as you well know, I am in the fullest
sympathy with the N.G.L. But there may be persons in
office in the future who will not be so entirely at one
as the present N.G.S.J.W. and myself are and it is well
to guard against future contingencies.

SOME REASONS FOR THE DECLINE OF GOOD TEMPLARY
IN THE UNITED STATES

[International Good Templar, May 1911]

Many things have contributed to cause the decline
of our Order in the United States. In the first place
it be noted that the character of our population has
greatly changed in the years that have passed since the
first Lodge was organized, and the United States of
to-day is very different from the United States of
sixty years ago. Good Templary was at first a purely
American institution and it is hardly probable that any
member of its early days ever in his wildest dreams
conceived the idea that it would become the great
world-wide organisation which it is to-day. The
comparatively small population of sixty years ago was
almost entirely an English-speaking people; the fashion
of "globe-trotting" had not been introduced, and people
from other countries were regarded with distrust and
sometimes with aversion.

A strong prejudice existed at first even against
those who came from Great Britain and Ireland, but the
fact that they use the same language has been a great
help in overcoming it.

The first immigrants were for the most part from
the British Isles. They brought with them their
drinking habits, and in the case of those who came in
the largest numbers [Irish Roman Catholics], they were
prevented from uniting with our Order, except in a few
instances, because their religion prohibited such
[secret] organisations. Later came the influx of
people from the continent of Europe bringing with them
their manners and customs and to most of these total
abstinence was a thing unheard of.

Good Templary in its earlier days had not developed the Missionary spirit which characterises it now,
and there was little, if any, effort made by American
Good Templars to draw foreigners into the Order. It
was not until after the Order was introduced into
Scandinavia, and Scandinavian Good Templars began to
come to the United States, that foreign-speaking Lodges
(with possibly a very occasional exception) were formed
in this country.

In the meantime other changes had taken place.
Villages had become towns and small towns had grown
into large cities. Places in which the Lodge room had
been the only resort outside of the home, were overrun
with new social organisations to which young people
were soon attracted. An organisation with rules as
strict as the Good Templars in the matter of dancing,

playing games, etc., could stand but little chance in winning the more frivolous of the young people in competition with the newer and less narrow societies.

Keeping pace with the growth of the social organisation has been the development of the institutional work of the churches. The various young people´s societies do not limit their effort to moral and spiritual uplift of the members, but provide for social intercourse and recreation as well. There is now no need to go outside of the church to be either edified or entertained.

All of these things have helped to make the advance of Good Templary difficult everywhere in America and some places impossible.

Some of the things which the Order takes pride in having originated have resulted in injury to itself. This is true of the Prohibition Party which withdrew from us many of our noblest men. The same may be said of the Anti-Saloon League, and while we rejoice in the fact that many of the best workers in these organisations were trained in our Lodges, we regret the loss to ourselves. In the effort to secure and enforce legislation, it has sometimes been forgotten that the less conspicuous work of developing and fostering the Temperance sentiment in a community is greatly needed and that Good Templary is just the thing to supply that need.

Another Society which has grown to large proportions, often at the expense of the Order, is the Woman´s Christian Temperance Union. Born in a Good

Templar Lodge room, fostered and nourished by Good
Templar women, it has become a great organisation. And
American Good Templary is the poorer by reason of the
fact that many of its ablest and most influential women
have been won from its rank to become leaders in the
W.C.T.U. And let it be whispered in passing that a
little less greed for office on the part of the
brothers and a little more readiness to give the
sisters the equal rights promised by the Order might
have prevented the defection of some of these good
women.

Looking at our topic from another point of view,
one is obliged to recognise the fact that the failure
to enrol the children in our Juvenile branch has had
much to with the decline of the Order in the United
States. If this work had been pushed as earnestly and
persistently as it has been in the British Isles, it is
certain that we should have an army of trained Good
Templars equal to those of any other nation. Something
has been done along this line, but not nearly as much
as there should have been.

Considering the question from still another aspect
we find a cause for the decline in that democracy of
which our honoured Brother Malins, P.I.C.T., once wrote
that it was "the bane of the Order." No one can prize
the democratic spirit of the Order more sincerely than
does the writer and no one can rejoice more sincerely
in the fact that "Good Templary, like the Gospel of
Jesus Christ, was given to the common people." But the
democratic spirit has its weak points and is probably
responsible for the idea that has gained prevalence in
recent years that <u>any</u> office is open to the aspirations

of <u>any</u> member. It is true that equal rights should prevail in the matter of office-holding, as in other things. But every office in the gift of the Order requires special qualifications in its incumbent. The possession of all these endowments by one individual is rare and it is folly for anyone to attempt to fill the post for which he is not fitted, just because he thinks he has earned the honour.

It has become customary to regard the office of Chief Templar as the most honourable one. Therefore, one who has all the qualifications to make him an admirable Secretary, Chaplain, Marshal, or other Officer, is not satisfied until he reaches the top and possibly makes a miserable failure. The really democratic attitude is that which regards one office as being just as honourable as another and realises that it is far better to be a good Sentinel than a poor Chief Templar. If we could only say of our members that they have "diversity of gifts but the same spirit," the spirit which would enable each one to do his best in the position for which he is best fitted, what strength and power would be added to our working force.

But with the ambition for office has come the use of unworthy means to attain the end desired. Methods in use at the Ward Caucus have been introduced, and candidates and their friends have sometimes lowered themselves and dishonoured the Order by taking part in the meanest of intrigues. It has even become a not uncommon thing for a candidate to endeavour to make capital for himself by slandering an opponent. Such things are foreign to the spirit of Good Templary and it is not an exaggeration to say that the Order has lost many good members by reason of them. And besides the visible result, it cannot be doubted that such departure from the true ideal must have caused the loss of the blessing of Almighty God. May it not be that the "glory has departed" because we have failed to live up to the true spirit of Good Templary?

But in discussing the question of the decline of the Order in the United States it is not right that we should look wholly upon the dark side. In mentioning some of the possible causes for the decline we have had the hope of uttering a warning cry to the newer jurisdictions. But let it be understood that there are still thousands of Good Templars in the United States who are living up to the highest conception of the obligation and whose worthy lives are examples of its ennobling power. Numbers are not always the true test of strength and anyone who attended the National Grand Lodge at Niagara Falls last summer [in 1910] could not fail to realise that while American Good Templary may lack in membership and in finances, it is still rich in men and women of high character and earnest purpose.

THE LATE BROTHER B. F. PARKER, P.I. SECRETARY: AN APPRECIATION

[International Good Templar, May 1912]

I have just read, with much regret, the announcement of the death of Brother Colonel B. F. Parker [1839-1912], P.I. Secretary, and feel that a few lines regarding him may not be out of place from one who was

for so many years (longer, I think, than any other
<u>living</u> Good Templar, except Brother Malins,
P.I.C.T.) associated with him on the I.S.L. Executive.

It sometimes happens that when one who has long
held an office retires from it, he is speedily forgotten, but this has not been so in Brother Parker´s
case. On the contrary, I believe that his many fine
qualities have stood out in bolder relief since his
retirement than during the many years he filled so
faithfully and patiently the arduous position of
Secretary to our great International organization.

Brother Parker was not what is called a brilliant
man; he was too much inclined to efface himself, and
one had to know him long and well before one could
properly appreciate him. But those who were privileged
thus to know him have many pleasant recollections of
his kindness and courtesy, his genuine and unselfish
love for the Order, and his loyal friendship.

My acquaintance with Brother Parker began before
the two branches of the Order united in 1887. I was
holding the office of Vice-Templar of the R.W.G. Lodge
of the World, and was editing our little organ, <u>The
Temperance Brotherhood</u>. I sent a copy containing what
I considered a rather smart article to Brother Parker.
Instead of the quiet contempt which I expected [from a
leader in the rival Right Worthy Grand Lodge] I
received a kindly little note acknowledging the paper,
and saying: "I think it extremely well edited." This
showed the spirit of the man; he could not approve the
article, but he could give a word of praise to the work
done, even by an opponent.

A further incident showing his readiness to appreciate the work of another came under my notice at the time of the Union session at Saratoga. A member of the newly-elected Executive remarked that Brother Malins had "his eyes all over the world," and Brother Parker quickly retorted, "So much the better for us. If Brother Malins had <u>not</u> had his eyes all over the world we should not now be an International organisation."

Those of us who were active in those days know how warmly Brother Parker seconded the efforts for union, although all do not know how much he did in a quiet way to help secure it. His loyal support of John B. Finch at that time was invaluable, and he gave the same loyal support to those who have followed that brilliant young chieftain in the chief chair of the Order. Mistakes he made sometimes, no doubt, for who is infallible? But his loyalty and fidelity to his leaders, his colleagues, and to the Order are unquestioned.

And now this kindly, quiet, hard-working, unassuming man has passed on to his reward, and his name will be held in affectionate and grateful remembrance with those of the many other noble ones who laboured for "God and home and every land" in the ranks of our Order.

"They rest from their labours, and their works do follow them."

DRINK VERSUS POVERTY

[International Good Templar, July 1912; reprinted in (Perth, Western Australia) Reformer and New York Templar, August 1912, and condensed in Scientific Temperance Journal]

Among the many assertions which are hurled at the advocates of total abstinence and prohibition, in an effort to refute their statements, is the one that poverty is the cause of drink. So common has the saying become that we have almost ceased to combat the argument. "Do away with poverty," says the Socialist agitator, "and you will do away with drunkenness." You point in vain to the many instances which have come within your experience of men of large means who have been drunkards; you tell the oft-told story of the two men who worked side by side in a factory, each receiving the same wage, the one man keeping his family in comfort, the other living in a slum with his hungry, ragged wife and children, the difference being that the one man was a total abstainer and the other a sot. Your arguments are ridiculed; your examples are referred to as "exceptions which only prove the rule," and you are silenced by the vehemence of your opponent. The old problem as to whether "the pig makes the pigstye, or the pigstye makes the pig?" [sic] is never solved, for even the most bigoted advocates of clean and respectable living are often obliged sorrowfully to admit that life in a city slum is not conducive to the realization of such an ideal.

It is hardly likely that, in these days, any careful student of social conditions, however rabid a

Temperance man he may be, will insist that drink is the
sole cause of poverty. But the sincere observer must
admit that it is a very large factor in bringing into
existence the terrible depths of want and misery in
which so many of our fellow creatures are submerged.
And sometimes it happens that one is able to study the
problem under conditions which must give the lie to the
assertion that without poverty there would be no
drunkenness.

The writer is now living in Western Australia in
conditions which enable her to know that the drink
traffic may flourish and prosper, with all its atten-
dant evils, in a country where poverty does not exist
to any appreciable extent. Western Australia is a
large, a very large country. It is about one-third of
Australia and consequently about one-third the size of
the United States. It contains nearly 1,000,000 square
miles of territory and has over 4,000 miles of sea
coast. Its population, at the present time, is not
more than 300,000, so there is, as yet, no need for
over-crowding. It abounds in all manner of valuable
products; indeed its natural wealth is not yet fully
discovered.

The people of Western Australia are brave,
progressive and enterprising. The capital city, Perth,
with about 60,000 population, is beautifully situated
and is fully up-to-date in almost every respect. The
smaller towns are not lagging far behind.

The climate is ideal: not hotter than in most
parts of the United States in the summer and without
the other extremes of cold and snow and ice. One could

live out of doors throughout the year without any very
great inconvenience.

The legislation is nearly all very favourable to
working people. The eight hour working day and the
Saturday half-holiday are established by law. In most
trades a minimum wage is fixed. Woman suffrage
prevails here as in all the other Australian States,
and there are many other good laws. Wages are high,
fully as high as in the United States; and living
conditions, owing to the climate, are much easier.
Educational facilities are good and are constantly
improving, and literature of all kinds is cheap and
plentiful. Churches are numerous, so there is ample
opportunity for spiritual culture, and the desire for
recreation is gratified by cricket, golf, tennis,
rowing and swimming clubs, picnics, river excursions,
concerts, theatres, and picture shows.

The misfortunes which cannot be avoided under the
most prosperous circumstances are provided for by
hospitals, convalescent homes, institutions for the
deaf and dumb, for the blind, etc.

It would seem that under such ideal conditions
there should be no poverty, and it may be confidently
asserted that there would be none, or that at least it
would be a negligible quantity, if it were not for the
drink. But the liquor saloon is on every corner. It
is licensed to keep open when all other trades must
close, and it is thronged constantly. It is a terrible
fact, and one which causes uneasiness to all sober
thinking people in the State, that the per capita
consumption of alcoholic liquor in Western Australia is

in excess of any other country in the world. And the results are just the same as in less prosperous countries: poverty, misery, disease, insanity, vice, crime and all the other evils which attend the dreadful traffic wherever it exists.

And here it must be said in behalf of Western Australians that the finding of gold during the last few years and the rush of people from other places in the goldfields is to some extent responsible for the size of the liquor bill. So also is the manufacture of wine and the licensing of wine shops, which become a snare to a class of people who would not enter the ordinary drinking saloon. But taking everything into consideration which may be said in excuse, the results are nevertheless appalling and must certainly prove that not alone in the establishing of prosperous conditions will the panacea be found.

There is still much for the Temperance man or woman to do in even the most prosperous communities; and while we do not withhold our sympathy for those who seek to abolish poverty, we have a right to claim their help in our struggle to stop the sale of the most potent cause of poverty, Strong Drink.

ONCE A GOOD TEMPLAR--ALWAYS A GOOD TEMPLAR

[International Good Templar, Dec. 1912]

I wish that more emphasis could be given to the fact that when a person is joining our Order he is taking a life-long obligation. I am inclined to think

that many members in these days do not regard the
matter so seriously as I, and thousands of old members
have always considered it. And now that so many young
people are being attracted to the colonies from the
British Isles, it is very necessary they should
understand that leaving their own country does not
cancel their relationship to Good Templary.

Among the numerous immigrants who are arriving in
Australia every week there must be many Good Templars.
Indeed, I sometime notice in the <u>Watchword</u> a line to
the effect that a certain brother is sailing on a
certain date, and I am sorry to say that is very often
all we hear of them. On two occasions recently I have
had letters from English Lodges recommending Good
Templar sisters to my good offices. In both instances
the sisters were met and were shown such attentions as
was possible. One young lady visited a Fremantle Lodge
after taking tea at the home of one of the members, and
since then the Order has seen no more of her. I wrote
to a member who lived in the town where the sister went
to reside and asked her to call upon her. The lady did
so but without result so far as the Order is concerned. The other young lady came to tea with me before
going to a situation in Perth. She seemed to be
greatly interested in the Order and had been a long
time a member, but I have never heard from her since.

When I left the Lodge in London to which I
belonged thirty-eight years ago and went to Boston,
U.S.A., I took my Clearance Card with me and I did not
feel happy or satisfied until it was safely deposited
in a Boston Lodge. I have so often testified to the
benefit I have derived from my membership in the Order,

that it is unnecessary to repeat the statements. But I
will say that I believe no other influence which has
come into my life has been so powerful in developing
whatever of good there may be in my character. And I
realise that if I had allowed my membership to lapse
when I left my own country, I should have been to-day
much the poorer, mentally, morally and spiritually.
Young people who are leaving home need every possible
safeguard and I am very sorry when they sever their
connection so lightly with our great Order.

Then the loss to the Order itself is something to
be considered. If every member who has left Britain's
shores in the last 38 years were still in active
connection with Good Templary, how much stronger we
should be in the other English-speaking lands.

I am not advising any addition to our initiatory
ceremony, but I do wish that something might be done to
make the words, "You have now undertaken a <u>life-long</u>
work" more impressive. And older members, who have
learned to value the Order, might do much by giving a
tactful little talk to those who are about to leave the
country.

During my many years' residence in Boston, U.S.A.,
my experience was much the same, that many of those who
came from the "Old Country" were not willing to cast in
their lot with their brethren in the new world. In
some cases the complaint was made that "the Lodges are
so different," and this is often true. But is that an
excuse for evading the responsibility which we assumed
when we assented to the Good Templar obligation? I
think not. One cannot change one's place of abode

without finding differences in our surroundings. The new Lodge may be less congenial than the old, but it is our duty to make the best of it and to do our part to render it useful and attractive.

THE PASSING OF SISTER CHARLOTTE A. GRAY: AN APPRECIATION

[International Good Templar, March 1913]

One of the saddest things connected with advancing years is that one must pause so often to pay the tribute of affection and respect to the memory of those with whom one has marched shoulder to shoulder in the ranks and who receive the call to "come up higher" before it reaches one´s own listening ear. And yet, to those who believe in the life beyond as giving opportunity for nobler and better service than can be rendered in the conditions surrounding us in this world, there must ever be a strain of rejoicing mingled with the grief. This must be especially so when, as in the case of our Sister Gray [1844-1912], the last days of our beloved comrade´s life have been a time of weakness [as a result of cancer] and of retirement from the labour she loved.

Knowing Sister Gray for so many years as I have; intimately associated with her as I have been many times and always realising her energetic spirit and her tireless activity, I have been impressed, as many others must have been, with the sweet spirit of patience and resignation with which she has borne the enforced withdrawal from the beloved work. To one who for many years has been "in the thick of the fight," it is not always easy to obey the command to lay down one´s arms and it is given to only a few to realise the truth of the words that "these also serve who only stand and wait." Who can say how much of the credit of a victory belongs to the one who, shut away from the scene of conflict, can yet follow those who are engaged in it with loving thoughts and ceaseless prayers? This was the task given to Sister Gray in her last days and there can be no doubt that it was fulfilled as faithfully and as earnestly as were the more strenuous duties of many previous years.

I first met Sister Gray when on my way to Stockholm to attend the Session of the Right Worthy Grand Lodge of the World in 1885. She was awaiting our party at Copenhagen and was soon at home with us. She was not at that time at work for the Good Templars in any official capacity, although even then her efforts to promote the cause in Antwerp were known to us. I remember how greatly she impressed me with her energy and zeal, but I suppose that few of us who met her then had any idea of the wonderful part she was destined to play in the propagation of the Order in Europe.

Her great work is a matter of history and it is all the more remarkable from the fact that much of it was accomplished in countries where, until very recently, a woman´s influence, outside of domestic affairs, has not been much regarded. But Sister Gray possessed peculiar gifts for such work. The wonderful facility with which she acquired languages has been often referred to; and with that was a remarkable ability of adapting herself to the varying conditions of life in the countries she visited and a breadth of

mind which enabled her to see that "mankind is one in
its rights and wrongs," and to recognise no distinctions of nationality, or tongue, or creed. Then there
was her wonderful tenacity of purpose, her courage and
her persistency. These and other qualifications used
for the glory of God, in a cause which she believed He
owned and blessed, enabled her to accomplish that work
which stands to-day as a monument for her.

Now while we praise the work and bless God for the
great harvest resulting from the faithful seed-sowing
of His servant, let us remember that this work was not
accomplished without much of cost to the worker. For
years she who loved her own land, was practically
exiled from it. For years she who knew so well how to
appreciate the joys of home and of fellowship with her
beloved ones, lived the life of a wanderer. Of
naturally quiet, domestic tastes, brought up with
strict ideas, loving refinement and the amenities of
life, she was yet willing to live as those lived whom
she wished to reach, so that "by any means," she might
"save some." Let it ever be remembered that in the
case of Sister Gray, as with all who labour sincerely
for the cause, the element of <u>self-sacrifice</u> was the
chief essential to success.[5]

---

5 Gray had a Scottish father but was born in Southampton. Her parents soon moved to London. For eleven
years Gray was connected with the Mariners´ Institute,
Antwerp. She started a Band of Hope there in February
1878. "In April, 1878, she became a member of the
Order, with the object of saving a poor drunkard."
Rev. James Mackenzie, in George W. E. Hill, <u>Hand Book
of Good Templary</u> (2nd ed., printed Ames, Iowa: Hodson
Bros., 1897), p. 24. In 1902 ill-health forced Gray to
retire from her Good Templar temperance missions on the
Continent.

THE POSITION IN WEST AUSTRALIA

[Scottish Temperance Annual (1914)]

The Labour Government [in Western Australia] has shown itself, to a certain extent, favourable to the Temperance movement, and a Bill is now before the House which offers full control over all licenses on a simple majority vote with the first poll in 1914. At the same time it is very plainly to be seen that both the Liberal and the Labour parties are in favour of the establishment of State hotels [public houses]. The promise is made by the present Government that when the hotels are established they will give the electors the power to vote them out of existence. "This," says one who is in authority on the Temperance question, "is so stupid that it might be regarded as a joke were it not for the fact that many of the well-meaning opponents of the traffic are willing to delay the final overthrow of the liquor evil to give State hotels the opportunity to show that the trade can be run in a respectable manner. They profess to believe that if the State owned all the hotels the cry of vested interest could not be raised, and the people could vote the whole traffic out." Needless to say that the experiment already tried in the State-owned hotels at Gwalia and Dwellingup fail to prove that the business can be run in a respectable manner, nor does their existence prevent the illicit sale of liquor in those towns.

Agitations are being carried on here by the Temperance people asking for an increased number of lessons on Temperance physiology in the public schools. At present the number of lessons per year is limited to four.

Another movement in which all classes of the community are uniting is to make the issue of a wine-shop license cover the sale of wine only. At present keepers of wine shops may serve lunches and teas, and sell fruit and confectionery. This makes them especially dangerous to young people, and to women who would not think of entering a public house.

Aside from local matters we are naturally rejoicing over the fact that the Minister of Defence has refused to allow the "wet" canteen to be restored to either the naval or military camps. And another cause for satisfaction is found in the fact that the Postmaster-General has definitely refused the request of the licensed victuallers to allow liquor to be sent through the mails.

WHAT THE TEMPERANCE MOVEMENT HAS DONE FOR WOMAN

[Presidential Address, WCTU of Western Australia, 1915, in New York Templar, Dec. 1915]

Few people realize what the temperance movement has done for woman throughout the world. They know that woman has done much for the temperance movement, but seldom think that in doing this work she has been unconsciously paying a debt. It may interest my readers if I set before them a few facts.

In 1851 the Independent Order of Good Templars was founded in Utica, New York State. Contrary to the one sex principle established by other organizations, the Good Templars began by admitting women on equal terms with men, giving them the right to vote upon all questions and to hold any office. It is claimed for Good Templary, and I think with truth, that it was the first equal suffrage society in the world. It was probably due to its equal rights feature that the Order grew so rapidly and became such a power in the United States. Women were found in every State of the Union ready and glad to accept the new dignity conferred upon them and in three or four States they reached, and filled successfully, the highest executive office. Mrs. Martha McClellan Brown, LL.D., the lady who founded the Woman's Christian Temperance Union, was Grand Chief Templar of Ohio when the Good Templars of that State numbered 90,000.[6]

In 1868 the Good Templar Order was introduced into the British Isles and the results were soon apparent in the fact that hundreds of women, who had the opportunity to open their mouths in public, acquired courage and confidence in the Lodge room and later became prominent speakers on temperance and other reforms. Mrs. Margaret Bright Lucas, sister of the Right Hon. John Bright, was a shining example of the value of an equal rights organization. I have met with many women, British and American, who have become prominent in the Woman Suffrage Movement, the Labor Movement, the

6   In fact the Grand Lodge of Ohio had 7,908 members on January 31, 1873. R.W.G.L., Proceedings (1873), p. 27. Brown became Grand Worthy Chief Templar of Ohio when the man elected to that office had been expelled from the Order for giving the password of his Subordinate Lodge to persons not entitled to it. Wisconsin Good Templar, Feb. 21, 1873, p. 4.

Socialist Movement and other efforts for the ameliora-
tion of the race, who have told me that they owed their
abilities as speakers or debaters, to their training in
the Good Templar Lodge.

In 1872 the movement known as the Woman´s Crusade
began in Ohio and its leaders, many of them, were Good
Templar women. "Mother" Stewart, one of those most
prominent in the Crusade, had been a Good Templar from
the time of the introduction of the Order into Ohio.

The Woman´s Christian Temperance Union was an
outcome of the Crusade and the first Union was formed
by Mrs. McClellan Brown and composed chiefly of Good
Templar ladies. Frances Willard came into the movement
soon after and in a short time became the leader of the
organization, retaining the position until her lamented
death occurred. Miss Willard was the founder of the
World´s Union. The British Woman´s Total Abstinence
Union was organized in Great Britain by Mother Stewart
in 1876 and a number of its first members were Good
Templars. It affiliated with the W.C.T.U. and is
included in the World´s Union of which [Rosalind
Howard] the Countess of Carlisle is the head.

The Good Templar Order was carried into Scandinavia about thirty-five years ago and in 1885 the
International body held its session in Stockholm,
Sweden. The writer held the position of Vice Templar
of the International Lodge at that time and objections
were made to any of the ladies being allowed to speak
at the public meetings for fear it might prejudice the
public against the Order. The objections were overruled, however, and the Vice Templar and one or two

other sisters were permitted to make brief addresses.
I paid a second visit to Sweden seventeen years later
and in the meantime the Order had grown to very large
proportions in that country. I was told that
thirty-five per cent of the membership was composed of
women and that the Grand Lodge was employing lady
lecturers and organizers. During this visit I had the
honor to represent the women of the Order in a deputation to the late King Oscar II. It will be readily
seen that the temperance movement has greatly helped
the cause of women in Sweden.

The same is true of Germany and it is interesting
to note that the Good Templar Order was introduced into
Germany by a woman, the late Charlotte A. Gray. Miss
Gray was a little, unassuming Englishwoman, but she was
gifted with a remarkable talent as an organizer, a
wonderful facility in acquiring languages, a strong
tenacity of purpose and a single hearted devotion to
the cause. The temperance movement has played a very
large part in the remarkable awakening of the German
woman in recent years. I was privileged to be present
in Dresden, a few years ago, at a great temperance
meeting when a mixed audience of over one thousand
people was addressed entirely by women, with the
veteran leader Miss Otilie Hoffman[n] in the chair.

The Prohibition Party of the United States,
organized in 1869, I think, was the first political
party in the world to put a Woman Suffrage plank into
its platform. People who are under the impression that
the temperance movement is narrow might study with
profit the platform of this party and learn that it
stands for other reforms besides the prohibition of the

liquor traffic. Some of the Prohibition organs published in the United States have done valiant service in exposing and opposing the White Slave traffic and other evils which chiefly affect women.

Many other facts might be mentioned to show that the temperance movement has had a very large share in advancing the cause of woman, but enough has been said to prove the case. I might add that the Woman's Christian Temperance Union in Australia has been the pioneer organization in enabling woman to come into her own. In Western Australia the W.C.T.U. was found to be advocating various reforms before the other woman's societies came into being and the securing of Woman's Suffrage in this State was mainly due to its efforts.

WILL GOOD TEMPLARY BE NEEDED IN THE FUTURE IN NORTH AMERICA?

[New York Templar, May 1919]

A friend writing from one of the Canadian jurisdictions says that many Good Templars seem to think it is not necessary to keep the Lodges alive now that Prohibition has been secured.

This is a very grave mistake, and one which in the future may lead to disaster. While it is true that Good Templary as an organization, has not led in the recent agitation for Prohibition in North America, it is no less true that the work of the Order in the past has developed and cultivated the sentiment which has produced such splendid results. When we claim that a

very large proportion of Prohibition agitators were
trained in Good Templar Lodges, we are only stating an
indisputable fact. The names of a multitude of men and
women occur to us who, although many of them have
ceased active connection with the Order, would very
willingly and gratefully credit much of their knowledge, earnestness and zeal to its teachings. One need
only cite the fact that Good Templary, from its
inception, has for nearly three-quarters of a century,
held steadfastly to its ideal of Total National
Prohibition, to demonstrate its right to be regarded as
an important factor in the great fight.

And now, what of the future? In a land where
intoxicating liquor is unknown; in which no longer
shall "the kindly fruits of the earth" be used to
produce a dangerous poison, will there by any need to
continue to agitate and educate against its use?

We have to remember that the legislation which has
banished this great enemy of mankind is the result of
many years of quiet, persistent effort and that many of
those who made that effort have passed, or are passing
from this world´s stage, leaving the gaps in the ranks
to be filled by untried recruits. And because "eternal
vigilance is the price of safety," it is necessary that
those recruits should be trained for service.

The liquor traffic is defeated for the present,
but we have no assurance that its upholders will accept
the defeat as final. There will always be attempts to
evade the law, or, even to secure its abrogation. The
work of Good Templary--the real work for which it came
into being--that of educating and training the young,

is as necessary as ever. Nay, it is even more necessary, for the young people who are growing up in Prohibition territory will not, happily for them, have the terrible examples before their eyes which in so many cases, have proved to those who preceded them an incentive to fight the evil, as well as a warning against its "deadly and seductive influence."

We can look forward to a land freed form the curse, purified from its demoralizing influence. We can hope for the future of our boys and girls a freedom from the deprivation and the disabilities which so many of the men and women of the past have suffered through the traffic. We may also hope for them that the temptations to wrong-doing which it offered to the weak ones will not exist. But this very immunity will make it more necessary to teach and to train the rising generation. "This liberty which we enjoy was won for us by the strivings and sacrifices of those who preceded us. It was bought by their labors and their prayers. It is ours to enjoy and it is ours to guard." Thus we must teach them and where can this teaching be more readily and effectively given than in the Good Templar Lodge or the Juvenile Temple?

So far from Good Templars suggesting that their Lodges may be given up, the present conditions should open the way for a revival of Good Templary all over North America. "Keep everlastingly at it," dear friends. Make your Lodges educational. Let Scientific Temperance be taught. Rejoice in the victories gained but remember that you must labor strenuously to **keep what has been won.**

THE WORTH OF GOOD TEMPLARY

[New York Templar, July 1925; reprinted Australian Temperance World, April 1927]

I have been interested in an article in a recent number of the Good Templars´ Watchword entitled, "What is Good Templary Worth to You?" Thinking it over I have been freshly impressed with the value the Order has been to me, and I have wished that I were a rich woman so that I could give tangible proof of my sense of its worth. But as I am not blessed with wealth, I can only say with the Apostle Peter, "Silver and gold have I none, but such as I have give I unto thee," and the gift consists in the warmest and strongest expression of appreciation of which I am capable. The best way of expressing my sense of the Order´s worth is, perhaps, to recall for the benefit of some of the younger members, what it has been to me during my more than fifty years of membership.

In the first place it has been a tremendous educational influence. When I joined the "Henry Ansell" Lodge in 1872 I was attracted to the Order by its social features. Although fairly well[-]educated I knew nothing about the temperance question beyond the fact that I had seen the evil effects of drink on one near and dear to me. The idea that total abstinence should be demanded of everyone seemed a very extreme measure, but in the lodge room, as I listened to the talks of members and visitors, I soon learned the reason for it.

Realizing my ignorance of the question, I began to read and study it, first in the organ of the Order and then in such other papers and books as I could secure. Soon the phases of heredity, environment, and social customs as related to temperance interested me. Later came the knowledge of the menace of the liquor traffic and the demand for its abolition, and for many years I have been an ardent prohibitionist. Those acquainted with my past record will know that I have always been a devout believer in the temperance training of the children, both in Juvenile Temples and kindred societies and by temperance instruction in the schools. And when added to this, I mention the knowledge gained of other countries, their people and conditions, I think that I may claim that the Order has been very much to me in the matter of education.

Another valuable feature of Good Templary is its power to awaken ambition and to inspire many of its members to cultivate their natural gifts. Many men and women who spoke their few first halting words in the lodge room with fear and trembling have become famous on public platforms; many others have been inspired to use their pens in advocacy of the great reform, as witness the innumerable articles, poems, and stories written by members. Then the knowledge gained of parliamentary law, of bookkeeping, of writing records, etc., has often been a material help to members in their business or professional lives, and the discipline of a well-conducted lodge has developed a love of law and order.

I mentioned that I was attracted to Good Templary by its social features, and that side is worth much.

When after a membership in London of about two years, I accepted the offer of a business engagement in Boston, U.S.A., I shall never forget the loneliness and home-sickness from which I suffered for the first few weeks, and it was in the Good Templar Lodge that I found solace. I formed friendships which lasted for many years, and my interests and enjoyments were all as-sociated with Good Templary. Later as I advanced in the Order, I met congenial comrades of many nationali-ties; and although, alas, some of these dear friends have "fallen asleep," there still remain some old and faithful co-workers, the correspondence with whom forms the chief happiness of my life. And I bless God for the many noble souls with whom Good Templary has brought me into touch.

Although feebly expressed, I hope that I have shown that Good Templary has been worth very much for me as an educational, inspirational and social factor. And I trust that these words, now that I am no longer able to take an active part in the work, may inspire others to make full use of the advantages offered by our great Order.

INTERNATIONALISM

["Auntie Jet," "Our Young People," West Australian White Ribbon, June 1928.]

Perhaps some of my boys and girls may wonder at my telling them about the good work going on so far away. But I think it is good to know and to be interested in the work in other parts of the world. It makes us feel that we are all united in the great cause and that a victory in one place is something for us all to rejoice over and to feel encouraged about, just as when we learn of mistakes in some places, we feel sorry and know that they are something for us to avoid. A great poet has said that "mankind is one in its rights and wrongs," and that is something for us to remember when we think of the struggle going on against intemperance in almost every country of the world.

A TRIBUTE TO THE SISTERS

[subtitle of article in series, "Incidents in a Good Templar Life," <u>Australian Temperance World</u>, August 1929]

Good Templars will all be ready to admit that the Order owes much of its success to the fact that so large a part of its membership is of the feminine gender. It is generally known that Good Templary at the beginning of its career allowed women to join on equal terms with men, and that it has the honor of being the first organisation to do so.

When the Order crossed the Atlantic the dignity it had conferred on the sex was extended to those in the British Isles, and when it became truly International the brethren in the Scandinavian countries were glad to welcome the sisters as co-laborers with them. In later years it has reached Germany, Holland, Switzerland, carrying with it the same slogan of equal rights for woman. It is not too much to claim that the Order's attitude in this respect has blazed the way for woman's

495

equality in other organisations, and has helped in the demand for woman suffrage.

Aside from its work in this respect, it cannot be questioned that the work in the subordinate Lodges has been mainly carried on by the sisters, and that in many of the smaller Grand Lodges much of the burden of holding the membership together and even of filling the offices has fallen on women.

During the many years in which I was honored with the office of International Superintendent of Juvenile Templars, I had reason to realise how active and efficient were those sisters who worked under my commission, and I look back with affectionate gratitude to those who gave such willing and gracious help to me.

The first who deserves mention is Mrs. M. B. O'Donnell, of New York, to whom belongs the credit of introducing the Juvenile Branch in the R.W.G. Lodge, and of insisting that the Supreme body should recognise its importance and its value. Mrs. O'Donnell was a highly gifted woman. She had a strong love for the Order, and her kindness and helpfulness were experienced by many of the younger members. She wrote a most cordial welcome to me when I first assumed the duties of my office, and she was a constant and faithful correspondent of mine until her death. I should like to speak at length of other dear women to whose friendship I owe much--for instance, Mrs. M. Mc-Clellan Brown, Mother Stewart, Amanda Way, Mrs. L. C. Partington, of Maine, Mrs. M. M. Ruslow, of New

Hampshire, and of many other dear friends.[7] These
have all passed away, and [I also speak gratefully] of
dear Mrs. Laura Rudy, who, although still living in
Philadelphia, is an invalid.[8]

In Great Britain and most of the foreign countries
the office of G.S.J.W. was usually filled by men, good
men and zealous workers, but this is intended as a
tribute to the sisters, many of whom have gone to their
reward. But in the countries that were far away from
me when I was in office there were two sisters famous
for the grand work they did for the children, and who I
was privileged to meet after I came to reside in Australia. One was Miss Marion Hall, of Sydney, N.S.W.,

---

7   Amanda M. Way (1828-1914), a Good Templar since
1854, had headed the Grand Lodges of Indiana and
Kansas. After writing the quoted letter, she was
elected Grand Chief Templar of Idaho. "IDAHO.--A
letter from Sister Amanda Way recently gave me great
pleasure. Writing from Boise, Idaho, she says: `A
little over a year ago I organized a Friends´ church in
this city. We have built a commodious church, also a
parsonage. We have thirty members, also a large
Sabbath school, a Christian Endeavor and a Junior
ditto, and also a good Lodge of Good Templars. This
meets every Monday evening in our church and we
contemplate organizing a Temple soon. That is news
that I know will please thee. Our Order is not doing
much in this state and cannot until we can get closer
together. The state is sparsely settled and mountains
intervene, so that each Lodge is almost alone, except
in the Boise Valley, where we have four Lodges near
enough to visit each other and have some communication. Prohibition sentiment is quite active and with
the woman´s vote we hope before many years to drive
out the saloon.´" Forsyth, "Right Worthy Grand Superintendent Juvenile Templars´ Department," _International
Good Templar_, June 1900, p. 187.

8   She died in 1930.

and the other Mrs. Brickhill, of Perth, W.A.[9] Both
these good women have gone to their rest in recent
years, leaving a record of faithful work well done.
Aside from these, most of the women who held my
commission, and whom I met personally, were in America. There were Mrs. Knapp of Michigan, Miss Steele of
Pa., Mesdames Henry of Indiana, Remington of Iowa,
Dietrick of New York, Wiley of Vt., Safley of Minn.,
Parlette of Md., and many others.

I love the Good Templar Order so well that I am
sorry to even hint at a criticism. But for a number of
years past the Order has departed from its lofty
standard of equality of the sexes. This criticism only
applies to the International Lodge, although I am
afraid that some of the European Grand Lodges have
failed to give the sisters due honor. But in the
Supreme body, for almost twenty years, the Executive
offices have been bestowed upon men. [A woman was
elected International Vice Templar in 1930.] I have no
complaint to make on my own account, for my record of
twenty-one years´ service of the I.S.L. Executive is

---

9   When Mrs. C. M. Brickhill succeeded Jessie For-
syth´s niece as G.S.J.T. of Western Australia, she
wrote that "I have held the position of S.J.T. in
N.S. Wales before coming to live in this state. I have
a family of seven, and all have been members of the
Juvenile Temple--four sons and one daughter having
since been transferred into the adult Lodge, the two
younger ones being members of the Temple which I have
had charge of lately, the Ark of Safety, Leederville,
No. 14. This Temple was instituted on the 9th of
February 1901, with 26 members. In a little over three
months it had a membership of 106, and during the time
of its existence we have administered the four-fold
pledge to 134 juveniles." Brickhill to Forsyth, n.d.,
in Jessie Forsyth, "Right Worthy Grand Superintendent
Juvenile Templars Department," International Good
Templar, July 1902, p. 226.

longer than that of many men. But I do not like my sex
to be slighted, and I am sure that there are many women
members now who are equally deserving of International
honors, and equally capable of fulfilling the duties
which go with them, as are the brothers who monopolise
the offices.

THE MEANING OF THE PLEDGE

[Australian Temperance World, "The Young Templar" page,
March 1932. Probably reprinted from an earlier
publication.]

In a quaint old church in a western town,
On a pleasant eve, as the sun went down,
Some boys and girls, and some women and men,
Heard the pitiful story told again
By a lady who spoke about the drink,
Of the ills it wrought and she bade them think
Of some work to do that would help along
The righteous cause, and defeat the wrong.
She said that the hope of the future lay
In the boys and girls of the present day.
And she begged that, to arm them for the fight
They would join the Temperance band that night.
Then a good old man rose and said: "I doubt
If these children know what it's all about.
You had better wait till they understand
'Bout a pledge for life, ere they join a band."
But a boy of seven, brave and ready,
Said, with eager voice, but with purpose steady:
"I know what it means; I mean to do it;
It is **saying a thing and sticking to it.**"

Index